ADMINISTRATIVE BURDEN

ADMINISTRATIVE BURDEN

POLICYMAKING BY OTHER MEANS

Pamela Herd and Donald P. Moynihan

Russell Sage Foundation   NEW YORK

LIBRARY OF CONGRESS
CATALOGING-IN-PUBLICATION DATA
Names: Herd, Pamela, author. | Moynihan, Donald P., author.
Title: Administrative burden : policymaking by other means / Pamela Herd and
   Donald P. Moynihan.
Description: New York : Russell Sage Foundation, [2018] | Includes bibliographical references
   and index.
Identifiers: LCCN 2018029435 (print) | LCCN 2018030618 (ebook) | ISBN 9781610448789 (ebook) |
   ISBN 9780871544445 (pbk. : alk. paper)
Subjects: LCSH: Public administration—United States. | Bureaucracy—United States. |
   Administrative agencies—United States. | Political planning—United States. |
   United States—Social policy. | United States—Economic policy.
Classification: LCC JK421 (ebook) | LCC JK421.H396 2018 (print) | DDC 320.60973—dc23
LC record available at https://lccn.loc.gov/2018029435

The paper used in this publication meets the minimum requirements of American National Standard for Information Sciences—Permanence of Paper for Printed Library Materials. ANSI Z39.48-1992.

Text design by Matthew T. Avery.

RUSSELL SAGE FOUNDATION
112 East 64th Street,
New York, New York 10065
10 9 8 7 6 5 4 3 2 1

We dedicate this book to the Wisconsin Idea and the University of Wisconsin Regents of 1894. Scholars "shall never be content until the beneficent influence of the University reaches every family of the state." That idea, attributed to University of Wisconsin president Charles Van Hise, can be fully realized only when accompanied by strong academic freedoms. The University of Wisconsin Regents of 1894, in their wisdom, offered the following defense of independent research: "Whatever may be the limitations which trammel inquiry elsewhere, we believe that the great state University of Wisconsin should ever encourage that continual and fearless sifting and winnowing by which alone the truth can be found." Although Wisconsin is no longer our home, we carry these values with us. On Wisconsin.

CONTENTS

LIST OF ILLUSTRATIONS

Box

Figures

Tables

ABOUT THE AUTHORS

PAMELA HERD is professor at the McCourt School of Public Policy, Georgetown University.

DONALD P. MOYNIHAN is the McCourt Chair at the McCourt School of Public Policy, Georgetown University.

ACKNOWLEDGMENTS

No single moment crystalized our decision to write this book, but a couple of candidates vie for the spot. One was when Don looked at a stack of immigration forms he had to fill out shortly after finishing his PhD. He asked himself, if someone with a PhD in public administration is struggling with the seemingly endless and contradictory requirements, how difficult must it be for an immigrant less familiar with bureaucracy? Another was when we both found ourselves frustrated at the barriers we had to overcome to get promised support from local and state government for our daughter who has a disability; the process sometimes seemed designed to limit support rather than provide help. Pam taught master's students in public affairs about these policies, as well as doing research on them, but found herself flummoxed when faced with stacks of eligibility forms and caseworkers who provided inaccurate eligibility guidelines. It was a wake-up call that it wasn't just the parameters of eligibility that mattered if we wanted policies to reduce inequality: the administration of those policies mattered too.

One of us (Pam) studies public policy and sociology, and the other (Don) studies public administration. As we talked about the frustrations that came from our interactions with the government, we were surprised to learn that no single theoretical framework reflected these common experiences. We set out to build that framework.

Part of what motivated us was the realization that such abstract frameworks matter. Scholars in our fields really do want our work to be relevant, to shape public understanding, and to influence policy. We also want to be good scholars and to hold true to the scientific principle by building on prior work. Research paradigms are important—they allow the gradual accumulation of knowledge. They can also become intellectual prisons, by defining what research questions are in and what are out. Paradigms flash a green light for some sort of research, but a red light for others.

We observed within the field of public administration an imbalance of attention to the experience of citizens relative to public managers, plus a paucity of research frameworks that allow scholars to connect policy with administration. We also observed in policy research in sociology, economics, and political science, especially that focused on inequality, an inattentiveness to the role of administration in shaping policy outcomes. As a result, questions that should be central to the study of public policy and administration are somewhat neglected: how does the state impose burdens on citizens? How are burdens created (and in particular what is the role of politics in this process)? What are the consequences of burdens for citizens? How do burdens shape inequality? How can we minimize the negative effects of administrative burdens while ensuring that the state is still able to use its power to achieve legitimate goals?

To ask and to answer such questions required us to build a new conceptual framework. We did so in baby steps: our first paper on the topic was published in 2010. We drew liberally from other domains in social science and the advice of many. The product of that effort is this book, which we view as an effort to understand one aspect of how a citizen engages with the state, limited to the domain of a few policy areas in the United States that we know well.

We also view this book as a starting point rather than a final version and hope that others take up the charge to apply, expand, and rethink the ideas we lay out here. In short, we want the book to be a green light to a new way to thinking about how to improve public policy. At the heart of this enterprise are a few simple beliefs we think most people would agree with regardless of their political leanings. Interactions with government should be no more onerous than need be. The state should not throw up unnecessary roadblocks that frustrate citizens. Good government means consistently looking for new ways to make the citizen experience of government be simpler, more accessible, and respectful.

This book benefited from generous research support from University of Wisconsin–Madison in the form of a Vilas award, funded by the William F. Vilas trust, the Office of the Vice Chancellor for Research and Graduate Education at the University of Wisconsin–Madison with funding from the Wisconsin Alumni Research Foundation, University of Wisconsin–Madison Institute for Research and Poverty, and a presidential award from the Russell Sage Foundation (G5825).

We also benefited greatly from collaborators who worked with us on early papers that developed this concept, specifically, Tom DeLeire, Hope Harvey, and Elizabeth Rigby. We also relied on diligent work of many students at the La Follette School who served as our research assistants, including Moira Lenox, Eric Hepler, Dan Marlin, and Virginia Andersen.

Any attempt to thank all of the people who gave us feedback along the way is too long to list and inevitably risks excluding someone. But we owe special thanks to Joe Soss, Carolyn Heinrich, Tim Smeeding, Richard Walker, and three exceptionally diligent reviewers at the Russell Sage Foundation. We are deeply grateful to Suzanne Nichols, our editor at the Russell Sage Foundation, who shepherded us through this process.

We also used presentations at many different universities as an opportunity to get feedback, and so we owe thanks to faculty and students at Aarhus University, the Danish National Center for Social Research, American University, Syracuse University, University of Leiden, the University of Minnesota, University of Southern California, University of Virginia, Florida State University, Florida International University, Indiana University, the University of Georgia, the University of Colorado Denver, and Renmin University. (Yes—it's a long list: we needed all the help we could get!) In 2011, at the University of Wisconsin–Madison, we hosted an event on the future of red tape research, with help from Richard Walker and Mary Feeney. The meeting was key in helping us think about how to extend existing public administration research to public policy. A bookend to that workshop was a slightly more glamorous meeting in 2017, hosted by Angel Saz Carranza and Marc Esteve, at ESADE Business and Law School in Barcelona, which proved invaluable in refining the concept. We are deeply grateful to the participants at both meetings.

INTRODUCTION

After September 11, amid unimaginable grief, victims' families found themselves awash in paperwork—applying to everything from workers' compensation to private charitable support and life insurance. Meryl Mayo lost her husband in the World Trade Center. In the days following his death, she spent countless hours finding out what financial resources she was eligible for, filling out forms, pulling together documentation, and dealing with officials who offered varying levels of help and sympathy. "'Everything was scattered all over the place. And then I thought about all the things I had to do and all the laundry that was overflowing from the hamper. And I felt so overwhelmed that I broke down so badly, I couldn't even catch my breath. I sat down on the floor, just like, 'I have to do this. I have to cry now.' And I did."[1]

Yet Mayo remembered one application process as being "refreshingly simple": Social Security. She just had to make a phone call and fill out a simple form online, or, if it were more convenient, she could get help at one of the more than 1,200 Social Security Administration field offices across the country. The first Social Security checks to victims' family members were mailed out on October 3, 2001.

This is a simple example of how we want government to work. A public agency offered a helping hand at a moment when help was desperately needed. All too often, our experience with government is the opposite, characterized by confusion, delay, and frustration. This book is about these administrative burdens, their political and organizational origins, how they affect citizens, and how governments can minimize them.[2]

The term *administrative burden* may evoke images of business regulation or basic bureaucratic encounters, such as renewing a driver's
license. But any context in which the state regulates private behavior
or structures how individuals seek public services is a venue in which
the state may impose burdens on its citizens. We focus on the costs
that people encounter when they search for information about public
services (learning costs), comply with rules and requirements (compliance costs), and experience the stresses, loss of autonomy, or stigma
that come from such encounters (psychological costs). All policies
that require citizens to engage with the state will, to varying degrees,
create such frictions. Although these burdens vary by policy and by
the person experiencing them, the experiences can be minimized in
a number of ways. One is to simply reduce burdens, such as trusting
someone's word that they are a citizen rather than requiring a document to prove it. Another is to shift burdens away from the individual, and onto the state, by, for example, requiring eligibility workers
to tap into administrative databases to establish whether someone
is a citizen.

Burdens matter. They affect whether people will be able to exercise
fundamental rights of citizenship, such as voting; they affect whether
people can access benefits that can improve quality of life, such as
health insurance. Burdens can alter the effectiveness of public programs. Social programs often reach only a fraction of their target
population, automatically weakening their effectiveness by shutting
out those who fail to negotiate the required procedure. Ultimately,
administrative burdens are the fine print of the social contract
between citizens and their government. They are the nuts and bolts
of policy design. The presence of administrative burdens makes the
difference as to whether government is experienced as accessible or
opaque, simple or bewildering, respectful or antagonistic.

Those who believe that government can act as a progressive force
for good in people's lives need to understand the role that administrative burdens play. Many have pushed hard for the expansion of
programs and policies that reduce growing inequality. But if those
programs bury people in paperwork and fill them with frustration,
it undermines not only policy outcomes, but also people's faith in
the capacity of government to do anything right. These burdens
might seem like the dull minutiae of administration compared with
the exciting possibilities in designing a new program, but policy

designs are not self-executing. Programs must be implemented. In our current age of polarization and declining faith in government, much can be done to improve governance just by focusing on how to reduce administrative burdens in policy design and implementation. Burdens should not matter only to those with an expansive view for the role of government. For conservatives who want government to work efficiently or to cast a less intrusive shadow on the lives of its citizens, understanding administrative burden offers a way to these ends.

Three simple themes reoccur throughout this book. First, burdens are consequential—they make a difference in our lives. The right to vote or access an abortion, or the ability to receive a needed state benefit may depend on the burdens we face. Second, administrative burdens are distributive. They affect some groups more than others, and in doing so, often reinforce inequalities in society. Third, burdens, like public policies themselves, are constructed. Administrative burdens are the product of deliberate choice occurring via political processes and a function of basic administrative capacity. Sometimes the implications of these choices and capacities are understood, sometimes not, but they can always be changed.

Burdens Are Consequential

Administrative burdens are pervasive and consequential in terms of the costs that citizens bear and, in turn, how those costs influence citizens' perceptions of government. We all face some sort of burden. Take taxes: "what we pay for civilized society," according to Justice Oliver Wendell Holmes.[3] Tax preparation takes time—a lot of it. The Department of Treasury, by itself, creates 6.7 billion hours of work for taxpayers each year, accounting for nearly 75 percent of the time citizens spend completing federal paperwork.[4] A recent analysis estimated the compliance costs of filing to be about $1.2 billion, or 1.2 percent of GDP.[5]

Taxes are also one of the most universal frictions adult citizens encounter with the state. It is no coincidence the Internal Revenue Service is one of the least popular agencies in the U.S. government.[6] Americans do not like paying taxes, but they also do not like the complex process that comes with it. Albert Einstein, when asked about managing his income tax reporting, quipped, "This is a question too difficult for a mathematician, it should be asked of a philosopher."[7] People's frustrations are justified because paying taxes could be made simpler.

Burdens matter for whether we gain access to vital resources, such as education. In the United States, burdens affect whether and where a student goes to college. The price of entry for any student requiring financial assistance for college is filling out the onerous Free Application for Federal Student Aid (FAFSA) form—and then understanding and navigating a complicated loan process subsidized by the federal government.[8] Low-income students are especially vulnerable to learning costs relative to their better-advised, higher-income peers. Lacking knowledge about expected financial aid benefits and their eligibility for application fee waivers, poorer students are less likely to apply to selective institutions. As a result, they lose out on the opportunity to win financial support provided by more selective institutions that would make college less costly.[9]

Burdens are also consequential in that they can, quite literally, determine who is and is not a member of society. Nowhere are these stakes clearer than in the area of immigration. For example, U.S. citizenship applications involve complex paperwork and demanding documentation, application fees, English proficiency, and a naturalization test that requires knowledge of U.S. history. Approximately half of individuals eligible for U.S. naturalization do not apply.[10] Some may simply not want to become U.S. citizens, but surveys suggest that administrative burdens—in the form of perceived language, personal, financial, and administrative barriers—are significant factors in their decision.[11]

Debates about how to address undocumented immigrants also center on burdens. Policymakers are more comfortable with immigrants gaining legal status only when they have overcome an array of barriers. For example, the 2013 Senate-approved bill that remains the closest bipartisan solution yet to this policy issue required immigrants to wait ten years before applying for legal status, plus three additional years for citizenship. Immigrants would also be subject to background checks, required to learn English, provide documentation that they had continuously lived and worked in the United States, and pay a $1,000 fine plus assessed taxes on top of the usual fees associated with the naturalization process.[12]

In the absence of a national framework for addressing unauthorized immigrants, states have passed their own laws, also using burdens to discourage immigration. For example, in 2010, the Texas Department of Health and Human Services stopped accepting a common and secure Mexican identification (ID) card. As a result, it became more difficult for Mexican nationals to obtain a birth certificate if they had a child in Texas. Having no birth certificate makes it nearly impossible for the child to establish U.S. citizenship and restricts access to public education and nutritional or health services that have long-term positive effects on development.[13] A simple decision on documentation thereby has potentially enormous consequences for these children and families.

For some immigrants, burdens are a matter of life and death. Take the case of Jewish people seeking to exit Germany and come to the United States in the run-up to World War II. Rather than publicly deny Jews access to the country, policymakers instead relied on the burdens inherent in immigration laws to exclude them. The United States had an annual quota of between twenty-six thousand to twenty-seven thousand slots for German immigrants between 1932 and 1938, but that quota was never filled before 1938—indeed, two-thirds of the quota was unfulfilled during that time.[14] Immigrants who sought to enter the United States were stymied by an almost impossible combination of bureaucratic demands from both the German and U.S. governments. A 1917 U.S. law that immigrants not be wards of the state was applied more aggressively with the onset of the Great Depression, requiring that immigrants had to either demonstrate ample financial resources or produce affidavits showing relatives or friends in the United States who could provide support.[15]

Would-be immigrants faced another set of administrative burdens from German officials, including ever more confiscatory fees to exit the country. Refugees had to pay a flight tax of 25 percent, which gradually increased until they were no longer allowed to remove capital when they exited. Under such circumstances, it became more and more difficult to demonstrate the resources necessary to satisfy U.S. immigration requirements, leaving immigrants in a catch-22. Simply collecting required documentation was also onerous. The U.S. Immigration Act of 1924 required the provision of police dossier, prison and military records, two copies of a certified birth certificate, and other government records. For a German Jew fearful of a Nazi regime, collecting such documentation was rife with risk and nearly impossible for those who had already fled the country. But the U.S. State Department was unwilling to waive documentation requirements, justifying these restrictions as necessary because of the perceived public safety dangers from potential criminals entering the United States.[16]

Such burdens put would-be immigrants at the mercy of a hostile German bureaucracy that made it difficult, if not impossible, to satisfy the demands of the unwelcoming American bureaucracy. Many seeking to exit found themselves trapped. Quotas remained unfilled. Between 1933 and 1944, just over one hundred thousand German and Austrian Jews made it to the United States, a fraction of those who could have been saved under a less burdensome process.[17] Most who stayed perished.

Burdens Are Distributive

Do burdens help or hurt some groups more than others?[18] If so, who are the winners and losers? We argue that those who are least advantaged tend to face more administrative burdens, even though they have fewer resources to manage and overcome them.

Burdens reinforce inequalities in access to rights, including the most basic of citizenship in a democracy: the right to vote. As discussed in chapter 2, burdens that make voting more onerous hit black voters, poor voters, and those with disabilities the hardest. Policies targeted toward the poor are more likely to be burdensome relative to universal policies that all use. Relative to the near 100 percent take-up for more universal programs, such as Social Security and Medicare, take-up rates by eligible beneficiaries of means-tested programs typically aimed at poor people in the United States are much lower: 40 to 60 percent for Supplemental Social Insurance, about 65 percent for the Supplemental Nutrition Assistance Program (SNAP, frequently referred to as food stamps), 30 to 60 percent of Unemployment Insurance benefits, about 50 to 70 percent for Medicaid.[19] For the Earned Income Tax Credit (EITC), a reimbursable tax credit tied to work for low-income earners, the take-up rate is about 80 percent.[20] Aid to Families with Dependent Children (AFDC) had an estimated take-up rate of between 77 to 86 percent. Participation rates declined dramatically after 1990s welfare reform. Its successor, Temporary Assistance for Needy Families (TANF), has a much lower take-up rate, between 42 to 52 percent.[21] Means-tested programs, that is, programs conditional on financial status, must do more to distinguish between the eligible and ineligible but, in creating administrative processes to do so, add more burdens. Yet, as we show in chapter 9, more accessible programs are not inherently simple; rather, they are constructed that way.

Resources matter in overcoming burdens. For example, low-income students seeking to go to college benefit more from the provision of help than their wealthier peers who are already better advised. One experiment—which provided students with information packets that included a summary of appropriate schools given the student's achievement, the net costs of different colleges for students at different income levels, and a voucher for free college applications—made low-income students 46 percent more likely to attend a selective institution than a control group that did not receive the information.[22] In some cases, having access to someone who can help negotiate the compliance burden of completing a form makes a difference. In another experiment, simply helping families complete the FAFSA form led to dramatic increases in applications and a 29 percent increase in actual college enrollment.[23] These examples illustrate both that individuals with fewer resources have more difficulty in overcoming burdens and that the resources needed to overcome burdens are not just financial. Forms of human capital, such as education, cognitive and noncognitive skills, or a social network, also matter.

For many Americans, especially poor Americans, the experience of government is the experience of burdens. Individuals applying for Medicaid are also likely to be applying for SNAP and possibly the EITC. These same individuals are also less likely to have IDs or live in neighborhoods that provide enough polling places, making it harder to access the right to vote. Poor women are disproportionately more likely to have unplanned pregnancies and also to need access to abortion services—which many states are making more difficult to access. If their children are to go on to postsecondary school, they can look forward to the overwhelming and frustrating financial aid process. In short, not only are policies targeted at the poor more burdensome, but the poor are also more likely to experience government as routinely burdensome.

Burdens Are Constructed

Administrative burdens are the product of administrative and political choices. In some cases, burdens are necessary to protect important political values, though those making these choices may fail to understand the implications that follow. But in many cases, as we make clear in the chapters that follow, political actors often see burdens as a policy tool to achieve an ideological goal.

Such political choices can be reflected in the maintenance of burdens even when changing circumstances call for governments to minimize them. The failure of the American administrative state to adapt Depression-era burdens on immigrants in the face of an increasingly desperate situation for refugees in Europe is an example of how not acting is itself a choice. Legislative bills to ease burdens on immigrants, such as exempting refugees from the need to document that they would not become a public charge, failed to get a hearing.[24] Once the war began, Congress and the State Department increased restrictions under the justification that immigrants posed a security risk as potential spies or saboteurs.[25] In 1943, the new State Department visa application form was four feet long.[26]

Political choices about burdens can be amplified or undercut by administrative actors. In the case of immigrants, the passive response of the U.S. government was compounded by a State Department that used its discretion to harden rather than relax administrative burdens. As early as 1930, consuls in Germany were directed by the State Department to limit the issuance of visas to no more than 10 percent of the allocated quota.[27] Administrative burdens became a mechanism to achieve this goal. As World War II came to a close, and the grim fate of Jews who had stayed in Germany became apparent, the Treasury Department issued a scathing attack on the U.S. government in general and the State Department in particular. In its "Report to the Secretary on the Acquiescence of this Government in the Murder of the Jews," the Treasury identified the power of individual administrators to obstruct immigration. For example, Breckinridge Long, assistant secretary of state, described as an anti-Semite and nativist, used his bureaucratic power to block a variety of efforts to help migrants.[28] For instance, he crafted a State Department memo in 1940 guiding the obstruction of visas. Long could take such actions in the knowledge that Congress "would certainly not object to administrative devices to limit immigration."[29]

These political choices are present not only in extraordinary circumstances. They are also present in the most mundane encounters with government that nearly all people experience. Let us return to our example of paying taxes. The friction of the tax process is largely unnecessary and represents a political choice. Taxes may be inevitable, but the process of paying them could be simpler for most people in the United States. Indeed, taxpayers in some other developed countries would find the U.S. process baffling. They do not encounter the array of forms or documentation requirements that Americans associate with April 15. For them, the cost of paying taxes is the taxes themselves. Americans pay the taxes, but also face the costs of a process that is bewildering and frustrating.

A less burdensome alternative exists. When we submit our tax returns, we are usually not giving the government much new information. Employers and financial organizations have already shared income data. For an estimated 40 percent of taxpayers, the situation is simple enough that the Internal Revenue Service (IRS) could pre-calculate the estimated tax liability or refund.[30] The taxpayer would be presented with a record of these data and decide whether they agree (by checking a box and completing the process) or not (requiring them to complete the traditional tax reporting process). Sometimes called *return-free filing*, this approach uses a strategy we discuss more in this book, which relies on a mixture of administrative data and technology to reduce burdens. A Brookings Institution report suggests that such a system could both save an estimated $2 billion and 225 million hours if implemented in the United States as well as reduce the anxiety that comes with the possibility that the taxpayer may not have included all of the relevant documentation.[31] Even taxpayers who do not use the pre-prepared form because of more complex tax situations would still benefit by being able to download government tax data, reducing their compliance burden.

In fact, such a system already exists in America, though few know about it or have benefited from it. Since 2005, the state of California piloted a program called ReadyReturn for a tiny fraction of taxpayers, usually less than one hundred thousand. Those who used it gave the system high marks for helping them save both time and money. ReadyReturn files are vastly cheaper for the state to process relative to paper returns, and taxpayer errors are minimized.[32] So why has this model not been adopted more broadly in other states or at the national level? The answer is that it faces intense opposition, driven partly by companies who benefit from the existing process and partly by political ideology.

As the Obama administration pushed to expand return-free filing, Intuit—the maker of the tax preparation product TurboTax—spent heavily in opposition, including $13 million in federal lobbying and a million dollars to oppose a candidate for the California comptroller who supported ReadyReturn.[33] Intuit has also invested in building the appearance of a local opposition to return-free filing by hiring lobbyists to persuade trusted community leaders to write op-eds and letters to Congress against it.[34] The designer of ReadyReturn had been contacted by other states interested in adopting this innovation, but those calls stopped in light of Intuit's opposition. "It was a huge signal to politicians everywhere how much Intuit cares about this. People in other states who had been interested in it started saying, 'We just don't want to pick a fight with Intuit.'"[35]

Intuit's opposition is understandable. Burdens for taxpayers are business opportunities for tax preparers. Such burdens are also viewed as valuable to the degree that they serve the political goal of eroding support for both paying taxes and for government itself. Conservative opposition to simplifying the process of paying taxes is not new. "Taxes should hurt," declared Governor Ronald Reagan when he opposed the adoption of withholding of state taxes in California.[36] The logic behind this opposition is that when the process of paying taxes generates a more memorable and negative friction, people are more aware of and less supportive of taxation itself. Americans for Tax Reform, the most visible and effective anti-tax group in the United States, has also campaigned against return-free filing.

The example shows how burdens can be imposed by government but can also be minimized by creative design to shift burdens away from citizens and onto the government. Such a shift would require an investment in government capacity and resources but give citizens real reason to believe their government is working to improve their lives. Austin Goolsbee, a former chair of the Council of Economic Advisers, has championed return-free filing: "For the cost of modernizing the computer matching system within the I.R.S. and the Social Security Administration, we could eliminate the compliance burden for more than one-third of American taxpayers."[37]

This same opportunity—investments in modernizing government's capacity in return for minimizing citizen's experience of burdens—exists in multiple policy settings. Throughout this book, we point to examples of burdens being increased and reduced, shifted from the citizen to the state and vice versa; in our concluding chapter, we provide a template for action. But the tax case also illustrates that burdens are often the function of political processes, sometimes maintained even when a better option is technically feasible. Further, it shows how political actors will use disingenuous arguments to rationalize the imposition of burdens. Anti-tax groups justify their opposition to simpler tax returns by saying that government cannot be trusted to estimate data it collects from its citizens, even though they must use the data reported to them by employers and made available to employees. An even more befuddling argument against simplifying tax preparation comes from Intuit: filling out needless tax forms is a form of citizen participation and empowerment.[38] By this logic, the most participatory democracy is the one that condemns citizens to spend their days wrestling with Kafkaesque bureaucracies.

Although politics matters, so does administrative capacity. Chapter 4's discussion of the Affordable Care Act (ACA), informally known as Obamacare, describes a natural experiment of sorts. States that politically opposed the ACA used administrative procedures to make it difficult for people to enroll in health insurance. The Trump administration limited ACA advertising and shortened public enrollment periods to achieve the same goal. But low administrative capacity also created burdens among governments supportive of the ACA. Most prominently, the Obama administration presided over a disastrous rollout of the federal exchange. State governments that wanted to take advantage of ACA struggled to make new processes accessible to citizens. The overriding lesson is that opportunities to shift administrative burdens away from individuals depends on a mixture of political will and administrative capacity. In some cases, that capacity comes not just from government but also from non-profit or private actors who can help the citizen shoulder burdens.

Basic Assumptions About Burdens

Are burdens always bad? Of course not! Some are unavoidable. The government has a legitimate interest in imposing some costs on citizens. The design of public policies reflects the often-competing values we expect from our government.[39] Citizens want government services to be efficient and free from fraud. It follows that an administrator tasked with implementing, for example, a means-tested program needs to distinguish between those eligible and ineligible for that program. Let us assume a happy scenario in which burdens deterred fraud and had no negative effect on program participation. In such a scenario, burdens are relatively easy to justify, though there may be ways that reduce costs while still protecting key values.

This book explores other cases, in which burdens are harder to justify. What about a second potential scenario, when costs imposed on individuals may provide some benefit, such as minimizing fraud, but impede other public values we care about, such as access, equality, or a program mission of reducing poverty? This is more troubling. It is fair to examine our tolerance for burdens under such circumstances. Is it justifiable if one case of fraud were prevented for each eligible person who no longer participated? Perhaps. What about one case of fraud for every ten or even one hundred eligible people who no longer received benefits? In such a case, we might decide that though burdens have an important value, the costs are too high, motivating us to find other ways to achieve the goal of deterring fraud, or even increasing our tolerance of fraud. But to make that decision, we first need a framework to identify burdens, their costs, and their benefits.

A third scenario is that burdens are imposed to achieve a purported goal but in reality have no tangible relationship with that goal. There might be little evidence of the fraud in the first place, making the burdens ineffective. Such is the case for laws that make voting harder, such as voter ID requirements (see chapter 2). It could be that the burdens are logically unrelated to the purported outcome. For example, burdens imposed on women seeking abortion are justified on the basis of protecting women's health, even though no evidence indicates that they do so, and some suggests that they may in fact worsen women's health (see chapter 3). In this scenario, it seems fair to conclude that limiting citizen access to a service is the tacit goal being pursued.

This book addresses all of these scenarios, but we focus on cases in which the value of burdens seems at best debatable and at worse entirely unjustified. Does this imply that the book strikes a normative stance? Yes: we make a number of normative assumptions that are worth being explicit about now, and return to them in the final chapter.

First, citizens are better off when public programs are designed to be simple, accessible, and respectful of the citizens they encounter. Most people would agree that if the public sector provides a service, it should be one that is visible enough to be seen, simple enough to comply with, and not psychologically taxing.

Second, burdens should be minimized to the greatest extent consistent with protecting important public values, such as cost and program integrity. Third, considerations of burden should be evidence based, identifying the multiple values involved and the likely effects of burdens on those values, and informed by logic and empirical evidence rather than by political rhetoric.

Fourth, because burdens can affect some groups more than others, we should be especially attentive to costs on those with limited resources or in programs that are specifically to help those with limited means. One corollary to this principle is that when policies affect large numbers of people, such as voting or Social Security, reducing burdens has a greater social benefit. Broadly accessible programs can reach more people, and therefore be more likely to achieve policy goals, whether it be reducing poverty, encouraging work, or fostering better health. A second corollary is that the public officials should explicitly consider the challenges for those who have the greatest difficulties in overcoming burdens. For any particular set of burdens, some groups will struggle more than others. For example, in chapter 6, we examine the particular challenges that older adults face in accessing SNAP benefits. When possible, burdens should be designed to be minimal enough to not exclude those that struggle with them the most. Having fewer hoops to jump through implies that those with fewer resources have a greater opportunity to participate and less risk of facing discrimination. If such populations still struggle, support should be provided to facilitate their participation.

Conclusion

Our goal in this book is to develop the concept of administrative burden as a framework for understanding how citizens and government interact with each other. In doing so, we illustrate the wide applicability of the concept across a variety of policy areas from welfare and health benefits to rights protected by the Constitution, such as the right to vote. Our examination of these policy areas shows that in some cases, political ideology or policy preferences lead politicians to use burdens to make government a source of hindrance rather than of help. In this respect, burdens contribute to dysfunction by design, making government an ineffectual and unwelcome presence in people's lives rather than an institution that solves problems.[40]

To implement the assumptions outlined in the previous section, we need to be able to ask, and answer, several basic questions. How would these principles work in practice? How do we determine when burdens are unjustified? How do we design and manage public programs in ways that shift administrative burdens away from citizens? Whose role is it to shine a spotlight on these burdens, and how do they make determinations?

To answer these questions first requires the type of conceptual language we present in this book. Chapter 1 takes on this task by offering a more detailed definition of administrative burden, and a deeper theoretical framing of how it works. Armed with that conceptual language, we make the case that although burdens are often a function of politics and power, their existence should be documented in a way that currently does not occur, tracking both their costs and benefits. State actors whose task it is to provide a rational provision of public services have a special responsibility here. We conclude by arguing for a professional norm of assessing burdens, under which policymakers and public managers regularly evaluate the benefits of burdens with a bias toward reduction, and that the administrative state should be refurbished to have the capacity to make government simple, accessible, and respectful.

UNDERSTANDING ADMINISTRATIVE BURDEN

1

The idea of administrative burden is not new. First, we identify how previous researchers have addressed the topic. But across this body of work is no common conceptualization of what it means. As a result, we are left with something akin to the parable of the blind men each describing a different part of the elephant but unable to make sense of the whole. Researchers across diverse fields are not talking to one another, key questions are not being asked, and research is not accumulating into actionable knowledge. A key goal of this book is to engage in concept-building that enables us to see the whole, by asking a wider array of questions and offering a more integrated approach to answering them.

Second, we lay out a broad framework to understand administrative burdens, built on three types of costs and the individuals' experiences when they come to interact with government. *Learning costs* arise from engaging in search processes to collect information about public services: Are there services that can fulfill unmet needs? Would one qualify for them? What are the requirements for the application process? *Psychological costs* include the stigma of applying for or participating in a program with negative characterizations, a sense of loss of personal power or autonomy in interactions with the state, or the stresses and frustrations of dealing with administrative processes. *Compliance costs* are the material burdens of following administrative rules and requirements. This is the time lost waiting in line, completing forms or providing documentation of status. It is the money spent on hiring an accountant to do your taxes, or the fees immigrants pay to process paperwork.

In addition to conceptualizing administrative burden, this framework maps the ways that politics relate to burden and identifies the role nonstate actors can play in buffering or amplifying the effects of burdens.

Antecedents of the Concept of Administrative Burden

Our framing of administrative burden as costs may imply a rational approach under which citizens weigh costs against expected benefits. A perspective from economics, which frames burdens as *ordeal mechanisms*, rests on such an approach: only those who truly derive a good deal of utility from a good or service will put up with the hassles that must be borne to receive it. Those who are not highly motivated to receive the good, such as wealthier people who value their time more highly and are unwilling to spend it negotiating burdens, will exit the process.[1]

The ordeal mechanism perspective warns us that burdens can be so great that people will simply opt out of dealing with processes they find too onerous. But it also has limitations. For one thing, unless elected officials deliberately design administrative processes with the rationing effect of burdens in mind, such effects are an unanticipated consequence of policy, rather than a deliberate feature. Second, the logic of ordeal mechanisms may be incorrect in its assumption as to why individuals falter when faced with burdens. For example, poorer people may have less resources available to negotiate burdens as they try to make ends meet. They lack the resources, for example, to pay for childcare, which would allow them to apply for multiple jobs or job training to maintain income supports. The more fundamental error with this approach is that it supposes that the willingness to negotiate burdens is a function of desire: that those who do not wait in line, turn up for an appointment, or complete a form simply do not value the resulting reward highly enough. As we argue later, human capital (or resources ranging from educational attainment, cognitive and noncognitive skills, to one's social networks) is another important explanation for people's ability to negotiate burdens.

Research from behavioral economics, in contrast, does not assume that individuals are necessarily rational. Indeed, such research shows that people rarely weigh benefits and costs in a fully rational fashion.[2]

This is because individual decisions depend on how individuals construe the world, not on objective measures of costs and benefits. This construal is shaped by contextual factors that frame burdens and interact with individual psychological processes, including cognitive biases that generate a disproportionate response to burden. This basic insight explains why burdens that seem minor and defensible when designed by the administrator can exert dramatic negative effects when experienced by a citizen.

Behavioral economics also helps identify particular cognitive biases that make burdens more consequential.[3] Individuals have biases in perceiving risk and probability, which in turn alter their willingness to overcome administrative burdens. For example, people who underestimate the risks of ill-health are also less likely to make the effort to overcome the burdens involved in enrolling in health insurance. Individuals also tend to overvalue the status quo of their situation, even if a different state is objectively superior. How institutions structure the default choice individuals face therefore has significant effects. For instance, changing the default on private savings plans from nonparticipation to participation has a large effect on take-up rates.[4] Individuals have biases in temporal planning, favoring the present and discounting the future. Avoiding burdens in the present may be preferred even if it means forgoing long-term net benefits. Another bias arises from choice overload or decisional conflict, which occurs when individuals feel overwhelmed by a multiplicity of choice, resulting in indecision, the selection of defaults, or poor decisions.

The advent of behavioral economics, and specifically its translation into policy *nudges*—structuring of choices to optimize outcomes— has drawn attention to how required procedures to access benefits influence policy effectiveness.[5] This research has shown, as we do in this book, that little burdens can have big effects and that policymakers and administrators should design public services with that risk in mind. The strengths of the behavioral approach—a focus on cognitive biases and choice architecture—are in some respects also weaknesses, in that the approach has given less attention to questions such as the origins of burdens, and specifically the broader political processes involved in their construction. It is easy to assume that the need for a nudge is simply the result of the choice architect being unaware of behavioral limitations. If so, once a better choice architecture is determined, it will be adopted.[6] We argue, though, that some programs are implemented to be burdensome, that the burden is a deliberate mechanism to undermine the original policy goal.

The nudge perspective has also been critiqued for leaving issues of inequality relatively untouched.[7] Nudges become an attractive mode of action when one has decided to ignore more structural shoves that influence societal inequality. For example, simplifying financial aid forms would have a less significant impact than making college free. This critique is ultimately unfair because the point of nudges is to improve the incremental effectiveness of existing policies. Yet, the focus on individual choice as the unit of analysis has given too little attention on the broader political processes that frame those choices. The focus on the architecture of choice also fails to account for how burdens may be targeted, either by policymakers or by front-level officials, at specific groups, again raising the specter of inequality. The programs targeted at poor people, from Supplemental Nutrition Assistance Program (SNAP) to Medicaid, tend to have the greatest administrative burdens.

The study of administrative burden is relatively rare in the field of public administration. The closest concept to administrative burden is red tape. The most widely used definition of red tape comes from Barry Bozeman: "rules, regulations, and procedures that remain in force and entail a compliance burden, but do not advance the legitimate purposes the rules were intended to serve."[8] This definition suggests that any rule that advances a legitimate purpose cannot be classified as red tape. In considering the definition of red tape, Bozeman and Mary Feeney note that "Red tape is bad. It is not an aid to accountability or legitimacy or a means of ensuring participation. Rules that appropriately hold organizations accountable may not be popular with the people constrained by them, but they are not red tape."[9]

By contrast, we assume that administrative burdens will often serve legitimate purposes and are not inherently bad. What might be onerous for the individual might reflect a legitimate interest of the state, and a full understanding of burdens requires understanding both the interests of the state and examining the experience of the individual. Another important distinction from red tape research is that although it focuses on the compliance burden generated by

Figure 1.1 *A Framework for Understanding State Construction of Burdens*

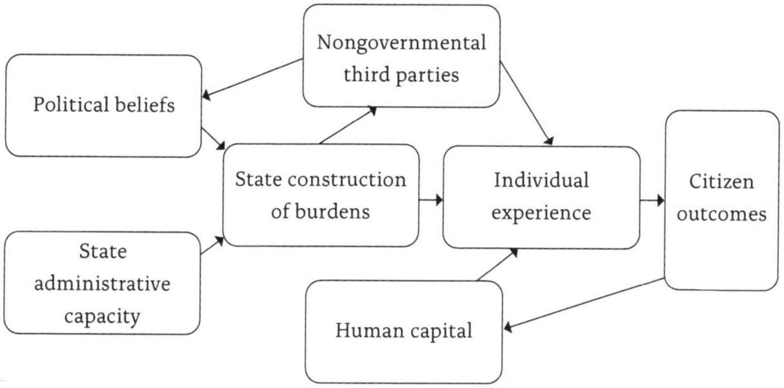

Source: Authors' compilation.

rules, we argue that it is just one component of a broader experience of burden, falling into the category of compliance costs. Perhaps because of the restrictive nature of the definition, little attention has been paid to the actual rules that citizens face; instead, research has centered on managerial perceptions of red tape.[10]

Another antecedent to our concept is research on ways in which rules or administrative discretion reduces access to programs. Such work is most prominent at the intersection of public administration and social policy, reflecting a broader concern with issues of "bureaucratic disentitlement" and equity.[11] This work is especially valuable in suggesting that burdens may be deliberately targeted at less powerful groups in society that are classified as "undeserving" and exercised by unsympathetic street-level bureaucrats. But this literature has retained a particular focus on social welfare policies targeted at poor individuals. Our goal is to broaden the concept to illustrate its application to an array of citizen-state interactions, whether it be a single mother trying to access Medicaid or an individual trying to vote.

Figure 1.1 lays out a broad theoretical model of administrative burdens that incorporates insights from existing literatures. To make the framework reasonably parsimonious in this discussion, not all possible causal pathways are specified, and not all of them are explored in equal detail. The framework establishes some boundary conditions of our approach, which in turn shape the cases we select, which are conceived as falling within the domain of public policy and administration. Although private-sector use of burdens are numerous and often ingenious—for example, requiring shoppers to mail in a rebate rather than provide it automatically—they are not considered here.

We also focus on the state construction of burdens that affects *individual citizens* who access public services. This may sound straightforward, but it is important to articulate, because much of the prior research on red tape in public administration has focused on the experience of bureaucrats, and that on regulation largely on private organizations.[12]

We do not discuss how burdens on businesses are problematic, simply because governments of all political ideologies are already responding to that message by building safeguards to protect private organizations from regulation. For example, President Ronald Reagan institutionalized a requirement for cost-benefit analyses to demonstrate that any new regulation provides a net social good. There is no equivalent for regulation of citizens beyond the Paperwork Reduction Act of 1980, which mandates that agencies track the time it takes for a citizen to complete a form but does not require that such burdens provide a net benefit.

Another protection for businesses is targeted reductions in regulations. For example, President Obama signed an executive order to reduce red tape. The European Commission committed to reducing regulations in the European Union by 25 percent. President Trump set a standard that every new regulation be accompanied by the removal of two regulations, mirroring similar mandates by the United Kingdom and Canada.

In all of these cases, the primary focus is on regulations that affect businesses. These examples point to the relative success that private organizations have had in lobbying for safeguards to protect against what they view as excessive regulation, a success that reflects not just their political influence but also economic orthodoxy, which counsels against overburdening organizations. International organizations such as the World Bank and Organization for Economic Cooperation and Development (OECD) encourage client governments to adopt a less burdensome regulatory regime.[13] The burdens on individual citizens are, by comparison, an afterthought.[14]

Given those parameters, our framework starts with a basic assumption that all encounters between citizens and the state generate some costs, even if minimal. Those costs will be borne by the state or the citizen, or are shared between the two parties. For example, does the state collect information from citizens via forms or its own administrative records? Does the state heavily advertise a program or service, or must citizens learn by themselves? A relatively neglected area in the study of government is how those costs are distributed across states and citizens, and how the state constructs or minimizes burdens. Are choices about costs made openly with a full discussion of consequences, or are they hidden either in recesses of bureaucratic implementation or via opaque policy justifications?

Policy design create burdens, and some burdens legitimately reflect the nature of the policy itself. For example, relative to universal policies, policies tightly targeted at specific groups are more likely to generate eligibility determinations that impose burdens. Consequently, individuals seeking benefits from the Social Security Disability program face more burdens than those applying to the Social Security Retirement Income program. Although the Social Security Administration is designed to administratively track employment and earnings histories, which is relevant for both benefits, the additional layer of proving one is disabled adds significant burdens on citizens. Policies that benefit larger numbers of people, or are more visible or easily understood will demand less effort on the part of citizens to learn about.

Policy implementation will also affect how people experience burden. The state can take action to provide information and reduce stigma through policy messaging about the program. Outreach efforts, and the availability and clarity of information, can affect learning costs. Choices about the design of customer service processes can make the wait time at a Department of Motor Vehicles (DMV) take twenty minutes in one state and two hours in another.

These design choices are limited by what is technologically feasible. As new options become possible, burdens can be restructured and minimized. For example, those buying groceries using electronic benefit transfer cards face lower compliance and psychological costs than those using traditional food stamps. Information technology makes sharing accurate information easier, potentially reducing learning costs. For services that require verifying identity and eligibility, combining a mixture of technology and administrative data offers the promise of fewer compliance burdens.

New technologies can be used either to diminish burdens but in some cases may make them worse. The use of information technology in bureaucracies may restrict the capacity of administrators to use their discretion to minimize the effects of burdens. For example, the automation of Food Stamp benefits in Indiana sidelined caseworkers, replacing them with unwieldy technological processes that many claimants struggled with, resulting in a decline in take-up of benefits, even as take-up was increasing in the rest of the country.[15]

Individual Experience of Burdens and Effects on Citizens

A simple definition of administrative burden is that it is an individual's experience of a policy's implementation as onerous.[16] A more specific definition is that administrative burdens are the learning, psychological, and compliance costs that citizens experience in their interactions with government. This definition is helpful for two reasons. First, it distinguishes between the actions of the state and the experience of the individual. As figure 1.1 makes clear, the state can construct rules and processes that give rise to the experience of burden, but the individual experience of burden is distinct from rules and process. Second, the definition allows for variation in the experience of burdens. To return to the example of the DMV, both the person who has waited twenty minutes and the person who has waited two hours have experienced burdens, but the costs imposed on the latter are greater. It may seem excessive to label twenty minutes as burdensome because it may reflect the most efficient service possible. But allowing for variation in the degree of burden provides for greater precision, enabling us to distinguish between experiences that are more or less burdensome.

To broaden the simple definitions given, we identify broad categories of costs that constitute administrative burden (see table 1.1). We also offer more detailed examples of these costs in the context of specific programs, which foreshadow many of the examples we study, and provides strong evidence of how burdens affect citizen outcomes that feature in figure 1.1.

Table 1.1 *The Components of Administrative Burden*

Learning costs	Time and effort expended to learn about the program or service, ascertaining eligibility status, the nature of benefits, conditions that must be satisfied, and how to gain access
Compliance costs	Provision of information and documentation to demonstrate standing; financial costs to access services (such as fees, legal representation, travel costs); avoiding or responding to discretionary demands made by administrators
Psychological costs	Stigma arising from applying for and participating in an unpopular program; loss of autonomy that comes from intrusive administrative supervision; frustration at dealing with learning and compliance costs, unjust or unnecessary procedures; stresses that arise from uncertainty about whether a citizen can negotiate processes and compliance costs

Source: Authors' compilation.

LEARNING COSTS

The effects of learning costs on whether people take up available benefits have been inferred in various ways. One approach is to document lack of knowledge about a program by its target population. People are frequently unaware of a program in general, whether they qualify, what is required to qualify, or the size of the benefits at stake. Individual knowledge varies across programs, but even for prominent programs such as job training and SNAP, about half of eligible nonparticipants believe that they are not eligible.[17] Surveys of nonparticipants suggest that they would apply for programs if they knew for certain they were eligible.[18]

Learning costs have also been evoked to explain the negative effects of other factors on take-up, such as living farther from administrative centers or having lower education or language barriers.[19] Learning costs also help to explain why those already in one program become more likely to access other services because applying to one program can generate knowledge about others.[20] Association with groups such as unions, veterans groups, or aid from private actors such as tax preparers has been shown to increase take-up because these third parties reduce learning costs by directly providing relevant information.[21] Field experiments have shown that simply providing information tends to increase take-up for programs such as the Earned Income Tax Credit (EITC) and SNAP, or financial aid for college.[22]

COMPLIANCE COSTS

Of the three components of burden identified in table 1.1, the strongest empirical evidence is for compliance costs.[23] Natural experiments have shown that new income documentation requirements reduce program participation among eligible participants.[24] Requiring applicants to undertake face-to-face interviews with caseworkers also decreases participation.[25] The experience of U.S. welfare reform in the mid-1990s provides persuasive evidence of the effects of compliance burdens. Participation in Temporary Assistance for Needy Families (TANF) sharply declined relative to its predecessor Aid to Families with Dependent Children (AFDC), which was partly the result of more stringent conditions of participation and the associated procedural barriers.[26]

Efforts to reduce compliance costs increase take-up. States that simplified reporting procedures and extended the time from six months to a year, until participants had to prove their eligibility again to stay enrolled, saw an increase in successful SNAP claimants.[27] The use of a single form for multiple programs is associated with increased take-up in Medicaid.[28] Similarly, having easy access to application materials increases take-up. The availability of electronic applications increased EITC and SNAP participation.[29]

The provision of help in completing applications also matters. Access to community-based application assistants increased certain groups' enrollment in Medicaid.[30] Providing application help has been shown to lead to an almost 80 percent increase in SNAP applications relative to those who were informed they were eligible but given no special assistance.[31] The most dramatic way by which the state can reduce application compliance burden is to auto-enroll eligible individuals into a program based on administrative data, which has also increased take-up of health insurance programs.[32]

PSYCHOLOGICAL COSTS

Work from social psychology points to fundamental aspects of human behavior that are relevant to understanding burden. Individuals have a basic need for autonomy over themselves and their actions.[33] Processes under which the state imposes burdens act as a source of external direction over individual autonomy. The more forceful that direction and the more at odds with the individual's intrinsic preferences, the greater the sense of loss of autonomy, which in turn will lower willingness to participate in and satisfaction with the process. Social psychology also points to the importance of procedural justice.[34] Individuals care as much or more about the process of their interactions with the state as they do about the outcome. Procedures perceived as consistent, fair, and equitable are fundamentally important to citizens. Administrative procedures perceived as arbitrary, unfair, and discriminatory leave us unhappy with our interactions with government.

If behavioral economics provides a logic for why cognitive biases make small burdens a big deal, social psychology suggests that violating basic psychological needs of autonomy and respectful treatment also exacerbate burdens. These insights align well with observational research, which shows how citizens value processes seen as respectful and empowering but respond negatively to those seen as unfair and demeaning.[35] Cross-national comparisons of citizen trust in government find that fair and equitable processes matter more than assessments of government performance.[36]

Different streams of research point to the ways in which psychological costs can emerge in the provision of social benefits. Economists have pointed to the stigma of participating in unpopular programs.[37] Research from political science and political sociology provides a logic for why programs serving recipients characterized as undeserving are unpopular.[38] Negative conceptions about those perceived as deviant or lazy become embedded political messaging. This is in stark contrast to programs of a more universal nature, such as Social Security and Medicare, where the broader base of beneficiaries are perceived of as deserving.[39]

Individuals may opt out of participating in unpopular programs to avoid damaging their self-identity or the negative treatments they believe are associated with participation.[40] For example, the stigma of using food stamps (as opposed to discount coupons) at a grocery store is a consequence of political perceptions of the program. In a survey of likely eligible individuals not receiving Food Stamp benefits, 27 percent said they would not apply. Among them, nearly half reported factors that indicated they wanted to avoid feeling ashamed, such as not wanting people to realize that they were poor.[41] This points to an example of how stigma can arise from societal constructions of a program and its recipients but also can be reduced or amplified by implementation processes. Here, using electronic benefit cards rather than traditional food stamps reduces the sense of stigma that arises from societal beliefs.

Interactions with the state may be experiences of power, or more precisely, the loss of power. Because the interaction is experienced as degrading, intrusive, or directive, it violates the basic need for autonomy. Receipt of benefits may be conditioned on required classes in, for example, financial literacy, which communicates to the individual that the state believes their financial distress is a function of poor choices. Alternatively, the individual must submit to processes normally reserved for citizens under suspicion of lawbreaking, further communicating a moral judgment being levied against them. Historically, social benefits to single mothers have been denied if caseworkers felt that claimants were not providing suitable homes. Such mothers were subject to close examination of their parenting, and even to "midnight raids" to verify that there was no "man in the house."[42]

Echoes of such extreme asymmetries in power persist in parts of the contemporary welfare system. For instance, fingerprinting applicants lowers Food Stamp application completion and some states have attempted to mandate drug testing as a requirement for benefits.[43] The questions claimants face may force them to provide what they see as private and unnecessary information, such as sexual partners or the income of co-habitants.[44] A sense of subservience and loss of autonomy is furthered when claimants feel that they must artificially alter their identity to be successful, contorting themselves into what they perceive as the caseworker's image of the deserving client,[45] or participate in requirements whose purpose they disagree with. For example, participants may view job-training programs as offering few skills to enable them to move out of poverty but feel they have no choice but to participate.[46]

Other aspects of citizen-state interactions can more subtly reinforce messages of power and standing. Welfare office waiting spaces tend to be systematically designed to convey certain messages to those who use them.[47] The simple act of waiting communicates that the state believes that individuals' time is of little value.[48] Such spaces may also be characterized by few amenities, the use of security, and partitions between claimants and caseworkers, further reiterating the limited standing of the claimant.[49]

Studies of welfare programs illustrate how the state may communicate that people are unable to determine how to live their lives and must conform to externally imposed processes and directives. Qualitative accounts find that welfare claimants are acutely aware of the disempowering effects of such processes and their relative lack of autonomy in the interaction, resulting in a sense of frustration, powerlessness, and degradation.[50]

In situations when the individual depends on the state for vital resources—provision of health services, income, immigration status—uncertainty about the receipt of those benefits, as well as frustrations in the process of seeking benefits, may elevate stress among individuals. For example, extensive research documents how caregiving of the old, sick, and disabled is associated with higher stress and poor health;[51] little effort has been made, however, to examine the degree to which stress is a consequence of negative interactions with the state while attempting to obtain benefits.

More generally, excessive compliance costs can cause high levels of stress, particularly among the more vulnerable. For example, it is not uncommon for parents of children with disabilities to identify the burdens they encounter when trying to access services for their children as a major source of stress.[52] A Kentucky mother trying to get Medicaid support for her blind and autistic daughter was stymied after the state demanded a pay stub for her eighty-eight-cent commission from Amazon for occasional blog writing. She noted, "I'm spinning so many plates. No wonder I feel overwhelmed and defeated."[53]

Dana Nieder, a New Yorker recertifying a disability parking permit for her permanently disabled daughter, was required to complete

multiple applications, provide paperwork from her daughter's physician, and see a city physician. Then the city sought additional
medical documentation, including a CT scan of her daughter's brain,
chromosomal labs, a neurology report, a psychological evaluation,
school documentation of her daughter's disability, and details of
her daughter's orthotics. After jumping through these hoops, she
received the permit only to realize it would be valid for just eight
months. She explained her frustration:

> Let me prove to you how different my daughter is and how many
> special needs she has and how it is permanent, it's permanent,
> and why must I keep telling you that she can't walk for long and
> her balance isn't great and everything is more work for her. And
> everything is more work for me. And she gets so tired. And I get
> so tired. *I am so tired.*
>
> I shouldn't have to fight annually for a parking permit. I need
> to fight for therapies, and to fight for school placements, and to
> fight for her rights over and over again. I need to fight insurance
> companies and to fight for assistive technology, and then to fight
> people to use the assistive technology that I fought for. I need to
> fight prejudices and fight ignorance and often fight her as she is
> pushed and challenged and learning to fight for herself (I hope).[54]

Understanding the imposition of psychological costs by the state
on its citizens is inherently important. However, the evidence of
how psychological costs matter to program take-up is less strong
than for other types of burdens. Although electronic benefit cards
can reduce stigma costs, evidence is mixed on whether such cards
have increased take-up.[55] A field experiment to reduce stigma with
the EITC (by sending mailings to eligible respondents that empha-
size higher peer use, or framing benefits as a reward for hard work)
did not increase take-up.[56] Evidence is also not strong that advertising campaigns that frame programs in positive terms matter to
take-up.[57] These results may indicate that opinions about programs
are difficult to change. We do not have experimental evidence on the
effects of negative treatments likely to induce psychological costs,
such as the effects of drug tests. Additionally, although psychological
and compliance burdens are conceptually distinct, it is often difficult
from a practical standpoint to separate them in the type of empirical

studies described here. Some of the benefits attributed to reductions of compliance burdens could be attributable to reductions in psychological costs.

EFFECTS ON POLITICAL PARTICIPATION

These examples leave little doubt, within the area of social policy at least, that administrative burdens have material impacts on whether individuals receive public services. Throughout this volume, we also provide evidence as to how burdens affect, indirectly, the health and economic security of citizens, and even their civic and political participation. For example, in chapter 2, we examine how burdens affect people's ability to vote.

Although not a central theme in this discussion, a broader policy feedback literature further suggests that citizen experiences of policies—and by extension the experience of burdensome processes that come with those policies—affects political efficacy and civic participation.[58] Such feedback effects can occur via two processes: first, the resources the state provides (such as education) that enable the citizen to gain civic skills, and, second, citizen interpretations of government rules and procedures they are exposed to, which convey "perceptions of their role in the community, their status in relation to other citizens and government, and the extent to which a policy has affected their lives."[59] Administrative burdens can affect both mechanisms. They can make resources more or less difficult to attain, and structure state rules and procedures to engender more or less negative interpretations among mass publics, or specific subgroups. Cumulatively, such effects matter beyond the individual, altering political participation, social capital, civic trust, or trust in government in broader society.[60]

Our focus is often on the costs of burdens, but this does not preclude positive effects. Positive interactions with the state can increase citizen confidence and knowledge of opportunities, and allow them to develop participatory skills.[61] For example, the development of Social Security played a crucial role in converting older Americans from being the least to the most politically active demographic group in U.S. society.[62] Chapter 9 illustrates the great care that the designers of Social Security made in ensuring that resources were broadly accessible via respectful processes. The GI Bill (formally the Serviceman's Readjustment Act of 1944) offers another example of the positive effects of a targeted program. Former soldiers experienced the program as conveying fairness and respect, engendering a sense of mutual civic commitment that saw them become more active citizens than equally well-educated veterans.[63] Although means-tested programs are generally assumed to convey more negative experiences, variation in implementation, even within the same program, can meaningfully alter the experience of a program to be more positive.[64]

Human Capital and Inequality

Burdens are not equally distributed. They are targeted toward some groups more than others. Thus, although interactions with the state can alter people's civic skills, their ability to negotiate those interactions will also be influenced by their existing skills. Human capital—such as education, money, social networks, intelligence, psychological resources, and health—matter to how people cope with administrative burdens. For example, a wealthier immigrant can hire a lawyer to manage the compliance burdens in citizenship application. The voter in better physical health is more likely to walk to the local polling station. People with more social connections or education have a greater ability to learn about a program and understand the requirements they need to satisfy in order to participate.

Human capital is not equally distributed. Those who may need services the most—those with lower income, less education, and fewer language skills—may therefore be most negatively affected by burdens. This group may also have lower access to forms of human capital resources that would help them overcome the burdens. Indeed, evidence indicates that burdens have differential impacts by class, race, and gender in social programs, education, voting registration rules, and immigration.[65]

The stresses of poverty may reduce cognitive capacity and exacerbate biases that amplify the effects of burdens, making people who feel threatened or exhausted more likely to make poor long-term choices.[66] It becomes harder to take a long-term perspective on financial choices when bills are overdue. For example, simply telling people to imagine that they face a large car-repair bill leads them to perform less well on IQ tests than those told to imagine they face a small bill.[67] In this fashion, as experiences with the state become stressful they may further undercut an individual's human capital and their ability to negotiate the administrative processes that gives rise to those stresses in the first place.

Part of the purpose of this book is to highlight the ways in which different forms of human capital have plausible or demonstrated connections to the effect of administrative burdens. The net effect of variation in human capital is that administrative burdens can exacerbate inequality. Administrative burdens can also contribute to inequality in another way if they are targeted at groups who already have limited resources. In the chapters that follow, we show that those seeking publicly funded income supports or health access are targeted with burdens. In general, those who lack political power or who are seen as undeserving tend to be less successful in winning benefits from the policy process.[68] The same insight applies to administrative burdens: those who are powerless or are categorized as undeserving are more vulnerable to burdens.

How Does Administrative Capacity Matter?

Thus far, we have discussed how the state establishes burdens, how citizens experience them, the effects on citizen outcomes, and the moderating role of human capital. We now return to the first link in the chain of effects presented in figure 1.1—how administrative capacity and political beliefs matter to the construction of burdens. Although the book pays greater attention to the role of politics, basic administrative capacity also plays an important role in shaping administrative burdens. Financial resources, administrative expertise, and organizational capacity all influence the degree to which the state can reduce administrative burdens on citizens.

Financial resources affect the ability of the state to minimize or shift burdens away from citizens. This trade-off is easy to miss if we examine government costs in the provision of services but neglect citizen costs. To give a simple example from chapter 9, efforts to save money by closing Social Security field offices or limiting hours shifts compliance burdens on to citizens. An administrator overseeing such cuts might not fully realize the implications, thus think that the cuts are more palatable than they are, or may have little choice in the matter.

Reduced budgets for such organizations and their overworked employees is itself a matter of political choice. Congress has consistently cut the Internal Revenue Service (IRS) budget since 2010, despite increased demands on the agency. As a result, citizens calling the IRS to get help filing might be greeted with a "courtesy disconnect"— 8.8 million callers were disconnected in 2015. In 2010, about 75 percent of calls got through and the average wait time was eleven minutes. By 2015, only 37 percent got through and the average wait time was twenty-three minutes.[69]

Capacity includes not just financial resources but also administrative expertise. Ultimately, individuals within organizations design the systems that clients interact with to obtain benefits. Those with more expertise can use those skills to design more easily accessible systems or to put more barriers in place. Chapter 9, which explores the creation of the Social Security program, demonstrates how skilled administrators, even when operating with low budgets, tight timelines, and political opposition, built a robust administrative machinery that ensured few burdens for the employers and citizens who interacted with the program.

General organizational expertise also matters. For example, the ability of programs such as Medicare (discussed in chapter 5) to automate aspects of eligibility assessments depends on functioning administrative data systems. Although less central to our interests, differences in implementation may be the product of other administrative factors, such as bureaucratic culture and motivation. Administrators who play an active role in creating and enforcing burdens and those directly providing public services to citizens may use their discretion to rigidly enforce, expand upon, or ameliorate the effects of burdens. Research on these street-level bureaucrats finds they are sometimes biased against different groups—reflecting personal bias or popular stereotypes—when they impose burdens.[70]

Just as administrators shape burdens, so may burdens matter to how administrators define their understanding of their organizational role. For example, because administrators motivated to help others believe their work causes them to impose unfair burdens, their organizational commitment, motivation, and effort may decline, and their sense of alienation and desire to quit may increase.[71]

How Do Political Beliefs Matter?

In some cases, burdens may arise inadvertently, through history, accident, or lack of foresight.[72] In many cases, burdens reflect legislative objectives, such as requirements that poverty-based policies serve those who are actually poor, and only those. However, relatively little attention has been paid to the politics of burdens. We propose that politicians will sometimes deliberately construct administrative burdens—as a complement or alternative to traditional forms of policymaking—to achieve their policy goals (although this is not the only way that burdens are created). Moreover, the politics of burden is a mechanism for understanding how the state shapes inequality.

A classic definition of politics—"who gets what, when, where, and how"—underlines its essentially distributive nature.[73] Administrative burdens play a central role in determining when, how, and where goods, services, and rights are distributed and, in practice, who is likely to receive them. It follows that political choices play some role in these processes. To understand such choices, we shine a light on a venue where politics matters and has played an underappreciated role.

Our argument consists of a few simple strands that, when woven together, offer new insights into the relationship between politics and governing. First, the creation or reduction of burdens is a venue where political values—and therefore political processes—play out. Second, partisan attitudes toward burdens are policy specific, and therefore relatively predictable once we know a party's stance in a policy area. Third, partisan attitudes are consequential to burdens, because elected officials use burdens as a substitute or complement for other forms of policy action. Fourth, the unobtrusive nature of burdens makes them an especially useful form of policymaking by other means. Finally, political stakeholders play an important role in determining burdens.

The first and most basic claim in our argument is that the creation and reductions of burden is a process in which politics plays out. Fights over burdens are fights about political values, such as access or program integrity, as well as the legitimacy of claims on the state made by some groups.[74] The venues of these fights are often within bureaucracies, where values are converted into bureaucratic logics and procedures.[75]

Welfare policies offer a straightforward illustration of how burdens reflect articulations of competing values. As far back as the Nixon administration, welfare programs have not been designed to balance take-up by eligible claimants with mistaken payments to ineligible beneficiaries; instead, administrative procedures have been used to reduce the former in the name of the latter.[76] Federal quality control guidelines offered states stronger incentives to avoid overpayment rather than to enroll eligible participants.[77] Contemporary performance evaluations of welfare programs maintain this tradition by rewarding reductions in fraud measures but neglecting beneficiary take-up.[78] Welfare is also a domain where the politics of race play out, with robust evidence that burdens fall disproportionately harder on black, relative to white, beneficiaries.[79] As we examine each policy, we identify the political values that arise in debates about burdens.

The second strand of our argument is that partisan attitudes about burdens in the abstract tell us little, but partisan attitudes toward specific policy areas are revealing and predictive. The conventional wisdom on the politics of government regulation is clear enough: conservatives seek to limit the dead hand of government from impeding on individual liberties and free enterprise, while liberals use the tools of government to correct perceived inequalities in society. We are accustomed to the image of Democrats pursuing policy goals via rules and regulations, and Republicans criticizing those rules as burdensome and inefficient. Republicans wear the mantle of laissez-faire champions, a status cemented in the 1960s, when states' rights issues bridged social conservatives and anti-regulation forces to establish the heart of the Republican coalition.[80] This image may be accurate for economic and regulatory policies to which businesses are subject, but it is clearly not the case for many of the policies we describe here.

Others have made a strong case for conservative paternalism in social policy, which justifies a detailed supervision of citizens' lives. The paternalism is strongest when directed at women, the poor, and blacks.[81] However, we show that the same pattern of strategic application of administrative burdens holds in other policy areas. We show that when partisans oppose a policy, or are unsympathetic to the beneficiaries, they apply burdens as a tactic to limit access rights or benefits.

The third strand of our argument is that political attitudes are consequential to burdens. The preferences of political actors— most prominently elected officials but also stakeholders, political appointees, public managers, and street-level bureaucrats—will often translate into actions governing the nature of burden in that policy area: whether it should be created or reduced, and the balance of burden between the individual and the state. This claim fits comfortably with a model of politics in which actors design administrative structures to serve political ends, even if the outcomes are operationally dysfunctional.[82] Policymakers can deliberately alter burdens to generate a behavioral response that aligns with their preferred policy outcome. In short, burdens are one of the tactics of contemporary political warfare about how policies are designed and delivered.

Fourth, we propose that the generally opaque nature of administrative burdens makes them valuable as a form of policymaking by other means that substitutes for or complements more overt policy change.[83] This point is important in an age of fierce polarization when, absent unified political control, parties look to nonlegislative ways to make policy. Indeed, administrative burdens form part of the "hidden politics" that Jacob Hacker argues have characterized battles about the role of the state in recent decades, where big policy changes have been made largely out of public view and without large formal policy choices.[84]

Although Hacker is most concerned that the welfare state has failed to evolve to reflect the contemporary risks individuals are vulnerable to, administrative burdens fits into the category of "subterranean political processes that shape ground-level policy effects," which he argues are both fundamental to understanding the evolution of governance and largely neglected.[85] One of the most striking examples is the use of burdens, such as unnecessary regulations for abortion providers, to prevent women's access to legal abortion.

When overt changes are unpopular (such as reducing benefits) or not publicly defensible (such as limiting the franchise), or when law constrains desired policy changes (such as Supreme Court decisions on abortion or federal policies in intergovernmental programs), administrative burdens offer a low-profile alternative, minimizing the need for political and legal processes of consultation and deliberation.[86] For example, directly changing social benefits requires legislative battles that will often be relitigated in court. By contrast, constructing complex, confusing, and time-consuming application procedures is a less visible form of policymaking that can effectively thwart people from accessing benefits, even if eligible by law. Because of these qualities, burdens are especially attractive policy instruments if they achieve goals that political actors are reluctant to explicitly acknowledge; they can also operate unobtrusively in policy areas mired by gridlock.

The unobtrusive nature of administrative burdens, relative to other policy alternatives, results from the combination of three qualities: opacity, controllability, and neutrality. Although issues such as eligibility levels for welfare programs are decided in high-profile debates played out in front of legislators and the media, the seemingly prosaic details such as the length of an application form are more hidden and complex, and their effects less likely to be observed or understood by outsiders. This is the quality of opacity.

Controllability means that such details are under the control of administrative actors—the details of programs generally considered to fall into the domain of administrative execution and are delegated to the executive branch. The controllability of rules relates directly to their opacity—as the nature and effect of burdens becomes clear, they become a matter of interest to other political actors, such as the legislature or higher levels of government. A third quality of administrative burdens is their apparent neutrality—changes in burdens can be presented as technical fixes without any specific policy intent, or as facilitating widely accepted political goals, such as the reduction of fraud.[87]

Although burdens may be unintended, occurring because of a lack of attention to their effects, we should not exclude the possibility that they sometimes represent an extension of political preferences. One might think that such an idea is already well documented, but that is not the case. Certainly, empirical evidence shows that politics affects welfare policy choices.[88] For example, the power of business interests explains variation in the generosity of TANF policies across states.[89] Partisan control of government influences bureaucratic discretion in terms of granting benefits but not in terms of how vigorously bureaucrats restrict claims.[90] Some research at the intersection of politics, inequality, and social policy has previously argued that burdens are imposed deliberately to limit claims on the public purse and targeted at groups with little political power.[91] Even so, the link between politics and administratively imposed burdens has not been widely explored.[92]

The Role of Third Parties

The final point about the politics of burdens is the role of non-governmental actors, or third parties. In writing this book, we were primarily interested in the relationship between citizens and the state, but it soon became clear that any account of American governance that ignores third parties—civic organizations, nonprofits, or for-profit organizations—is incomplete. These nonstate organizations play multiple and, in some policy areas, central roles in constructing and reducing burdens in policy design, and mediating or amplifying their effects in implementation.[93] We document the role of third parties as falling into four broad categories.

First, they can act as political stakeholders that lobby to impose or reduce burdens. The tax preparation industry lobbies aggressively to maintain complexity in the current tax reporting system. As chapter 8 shows, the same industry has lobbied to make the EITC broadly accessible—though still complex enough to justify the use of their services as tax preparers. The approach of these actors is not based on any overriding conviction about the burdens citizens should face in the tax system but instead reflects simple profit incentives.

Second, third parties can alter the costs citizens face in their interactions with government. Most obviously, they can change learning costs by explaining a policy in ways that either increase or reduce knowledge about a program, the citizen's legal rights, and how to acquire services. They can reduce compliance costs by helping people navigate bureaucracy or acquire documentation.

Burdensome procedures create financial incentives for third parties who can help others overcome burdens. Hospitals have an incentive to help patients enroll in public health insurance programs such as Medicaid, thereby reducing the financial costs of providing charitable care. At a more micro level, Howard Becker describes the use of informal fixers in Brazil known as *despachante*: "the guy who knows how to get impossible things done ... who, in short, knows how to get unresponsive bureaucrats to do what they should do cheerfully and willingly as a matter of course but seldom do."[94]

Faith-based or civic groups can reduce burdens for members. For example, veterans seeking disability benefits tend to be more successful if they live in a state with more active veteran's groups that can help them with the process.[95] We should not assume that match between the needs of populations for third-party help and the presence of helpful third parties is carefully calibrated. Some populations may find themselves facing burdens with limited third-party supports, reinforcing inequality across groups. For example, those who struggle to manage newly imposed voter ID laws because of difficulties with documentation cannot turn to an obvious nonprofit organization that would offer specialized support. This creates a challenge—and opportunity—for the philanthropic community: identify communities facing significant administrative burdens but without strong networks of support to help minimize the costs they experience.

In less obvious ways, third parties can alter psychological costs by conveying messages about a program. For redistributive programs, they can convey that the program is valuable and that recipients are deserving. When they oppose the program, they can portray the policy as serving the undeserving or as inconsistent with liberty. For example, opponents of the Affordable Care Act funded nonprofit organizations to target younger potential users to discourage them from enrolling in the program.[96]

Third, nongovernmental actors can alter costs in their role of service providers. Many public services are provided by third parties, who have the opportunity to buffer or amplify burdens just as public employees can but with greater flexibility to follow individual beliefs or financial incentives. As chapter 5 shows, the complex array of health insurance choices by Medicare beneficiaries, due to the large number of plan options and providers, increases profits for insurers and reduces benefits for beneficiaries.

Private service providers may also use burdens to engage in the cream-skimming of more profitable clients by placing more barriers in the place of less attractive clients. A simple illustration is in welfare-based job-training requirements, when one Florida company contracted to provide these services believed it could increase profitability by adopting new administrative burdens to exclude clients who "were not serious enough." They required daily attendance of classes for a week before they could even submit applications for benefits, sent discouraging signals in meetings with clients about the time investments required and the limited assistance on offer, more aggressively imposed sanctions on clients not following requirements, and added new barriers to get back on the program if the client was sanctioned: "Under the new system, only one local staff member (known among the staff as the Sanction Queen) was given authority to sign off on the return of a sanctioned client, and this staff member was made available to clients on only one day each week, for two hours. Sanctioned clients who missed this window would have to wait another week to return." Missing any step of the process, such as a skipping a class, would require the client to restart the process from the beginning.[97]

Fourth, third parties can be the object of administrative burdens. The state can influence the role of third parties by, for example, creating incentives to either limit access or offer help, or by regulating their actions to make such help difficult or risky to provide. In the case of abortion, states have burdened third-party service providers in an effort to limit access. Conservatives have charged that the IRS has played a similar role in restricting first amendment rights by imposing burdens on political groups.

Conclusion

The idea of administrative burden is intuitive. We recognize it from our experience as citizens engaging with the state. It reflects our hours at the DMV, or the lines when we vote. For some, it also reflects the difficulties in accessing vital public services such as income supports or health care. Despite the centrality of administrative burdens in the relationship between the citizen and the state, it is not a well-defined concept, and as a result, there is not a well-articulated agenda for managing and reducing burdens. We do not, for example, train those who enter into the public service to think of administrative burden as a factor to consider in program design in the same way that we coach them to consider efficiency.

This chapter establishes a broad conceptual framework for administrative burdens, and consequent implications for how we are governed. Different aspects of the framework we identify in figure 1.1 have been addressed, but not systematically, and almost entirely within the field of social policy. Others are relatively neglected: the political origins of burdens, bureaucratic relationships with burdens, and the role of third parties. A comprehensive approach requires building knowledge about all these different dimensions of governance. We cannot fully detail or resolve all aspects of administrative burdens in this book, but simply mapping how they are connected is important.

The understudied aspects of administrative burdens also influence how we chose the cases that follow on voting rights, abortion access, health policy, and income supports. We select cases that are instrumentally important: they are important policy areas in their own right, even as they offer us a deeper understanding of how administrative burdens arise in policies.[98]

The importance of these topics should be self-evident: voting and abortion are tied to constitutional rights. Health and income supports are cornerstones of a basic standard of living, part of what Thomas H. Marshall describes as social rights.[99] Although what constitutes rights is itself contestable, the Supreme Court ruled in 1970 in *Goldberg v. Kelly* that welfare benefits are similar to a form of property when it comes to guaranteeing some due process rights.[100] They cannot be removed simply on the basis of suspicion of fraud, for example. Health and income supports are also where the federal government spends the majority of its money. In 2015, 23 percent of the budget went to Social Security, 14 percent to Medicare and another 14 percent to other health spending, while 13 percent went to income supports.[101]

We are also interested in the politics by which burdens are made. We therefore order the chapters to fit with our argument that burdens are constructed. We start with cases featuring overt efforts to introduce burdens, and these efforts have become a visible part of politics—elections and abortions. We move on to cases in which the politics of burdens is both more mixed—featuring efforts to both increase and reduce burdens—and less visible. These include the Affordable Care Act, Medicare, and SNAP.

We conclude with three cases that involve efforts to shift burdens away from citizens: an expansion of Medicaid in Wisconsin, the Earned Income Tax Credit, and Social Security. In each, we focus on a time when the construction of burdens is most salient. In cases such as the EITC and Social Security, this demands a historical understanding of how each program was designed and evolved over time; in other cases, though, we offer a snapshot of a more limited time frame. Collectively, the cases illustrate how the imposition or reduction of burdens, or the shifting of burdens between the citizen and the state, have been a matter of political choice, though this choice has often been made out of public view and justified by political values others than the ones being pursued.

By focusing on burdens in income supports, health access, abortions, and voting, our case selection is also intended to challenge a political stereotype, which is that political parties have relatively fixed attitudes toward burdening citizens: Republicans opposing and Democrats being more willing to tolerate regulation that fosters other policy goals. Instead, we show that conservatives are skilled users of rules and regulations to achieve their policy goals. Although our focus is mostly tied to issues of concern to progressives, the framework of administrative burdens is no less salient to conservative critiques of the use of state power in other areas, such as the use of administrative burdens to regulate political speech or gun rights.

THE RESURGENCE OF BURDENS IN VOTING

2

RACE, BURDENS, AND ACCESS
TO POLITICAL RIGHTS

We have assumed that voting is a costless act, but this assumption is self-contradictory because every act takes time. In fact, time is the principal cost of voting: time to register, to discover what parties are running, to deliberate to go to the polls, and to mark the ballot. Since time is a scarce resource voting is inherently costly.

—ANTHONY DOWNS

We start our substantive analysis with elections, partly because voting is one of our most basic democratic rights, partly because it illustrates how partisan divides matter to the construction of burdens, and partly because voting influences which policies are adopted and how they are implemented. Higher voter participation tends to increase the share of low-income voters, resulting in more generous welfare services, greater equality, more progressive taxation, and less restrictive welfare participation rules.[1] If policymakers and administrators use their authority to influence who votes in elections, they are also influencing the policies that will be adopted after the election, and the burdens that accompany those policies.

On June 22, 2013, the Supreme Court struck down the preclearance provisions of the Voting Rights Act of 1965. Chief Justice John Roberts penned the 5–4 majority opinion in *Shelby v. Holder*, which removed a requirement for fifteen state governments with a history of suppressing black voters to seek preclearance from the federal government before changing their election policies. "History did not end in 1965," said Roberts, reasoning that the formula used then to determine which states sought preclearance was outdated and could not justify disparate treatment of states decades later. Justice Ruth Bader

Ginsburg, in dissent, warned that tossing aside the preclearance provisions was akin to "throwing away your umbrella in a rainstorm because you are not getting wet."[2]

At the heart of the conflict in *Shelby v. Holder* are competing visions about what role burdens should play when people exercise their right to vote. Both Roberts and Ginsburg agree that burdens were used to discriminatory ends in the past. In this chapter, we detail some of the subtle and less-than-subtle ways that legislators and local election officials made the process of voting systematically more difficult for African Americans. Fighting overt and racially motivated use of administrative powers to limit voting was central to the civil rights struggle, with progress largely depending on the willingness of federal courts to intervene.

Where Roberts and Ginsburg disagreed is the relevance of this discriminatory past for today's elections. Roberts drew a line under the past. Ginsburg drew a direct line from the past to the present. She warned that although crude "first-generation" barriers of the civil rights era may have disappeared, they have been replaced by "second-generation" burdens.

This chapter examines the competing visions of Roberts and Ginsburg, which go far beyond *Shelby v. Holder*; these disagreements illustrate deep ideological and partisan divisions about how people vote in America. Republicans have altered election laws in the name of protecting the integrity of the voting process, arguing that the burdens imposed on citizens are marginal and justified by the benefits the burdens offer. For example, President Trump established the short-lived Commission on Election Integrity "to promote fair and honest Federal elections."[3] Democrats argue that such changes are deliberately intended to limit access to the polls, and that such burdens should not be tolerated. Behind the battles about integrity and access are partisan calculations about which policies best help their electoral fortunes. Third-party organizations that seek to register voters are sometimes caught up in these battles, discouraged from helping citizens register to vote.

To sort through these competing claims, we look for empirical evidence regarding key questions: How have burdens historically been used to restrict access to voting? What led to the collapse of a decades-long bipartisan goal of increasing turnout? How significant are the burdens that these new laws pose? What are the effects on turnout and the composition of the electorate?

Burdens in the Pre–Voting Rights Era

Accusations that administrative burdens are being used to limit democratic rights today sound an uncomfortable echo with the post-Reconstruction American South. In the aftermath of the Civil War, Reconstruction compelled southern states to allow freed blacks to vote as a condition for rejoining the union. To limit the actual exercise of this franchise, whites in the South applied administrative burdens selectively to blacks.

One tactic was the use of extralegal methods to terrorize or punish potential voters.[4] The process of registering to vote was associated with psychological costs that arose from very reasonable fears of retribution from agents of the state, such as local police, or private actors, such as landlords, or terrorists such as the Ku Klux Klan. As federal supervision of Reconstruction faded in the 1870s, Southern whites no longer relied exclusively on informal techniques such as violence or voting fraud. They now had enough legal power to employ more formal barriers: the poll tax, literacy tests, secret ballot requirements, confusing ballot arrangements that were de facto literacy tests, and complex registration requirements. So that these policies would achieve the fullest effect, they relied on public officials using their discretion to both target and amplify the effects of burdens on blacks while exempting poorer or illiterate whites from the same requirements.

One example of selective application of administrative discretion is that officials could correct or ignore errors in registration paperwork for whites but enforce requirements for blacks. They could make the process of paying poll taxes easier for whites but more difficult for blacks, or simply refuse to provide the needed receipt of payment. Clerks could also discourage registration applications by working so slowly that applicants would have to wait for hours to register, or by refusing to offer any assistance in completing applications. Clerks might also require that black applicants bring at least two whites who would vouch for their status.[5] Requiring more frequent registration and demanding registration processes were applied selectively to black voters.[6]

Literacy tests were common from the 1890s to 1960s and formally applied to everyone. Administrators could choose who would take to test, however, as well as the standards necessary to pass. The process of taking the test itself might be stressful: a black applicant could assume that the official imposing the test wanted him to fail, and might even rig standards to ensure that outcome. For example, officials applying a literacy test in Alabama sought not only to include the capacity to write and read a section of the Constitution but also to interpret its meaning. This would, according to a Democratic leader at the time, "give certain discretion to the Board of Registrars and prevent them from registering those elements in our community which have not yet fitted themselves for self-government."[7] In other cases, examiners could choose to pose extraordinarily specific questions that very few citizens could answer, such as "what is meant by the pocket veto?"[8]

As formal methods of discrimination were struck down by courts, the burdens state actors used depended ever more on administrative discretion. Pressure to make literacy tests less discriminatory led to the adoption of formal written tests to minimize the use of this discretion. Even so, test questions could be structured to be ambiguous enough to enable discrimination in the interpretation of the answers. One extreme example comes from a parish in the state of Louisiana just a year before the Voting Rights Act was passed.[9] One question asked test-takers to "Spell backwards, forwards." The test taker could answer "backwards" with or without a comma, or "backwards, forward." Three answers could be plausibly interpreted as correct, or incorrect, depending on the preferences of the test examiner. Another question was "Write right from the left to the right as you see it spelled here" offered even more potential answers. Such vague questions did little to test literacy but gave administrators enough discretion to punitively apply a burdensome tool on black citizens.

Even after the voter was registered, election officials could find ways to remove them from voter rolls. For example, one city in Georgia once purged the registration rolls of voters, requiring black voters, but not whites, to come to a courthouse to verify their status.[10]

The Voting Rights Act of 1965 blocked burdensome tactics such as literacy tests, summarized in table 2.1. States and counties with a

Table 2.1 *Comparing Burdens in Pre–Voting Rights Era and Today*

Pre–Voting Rights Act Era	Today
Learning costs	
Knowledge of requirements, substantive and esoteric information requested (such as details of the U.S. Constitution) as part of a literacy test; costs higher if administrators chose not to share information about registration	Knowledge of registration policies, documentation required and deadlines, polling place location
Compliance costs	
Poll taxes; requirements to bring documentation of status, witnesses, extra time, and financial costs resulting from delays imposed by discretionary requests of local officials	Time and effort to travel to register and vote; providing appropriate documentation
Psychological costs	
Stress of registering and voting because of overt discrimination; stresses of participating in rigged literacy tests; concerns about intimidation and violent retribution	Concerns about validity of ID

Source: Authors' compilation.

history of discriminatory electoral practices now had to seek federal permission before introducing new election procedures. The act also gave the federal government a way to police informal discrimination: observers could witness how election officials did their job. The act led to dramatic increases in registration in affected states and was hailed as a milestone, though it was "a curious milestone to be sure, since the essence of the act was simply an effort to enforce the Fifteenth Amendment, which had been law for almost a century."[11] The true effect of the Voting Rights Act was to vastly restrict the use of state and local discretion to ignore constitutional rights, just as the federal government had done during Reconstruction.

Administrative Burdens in the Voting Wars

As table 2.1 illustrates, administrative burdens in voting procedures have generally become less onerous over the course of U.S. history. The franchise has been extended, election procedures made more uniform, registration has become easier, and voting more convenient.[12]

This experience has not been uniform—the disenfranchisement of felons has become more widespread over time, even as 8 percent of all adults and 33 percent of all African American men have felony convictions in the United States today.[13] But the latter part of the twentieth century largely saw a gradual expansion of access to the ballot through the Voting Rights Act in 1965, the Voting Accessibility for the Elderly and Handicapped Act in 1984, the Uniformed and Overseas Citizens Absentee Voting Act of 1986, and the National Voter Registration Act (NVRA) of 1993. Each law was driven by concerns of declining voter turnout in aggregate, as well as the barriers faced by particular groups, such as the military serving overseas or the disabled.

The immediate aftermath of the 2000 election reflected the bipartisan concerns about voter access that characterized the late twentieth century. The Help America Vote Act of 2002 offered a technocratic approach to modernizing the polling place, though it did include new provisions that increased punishment for providing false information on voter registration forms. State governments remained interested in increasing access to the polls. Early voting has been, by far, the most popular innovation aimed at reducing burdens in the election process in recent years. In the 2016 presidential election, 39 percent of voters took advantage of early voting, which is allowed in more than half of all states, compared with 7.5 percent in the early 1990s.[14]

The bipartisan consensus around elections was already disintegrating when the Help American Vote Act was passed, fueled by a conservative reevaluation of election policies. The issue of how Americans vote has been transformed, starting a period that election scholar Rick Hasen has dubbed "the voting wars."[15] The closeness of Presidential elections, especially in the state of Florida in 2000, illustrated the degree to which election policies and administration mattered to political outcomes.

Republicans now expressed concern that expanded access at the polling place undermined the integrity of elections. Members of the George W. Bush administration articulated these concerns, including the president's advisor Karl Rove, who warned of "an enormous and growing problem with elections in certain parts of America today. We are, in some parts of the country, I'm afraid to say, beginning to look like we have elections like those run in countries where the guys in charge are, you know, colonels in mirrored sunglasses."[16] Bush's Department of Justice was led by John Ashcroft, whose supporters argued that he had been the victim of voter fraud in his failed 2000 Senate bid. Ashcroft replaced or reassigned civil rights lawyers with lawyers who were more concerned with voter fraud and largely antagonistic to traditional concerns about racial discrimination.[17]

Republican state governments followed suit, adopting laws that promised to protect electoral integrity. A trickle of new state election laws became a deluge after the 2010 midterms that saw Republicans take control of eleven new governorships and twenty-one legislative chambers. The most obvious, and fiercely debated, result was a number of voter ID laws, almost all of which faced court scrutiny. But requiring an ID to vote is only one of a broad array of weapons in the voting wars.

REGISTRATION

When we think of voting, we think of the citizen casting their ballot at a polling site. But voting is just the final stage in the election process. As the brief history of the pre–Voting Rights Act era makes clear, registration is the more consequential part of the election process when it comes to burdens. About 10 percent of citizens view registration as difficult, but these numbers are higher among minorities and the young.[18] Table 2.2 outlines burdens in registration and how they might be increased or reduced by policymakers.

How much does registration matter to turnout? One study that analyzed the historical introduction of registration requirements in New York and Ohio counties estimated a 3 to 4 percentage point long-term decline in participation.[19] Another approach is to compare turnout rates for states that allow voters to register on Election Day, versus those that do not, controlling for other factors. Such analyses generate a higher range of estimated effects, from 3 to 7 percentage points.[20]

A field experiment from France examined the effects of making registration easier.[21] Relative to a control group, citizens who had campaigners come to their homes and offer information and help to register were more likely to vote by about 4 percentage points. Those

Table 2.2 *State Actions to Reduce or Increase Burdens in Voter Registration*

Reduce	Increase
· Election day registration and same-day registration allow one-stop shopping · Registration opportunities at routine interactions with state (DMV, welfare providers, high schools for preregistering individuals below age eighteen) · Online registration: does not require special trip to register but usually requires ID · Automatic registration: using administrative data to register citizens, changing default from opt-in to opt-out	· Requiring proof of citizenship to register · Reducing Election Day and same-day registration opportunities · Purging the rolls, requiring citizens to reregister · Discouraging third parties from registering voters · Lengthening the state residency requirement

Source: Authors' compilation.

who were given help registering, thereby minimizing compliance costs, were more likely to vote than those who just received information. The analysis offers strong causal evidence that both learning and compliance costs are barriers that lower registration, and that reducing those costs increases turnout.

As voters learn about registration, they become more likely to register.[22] A study of Google searches for the phrase "register to vote" in the weeks before the 2012 presidential election found a high correlation with the daily total of newly registered voters. That study also illustrated how learning about deadlines was valuable only if citizens could act on that knowledge. The correlation between searches for registration information and actual registration occurred only in states where it was still possible to register. An estimated three to four million additional citizens would have registered if they did not face state registration deadlines.

Allowing people to register on Election Day or during early voting periods therefore removes a consequential barrier to voting, turning it into a form of one-stop shopping. It also takes advantage of the social encouragement of campaigns, allowing marginal voters who might only become interested in the waning days of a campaign to still vote.[23]

An alternative to allowing Election Day registration is to let people register in routine interactions with the state, thereby removing the compliance costs that come with a separate trip to a registration site. That was the goal of the NVRA, which was modeled on state laws. The NVRA allowed all citizens to register to vote when they received or renewed a driver's license, and hence is popularly known as the motor-voter law. A less well-known NVRA requirement is that agencies providing federal welfare benefits—such as the Supplemental Nutrition Assistance Program, Medicaid, and disability benefits—share voter registration forms and provide help in completing them, verifying applicants' identification and helping them enroll in benefits. However, the requirement to encourage registration through the provision of social benefits has been implemented haphazardly and unevenly across states.[24] Consistent with these two records of implementation, evidence shows that historically the motor-voter program increased turnout but that agency-based registration did not.[25] However, recent legal efforts to compel states to fulfill their statutory responsibilities for agency-based registration have seen millions of new voters added to the rolls, pointing to the untapped potential of this approach.[26]

Another way to reduce the costs of registration is to preregister young voters before they turn eighteen. Not surprisingly, states that introduce preregistration see a rise in the turnout of young voters.[27] A dozen states allow preregistration, and until recently it was an uncontroversial policy option. For example, it was passed with broad support in North Carolina in 2009. Just four years later, the law was repealed as part of a broader Republican package of laws that restricted voting, though it was ultimately restored by a federal court in 2016.

Online registration of voters has become increasingly popular as a policy option that increases access and reduces election administration costs. In 2008, just two states allowed online registration, but twenty did by 2014, covering about half of eligible voters.[28] In some cases, the adoption of online registration was offered as a substitute for other registration options. Wisconsin adopted online registration in 2016, but in the same bill eliminated the ability of community special deputies to register voters.

Third parties help reduce the costs of registration. By helping citizens gather the information necessary to register to vote and assisting them in filling out registration forms, these groups remove the need for citizens to go to a specific office to register. Such groups are targeted by those who believe fraud is rife in elections, however, because it is easy to include false information in registration drives. Some policies and procedures are intended to make it more difficult for such groups to operate by shifting burdens and risks on them, including potentially ruinous fines for providing false information.

In 2011, Florida passed House Bill 1355, which extensively regulated third parties with fines, civil punishments, and even the threat of prison. For example, failing to turn in a registration signature within forty-eight hours would generate fines of $50 per application. The bill's sponsor said, "I have to tell you, I don't have a problem making it harder. I want people in Florida to want to vote as bad as that person in Africa who walks 200 miles across the desert. It should not be easy."[29] The League of Women Voters subsequently stopped their registration drives in the state because, according to the president, "It's too cumbersome. There is too much red tape and regulation."[30] As a result, voter registration in the Florida dropped precipitously across all groups after the law was passed, the decline was greatest among younger citizens and Democrats.[31]

States can also make registration more burdensome by requiring longer residency before registering, or by asking for more documentation. Alabama, Arizona, Georgia, and Kansas have passed laws requiring individuals provide documentary proof of citizenship to register. When federal courts invalidated this requirement for federal elections, Kansas introduced a two-track registration process, one for federal elections and another for state elections that excluded those who did not provide required citizenship documentation.

Election official discretion can be used in other ways to increase burdens and limit registration. Officials can decide to aggressively purge the registration rolls of suspected felons or those who have not voted recently. Florida chose to purge felons in 2000, applying a law that originated in the post-Reconstruction era as a way to curb the participation of newly freed slaves. State officials identified fifty-eight thousand names of possible felons to remove from the rolls in a state where 44 percent of felons but only 11 percent of registered voters were black.[32] The names were generated from a cross-match between the state felon database and county rolls. The state Division of Elections was warned by the contractor performing the match that they were generating false positives but were told by a state official, "Obviously, we want to capture more names that possibly aren't matches and let the supervisors make a final determination rather than exclude certain matches altogether." Local election officials were influenced by their partisanship in how they used this discretion. Local Republican election officials were much more likely to aggressively use the list to remove potential voters.[33] An estimated twelve thousand nonfelons were mistakenly removed, preventing them from participating in a state that George W. Bush won by 537 votes.[34]

Many states already share registration data to identify potential double-voters who are registered in two states. This Interstate Crosscheck System matches people based on name and birth date and was championed by members of President Trump's commission on election integrity. However, the system is rife with false positives from people who have the same name and birth date. One analysis found that purging on that basis would lead to three hundred legitimate registrations to be dropped for every registration associated with a double vote.[35]

Another technique to make registration more burdensome is to remove infrequent voters from the rolls, requiring them to reregister. The state of Ohio, to take one example, purged those who had not voted in three elections and failed to return a postcard verifying their status, removing two million people over five years. Because poorer voters are less frequent voters, they are more likely to be purged.[36] When the Supreme Court upheld Ohio's approach in 2018, it gave a green light for others to follow, opening a new front in the voting wars. Requiring citizens to continuously vote, or to fill out postcards, makes the right to vote contingent on completing administrative burdens, which themselves are tied to some notion of deservingness. "If this is really important thing to you in your life, voting, you probably would have done so within a six-year period," said Jon Husted, the Ohio secretary of state who led the purge.[37] The view that voting is reserved for the civically worthy justifies the adoption of burdens such as returning a postcard, even when less burdensome and more accurate administrative options exist. States could shift the burden onto themselves and use administrative data to keep the rolls accurate.

Table 2.3 *Policy Checklist to Reduce or Increase Burdens in Voting*

Reduce	Increase
· Vote by mail and mail absentee voting reduces learning and compliance costs · Early voting, weekend voting, in-person absentee voting or making Election Day a holiday increases the convenience of voting	· Reducing the number of days of early voting, limiting its overlap with registration, reducing weekend voting · Voter ID laws create learning and compliance burdens to acquire IDs

Source: Authors' compilation.

VOTING

Voting is an infrequent experience patterned by a sporadic set of routines. Political campaigns and media remind us when to vote, though we might have to search out where. Although many are motivated by a sense of civic duty or caught up in the issues of the campaign, others are less dedicated, or may believe that their individual vote matters little. Under such conditions, a small learning or compliance cost might be enough to discourage voting (see table 2.3). For example, a relatively small increase in distance to the polling place is enough to lead to a significant decline in turnout, especially among households without a car.[38]

One way to get a sense of these costs is to examine what happens when polling places change. Such changes provide natural experiments that test how much seemingly little disruptions matter. Two studies of the consolidation of polling places, one in New York State, the other in Los Angeles, found that changing the location of the polling place led to a significant reduction in voting—by about 2 percentage points in the Los Angeles example and 7 percentage points in New York.[39] By using the change in distance between voters and the new and old voting place, the authors were able to assess the degree to which these declines were the function of compliance costs of having to travel further, or the learning costs of finding out about and traveling to an unfamiliar location. In both cases, the learning costs had a greater effect than the increase in distance to be traveled.

A number of policies can make voting easier. Voting is harder for those with health difficulties or mobility restrictions, because traveling to a local polling place may be prohibitive.[40] States generally help such citizens by allowing vote by mail, though typically the individual has to request such a ballot. Oregon, Washington, and Colorado have moved further, turning their elections entirely into vote-by-mail affairs under which registered citizens are automatically sent a ballot. More states allow all-mail voting for local elections. The net effect of all-mail on turnout is positive, increasing participation in the range of 2 to 4 percentage points, and even more for less habitual voters.[41] Some research, however, does suggest that the effect fades over time or is limited to lower-turnout elections.

The most widely adopted innovation to make voting easier in recent decades has been early voting, which extends the voting period to days or weeks before Election Day. However, although it may make voting more convenient, it largely benefits likely voters, rather than marginal voters who show less interest in a campaign until after the registration date has passed.[42]

Voter ID laws are the battlefront of the voting wars and thirty-four states have adopted them.[43] Proponents note that IDs are required for many aspects of daily life, such as opening a bank account. But the United States is not a country with universal identity cards, or much appetite for such a standard, and about 12 percent of the eligible voting population lacks an acceptable form of ID.[44] For those voters, requiring new IDs imposes a new burden. As a result of the wave of voter ID laws passed before the 2012 election, an estimated five million voters faced new difficulties in casting ballots.[45]

For someone who either was never issued or lost a birth certificate, it becomes significantly more difficult to get ID. One Wisconsin octogenarian, Ruthelle Frank, who voted in every election since 1948 but who was never issued a birth certificate, testified about the burdens she faced to get a new ID. She would have to seek out and pay for a birth certificate from the register of deeds. Because of a spelling error in the registration form recorded by the physician when she was born, she would have to petition the courts to correct it, requiring weeks of additional effort and hundreds of dollars in additional costs.[46] Frank, who joined what became an unsuccessful American Civil Liberties Union suit against the new law, described her experience at the Department of Motor Vehicles (DMV), where she said that a clerk asked,

> "How do I know you're not an illegal alien?!" That really hurt. I'd lived in the same house for 85 years, I'd served on the village board for 18 years, and then they told me that I wasn't going to be allowed to vote. I always voted. I've been registered to vote since I was 21 [the voting age wasn't 18 until later], and I have never missed a presidential election.... I left the DMV and thought, "It just isn't right." I felt so downtrodden.... it just felt like I wasn't as good as anyone else. I did try to get a birth certificate after that. Eventually, they told me I could get one, but I'd have to pay anything from $20 to $200, since there was a mistake with my name that had to be corrected. That's a lot of money! I'm so old now, what am I going to do with a $200 birth certificate? Hang it on the wall? No one should have to pay a fee to be able to vote.[47]

States vary in their willingness to accept some state-issued identification, more recent voter ID laws tending to be more restrictive. Perhaps the most glaring example is the willingness of the state of Texas to accept gun carry permits but not student IDs from state universities.

An individual might have what they believe is a valid ID but be mistaken. For example, if the ID is expired, or from another state, it could be rejected. If the ID does not align with registration records because of a misspelling, a stray initial, or a name change before or after marriage, the voter could be denied.

Given state variation in requirements, the introduction of voter ID laws increases learning costs. Voters have to be aware of the requirements of the new law in their state, whether they satisfy them, and if not, what is needed to remedy their status. These costs are higher for the estimated seven million Americans who move across state lines each year.[48] Such learning costs may be enough to encourage voters not to bother with the voting process. One survey of registered voters in a Texas district following the introduction of voter ID found that 6 percent of those surveyed said that the primary reason they did not vote was because they did not believe they had one of the seven accepted form of IDs. However, interviewers found that the vast majority of these voters did in fact have these IDs. The effect of the law was simply to sow doubt among registered voters, especially Latinos, who incorrectly believed that they did not have the necessary photo identification.[49]

Voter ID laws do therefore impose burdens on citizens. Whether those burdens actually reduce turnout is more difficult to answer. In part, this is because strict voter ID laws are relatively recent. Defenders of such laws like to point out that in states such as Indiana, their introduction was not associated with a downturn in turnout, especially among minority voters. But it is difficult to separate the effects of the laws from other factors that altered turnout in a small number of elections, including the presence of Barack Obama on the ballot. Some evidence suggests of a backlash effect from the introduction of the laws that may have temporarily increased voter motivation to overcome new burdens.[50]

Nonetheless, some evidence also indicates that voter ID reduces turnout. A survey found that 9.3 percent of nonvoters in the 2008, representing about 2.2. million voters nationally, pointed to problems with identification as a major factor in resulting in their not voting.[51] The Government Accountability Office estimated that voter ID laws in two states reduced turnout by 2 to 3 percentage points.[52] A study that compared changes in turnout between the 2012 and 2016 election found an increase of 1.3 percent in states with no change in their voter ID laws, an increase of 0.7 percent in states that adopted more lenient voter ID laws (Alabama, New Hampshire, and Rhode Island), and a decline of 1.7 percent in states that adopted strict ones (Mississippi, Wisconsin, and Virginia).[53] Such burdens may not fall equally across all voters, however.

DISTRIBUTIONAL EFFECTS OF VOTING POLICIES AND IMPLEMENTATION

The history of voting in America is one of unequal access across groups.[54] The distribution of learning and compliance costs reflect this pattern today. As a general rule, new burdens have the least effects on habitual, middle-aged, white, and high-income voters. Alleviating burdens can enhance the participation of poorer, younger, and minority voters.

Higher-income groups vote more than lower-income groups. But what appears to be a voting gap is really a registration gap. Registered low-income citizens vote at rates similar to registered wealthy citizens. Those earning $10,000 to $15,000 per year are the least likely to vote, 52 percent less likely than those earning $150,000. That gap declines to 16 percent for registered low-income citizens.[55]

Higher-income groups also face lower learning and compliance burdens in the act of voting. A study of Los Angeles neighborhoods found that Election Day polling places tended to be of a lower quality—less visible, less stable, and more difficult to find and navigate—in poorer neighborhoods, resulting in lower turnout for residents.[56]

Policies that make registration easier facilitate the participation of low-income and minority groups.[57] The greatest beneficiaries of a French initiative to help people to register from their home tended to be immigrants, those who did not speak French at home, and younger and less educated citizens.[58] The implementation of the Voting Rights Act preclearance provisions in North Carolina is estimated to have increased African American registration by 14 to 19 percentage points and turnout by 10 to 19.[59] A study of changes to U.S. election policies between 1978 and 2008 found that easing the registration process, through the motor-voter law or allowing Election Day registration, increased the share of low-income voters.[60] Intuitively, this finding is unsurprising for a couple of reasons: those with less stable housing situations are more likely to need to reregister frequently to stay on the rolls, and so registration is a higher burden for them than for citizens who are in a stable home environment.

As with other burdens described in this book, the barriers to registration may loom larger for voters with fewer resources or who have less connection to the state. There are also implications for partisan turnout. An analysis of the 2004, 2008, and 2012 found that counties with Election Day registration had consistently higher Democratic turnout.[61]

Sometimes efforts to expand access to the ballot increase, rather than decrease, the income bias in voting.[62] Early voting is an example: early voting tends to be used by wealthier voters, increasing Republican vote share.[63] Early voting sites are also less frequent in locations with high black populations.[64] Those who favor early voting as a means to increase access therefore should focus on the implementation of the law, specifically the location of polling places. An anecdote from the 2016 election is instructive. The city of Madison, Wisconsin, expanded early voting sites in the 2016 election. Madison ended up with more early voting sites available than nearby Milwaukee, despite having less than half its population. Madison's turnout increased slightly from the 2012 election even as Milwaukee's declined by about sixty thousand votes in a statewide election determined by twenty-seven thousand votes.[65]

The negative effects of early voting can also be reduced if it is paired with same-day registration, but some states have refashioned their early voting laws in ways that seem targeted to limit minority participation.[66] Churches with black congregants have taken advantage of early voting on the Sunday before elections to organize "souls to polls drives." In revising the days that early voting was available, legislatures in Florida, North Carolina, Ohio, and Wisconsin cut the Sunday before Election Day; Ohio also cut the "golden week" that allowed both early voting and same-day registration.

The costs of voter ID laws are borne most heavily by minority, low-income, and elderly groups that are less likely to have acceptable forms of identification.[67] The most commonly held form of state-issued ID is a driver's license. However, many younger low-income voters do not have a car and therefore no need for a driver's license. The lack of cars and IDs falls across familiar racial divides. Whites are more likely to have a driver's license at younger ages: 79 percent of eighteen- to twenty-year-old whites have a license, versus 55 percent of blacks and 57 percent of Latinos.[68] Therefore, if a voter ID law is introduced, most younger whites will face fewer barriers than their black or Latino counterparts.

Voter ID laws have been decried as an unconstitutional poll tax because they require eligible voters to pay for an ID that they may not otherwise need before they can access the vote. To avoid this charge, states have generally offered free IDs if citizens need identification for voting. Still, voters face the learning costs of finding out about such exceptions (which states have not been active in communicating), and the psychological costs of pleading financial need to request free identification. Even a free ID brings its own costs. The compliance burdens required in seeking out identification are estimated to be between $74 and $175 in strict voter ID states.[69]

Officials can use their discretion to discriminate whom they help overcome learning and compliance costs. Researchers who contacted more than seven thousand local election officials who provided information on election requirements found that emails from (fictional) Latino citizens were about 5 percent less likely to receive a response, and that the quality of the information was lower relative to emails from white-sounding names.[70] At a basic level, white and minority voters face different learning costs because they receive different degrees of help from election officials. Once they get to the polling place, the application of bureaucratic discretion varies for different groups. Minority groups are consistently more likely to be asked for IDs, and the differences are more pronounced in states where poll workers had greater discretion.[71]

It is reasonable to assume that minority and low-income groups' facing higher burdens with voter ID will affect turnout on Election Day. Indeed, voting districts with stricter voter ID laws tend to have lower turnout among low-income groups.[72]

The Politics of Burdening Voters: Fraud, Partisanship, and Race

What drives the politics of burdens in election administration? Because elections are run primarily at the state level, we can examine state-by-state changes to law to answer the question. Unlike burdens in social policies, elections have such clear importance to partisan interests that basic details are enshrined in statute.

However, a clear legislative record does not necessarily mean that citizens know what is motivating elected officials' positions. States have a legitimate interest in ensuring the integrity of elections, and a majority of citizens consistently express support for voter ID requirements. But support for such measures declines when people are told that they will make it harder for eligible voters to participate.[73] Given evidence that burdens do indeed reduce the participation of eligible citizens, to what degree do they actually protect against fraud?

ASSESSING THE THREAT OF FRAUD

The "largely uncontested conclusion within social science circles is that deliberate, systematic electoral fraud is extremely infrequent" say Keith Bentele and Erin O'Brien in a review of the adoption of new voting laws.[74] This is also the conclusion drawn by successive presidential commissions on election reform.[75] But no such consensus exists in political circles. President Trump warned that "voter fraud is very, very common."[76] The United States certainly has colorful historical examples of election rigging, as well as contemporary problems such as bogus names included in voter registration drives (such as Mickey Mouse), or failure to remove the dead from voting rolls.[77]

However, there is simply no evidence of wide-scale fraud from recent decades. Population-based estimates of voter fraud indicate that it is extraordinarily rare, though may appear to be more frequent because of administrative errors.[78] A comprehensive assessment found just thirty-one credible allegations of in-person voter impersonation—not successful prosecutions—among the more than one billion ballots cast between 2000 and 2014.[79]

Although those registering voters might fill out a form for Mickey Mouse, actual voter fraud requires someone claiming to be Mickey Mouse to turn up at the polling place. Voter impersonation carries real risks. It is a felony, and someone impersonating another voter on the rolls runs the risk of being detected if that voter has already voted. Organizing large-scale fraud via in-person voter impersonation is so difficult and expensive as to be impossible. It would involve large numbers of individuals agreeing to falsely represent themselves at the polls. The financial incentive to do so would have to be high given the risks, making the process expensive. Because many would need to be recruited, it would be difficult to keep the conspiracy a secret. Even then, the organizer of the conspiracy still would not know for certain how the paid voters actually voted.

Evidence of voter fraud is largely anecdotal or absent. One staple claim is that busloads of illegal voters (sometimes from out of state, sometimes from outside the United States) are traversing the country.[80] At a time when any notable public behavior is recorded and uploaded to social media, these buses remain mysteriously invisible even as their fraud is recounted on conservative media outlets and social media.

Believers in voter fraud argue that it is impossible to detect because those engaging in it know it is a crime and have an incentive to cover it up. What makes this line of reasoning problematic is that it cannot be refuted: there is no way to falsify the claim. But falsification is a basic tenet of science: if I cannot falsify your claim, I likewise cannot prove it. It belongs in the realm of faith and conspiracy rather than fact. Indeed, those who believe in voter fraud tend to be more conspiracy-minded than others.[81]

Of course, authorities can crack down on illicit behavior if determined to do so. Nevertheless, legal efforts to identify fraud have been strikingly unsuccessful. The Bush administration Department of Justice made prosecuting voter fraud a priority; rather than widespread election rigging, it found individuals who appeared to have been confused over eligibility, consistent with the majority of cases of documented fraud.[82] For example, a woman in Wisconsin who voted while on probation was sent to prison. Another case saw a sixty-eight-year-old Pakistani national and legal U.S. resident deported when he mistakenly filled out a voter registration card while renewing his driver license.[83] Perhaps one should expect that felons and immigrants should be aware of their voting eligibility and rules, but surveys reveal that even the election officials charged with implementing the rules often have a limited grasp of them.[84]

A common mistake that looks like fraud on first blush is the voter who mails in an absentee ballot and then also shows up to vote in person on Election Day, either because they forgot they had mailed their ballot, or doubted that the Postal Service would deliver it on time. But clerks will catch multiple votes under the same name, so the risk to electoral integrity is minimal.

Social scientists have developed techniques to detect illicit behavior. One such approach is a list experiment, where respondents identify that they participate in a specific number of behaviors from a longer list, without identifying which behaviors they engaged in. These results are then compared with those from another group, who are given the same list plus one additional item (in this case, admitting one has engaged in in-person voter impersonation). The method allows someone to convey information that they have engaged in a certain behavior without fear of punishment or social judgment. The difference in the number of reported behaviors between the two groups provides a credible estimate of the likely prevalence of the behavior in the general population. The use of this technique confirmed prior studies: voter fraud is vanishingly rare, the reported rate of in-person voter impersonation being equivalent to the reported rate of alien abduction.[85]

Researchers have also examined registration records to detect fraud, assuming that fraudsters will strategically impersonate infrequent voters who are less likely to turn up at the polls. Unusual patterns such as voters who turn up in low-profile but not high-profile elections suggests fraud. This auditing approach was applied in multiple local elections in three states, and successfully identified two cases of previously known fraud but no others, leading the researchers to conclude that "Anomalous data patterns regularly crop up in a few cases, but in each case, innocent explanations, rather than fraud, provide the best explanation of the patterns. Our results suggest that little evidence supports the claim that voter ID laws are needed to combat electoral fraud."[86]

One form of voting fraud is somewhat safer to perform, and that is to secure and complete the absentee ballot of another person, avoiding the personal risk of detection that comes with going to the polls.[87] Others have argued that a plausible way to engineer systematic fraud would be to manipulate the software of e-voting machines.[88] But neither voter ID requirements nor registration restrictions do anything to prevent these threats. Nor do voter ID laws do much to stop noncitizens or felons who can access these IDs but are ineligible to vote.

PARTISANSHIP AND RACE: THE CASE OF VOTER ID

Voter ID laws fit into a broader category of policies that make voting more burdensome, including shortened early voting periods, restrictions on same-day registration, stronger regulations on registration efforts, and restricting the ability of felons to vote.[89] If such laws impose burdens but do little to reduce fraud, why have they been adopted?

The most straightforward explanation is party politics. As Republican control of state legislatures and governorships increases, so does the adoption of more restrictive practices. All new strict photo ID restrictions between 2006 and 2012 were passed in Republican-controlled legislatures, Rhode Island excepted. The adoption of restrictive laws was higher under Republican control if the state was also a possible presidential swing state, suggesting that the use of burdens is at least partly driven by a desire to make a state less competitive in presidential elections.[90]

If the strategic intent to restrict voting is clear, a concern about voter fraud provides an acceptable political frame. In Wisconsin, for example, Governor Walker has repeatedly presented voter ID as a change that will make it "easy to vote, but hard to cheat." He has also connected cheating to partisan goals, suggesting that a relatively large amount of fraud is occurring to the benefit of Democrats: "I've always thought in this state, close elections, presidential elections, it means you probably have to win with at least 53 percent of the vote to account for fraud. One or two points, potentially."[91]

Media coverage reflects the strategic use of fraud for partisan purposes. Because voting fraud is such a rare event, individuals almost never experience it directly and make judgments based on information they receive from others and their own beliefs. Media coverage of voter fraud has increased sharply in recent elections. Such coverage seems to be driven by electoral competitiveness (it is higher in presidential swing states) and the passage of restrictive voting laws.[92] A review of media coverage on voter fraud concluded that GOP "campaigns sought to place voter fraud on the issue agenda before the election in strategically important states."[93]

In addition to partisan motivations, a variety of evidence suggests a racial motivation to burdening voters. More restrictive laws have been proposed in states with higher proportions of blacks and non-citizens, and are more apt to occur in states where African Americans and poorer citizens are more likely to vote.[94] At the individual legislator level, Republicans with large proportions of black voters in their district are likely to support voter ID and Democrats are likely to oppose.[95]

Beliefs about voter fraud are tied to racial beliefs among both legislators and the public. Among the public, conservatives and consumers of Fox News are more likely to believe that voter fraud is a substantial problem.[96] While blacks oppose voter ID laws, non-black voters who demonstrate racial resentment are more likely to support laws.[97] Racial views may also be a function of unconscious bias. One study showed how racial frames affect support for voter ID.

In an experiment, individuals were asked about their support for voter ID laws. Some were just asked the question; others were asked the question alongside pictures of black and white voters standing next to a voting machine. Support for voter ID laws increased significantly when a picture of the black voter was used, even after controlling for political ideology and racialized attitudes.[98] Another experiment suggests that racial frames may not be necessary to invoke racial beliefs; simply inducing fearful emotions among whites increased their willingness to support voter ID.[99]

Legislators supporting voter ID also show signs of racial bias. In an experiment, legislators in fourteen states were sent emails, some from fictional Latino individuals (Santiago Rodriguez) and some from a white-sounding name (Jacob Smith).[100] Emails from the Anglo name received a significantly higher response rate from legislators who had supported voter ID laws. By contrast, the response rates were virtually identical among legislators who did not support voter ID laws.

THE JUDICIARY STEPS IN: THE ROLE OF EVIDENCE IN WEIGHING BURDENS

Given the constitutional importance of voting, the voting wars inevitably found their way to the courts. One of the defining features of judicial oversight is that judges are compelled to use evidence and reason in their decisions to a degree not required by legislatures. Nevertheless, they have struggled to determine how to weigh the costs and benefits of burdening voters.

Even as the Supreme Court upheld an Indiana voter ID law in 2008, the plurality opinion accepted that the problem the law sought to address—in-person voter impersonation—had never been recorded in the history of the state. However, the Court reasoned that voters should endure the burdens that come with getting an ID, setting a standard that if it is possible for citizens to overcome burdens, the law is constitutional. Sometimes courts also accept a related legislative claim that though there might not be evidence of fraud, public concern about voter fraud justified greater restrictions. Again, this is a dubious claim. It assumes that the citizens of states with voter ID laws will be more confident in elections and that perceptions of fraud reduce likelihood of voting. Surveys show neither of those assumptions to be true.[101]

When deciding the Indiana case, the courts lacked access to the more recent research on voter ID. There was simply little evidence to weigh. Judge Richard Posner wrestled with this issue when presented with the Wisconsin ID law in 2014. Posner's perspective is significant for several reasons. Apart from being a widely cited Reagan appointee, he also penned the majority opinion supporting the Indiana law that the Supreme Court later relied on. However, in an act rarely seen in the courts, or in public life generally, Posner characterized his earlier judgment as wrong or, perhaps more accurately, proven wrong by evidence that emerged in the ensuing years. The majority did not accept Posner's view, and his blistering dissent sought to offer guidelines for how courts should weigh evidence in their decisions:

> The panel is not troubled by the absence of evidence. It deems the supposed beneficial effect of photo ID requirements on public confidence in the electoral system "'a legislative fact'—a proposition about the state of the world," and asserts that "on matters of legislative fact, courts accept the findings of legislatures and judges of the lower courts must accept findings by the Supreme Court." In so saying, the panel conjures up a fact-free cocoon in which to lodge the federal judiciary. As there is no evidence that voter impersonation fraud is a problem, how can the fact that a legislature says it's a problem turn it into one? If the Wisconsin legislature says witches are a problem, shall Wisconsin courts be permitted to conduct witch trials? If the Supreme Court once thought that requiring photo identification increases public confidence in elections, and experience and academic study since shows that the Court was mistaken, do we do a favor to the Court—do we increase public confidence in elections—by making the mistake a premise of our decision? Pressed to its logical extreme the panel's interpretation of and deference to legislative facts would require upholding a photo ID voter law even if it were uncontested that the law eliminated no fraud but did depress turnout significantly.[102]

In short, Posner urged the Court to weigh actual evidence about costs and benefits of burdens, rather than partisan beliefs unwedded to facts, an approach consistent with how the Department of Justice had considered preclearance motions before they lost this authority when the Voting Rights Act was struck down. For example, in blocking a 2011 voter ID law in South Carolina, the Justice Department required the state to identify the number of individuals affected, identify the number of minority voters without an ID, and estimate the likelihood that more of them would be less likely to vote. Whether one agrees or disagrees with the rationale of the Justice Department, it was at least an exchange based on evidence of costs and benefits.

Courts that have explicitly used the type of balancing test Posner proposed tend to strike down voter ID laws. In the Wisconsin ID case, Judge Lynn Adelman undertook an exhaustive review of evidence of fraud from the 2004 election, finding seven cases, all of which featured felons casting votes—a form of fraud that voter ID does not prevent. By contrast, Adelman noted that an estimated 9 percent of eligible voters did not have the appropriate ID, and that these citizens were disproportionately poorer and members of minority groups. Adelman concluded, "it is absolutely clear that Act 23 will prevent more legitimate votes from being cast than fraudulent votes." He rejected that the state should impose actual burdens to address concerns that were only "theoretically imaginable."[103]

A Pennsylvania trial court applied similar judgment: "a vague concern about voter fraud does not rise to a level that justifies the burdens constructed here."[104] In blocking the Texas voter ID law, a federal district judge ruled that not only was the law discriminatory— relative to whites, blacks were about three times more likely and Hispanics about twice as likely to lack a valid ID—but also that this discriminatory effect was intentional. Although the Supreme Court allowed the law to go into effect, the Fifth Circuit required the state to allow individuals to vote if they signed an affidavit that they faced difficulties in accessing the documents necessary for an ID (the Texas attorney general swiftly promised criminal prosecutions if voters lied on those affidavits).[105] North Carolina's sweeping law was also struck down. Judges pointed to the discriminatory intent of a law designed to "target African Americans with almost surgical precision," citing evidence such as legislative requests to identify the racial breakdowns of registered voters lacking ID.[106]

Policy Option: Universal Voter Registration

For those interested in increasing voter access, the evidence cited in this chapter directs attention from the act of voting itself to registration as a crucial first step. Where registration is onerous, voting declines. Expanding Election Day registration and same-day registration laws are straightforward and proven ways to increase turnout by reducing administrative burdens.

Another policy option would be to use administrative data to automatically register voters. This option is similar to the option of auto-enrollment used in other policy areas (see the discussion of Medicaid in chapter 7). It is also an extension of the logic behind the motor-voter law: citizen interactions with the state allow a non-onerous way to verify voter eligibility.

Some states have begun to pursue auto-enrollment, which has become known as universal registration. The costs of being automatically registered seem minimal, and the potential benefits are quite large. In 2015, Oregon became the first state to put in place automated registration by sharing state DMV records with the secretary of state. Oregon estimated that three hundred thousand new individuals would be added to the rolls. Other states, including California and Vermont, soon followed. Partisanship has also affected the adoption of universal registration policies, which face more opposition from Republicans.[107]

The United States is unusual in how it manages data registration processes. In most developed countries, the burdens for registering are left to the state, not to individuals or partisans. States have shown a capacity to use administrative data to verify eligibility issues in other areas, including citizenship, and they could do the same for voting. But a simpler approach would be a federal standard based on administrative data such as tax records, and preregistering sixteen-year-olds via high school and DMV records.[108] Although the federal government does not run elections, it is perhaps best placed to develop a national standard and to invest in an information technology infrastructure to register all citizens.

Conclusion

Contemplating how burdens matters to the basic right of voting recalls William Faulkner's observation that "The past is never dead. It isn't even past." The history of burdens in the post-Reconstruction South holds striking parallels with the present. Laws and procedures were adopted with clear discriminatory intent and effects. The implementation of those laws, and the beliefs of bureaucrats tasked with implementation, may be just as important as the laws on the books. The empirical evidence reviewed in this chapter suggests that these central features remain salient to the experience of voting today. Contemporary election policies are motivated by race—more restrictive laws are passed in states with higher populations of politically active black people. Some of these policies will create burdens that make it less likely that citizens will vote. And low-income and minority voters are more likely to experience these burdens relative to other groups—they are less likely to get help in terms of information or support, less likely to have a polling place close by, and are more likely to be required to prove their identity.

In short, the evidence largely supports Ginsburg's vision of elections. It took the strong medicine of the Voting Rights Act to end widespread discrimination. As soon as the preclearance requirements were deemed unconstitutional, newly liberated states and localities moved quickly to put restrictions in place. Florida reinstated a process that reviewed registration lists to remove noncitizens, which opponents argued was targeted toward Hispanic voters and would place burdens on citizens to prove their standing. Texas put in place its voter ID law, which had previously been blocked, as did Mississippi and Alabama, which had passed laws that had not completed federal review. Once the Shelby decision was handed down, the North Carolina General Assembly switched from a voter ID bill to a much more extensive set of limits, which disallowed student ID, preregistration, same-day registration, and reduced early voting.

Although changes in state law received the most attention, the Shelby decision also triggered changes in local administration. For example, black pastors in Jacksonville protested the replacement of a heavily used polling center by one that was not near public transportation. Galveston County in Texas moved ahead with a plan previously blocked by the federal government to consolidate its voting districts, reducing the number of easily accessible polling places.[109] Such local changes are less visible and require little justification, even as history shows that they are important in shaping access to the polls.

Congress could reinstate the preclearance provisions of the Voting Rights Act in some fashion, though the politicization of election processes makes this unlikely. The voting wars seem likely to continue on many fronts, especially voter ID laws, but universal registration could gain bipartisan support. For those sincerely concerned about fraud, automating registration offers the chance to both discard the symbols of fraud (those Mickey Mouse signatures that arise in registration drives) and generally provide a strong state-backed guarantee of the integrity of the process. For those concerned about access, it would expand the pool of potential voters and address a proven barrier to voting turnout.

FALSE CLAIMS AND TARGETED BURDENS

3

THE CASE OF ABORTION RESTRICTIONS

Abortion remains one of the most divisive issues in American politics. Its status as a right was conferred not by a referendum or legislative action but by the Supreme Court's reading of the Constitution. Elected officials who favor an outright ban on abortions therefore find themselves constrained by the courts. As a result, they turn to other methods to achieve their policy goals, which include policy actions that the courts will permit, such as blocking public funding for abortions and banning certain types of late-term abortions. But other changes limit access by making the process of seeking or providing an abortion more burdensome. Collectively, these tactics have transformed the landscape of reproductive rights. In much of the United States, a woman seeking an abortion must negotiate a thicket of administrative barriers.

State laws that seek to make abortion more burdensome have required women to undergo waiting periods and mandatory counseling (including descriptions of the procedure, the development of the fetus, and fetal pain), make multiple clinic visits, gain parental consent, and take and view an ultrasound. Some legislatures have required that providers be situated within a fixed distance from a hospital, have admitting privileges to that hospital, ensure the physical presence of one or more licensed physicians during the procedure, or be located in an ambulatory surgical center, even if the patient is not undergoing a surgical abortion. Such requirements have resulted in the closure of clinics, which in turn increases compliance burdens for women who have to travel farther and wait longer to gain access to fewer abortion providers.

These restrictions vary by state but affect a large number of women. The Guttmacher Institute, whose data on abortion policies is used by both pro-life and pro-choice advocates, estimates that one in three women seek an abortion over the course of their lives.[1] Most are poor: about half live below the federal poverty line, and another quarter fall between 100 to 199 percent of the poverty line.[2] Because of policies that ban or make it difficult for women to use health insurance to cover abortions, the majority end up paying out of pocket, including three-quarters of those in states where Medicaid places significant limits on reimbursement for abortions.[3] Administrative burdens that indirectly increase the costs of abortions—by imposing travel and accommodation costs to reach clinics, or by requiring women to take more time off work and find childcare to allow for multiple visits—fall most heavily on poor women. Delays in access to services result in a higher number of more expensive and invasive late-term abortions.

The role of third parties is central to the story of administrative burdens for abortion. Governments do not provide abortions directly. Instead, pro-life policymakers use governmental power to regulate private actors—abortion providers and private insurers—in a manner that makes it harder for women to receive abortions.

Precisely because abortion is such a divisive political issue, it is especially illustrative of the politics of burden. Pro-life policymakers and stakeholders are so motivated by this issue that they have creatively developed detailed burdens to facilitate their policy goals. Decisions that in other policy settings would be delegated to professional standards, provider discretion, or executive branch regulation—such as the words a doctor tells a patient or the precise width of corridors of service providers—are instead legislated, leaving a clear record of where political parties fall on the issue. The Guttmacher Institute estimates that states adopted 288 such provisions between 2010 and 2015— as many as had been passed in the previous fifteen years. Such laws are only adopted in states with Republican control, making this a policy area where the relationship between partisan politics and the implementation of burdens is clear.

The politics of abortion also illustrate how the generally opaque nature and apparent neutrality of administrative burdens offer a fig-leaf justification to engage in policymaking by other means. Pro-life policymakers know they cannot get away with promising to violate constitutional rights, so they offer an alternate value-based justification—protecting women's health—even as medical research suggests that such claims are unjustified. Abortions are safer than other common and less regulated forms of medical procedures, including colonoscopies, the removal of wisdom teeth, and even childbirth itself.[4] Similar to the administrative burdens placed on voting, the stated goal differs from the actual goal.

Ultimately, as is the case with voting, the courts are required to make sense of it all. *Roe v. Wade*, which legalized abortion nationally in 1973, followed a series of changes at the state level, starting in the 1960s, that legalized abortion services in an incremental fashion.[5] More recently, the wave of restrictions passed in state legislatures in the aftermath of the 2010 elections met with a judicial response in 2016; the Supreme Court found that some of those restrictions amounted to an undue burden in the case of *Whole Woman's Health v. Hellerstedt*.[6] This case, like the voting case, shows how courts wrestle with the concept of burden in citizen-state interactions.

The Nature of Burdens in Abortion Access

Battles about abortion have been waged on multiple fronts and in multiple ways. For some policies, such as limiting public funding, restrictions on certain types of late-term abortions, or gestational limits (tying restrictions to the duration of the pregnancy), policymakers are explicit in their goal in preventing abortions. Some restrictions may be deliberately adopted to test the willingness of the Supreme Court to provide states more discretion, but there is little subterfuge in the goals being pursued or the process employed. These restrictions certainly make it harder for women to get an abortion but do not change the processes of accessing the procedure.

Direct Burdens on Women

We limit our attention to policies that embed new barriers into the process of providing or receiving abortions. A woman can technically still access the service, but these barriers—sometimes referred to as targeted regulation of abortion providers (TRAP) laws—make the process more burdensome (see table 3.1). They are targeted at

Table 3.1 *Burdens Targeted at Women Seeking Abortions*

State Policy	Potential Costs
Limitations prohibiting private insurance (eleven states)	Learning costs to understand what is covered, compliance costs via out-of-pocket spending
Documenting rape, incest, or risk to life to use health insurance	Psychological and compliance costs for women to document these conditions
Waiting periods (twenty-seven states)	Compliance cost for both women and providers arising from additional appointments
Abortions after a specific point in the pregnancy must be performed in a hospital (nineteen states)	Compliance cost for women who have to go to a more expensive setting for an abortion
Physician must be physically present to administer medical abortion (nineteen states)	Compliance cost for both women and providers arising from additional appointments
Mandatory scripted counseling (eighteen states)	Psychological costs for women and potential learning costs if given incorrect information; psychological costs for providers
Required ultrasounds (twenty-six states)	Psychological costs on women, compliance and psychological cost for providers
Parental notification (thirty-seven states)	Psychological costs on women, compliance cost on provider seeking permission

Source: Guttmacher Institute 2017.

women seeking abortions, but some also impose costs on the abortion providers.

COMPLIANCE COSTS

Seeking an abortion generates a series of compliance costs, starting with monetary ones. Because these costs are set by private providers, they are not state-generated administrative burdens per se. However, the ways in which the state regulates providers and insurers affects the costs that women face, as well as the resources on hand to meet those costs.

Federal funds, including Medicaid, cannot be spent on abortion except if there is a threat to the life of the mother or in cases of rape or incest. Some states allow the state portion of Medicaid to be used for abortion, but others have restrictions similar to those imposed by the federal government, which also apply to those in Affordable Care Act (ACA) marketplaces in many states. Because of these cumulative restrictions, most women have no insurance for a medical service that many will use over their lifetime. In 2008, only 12 percent of abortions were paid for by private insurance.[7] Many with health insurance still end up paying for the service. One survey of women at abortion clinics found that though only 36 percent of the sample had no health insurance, 69 percent were paying for the service out of pocket. The 46 percent of women who did not try to seek reimbursement believed (often correctly) that the service was not covered.[8] For these women, the average out-of-pocket costs for an abortion was $485, increasing to $854 for a second trimester abortion. Lost wages (an average of $198), transportation costs ($44), childcare costs ($57), and other costs ($140) drove the compliance costs higher.[9]

Some costs are unavoidable, and they increase as states mandate waiting periods and additional procedures that generate multiple visits. In most states, women must wait a specified time after receiving mandatory counseling before having an abortion. In some states, legislators have found creative ways to extend waiting periods beyond the twenty-four to seventy-two hour standard, such as only counting work days in the waiting period. Women in nineteen states must go to a hospital after a specific point in the pregnancy, creating a compliance cost of going to a more expensive setting for an abortion.

State restrictions have especially targeted medication abortions, a first-trimester abortion that uses medication to induce a miscarriage. Physicians must be present to watch the patient take the medication pills, even though this is not clinically necessary. As a result, patients must make multiple clinic visits, increasing compliance costs. In Wisconsin, a law required that the *same* physician be present for two appointments, in part to determine that the patient was not under coercion. The latter requirement was vague enough that Planned Parenthood stopped providing medication abortions, which represented one-quarter of abortions in Wisconsin the previous year.[10]

States have also targeted medication abortion by requiring that providers only deliver the medication using protocols approved by the Food and Drug Administration (FDA). The protocols, approved in 2000, called for a higher dosage of the active drugs and three visits within the first seven weeks of pregnancy. Since those protocols were established, research has shown the drug to be safe and effective for longer periods at lower doses. Doctors could not use that evidence to inform their treatments in states that followed the FDA mandates, effectively requiring more visits within a shorter time. In March of 2016, the FDA updated its protocols to align with evidence on the drug, effectively thwarting state efforts to enforce the older and more restrictive FDA guidance.[11]

LEARNING COSTS

The compliance costs, in turn, create learning costs for women seeking to understand their rights and options. Simply understanding the availability of insurance can be difficult. Private insurers in eleven states are required to treat abortion as a separate form of medical insurance, offered as a supplemental rider rather than included in primary coverage. Because federal guidelines do not treat abortion as a common health-care event, insurance providers are not required to disclose that they do not cover it. Women thereby face learning costs given that coverage is opaque at time of enrollment, and many may not find out until they need an abortion that it is not covered by their insurance. Twenty-nine percent of women surveyed at an abortion clinic said they were unsure if they had coverage.[12]

The social stigma associated with abortion amplifies learning costs, creating a reluctance to seek information and a vulnerability to accessible but inaccurate information, including from government. A study of state Medicaid helplines and Medicaid managed care organizations found that in 18 percent of cases, women were given incorrect information.[13] Government requirements may compel abortion providers to offer misleading information in mandatory counseling. In five states women are told that there is a link between abortions and breast cancer, and in eight they are told that abortion damages mental health. Women in thirteen states are required to be told that fetuses can feel pain. Evidence does not support any of these claims.

Some women seeking abortion may already be starting with a low level of knowledge. A doctor serving women in Texas, which emphasizes abstinence in public education, noted that a lack of sexual education is one reason unplanned pregnancies occur: "Even just today, I saw a few patients that are in their mid-twenties and still don't know how birth control works or what their options are or had some questions about their anatomy. The lack of education is sort of a lack of power for a lot of people."[14] A survey of eighteen- to twenty-nine-year-olds confirmed this impression—the majority of those surveyed said they know little or nothing about birth control pills or implants. Half of unmarried women believed that birth control pills could cause cancer, making them less likely to use this method of contraception.[15]

PSYCHOLOGICAL COSTS

Abortion is perhaps the best example of an individual being guaranteed a legal right to make a choice that society stigmatizes. Abortion stigma has been defined as "a negative attribute ascribed to women who seek to terminate a pregnancy that marks them, internally or externally, as inferior to ideals of womanhood. While definitions of womanhood vary depending on local cultures and histories, a woman who seeks an abortion is inadvertently challenging widely-held assumptions about the 'essential nature' of women."[16]

Abortion stigma in the United States is pronounced enough to create a startling disconnect between the commonness of abortion and women's reluctance to talk about it. Carol Sanger notes that for many women, talking about the experience of abortion "is too personal, too risky, too stigmatizing." This stigma gives license for legislators to act punitively, but, limited by *Roe*, "the general strategy has been to make abortion harder to get: harder legally, financially, emotionally, and practically."[17]

Stigma varies by community, and this matters to how women experience abortion. Women that perceive lower community support for a right to abortion report a heightened sense of shame.[18] As they perceive more stigma, they become less likely to share their condition with others and feel more distress.[19] Opponents of abortion are organized and able to broadcast their opposition via powerful institutions, such as political parties and churches. Abortion is the only health procedure where the patient can expect to face a phalanx of protestors at the point of care. The rights of protestors are guaranteed by law, regardless of the psychological burdens it places on women or providers, illustrating that the experience of stigma is partly structured by laws.

State decisions can increase the psychological costs of seeking access to abortions. In a state with the full array of restrictions, women face a daunting gamut of psychologically taxing demands. Minors in thirty-seven states must provide parental notification; in some states, they must also receive consent. Required counseling may offer some emotional help to women, but it is also a way that the state can communicate its moral judgment of the woman's choice by, for example, communicating that fetuses can feel pain.

In some states, women are required to look at the ultrasound, and the provider is required to describe the fetus. Such requirements offer no medical benefit. Nor do they cause women to change their minds.[20] One study found that among women who selected to see ultrasounds, 98 percent continued to have an abortion, versus 99 percent among those who did not have an ultrasound. Only the very small percentage of women who had already expressed some uncertainty appeared to have been influenced by ultrasounds.

Mandatory requirements such as ultrasounds ultimately seem designed both to facilitate feelings of guilt rather than alter a women's choice, and to communicate to women the limits of their autonomy to make this decision. One provider recounts how mandatory scripts creates stress for patients: "There was a patient who—she just found out that her precious baby had a life-threatening problem and decided to terminate and then they had to listen to this ridiculous script.... She started crying and just saying, 'I can't do that. I can't believe I have to go through this again.'"[21]

Laws that create delays and the need for multiple visits compound psychological costs. A thirty-five-year-old mother published an anonymous account of managing administrative barriers imposed after the passage of Wisconsin's restrictive abortion laws:

> I am shaken. I am embarrassed. I am scared. I am tired of waiting.
> I am now called into a room. I can bring Hubby this time. We are

told to watch a video, again required by state law. The video talks about adoption, foster parenthood, the dangers of abortion, my rights. It drags on. I feel like a small child. Husband looks concerned and helpless. I sign a form indicating my understanding of the information presented on the video. We wait. A nurse finally comes back in. Time to go back to the waiting room. We'll call you in a short while.

I stare aimlessly into space. How did I get here? Why is this such an awful experience? Why do only two clinics in the state do this? How did our country get to this point where a small group of people in our state legislature can decide what I must or must not do with my uterus?

I am called back for lab work. Finger pricked, questions asked of me. Do I have any questions? Yes. How long is the wait for the next appointment? I know there's a 24-hour waiting period, but there's a weekend. Can I come back Monday? Um ... no. We only do the procedure on Tuesdays and Wednesdays, so we'll be able to schedule you the 16th.

The room starts spinning. The 16th? That's twelve days away. That's like two chapters in *What to Expect When You're Expecting*. I need to wait and experience all the things that come with pregnancy over the next two weeks, knowing I have that appointment on the calendar?

How is this happening to me?! How will I survive? I don't hear anything the nurse says. She and my husband ask if I'm okay. Apologies for the wait. The holidays led to backups. Are you still with us? Do you have any other questions?

The rest of the appointment is a blur. I don't understand. Can I crawl into bed for two weeks until I come back? Can I take off work? Can someone watch my kids?

A doctor hands me a list of clinics in neighboring states I can call if I can't wait. Insurance won't cover it, but they have less restrictive laws so it's worth a try. I cry. I beg. I start shaking. Isn't there anything I can do? No, sorry, this is how it is now in our state.

Husband walks me to the car. I spend the next two days in bed alternating between crying uncontrollably and going completely numb. I go to a birthday party, hoping it will be a good distraction. I mumble about being sick. I am a shell of a person, with no expression and no sense of what is happening in my life. Somehow I go to work for a day. People comment on how tired I look. Is everything okay? Are you sick?

I call the other clinic in the state. Can you see me earlier? No, we have a three-week wait. I call the neighboring state's clinic. Yes, we can see you in two days. No, your insurance won't cover you here.

I book the appointment. I have a credit card; I can worry about the money later. The clinic is 2–½ hours away, and I have an 8 a.m. appointment, so I book a hotel room for the next day. More money, but there's no way I can leave my home before 5 a.m. The gas, food and other expenses will add to the financial burden, but I feel I have no other choice. I cannot work, parent, or survive another week and 2 days of this hell.[22]

Women seeking to use health insurance in states that only allow coverage of rape, incest, or maternal risk also face the psychological burden that comes with verifying these conditions, often requiring documentation provided via a physician or law enforcement. Although federal law specifies that women do not need a police report of rape, state statutes may require that the woman has reported the rape.

Medication abortions can help to reduce psychological costs. This procedure is less invasive and offers more privacy than a surgical abortion, especially if the second treatment can be completed at home. Nicole Safar, the public policy director of Planned Parenthood Wisconsin, noted that "More than the physical piece, for many women medication abortion is the right choice for her entire self— emotionally, psychologically. Many women would prefer to go through the process at home, with their family. That's a huge piece of it you can't really quantify."[23] As noted, requirements to have doctors present to witness the medication abortion, or to follow outdated FDA protocols, make this option less available to women.

Requiring clinics to have the standards of ambulatory surgical center is another way to limit the ability of staff to provide women with some psychological support:

The necessity to have even first-trimester abortion procedures take place in a hospital-like environment has meant that the small touches developed over the years to comfort the patient— cozy fleece blankets, specially selected calming herbal teas, use

of heating pads, journals where women could discuss their feelings about their procedures as well as write messages of support
to other patients, and soothing art on the walls—have had to be
abandoned in the name of sustaining a sterile environment.[24]

EVIDENCE OF THE EFFECTS OF BURDENS
ON ACCESS TO ABORTIONS

The effects of burdens are interactive. As compliance costs compel
more clinics to close, patients must travel longer distances. Mandatory
wait times mean that multiple trips are needed or that the patient
has to find a place to stay. The crowding of more appointments and
women into fewer clinics creates another problem: it becomes harder
to have an early abortion. In oral arguments regarding the Supreme
Court discussion of a Texas law, the U.S. solicitor general noted that
the existing abortion providers would have to process four to five
times more abortions to make up for the providers forced to close.[25]

Because burdens imposed by states create scarcity among providers and barriers for patients to overcome, the delays become
extraordinarily consequential. Instead of taking a pill in a health-
care location closer to home, women are more likely to have to travel
farther to endure a surgical procedure or to miss the cut-off date and
be forced to bring an unwanted pregnancy to term. One study from
Texas estimated that if the waiting period to receive an appointment
were increased to twenty days because of the closure of facilities, the
rate of second-term abortions would almost double.[26]

Women who had abortions near the legal gestational limit point
to compliance costs as a reason for delay: a survey found that
67 percent of such women identified travel and procedure costs, as
did 58 percent of turnaways (women who passed the gestational
limit and were barred from receiving an abortion). Confusion and
problems with insurance were also a significant barrier, cited by
35 percent of women who had abortions near the gestational limit
and 37 percent of turnaways. Learning costs were prominent. Among
women who had abortions near the legal limits, 34 percent pointed
to not knowing where to get care and 23 percent cited not knowing
how to get a provider; the respective percentages for turnaways
were 34 percent and 30 percent.

Another study found that laws that compelled multiple visits increased the financial costs of abortion by 19 percent and reduced abortions by between 13 and 15 percent. Having multiple TRAP laws in place was estimated to increase the cost of abortions by 25 percent and reduce abortions by 17 to 19 percent.[27] Policies that increase these costs are also therefore likely to generate delays in abortions, and increase the number of later-term abortions and unwanted pregnancies.[28] Put another way, increasing the financial costs of abortions makes it unaffordable for poorer women.

Abortion restrictions appear to be encouraging a return to dangerous self-administered abortions.[29] Do-it-yourself (DIY) abortions are a social behavior difficult to identify because they are illegal. However, Google searches are a way of tracking both whether individuals are seeking information about how to perform DIY abortions and when and where these searches take place. After a wave of abortion restrictions, 2011 saw a 40 percent jump in searches related to DIY abortions, such as "how to self abort," "buy abortion pills online," "how to do a coat hanger abortion." In 2015, searches about DIY abortions totaled some seven hundred thousand, compared to about 3.4 million searches for abortion clinics and about one million for legal abortions. Such searches were more likely to occur in states with greater administrative burdens: eight of the ten states with the highest rate of searches were rated as hostile to abortion by the Guttmacher Institute.[30]

Burdens on Providers

Although the direct burdens that women face are significant, policymakers have also sought to limit access to abortion by targeting private third parties, that is, abortion providers and insurers. In many cases, the same provisions that are onerous for women also generate costs for these third parties (see table 3.1). For example, private insurers are directly affected by state and federal regulations. The Affordable Care Act prohibits the use of federal money for abortions. Private insurers operating in the exchanges created by the ACA must keep separate accounts for reimbursements in order to demonstrate that no federal subsidies were used to cover abortion services, and insurers have struggled to comply with these requirements.[31]

For providers, mandatory waiting periods mean extra appointments. Requiring a physician to be present to observe the provision of medications generates a compliance burden for abortions that is not in place for riskier outpatient procedures. Preventing clinics from employing lower cost but qualified staff (such than a physician's assistant or nurse practitioner) or technology (such as telemedicine) increases clinic costs, even as the complication rates for both medical and surgical abortions is similar for physicians and other clinical staff.[32]

Requiring medically unnecessary procedures may also generate psychological costs for staff. Employees who join an organization with a motivation to help others become demotivated if their work environment stops them from fulfilling their goals.[33] Clinic employees already have to deal with protests, harassment, and the threat of violence. Providers also face the psychological costs of forcing patients to undergo mandated services that they know are neither wanted nor medically beneficial. They must repeat scripts about the procedure that are at odds with their demonstrated commitment to making abortions available and which often contain what they know is medically questionable or incomplete information. The result is to weaken patient-physician trust and rapport.[34]

One provider reflected on the growth of TRAP laws: "All of them increase the stress on providers. They're just laws that can catch me accidentally doing something wrong legally, not doing anything wrong medically."[35] Carol Joffe, who has interviewed employees at clinics, describes staff as "bewildered" by aggressive inspectors that monitor their work: "As a veteran manager put it, the newer employees began to 'internalize' the critiques of the clinic's opponents, wondering if, indeed, "we were doing something wrong."[36]

Table 3.2 identifies burdens that are directly targeted at abortion providers. Providers have to know about these rules so some learning costs are involved, especially when they change frequently. But the main costs are compliance costs.

Abortion providers in many states find themselves in a Kafkaesque quandary that mixes regulatory zeal, excessive formalism, and ambiguous expectations. Individual employees may find that their status and record may be subject to intense scrutiny. For example, Mississippi requires that "each employee shall have a pre-employment health examination by a physician. The examination is to be repeated

Table 3.2 *Burdens Targeted at Abortion Providers*

State Policy	Type of Burden Created
State oversight of employee records	Compliance costs to satisfy requirements, psychological costs of close scrutiny on employees
Physical design and function of the regulated facility (nineteen states)	Compliance costs that may require a move or renovation
First-trimester abortions must be performed near a hospital (eight states)	Compliance costs that might require a provider to move
Admitting privileges at nearby hospital (eleven states)	Compliance costs to seek such privileges
Licensing not required of other physicians (thirty-seven states)	Compliance costs in the form of extra documentation
Requirement of unusually detailed formal policies and procedures	Compliance costs of establishing and enforcing such rules
Ambiguous standards	Learning costs to interpret ambiguous laws, compliance costs to enforce them as organizational rules

Source: Guttmacher Institute 2017.

annually and more frequently if indicated to ascertain freedom from communicable diseases."[37] Clinics face a compliance cost to maintain records and make employees available for testing; employees face the psychological costs of knowing they are under a scrutiny not applied to other health providers.

States can increase compliance costs by requiring clinics to have certain layouts and facilities. Nine states specify the size of the procedure rooms, and seven states specify the width of the facility corridors. The most common requirement is for ambulatory surgical centers to be on-site. Even facilities that only dispense oral medications for medication abortion, rather than provide surgical procedures, are still be required to have a surgical center in eighteen states.

Clinics can also be mandated to have a relationship with local hospital. They may be required to be within proximity of a hospital (usually ranging from fifteen minutes to thirty minutes or thirty miles), or have admitting privileges at a hospital (eleven states). This requires the cooperation of hospitals. Hospitals in states that pass these TRAP laws are reluctant to be associated with an unpopular activity, especially if the hospital is affiliated with a religious entity. For example, abortion providers in Mississippi tried to satisfy the admitting privilege requirement after a 2012 law but were unsuccessful in finding cooperative hospitals, leaving only one viable provider in the state. In Texas, some hospitals declined to provide admitting privileges for their own doctors.[38] Clinics that rely on visiting doctors are especially vulnerable to these provisions. Visiting doctors can provide care in parts of a state that might not otherwise be served, but they are less able to gain admitting privileges with hospitals.

Admitting privilege requirements have the effect of giving hospitals a de facto veto over the provision of health services they do not actually provide. Medical associations have stated that such privileges or the requirement for surgical facilities are unnecessary, offering no additional guarantee of care. Federal law already requires that any woman experiencing a complication be admitted to an emergency room. Laws that require admitting privileges therefore do not solve any particular problem. A review of the medical evidence on complications from abortion found only one instance where admitting privileges were necessary.[39] In the Supreme Court oral arguments on the merit of such privileges in Texas, Judge Breyer asked, "What is the benefit to the woman of a procedure that is going to cure a problem of which there is not one single instance in the nation, though perhaps there is one, but not in Texas?"[40]

As providers find themselves undertaking tasks they disagree with, both individual employees and provider organizations may stop providing the service. Such a threat comes in the context of a long decline in the number of abortion providers. In the aftermath of the *Roe v. Wade* decision, fewer and fewer OB-GYNs were willing to perform a role characterized in some quarters as that of a murderer or butcher. In 1973, eight in ten abortions were performed in hospitals. By 1996, the situation had reversed: nine in ten were performed in clinics.[41] The shift to a clinic-based approach enabled patients to receive services at lower costs in a setting focused on reproductive rights. But it also marked abortion providers as outsiders in the medical profession, more visible and more vulnerable to public and political attack.

Provider compliance costs also crop up at the intersection of clinical practice and public health insurance programs. The experience of abortion providers interacting with state and federal Medicaid administrators is different from that of other health-care providers. Medicaid will, in theory, provide payment for abortions in states where state law does not prohibit that payment and for abortions that are eligible under the exceptions established in federal law. In reality, however, abortion providers find it difficult to access Medicaid reimbursements.

Medicaid administrators sometimes demand documentation from abortion providers beyond what the law requires. In seeking reimbursement for public funding for permitted abortions (arising from rape, incest, or a risk to the mother's health), clinics face difficulties. This may include such hurdles as requiring the submission of a police report for verification of rape. One study found that only between 54 percent (in states that have their own version of these restrictions) and 62 percent (in less restrictive states) of Medicaid reimbursement requests were successful.[42] Because of the heightened scrutiny under which abortion providers operate, they sometimes add their own layers of documentation for women that exceed those required the law.[43]

In some cases, the state requires that the abortion provider formalize processes that otherwise might not be in place, or might exist only informally. For example, in South Carolina, written policies and procedures must be developed by the clinic on "1. Safety rules and practices pertaining to personnel, equipment, gases, liquids, drugs, supplies and services; 2. Provisions for reporting and investigating accidental events regarding patients, visitors and personnel and corrective action taken; 3. Provisions for disseminating safety-related information to employees and users of the facility."[44]

Some laws are difficult to interpret and it is impossible to fully document compliance. For example, Texas requires that licensed facilities ensure that all patients are cared for in a manner that "enhances [the patient's] self-esteem and self-worth."[45] South Carolina reserves the right to fine licensed facilities for taking any other actions that "are against the best practices as interpreted by the

[Health] Department."[46] In Wisconsin doctors must, under threat of criminal penalty, verify that the patient is not being coerced into have an abortion. Providers face not just compliance costs but also learning costs to demonstrate adherence to uncertain regulatory standards.

When Burdens Become Politics: Protecting Women's Health Versus Access to Abortion

Abortion policies illustrates the potential for administrative burdens to serve as a form of politics by other means. Because the Supreme Court has eliminated the possibility of state legislatures simply banning the procedure, the turn to other policy tactics—and a disingenuous framing—becomes more attractive.

Abortion is a relatively safe procedure. The rate of medical complications that arise is less than 0.3 percent, according to the American Medical Association, lower than outpatient procedures that are not subject to the same demands. Another recent study found that 0.23 percent of abortions had major complications, and another 1.88 percent had minor complications.[47] As soon as a woman becomes pregnant, the risk of complications and mortality goes up, and increases each week through gestation until childbirth. In purely health terms, delays in receiving abortions therefore increase maternal risk. Childbirth itself is estimated to be fourteen times less safe for the mother than a first-trimester abortion.[48]

In some cases, pro-life advocates argue that abortion undercuts women's mental health. A review of existing studies by the American Psychological Association found no such connection after other factors, such as prior mental illnesses, were accounted for.[49] Indeed, bringing an unwanted pregnancy to term can create negative long-term mental health outcomes. A longitudinal study of the pre-*Roe* era found that women with unwanted pregnancies had worse mental health even decades later (controlling for observable confounders such as education, health, and income).[50] Another study compared women who received abortions just before the legal cut-off and women turned away immediately after. The turnaways were less likely to have aspirational goals such as further education or career goals, and were more exposed to domestic violence from the father of their child.[51]

Policies that delay abortions or encourage childbirth can be argued on other grounds, including sincerely held beliefs on the sanctity of life. But such policies do not improve the health of the mother. Indeed, forcing the closure of women's health clinics is likely to worsen women's health. Texas has the highest maternal mortality rate in the developed world, a rate that has only increased with the introduction of TRAP laws.[52] The sudden uptick in the adoption of TRAP policies did not come as the result of any new medical insights or research on women's health but from a political change: the 2010 election that saw Republicans take control of over twenty-six state legislatures and twenty-nine governorships.[53]

Why should policymakers bother with such an easily disproved claim in the first place? Pro-life legislators seeking a realistic chance of passing laws that will be upheld by the courts cannot explicitly state their true policy goals of reducing abortions. Instead, the restrictions must have some rational association with another interest of the state, which most commonly has been expressed as the health of the woman. For example, in signing a law that restricted abortions in Louisiana, Governor Jindal called it "a common-sense bill that gives women the health and safety protections they deserve."[54]

Ironically, the women's health claim echoes one of the primary justifications for making abortion accessible in the first place. The women's movement made the right to control one's own body a central argument for legalizing abortion, but another concern was women's health. Women were dying—and many more faced lifelong health challenges—as a result of unregulated and unsafe abortions. Developing countries still feature such grim conditions. One analysis published in The Lancet labeled this lack of access to safe abortions as a "preventable pandemic," resulting in an estimated sixty-eight thousand deaths annually. The authors concluded that "access to safe abortion improves women's health."[55]

The co-opting of women's health as an argument to limit abortions reflects the plasticity of administrative burdens. Such burdens are opaque enough that they can be asserted to achieve goals they have little real relationship with. They can be framed as a common-sense tool to protect citizens by regulating a service, rather than as an overt effort to stop citizens from choosing that service. Directives that require hospital admitting privileges, ambulatory surgical centers, or following FDA guidelines sound like reasonable precautions to protect women. Only those who know the policy context can gauge the likely impacts on women and providers. Other directives—such as requiring women to have sonograms—draw more attention because their lack of a health benefit is more immediately apparent.

In some instances, the mask about women's health drops. Representative Henry Hyde, who skillfully limited federal funding for abortion, made no such claim: "I certainly would like to prevent, if I could legally, anybody having an abortion, a rich woman, a middle-class woman, or a poor woman. Unfortunately, the only vehicle available is the . . . Medicaid bill." More recently, a board member of the advocacy group Pro-Life Mississippi framed TRAP laws as "part of a greater strategy to end abortion in our country. It's part of it, and one day, our country will be abortion free."[56]

As these laws are struck down, their proponents become less guarded in their responses. After Oklahoma's admitting procedures requirements were blocked, its governor responded by saying, "I will always fight for the rights of the unborn."[57] The day that Texas restrictions were deemed unconstitutional by the Supreme Court, Texas Governor Greg Abbot released a short statement saying, "The decision erodes States' lawmaking authority to safeguard the health and safety of women and subjects more innocent life to being lost. Texas' goal is to protect innocent life, while ensuring the highest health and safety standards for women."[58] Governor Scott Walker of Wisconsin, whose own restrictions were affected by the Texas decision, tweeted, "Core of WI's law remains—require access to medical images & info about their unborn children. A positive, pro-life solution remains in WI" and "We're disappointed an activist court overturned common sense standards on abortion providers, we will continue to protect [the] sanctity of life." Such statements either balance claims about women's health with the language of the pro-life movement, or abandon them altogether for the former in favor of the latter.

The pro-life movement has long overlapped with the Republican Party. Pro-life advocates, such as Americans United for Life, develop model legislation for state legislators to introduce whether they are to demonstrate their commitment to the cause.[59] TRAP laws are the culmination of decades of trial and error to find tactics that are legal, feasible, and effective ways to minimize abortion. As a simple matter of political strategy, administrative burdens that center on protecting women's health have been more successful in limiting access to abortion than direct assaults that focus on the rights of the unborn, such as laws that convey "personhood" status on a fetus.

Pro-choice stakeholders also played an important role in monitoring the diffusion of such bills and alerting their supporters. Pro-choice stakeholders contested the claims that burdens facilitated women's health, and documented the likely effect of TRAP laws on access. These stakeholders include providers, such as Planned Parenthood, and advocacy groups, such as NARAL Pro-Choice America. In a policy area that was more one-sided, lacking well-organized stakeholders who could understand and raise alarms about opaque policy proposals, the strategy of relying on administrative burdens would have been even more successful.[60] Instead, the debate—over whether TRAP laws served women's health, or were instead intended to limit access to abortions—would return to the courts.

THE ROLE OF THE COURTS

Since *Roe v. Wade*, the politics and practical implementation of abortion have been inextricably tied to the courts. Much of the vulnerability of abortion rights rests on the fact that it is not a positive enumerated right but instead one carved out of a right to privacy. A series of decisions—most notably *Harris v. McRae* (1980), *Webster v. Reproductive Health Services* (1989), and *Planned Parenthood v. Casey* (1992)—gave state governments significant power in regulating reproductive services.[61] Indeed, the *Roe* decision specified that protecting women's health was a justifiable basis to place restrictions on access to abortions. TRAP laws therefore offer an invitation to the courts to grant states even more authority to regulate abortions.

It is ultimately up to the courts to balance individual rights versus state authority. The court has articulated this balance by applying a legal concept of *undue burden*: the state cannot place excessive barriers on individuals seeking to access a good or service. This concept of undue burden points to a legal standard for courts to apply generally in considering administrative burden as well as to the practical difficulties in determining when such burdens are too great.

The undue burden standard was outlined in *Planned Parenthood v. Casey*. The Supreme Court declared that "the State may enact regulations to further the health or safety of a woman seeking an abortion, but may not impose unnecessary health regulations that present a substantial obstacle to a woman seeking an abortion.... An undue burden exists and therefore a provision of law is invalid if its purpose or effect is to place substantial obstacles in the path of a woman seeking an abortion before the fetus attains viability." From the beginning, the meaning of this standard was unclear. The Court ruled in *Casey* that a twenty-four-hour waiting period and parental reporting requirements were not undue burdens, but that spousal notification was excessively burdensome because it gave husbands an effective veto over their wife's decision and created a risk of spousal abuse.[62]

Legislatures and courts have grappled with what constitutes an undue burden. Judges have most often focused on compliance costs, such as financial costs required to travel to a provider. They have also disagreed on how those costs should be balanced with a consideration of benefits. One perspective, articulated by Judge Richard Posner in the Seventh Circuit Court, calls for a balancing test between the benefits and costs of state policies: "If a burden significantly exceeds what is necessary to advance the state's interests, it is 'undue,' which is to say unconstitutional. The feebler the medical grounds (in this case, they are nonexistent), the likelier is the burden on the right to abortion to be disproportionate to the benefits and therefore excessive."[63]

In assessing Wisconsin's restrictions on abortions, Posner also noted that burdens are unevenly distributed, having a greater impact on low-income women:

> more than 50 percent of Wisconsin women seeking abortions have incomes below the federal poverty line and many of them live in Milwaukee (and some north or west of that city and so even farther away from Chicago). For them a round-trip to Chicago, and finding a place to stay overnight in Chicago, should they not feel up to an immediate return to Wisconsin after the abortion, may be prohibitively expensive. The State of Wisconsin is not offering to pick up the tab, or any part of it. These women may also be

unable to take the time required for the round trip away from their work or the care of their children.[64]

Posner's perspective on undue burdens calls for evidence on whether the law is likely to achieve its claimed benefits. Other courts took a different approach. The Fifth Circuit Court approved restrictions from Texas that were similar to Wisconsin's, explicitly declining to judge the efficacy of the law. Instead, judges focused on whether it was possible for a woman to overcome the burdens rather than whether the burdens are justified. In that context, the court did not see the prospect of clinic shutdowns leaving nine hundred thousand women more than 150 miles from the nearest clinic as an undue burden. In 2013, Texas had forty-one abortion clinics. This number dwindled to eighteen by 2015, and was expected to decline to ten if the law was put into effect. The Court returned to the *Casey* decision that called for a "large fraction" of women to be affected before a burden could be considered undue. That nine hundred thousand women could be clearly burdened by the loss of services, but that the law itself was not deemed to produce an undue burden, seems both illogical and at odds with the spirit of the original *Casey* decision, which also referred to a "significant number" of women as a consideration.[65]

In resolving these disagreements, the Supreme Court sided with Posner's view of undue burden in *Whole Woman's Health v. Hellerstedt* (2016). The Court concluded that a determination of undue burden required both a consideration of the benefits of the law, as well as its costs. Writing for the majority, Justice Breyer concluded that the Texas law failed to offer "medical benefits sufficient to justify the burdens upon access that each imposes. Each places a substantial obstacle in the path of women seeking a pre-viability abortion, each constitutes an undue burden on abortion access, and each violates the Federal Constitution."[66]

The majority opinion carefully documented evidence of the costs those burdens, while noting the lack of evidence on benefits. Breyer was also explicit on the role of evidence itself, arguing that the Fifth Circuit was "incorrect" to suggest that

a district court should not consider the existence or nonexistence of medical benefits when considering whether a regulation of

abortion constitutes an undue burden . . . The statement that legislatures, and not courts, must resolve questions of medical uncertainty is also inconsistent with this Court's case law. Instead, the
Court, when determining the constitutionality of laws regulating
abortion procedures, has placed considerable weight upon evidence and argument presented in judicial proceedings.[67]

In short, courts are not obliged to uncritically defer to legislative claims, especially when such claims are at odds with evidence.
Justice Ginsburg went even further than Breyer, concluding that
"it is beyond rational belief that H.B.2 could genuinely protect the
health of women." Instead, the law "would simply make it more
difficult for them to obtain abortions." She concluded by warning
that "Targeted Regulation of Abortion Providers laws like H.B.2 that
do little or nothing for health, but rather strew impediments to
abortion," cannot survive judicial inspection.[68]

Conclusion

What do policymakers do when the law limits them from banning a
practice they see as immoral? In the case of abortion, the answer has
been to impose administrative burdens as a form of policymaking
by other means. The deep partisan divisions around abortion have
meant that the exercise of such restrictions have become overtly
political, decided in legislatures and the courts, and patterned on the
distribution of power in the U.S. system of government. The claim of
women's health was little more than a rhetorical fig-leaf to obscure
the true intent of the policy. The partisan legislative record on this
issue, the failure to apply similar burdens to riskier medical procedures, and the statements of pro-life stakeholders and politicians all
point to the use of burdens as a means to reduce the number of
abortions.

The *Roe v. Wade* decision saw courts significantly constrain state
discretion, while still leaving room for more conservative states to
test the boundaries of that discretion via the adoption of administrative burdens. The *Whole Woman's Health v. Hellerstedt* decision
signaled to states that using burdens to limit access to abortion was
an abuse of their discretion. The *New York Times* greeted the decision

as "the court's most sweeping statement on abortion since *Planned Parenthood v. Casey*," underlining how administrative burdens have been the central battleground on abortion policy in recent decades.[69]

Even as *Hellerstedt* offered a moment of victory for pro-choice activists who saw specific types of burdens struck down, the pro-life movement continues to advocate for additional burdens. For example, Indiana and Texas adopted laws, in 2016 and 2017 respectively, to require fetal tissue to be buried or cremated, no matter the state of development. Even if these laws, in turn, will be deemed unconstitutional, they signal the centrality of administrative burdens to the politics of abortion.

THE AFFORDABLE CARE ACT   4

FEDERALISM AS A SOURCE OF BURDENS

The cases of voting and abortion described in the preceding chapters demonstrate how burdens can be embedded in statute to achieve policy change. The implementation of the 2010 Patient Protection and Affordable Care Act (ACA) presents a more nuanced case where partisanship and politics matter. It also highlights the role of administrative capacity and the potential for burdens in a federal system. Moreover, it provides a template not only for the construction of administrative burdens, but also for their deconstruction.

The passage of the ACA, frequently referred to as Obamacare, led to the largest reduction in the uninsured population since the implementation of Medicare in 1965. Between 2013 and 2016, the proportion of the uninsured under age sixty-five dropped from 20 percent to 11.5 percent.[1] Most attention concerning how the ACA increased the number of individuals with health insurance has focused on the policy expansions: these include changes to Medicaid such as increasing income eligibility thresholds and removing asset tests, as well as the provision of subsidies that allow individuals with low incomes who do not qualify for Medicaid to purchase private health insurance coverage. We examine an aspect of the ACA that has been given less attention but may be no less important in reducing the rate of uninsured: the administrative burdens faced by citizens as they attempted to access health insurance.

The ACA is not a health insurance model anyone would design from scratch. The bill expanded access to what is already a complex health-insurance system in a way that satisfied existing stakeholder interests in maintaining that system and reflected the intergovernmental distribution of power. The inherent complexity of the U.S. health-care system ensures that accessing insurance using the ACA would be burdensome. The question became who would bear the burden—the state, beneficiaries, or possibly even third-party providers such as health insurance companies?

Embedded throughout the ACA were policy requirements and flexibilities focused on reducing burdens for individuals seeking private plans and Medicaid. The importance of these administrative reforms did not go unnoticed by opponents of the ACA. Policymaker efforts to expand or minimize burden in the implementation of the ACA were driven by partisan attitudes toward the bill itself. The ACA passed Congress without a single Republican vote. Republicans who once supported elements of the law, such as the individual mandate, now called it unconstitutional, and in the years following its passage made the repeal of Obamacare a defining feature of political campaigns. In the years since its passage, the Obama administration and states supportive of the law sought to shift burdens in accessing health insurance away from beneficiaries; the Trump administration and states opposed to the law have tried to make access to health insurance afforded under the ACA more burdensome.

The implementation of the ACA reflects how federalism—the intergovernmental distribution of power—creates opportunities for different levels of government to work at cross-purposes. Under President Obama, many state governments sought to hinder the ACA by increasing burdens, either by withholding cooperation or by deliberately introducing burdens into policy domains under their control. Under President Trump, states supportive of the law looked for ways to soften burdens created by the Trump administration. Administrative capacity is also part of this story. In some cases, state governments that wanted the program to succeed imposed burdens because of an inability to quickly master the novel challenges the ACA posed. Such variation in government capacity at the state level is also an inherent aspect of federalism.

We focus in particular on how these factors played out in one venue—the health-care exchanges where insurance could be purchased or Medicaid eligibility could be determined. The federal exchange offered via Healthcare.gov proved almost impossible to navigate on its creation but gradually improved as the federal government moved to ease burdens that beneficiaries faced. As we detail, a key challenge involved better managing federal coordination with the states to ensure rapid enrollment. The legislation, designed around the assumption that nearly all states would create their own exchanges, ran into state and federal coordination issues when many Republican governors refused to do so in protest over the legislation.

Certain design choices were critical to fixing the federal exchange. For example, Healthcare.gov linked to tax records to verify income eligibility for the subsidies for those purchasing private plans. Individuals are not required to file any documentation. Moreover, they are not required to wait for eligibility to be determined. This verification is done nearly instantaneously on Healthcare.gov (or in the state system). Individuals are also automatically reenrolled in their existing plan if they do not reenroll themselves into a different plan. Moreover, if a particular plan is discontinued by an insurer, individuals will now be automatically enrolled into a plan that most closely matches the discontinued plan. Such design features seek to reduce burdens in reenrollment.

We also focus closely on the role of *navigators*—third parties funded by the ACA to reduce the burdens that people faced in the new health insurance system. Their effectiveness was hampered by limited resources as well as by some Republican-led state governments that made it harder for navigators to reduce learning and compliance costs for citizens. Navigators were further hampered by the near-elimination of financial support for the program by the Trump administration.

The Exchanges

The ACA is a sprawling piece of legislation, impossible to summarize in a single chapter. Table 4.1 details the basic costs that individuals experience in seeking access to health insurance via the ACA. To understand how administrative burdens played a role in its implementation, we focus here on health-care exchanges.

The exchanges are where people seeking subsidized individual market plans and Medicaid coverage encountered the ACA's burdens. Those seeking health insurance coverage could use the exchange to sort out their varying options and enroll in a plan. Individuals could apply online, over the telephone, by paper enrollment, or by having a

Table 4.1 *Burdens in Seeking Health Insurance via the Affordable Care Act*

Learning costs	Finding out about eligibility, level of support, and appropriate plan, exacerbated by uncertainty about the status and content of the law and multiple eligibility procedures
Compliance costs	Delays as a result of dysfunctional exchange websites; slow coordination between federal, state, and local eligibility verification procedures
Psychological costs	Stress; frustration with delays in process and uncertainty of access

Source: Authors' compilation.

navigator complete enrollment for them. The Obama administration hoped the exchanges would facilitate high enough participation to avoid the death spiral that results if only the sickest with the highest medical expenses enroll.

The 2013 rollout of the exchanges was immediately threatened by partisan state government reactions to the legislation. The ACA was designed with the assumption that states would run their own exchanges. The Department of Health and Human Services (HHS) expected that only eight states would participate in the federal marketplace.[2] Instead, only sixteen states chose to run their own exchanges, seven more partnering with the federal government, leaving 59 percent of the uninsured living in states that did not run their own exchange.[3]

The partisan division in how states responded to the exchanges was clear. Eighteen of the state-run or federal-partnership exchanges were in states with Democratic governors, including five of the seven in the federal-partnership exchanges, and seventeen had Democratic legislatures. By contrast, Republicans controlled the governorship in twenty-five of the twenty-seven states that opted out. Republican governors who normally warned of the dangers of federal control chose not to set up their own exchanges even as they used antifederal rhetoric to defend their decision. Governors Kasich in Ohio and Deal in Georgia complained that the state-run exchanges would lead to a "high federal burden" and that these "one size fits all approaches" did not allow for "flexibility."[4] Refusing to adopt the state exchanges became a way for those opposed to the ACA to express that opposition.

The absence of state exchanges created complications because of the intergovernmental dynamics of Medicaid. Although Medicaid is subsidized by federal dollars, it is run primarily by state governments. Eligibility rules—and insurance regulations—are determined by the state. Thus, having states administer enrollment was consistent with established practice for Medicaid. State-run exchanges could reduce learning and compliance costs for participants by allowing for a one-stop shopping experience. The purchaser could consider private individual insurance plans, subsidies to purchase those plans, and eligibility and enrollment in Medicaid, all in a single venue. In the federal exchange, individuals would be able to buy private insurance, apply for the federal subsidy based on their income, and see whether they might qualify for Medicaid. But there was no clear plan about how Medicaid enrollment, which is administered by states and counties, would work for those using the federal exchange.

INTERGOVERNMENTAL COORDINATION CHALLENGES

The unexpected refusal of states to run exchanges created a series of implementation and administrative challenges that resulted in more burdensome participant experiences, particularly in the first few years.[5] A central challenge was coordinating individual information across multiple levels of government and private insurers. Significant communication issues arose between the federal exchange and states, and in some cases, even within states, when county agencies were tasked with Medicaid enrollment. These issues created difficulties for applicants. For example, an individual could apply for coverage via the federal exchange and be given a notice of eligibility for the state Medicaid program. The federal government then transferred the file to the state. The state then determined eligibility. This process, in most cases, took months.[6] In May of 2014, nearly 2.9 million people found themselves caught in this backlog.[7] In many instances, after waiting for months, states asked individuals for the same information that they had already provided to the federal exchange. Even in states that used the federal data, outdated information systems often hampered the automated transfer of records, leaving caseworkers to manually input information received from the federal government, exacerbating time delays.

The largest backlogs occurred in states where counties determine eligibility. By contrast, during this same period, states such as New York and Kentucky avoided delays by having the same state agency make all eligibility determinations, from Medicaid to the income-tested subsidy for private health insurance.[8] The backlog was reduced, but considerable variance remains in states that use the federal exchange regarding how long it takes to determine eligibility and the additional work required by beneficiaries.[9]

If an individual was deemed ineligible for Medicaid, the state returned the case to the federal government. The individual was then notified of eligibility for the income subsidy rather than Medicaid. Applicants often faced months of uncertainty before they could enroll in subsidized health insurance. Those who enrolled in a federal health plan on the Healthcare.gov exchange, but then applied for Medicaid directly through their state, could also face costly and confusing burdens. The federal government, unaware the individual was enrolled in Medicaid, would automatically reenroll them in a private plan. The consumer, unaware, would be simultaneously enrolled in two plans and would be required to pay the premiums for the private plan, creating further confusion and financial costs. Users of the federal exchange experienced frustrating problems and delays but lacked an understanding of what was causing these problems, making it easy for them to point the finger at the Obama administration.

The difficulties in coordinating on multiple levels were compounded by the complexities of the task. Here, the federal government simply lacked the capacity to roll out a new and untested Healthcare.gov website that would seamlessly capture user information. The resulting delays, and requirements to provide the same information multiple times, created a compliance burden. The burden was compounded when Healthcare.gov crashed almost as soon as it was open for business, leaving long and frustrating waits for applicants. Only six people managed to access insurance on the first day the site opened.[10]

The planning for Healthcare.gov was plagued by mismanagement, according to a comprehensive assessment by HHS's inspector general, but the failure of state governments to establish their own exchanges exacerbated these problems.[11] In the days preceding the launch, HHS officials scrambled to find ways to meet unanticipated capacity demands for the federal exchange; they had assumed state exchanges would be managing far more of the demand.

HHS also prioritized pushing the website out on schedule, despite evident problems, concerned that congressional critics would use any delay as a basis for pursuing a repeal of the law. Compounding these issues, the day the website launched was the first of a sixteen-day federal government shutdown, which was partly motivated by House-Senate disagreements about delaying the ACA. Only a fraction of pre-shutdown staff was available to identify and address problems. Relatively few pretests and lack of a soft website rollout increased the demands on staff to identify and resolve problems during the rollout.[12]

As a general rule, bureaucracies are better at fixed tasks than at novel tasks. Over time, the federal government found ways to improve the user experience. One of the best fixes to the coordination issue, which eight states used, was allowing the federal government to determine final eligibility for the state-run Medicaid program but then transferring files to the state to complete enrollment.[13] The eight states taking this approach were Alabama, Alaska, Arkansas, Montana, New Jersey, Tennessee, West Virginia, and Wyoming. This process reduced the differences in administrative burdens between states that ran their own exchanges and those participating in the federal exchanges. For example, in these eight states, as in the states that run their own exchanges, three-quarters of people who provide assistance with exchange enrollments say that Medicaid enrollment is timely, relative to just one-third of their counterparts in states that participate in the federal exchange but do not allow the federal government to determine eligibility.[14]

Overall, the enrollment into private plans became relatively straightforward and streamlined, although Medicaid enrollment in states where the federal government cannot determine eligibility remained a problem. Table 4.2 summarizes key actions to reduce burdens that were used in this and other processes, as well as practices used to increase burdens.

The Obama period was characterized by attempts to reduce administrative burdens to ensure the long-term success of the ACA. The Trump administration took the opposite tack. Trump's first HHS secretary, Tom Price, outlined an early blueprint to undermine the ACA if

Table 4.2 *Government Actions to Reduce or Increase Burdens in the Affordable Care Act*

Reduce	Increase
Learning costs · Funding of navigators · Outreach · Longer sign-up times Compliance costs · Allowing navigators to complete enrollment · Federal investments in state capacity to upgrade enrollment and eligibility systems · Automatic reenrollment into existing or similar plans on exchange · Link to federal or state administrative data, rather than require documentation, to verify eligibility, provide assistance, renew enrollees · Allowing federal government to determine Medicaid eligibility · Real-time verification of eligibility · Universal application for CHIP/ Medicaid and subsidies · Eliminating in-person interviews for Medicaid · Use SNAP data for Medicaid enrollment · Expanded use of presumptive eligibility and automatic enrollment for Medicaid · Extending child Medicaid eligibility to twelve months · Limiting frequency of renewal processes	· Shortening sign-up times, reducing the availability of Healthcare.gov · Delaying enrollment until multiple levels of government verified eligibility · Requiring background checks and licensing of navigators or other third parties · Limiting resources for navigators and outreach · Political messaging that creates confusion about the status and value of the program · Increasing Medicaid premiums and copayments

Source: Authors' compilation.

legislative efforts to repeal failed, in large part by increasing administrative burdens on participants. He suggested shortening the period when people could enroll for the ACA, tightening grace periods for individuals to pay late premiums, and requiring more documentation to enroll during special enrollment periods.[15] HHS implemented some of these proposals, such as shortening the enrollment period from three months to forty-five days. It also made Healthcare.gov less accessible via more frequent shutdowns, and largely eliminated advertising of the program during the enrollment period.

Some of the efforts to reduce burdens listed in table 4.2 occurred at the state level. Many states continued to improve their administrative capacity, and reduce burdens, in a pattern of incremental problem-solving. Colorado is such an example. The state initially required that individuals be rejected from receiving Medicaid before they could check eligibility for the federal subsidy to buy private insurance. However, this determination did not happen in real time via an automated eligibility system, leading to enrollment delays.[16] State officials quickly shifted to automatic eligibility determination based on adjusted gross income.

States like Minnesota, where enrollment is at the local level, needed to improve communication among state and county agencies when it came to eligibility and enrollment in Medicaid.[17] Colorado and Minnesota are examples of states that faced administrative capacity challenges but ultimately saw some of the largest reductions in the percent of uninsured children between 2013 and 2014.[18] In both states, administrators had political support to identify and resolve implementation processes that were creating burdens.

Regardless of what was happening at the federal level, state elected officials opposed to the ACA often chose to make the implementation process more burdensome, most directly by failing to set up state exchanges. Governors could also decide to abandon a functioning exchange. Kentucky was one of the early success stories, creating a highly effective state exchange and outreach campaign, which contributed to some of the largest increases in health insurance coverage in the country. A newly elected Republican governor, however, shuttered the state exchange in 2016 on the basis of a campaign promise to repeal Obamacare.[19] Governors could also decide to object to federal efforts to simplify the experience. For example, Wisconsin threatened private insurers with legal action if they obeyed the Centers for Medicare and Medicaid Services (CMS) mandate to automatically enroll individuals in a similar plan if the participant's existing plan is discontinued. As we describe in the next section, state politicians also targeted information and outreach efforts.

Information and Outreach

The quantity and quality of outreach at the state level offered a way to influence enrollment. The ACA included provisions and funding for public and private entities to assist or actually enroll individuals into health insurance plans.[20] Such outreach not only helped people navigate procedural barriers but also provided an opportunity for the state to facilitate and actively engage people, especially those who felt forgotten by government.

People needed help and advice to manage the learning and compliance costs of the ACA. More than one-third of uninsured adults reported the process of enrolling via the health-care exchanges to be difficult or confusing.[21] The sustained publicity stemming from the political opposition to Obamacare might be expected to help reduce learning costs. But general awareness of the program, and even targeted outreach efforts, did not eliminate significant learning costs that come from determining individual eligibility and benefits for a new and complex program, or from sorting through the suitability of competing plans. A Commonwealth Fund survey found that nearly half of those uninsured were simply unaware of the Medicaid expansion or financial subsidies for private marketplace plans.[22] A 2017 poll found that one in three people did not know that Obamacare and the ACA were the same policy, the highest confusion being among those with lower incomes.[23]

Providing help to potential applicants mattered to enrollment. A 2014 Urban Institute survey found that, among previously uninsured adults, those who had benefited from application assistance were more likely to have enrolled through the marketplace—more than half of enrollees had used assistance, relative to less than a third of non-enrollees.[24] A 2016 survey found that, among those income eligible and with similar demographic differences, the rate of enrollment was 77 percent for those receiving assistance,

---

Box 4.1 *Legalese in Health Insurance: Policy Provision from a Rhode Island Insurer*

Benefits are payable for Covered Medical Expenses (see "Definitions") less any Deductible incurred by or for a Covered Person for loss due to Injury or Sickness subject to: a) the Maximum Benefit for all services; b) the maximum amount for special services; both as set forth in the Schedule of Benefits; and c) any coinsurance amount set forth in the Schedule of Benefits or any endorsement hereto. The total payable for all Covered Medical Expenses shall never exceed the Maximum Benefit stated in the Schedule of Benefits. Read the "Definitions" section and the "Exclusions and Limitations" section carefully.

Source: ConsumersUnion 2009.

---

compared to 60 percent for those who did not receive assistance.[25] Administrative data obtained from CMS also found that, among those uninsured who visited the marketplace, the biggest difference between those who enrolled and those who did not was in whether they had received personal assistance.[26] Outreach and messaging therefore had a positive effect on giving citizens access to a product that could significantly improve their quality of life.

Personal assistance is especially important if online marketplaces provide information written in legalese. The average citizen reads comfortably at an eighth grade level, yet health plans typically assume college-level reading skills, numeric literacy, and familiarity with specialized terms such as *deductible*, the practical meaning of which varies from one plan to another (see box 4.1).[27]

A Kaiser Family Foundation survey of eligible low-income nonparticipants in the ACA highlighted the importance of learning costs. Although media coverage of Healthcare.gov problems had been extensive, "logistical issues in applying for coverage do not appear to be a leading reason why people went without insurance in 2014. Rather, lack of awareness of new coverage options and financial assistance appear to be a major barrier."[28] The majority of these individuals perceived the cost of health care as too high and were unaware of the availability of subsidies to make such coverage low- or zero-cost. The same survey also pointed to significant confusion about eligibility, many individuals incorrectly assuming that they were ineligible for financial subsidies.

The ACA illustrates that though a program might be well known, individuals still need help to learn about and manage the details of gaining access. Take the following example of a cancer patient attempting to gain insurance:

> She was in her early 60s and had been diagnosed with cancer, which had prevented her from working for more than a year. She was enrolled in Medicaid's 'medically needy' program, which offers some level of coverage for people with serious illnesses, but doesn't satisfy the health reform law's individual mandate. It was too expensive anyway; she'd been skipping radiation and hadn't seen a doctor for two months.
>
> The woman wanted to find out if she qualified for an exemption so she wouldn't have to pay the mandate penalty. She had already called the state's Medicaid office, and they had told her that she didn't qualify for any coverage except the medically needy program (Florida has not expanded Medicaid under Obamacare).
>
> But that wasn't right. The woman qualified for Obamacare's tax credits to help her purchase a private plan. She eventually bought a plan that would cost her $19 a month. The woman was in tears by the time she finished signing up.
>
> "Why didn't anybody tell me?" . . . It's a [common] situation: Great confusion about the health law and what it takes to sign up. "It's not explained well anywhere," she said. "Most people have no idea."[29]

WHO PROVIDED SUPPORT? BROKERS AND NAVIGATORS

So, who actually provided the assistance that is so critical for enrollment? Two sources of help were available: traditional private insurance brokers and navigators funded by federal and state governments.

Traditional insurance brokers and agents could provide support if they had a formal arrangement with the exchange. They received training regarding plan options, subsidies, and privacy and confidentiality laws. Brokers and agents could assist individuals with both buying plans through the exchange and with applying for advance premium credits, reducing both learning and compliance costs.[30] However, this arrangement had problems. The ACA capped administrative costs at 20 percent for insurance companies (80 percent of operating revenue must be spent on health care), effectively reducing broker fees even as the time involved in supporting clients to navigate the exchange and ACA increased. In a 2016 Kaiser Family Foundation poll, 49 percent of brokers reported that some insurance companies were no longer providing commissions for ACA plans.[31] Nearly 33 percent reported that virtually all of the exchange plans they sold now had reduced commissions.

In contrast to the private market approach, the Navigator Program provided public dollars for outreach and enrollment assistance. In 2013, $54 million was made available to states that participated in state and federal run exchanges to hire individuals—known as *assisters*—in local community organizations, social service agencies, and advocacy groups.[32] Assisters had to be independent of health insurance companies and were required to receive twenty to thirty hours of training and pass a test developed by CMS. The specific tasks of navigators included

- maintaining expertise in eligibility, enrollment, and program specifications;
- conducting public education activities to raise awareness about the Marketplace;
- providing information and services in a fair, accurate, and impartial manner, including information that acknowledges other health programs such as Medicaid and the Children's Health Insurance Program;
- facilitating selection of a qualified health plan;
- providing referrals for enrollees with questions, complaints, or grievances about their health plan, coverage, or a determination under such health plan or coverage to any applicable office of health insurance consumer assistance or health insurance ombudsman or any other appropriate state agency or agencies;
- providing information in a culturally and linguistically appropriate manner, including to persons with limited English proficiency; and
- ensuring accessibility and usability of Navigator Program tools and functions for persons with disabilities.[33]

Traditional insurance brokers have played a role in the exchange, but the Navigator Program showed how government-funded outreach could access groups who would otherwise be overlooked. For example, although 76 percent of assisters offered outreach, only 40 percent of brokers did. Fewer than 50 percent of brokers helped poorer individuals eligible for Medicaid, but almost 90 percent of assisters did. Administrative factors played a role in this difference. In states that managed their own exchanges and better integrated Medicaid enrollment into the exchange, brokers were much more likely to provide assistance with Medicaid enrollment. In general, however, the Navigator Program provided more service to poorer individuals, minorities, immigrants and those who were more likely to be uninsured and faced more challenges with enrollment.[34]

Some issues with the outreach programs have weakened its effectiveness. One is a lack of resources.[35] The assistance needed for each client was greater than was initially anticipated. A 2015 survey conducted by the Kaiser Family Foundation found that more than 60 percent of navigators indicated that it took one to two hours per person to provide enrollment assistance, and 23 percent reported that it took more than two hours. Nearly 40 percent of Navigator Programs polled reported that they could not provide support to all of those who had sought help.[36] In the final weeks of open enrollment in 2016, one in four assisters reported that need far exceeded demand, and they were turning away large numbers of people seeking support. Being unable to help those directly seeking support also meant that navigators had little opportunity to reach out to subgroups who were unlikely to be aware of how they could benefit from the ACA.

Even the assisters struggled with the administrative burdens built into the program, which weakened their ability to reduce learning and compliance costs for beneficiaries. In a 2014 poll, nearly 90 percent of navigators indicated that some enrollee questions could not be answered because specific plan information was not available in the Exchange Marketplace.[37] In 2016, assisters indicated that among clients who considered or purchased private health insurance, many struggled to find answers about health insurance plans: 51 percent sometimes had a problem, 26 percent often had a problem, and 11 percent almost always had a problem.[38]

Assisters faced their own difficulties managing technical issues with online enrollment systems, which often necessitated time-consuming workarounds to ensure enrollment for a client, such as doing direct enrollment in state Medicaid programs instead of going through the federal exchange. One significant challenge was verifying the identity of some clients, such as immigrants and young people, who lacked established credit histories. Difficulties for navigators made them less able to help clients overcome burdens, requiring the need for paperwork and documentation to verify eligibility.

Although some of the burdens navigators faced were unintended, a few state legislatures added requirements that significantly increased burdens for navigators.[39] Insurance brokers lobbied for such restrictions to limit competition for commissions.[40] Partisan politics also played a role. Those ideologically opposed to the ACA saw undermining outreach as a way to hobble Obamacare. The insurance commissioner in Georgia spelled out this approach: "Let me tell you what we're doing. Everything in our power to be an obstructionist. We have passed a law that says that a Navigator, which is a position in that exchange, has to be licensed by our Department of Insurance. The Obamacare law says that we cannot require them to be an insurance agent, so we said fine, we'll just require them to be a licensed Navigator. So, we're going to make up the test, and basically you take the insurance agent test, you erase the name, you write 'Navigator test' on it."[41]

Thirteen states adopted regulations that hindered assisters, such as additional fees, residency requirements, and background checks including fingerprinting, training and examinations, and evidence of financial responsibility.[42] Ten of those states had Republican legislative control; two others had split-party legislative control and Republican governors. Although the ACA prohibited requiring navigators to carry malpractice coverage, some states asked navigators to show financial capacity to protect themselves against liability. Eleven states limited what navigators could discuss with clients, including advice regarding the benefits, terms, and features of the health insurance plans, or making comparisons between plans, which heightened client learning costs.[43]

Some states passed additional restrictions that limited non-navigators from providing help. Tennessee extended advice restrictions targeted to navigators to "any person, other than an insurance producer, who . . . facilitates enrollment of individuals or employers in health plans or public insurance programs offered through an exchange."[44] This particular rule could therefore cover any good Samaritan, such as a church group, who voluntarily helped another person make sense of the Healthcare.gov website.

What makes this political opposition so striking is that the Navigator Program was modeled on an approach that enjoyed bipartisan support: the State Health Insurance Assistance program. Indeed, this program had been in place since 1990 and was a key way the George W. Bush administration pursued outreach when it added prescription drug benefits to Medicare. By contrast, navigators had to worry they might face personal attack from conservative social media. For example, the Kansas *Watchdog* published a story online about a navigator, including her name and picture, attacking her for a past bankruptcy and resulting arrest warrant—ironically for unpaid medical bills due to a hospital stay.[45]

Partisan politics also played a role in limiting the organizational capacity for other forms of outreach in many states. In most states with federal exchanges, especially those that opposed the ACA, outreach was organized at a grass roots level. Individual community groups and agencies had to self-coordinate and generate applications to the federal government for resources. Without the state to act as a central organizing force, generating working networks was more difficult.[46] In such states, the federal government awarded outreach grants to national organizations that often had no relationships with grassroots organizations, with limited effect.[47] By contrast, states that developed their own marketplaces had a more centrally organized process to develop outreach plans and networks.[48]

States that chose to not set up their own exchanges also devoted fewer resources to ACA outreach, education, and advertising.[49] For example, states without exchanges spent $11.49 in application assistance per person eligible for a Medicaid-federal subsidy, whereas states with their own exchanges spent $30.[50] Given evidence of an ongoing lack of knowledge about the Medicaid expansions and the federal health insurance subsidies, this failure to fund outreach likely reduced take-up by increasing learning costs.

Even in higher-spending states, funding for outreach soon declined. A survey of state-based marketplaces found that two-thirds had reduced funding by 2015.[51] In theory, insurance brokers and agents could fill the gap, but brokers and agents are less likely to serve disadvantaged populations.[52]

The election of President Trump further accelerated declines in support. Since 2017, the federal government substantially curbed outreach. The Trump administration quickly canceled spending on advertising immediately following the inauguration, affecting the final weeks of enrollment in January of 2016. He then cut the ACA outreach budget by 90 percent. New HHS promotional materials featured videos of people explaining how the ACA had harmed them. HHS told its own regional staff to no longer participate in enrollment events designed to reach the public. They also cut ACA promotional partnerships with organizations that had direct access to potential beneficiaries, such as companies whose low-wage employees might be eligible, faith-based organizations, and medical groups. Finally, HHS ended contracts with private firms that provided in-person assistance for enrollees, and cut the Navigator Program budget by about 40 percent.[53] Nonetheless, the federalist system has partially undermined President Trump's efforts to undercut the ACA. States such as California extended their enrollment period and continued to spend significant sums on outreach and advertising.

In aggregate, the actions of the Trump administration have likely led to enrollment declines. Between 2016 and 2018, enrollment declined from 12.7 to 11.8 million. Although states that ran their own exchanges saw a total decline of 3 percent, representing one hundred thousand people, the decline in federally run exchanges was 9 percent, or nine hundred thousand. Indeed, states that ran their own exchanges saw no decline in enrollment between 2017 and 2018, but those that participated in the federal exchanges saw a drop of five hundred thousand.[54] In short, states found ways to stem the decline of enrollees despite the opposition of the federal government.

Shifting Burdens in Medicaid

The ACA's broader goal of expanding access to health insurance involved adding people to private health insurance (with financial subsidies) and to the Medicaid program. More than half of the previously uninsured Americans who received health insurance coverage under the ACA enrolled in Medicaid.[55] This is particularly striking given that nineteen states failed to expand their Medicaid programs after the landmark Supreme Court decision in *National Federation of Independent Businesses v. Sebelius* (2012), which allowed states to skip the expansion while continuing to receive federal subsidies for their existing Medicaid program.[56]

Although Medicaid's eligibility expansion has received much fanfare, the ACA also targeted Medicaid's administrative burdens via a series of requirements and flexibilities granted to the states. Collectively, these changes have shifted learning and compliance burdens away from individuals and onto government. Here, the ACA reflected best practices already in place in states with substantial success in increasing enrollment rates. Moreover, federal funding was made available to states to upgrade their eligibility and enrollment systems to meet these new federal requirements. As with other aspects of the ACA, however, political resistance at the state level partially undermined aspects of these efforts.

The ACA significantly changed enrollment procedures in state Medicaid programs.[57] States were required to expand Medicaid enrollment mechanisms. States added telephone and online enrollment options to existing in-person and mail options. By 2016, nearly all states had implemented these changes.[58] Some online systems are easier to negotiate than others, however. For example, although nearly all states allow individuals to start and stop the application process without losing information already entered, thirty-three states allow individuals to actually upload required documentation and thirty-five allow for the renewal of coverage online. To facilitate outreach, twenty-four states allow advocates or third-party assisters to complete online applications for beneficiaries.[59]

The Obama administration encouraged, and sometimes required, states to draw on existing state administrative data to verify eligibility criteria. States were given the option to eliminate documentation for some eligibility criteria, including birth dates, state residency, and household composition.[60] For other criteria, including income and citizenship, verification was required. States, however, could access existing administrative data for verification. A federal database was created for this purpose, featuring data from the Social Security Administration, the Internal Revenue Service (IRS), and the

Department of Homeland Security. States could also draw on their own sources. Nearly all states use their wage and unemployment compensation data to verify status. About half of states use vital data services and a smaller fraction draw on records from the Department of Motor Vehicles.[61]

In addition to using administrative data to reduce compliance costs, the ACA helped make real-time determination of eligibility a benchmark for states.[62] By 2016, thirty-seven states offered real-time eligibility determination. However, even in states offering this standard, it was not done for all applications. Some states completed fewer than half of their applications in real time; others completed as many as three-fourths.[63]

One key way that the ACA reduced administrative burdens was to expand the use of presumptive eligibility. Presumptive eligibility allows for qualified entities, such as health-care providers, hospitals, and schools, to screen eligibility based on gross income and immediately enroll individuals. Prior to the ACA, presumptive eligibility was allowed for pregnant women and children, but the ACA allowed it for all categorical eligibility categories. States varied in the use of this flexibility, without obvious partisan patterns. For example, although twenty-nine states employ presumptive eligibility for pregnant women and eighteen do for children in traditional Medicaid, only seven do so for parents and just six for adults.[64]

Three other options—express lane eligibility, fast-track enrollment using Supplemental Nutrition Assistance Program (SNAP) data, and fast-track enrollment for eligible parents of children already enrolled—have further eased enrollment experiences in some states.[65] Express lane eligibility allows states to automatically enroll children already enrolled in programs like SNAP. For example, a child with an already accepted SNAP application can be enrolled in Medicaid without providing any further information or application materials. Starting in 2013, CMS also allowed states to enroll parents into Medicaid using SNAP data. In states that have expanded Medicaid eligibility, eligibility guidelines for SNAP and Medicaid are nearly identical, showing only slight differences in how income and household size is calculated. States contact individuals based on their SNAP eligibility, ask them if they wish to enroll in Medicaid, and then follow up with a few questions. If eligible, they are immediately enrolled without additional paperwork or procedures, thus reducing duplicative compliance costs. A similar process is in effect for eligible parents of enrolled children. These parents are identified and then contacted, and after providing consent, enrolled. Fast-track enrollment both increases participation among those eligible, as well as reducing administrative financial costs.[66]

Reenrollment in the Medicaid program is another avenue through which administrative barriers can be reduced to increase access. The ACA placed new requirements on states to use existing data to reenroll individuals without imposing more paperwork or eligibility verification. By 2016, thirty-four states used this automatic reenrollment, though it is unclear for what proportion of applications. If participants are not automatically reenrolled, states are required to send applicants forms with pre-filled information. By 2016, forty-one states reported that they did.[67] The same number of states also allowed renewal over the telephone.

The scale of learning and compliance costs matter for take-up, as does the frequency that individuals encounter these costs. Reenrollment periods elicit a high churn of participants off programs. Simply reducing the frequency of eligibility renewals therefore reduces burdens. Some states had required renewals every six months, but the ACA limits them to every twelve. Moreover, it also gives states the option to provide continuous enrollment for up to twelve months; if income changes in this period, individuals can retain coverage. Nearly half of states took this approach for children enrolled in Medicaid. Finally, seven states use SNAP data to process reenrollments.[68] The ACA also eliminates an asset test when determining eligibility, in turn reducing the compliance costs that accompany documenting assets.

Although the ACA compels many states to reduce learning and compliance costs, it remains an intergovernmental program, and states retain discretion to adopt requirements that actually increased compliance costs, most obviously in the form of Medicaid premiums and copayments. Individuals in the thirty states that require those payments could be forced off the program if they fail to pay a premium, though a thirty- to ninety-day grace period applies, depending on the state. Premiums add burden not just because of the financial costs but also by adding another layer of compliance. The Medicare program has premiums, but because they are automatically deducted from people's Social Security checks, forgetting to pay a premium or not getting a bill never leads to losing coverage. By contrast, Indiana imposed Medicaid premiums and dropped twenty-five thousand adults from the program for failure to pay. Only half of those individuals regained insurance.

States can layer other conditions onto programs if given permission from the federal government through Medicaid waivers. For example, Iowa and Michigan adopted wellness programs under which premium payments would be waived for healthy behaviors, such as undertaking a health risk assessment. But such programs can fall short because of the learning and compliance costs involved. A review of Michigan's program found that though many beneficiaries had undertaken a health risk assessment, most were unaware of the connection between it and reduced payments, or that such a benefit even existed, making it unlikely they would take advantage of it.[69]

The experience of wellness programs illustrates how efforts to restructure Medicaid to serve ends beyond providing health coverage end up creating another form of administrative burden. This point holds true of the copayments themselves, or versions of health-care savings accounts, such as Arkansas's Health Independence Accounts. Such initiatives are intended to encourage clients to act as consumers, taking financial responsibility for their use of health services. But the ideal of personal responsibility that motivates such policies presupposes that people will have the persistence to manage the accompanying bureaucratic hurdles. Even so, the Trump administration signaled that such plans are welcome modifications to Medicaid.

Eligibility changes that exclude some populations are not administrative burdens. However, the process of making such changes, and changes that add more complexity to a program, can create new learning and compliance costs even for those who remain eligible. For example, prior to the ACA, Wisconsin had covered parents of children up to 200 percent of the poverty level. After the ACA, the state changed this coverage to 100 percent, likely reducing the participation of those children between 100 and 200 percent who remained eligible under the new eligibility rules.[70] One of the challenges Colorado faced with enrolling individuals in Medicaid under the exchange was that Medicaid eligibility criteria varied for different members of the household. People in this situation found navigating the Colorado exchange especially challenging.

The Trump administration also adopted a new tactic to increase Medicaid burdens: work requirements. At a meeting of the National Association of Medicaid Directors, CMS Administrator Seema Verma welcomed work requirements by saying, "The thought that a program designed for our most vulnerable citizens should be used as a vehicle to serve working age, able-bodied adults does not make sense.... These are individuals who are physically capable of being actively engaged in their communities, whether it be through working, volunteering, going to school or obtaining job training. Let me be clear to everyone in this room, we will approve proposals that promote community engagement activities."[71] Ten states, all led by Republican governors, quickly sought waivers from the Trump administration to impose work requirements.[72] The actual work requirements vary across states, though all are required to exempt people with disabilities, pregnant women, and the elderly. Individuals exempt from these requirements will need to document and prove those exemptions.

Kentucky, which was granted the first waiver, demonstrates how this eligibility change substantially increases administrative burdens. Individuals are required to work, train for a job, or volunteer at least twenty hours a week. The challenge is documenting this participation. Ten regional workforce boards are tasked with monitoring compliance.[73] People will be required to upload the necessary documentation to verify their activities. But 30 percent of low-income adults most likely to be on Medicaid report they never use a computer, 28 percent say they do not use the internet, and 41 percent do not use email.[74] It is unrealistic to expect that such a population will have the technological literacy to navigate online documentation processes.

Sarah and Matt Burress offer an example of the difficulties involved. The Medicaid coverage they gained after Matt started his lawn care business was crucial: his glaucoma would have led to blindness without treatment. But the informal, irregular, and seasonal nature of his work does not align well with new documentation requirements. Sarah noted, "Do his clients have to say, 'Yeah, he mowed my grass this week?' Part of it feels like they're trying to catch you, by burying people in paperwork and making it a huge inconvenience."[75] Their case is not atypical. Bill Wagner, who manages primary care clinics in poorer Kentucky neighborhoods, had been helping people enroll in Medicaid prior to the Trump administration. Now, he notes, "We're shifting our focus from helping people gain coverage to helping people keep it."[76]

In some instances, new documentation requirements seemed designed to fall harder on some people more than others. Michigan proposed to limit work requirements to counties with low unemployment, exempting those with higher unemployment.[77] As a result, residents in high-unemployment cities that fall in low-unemployment counties—such as Detroit and Flint—would be subject to the new requirements. A higher proportion of blacks live in such cities. Even as they face unemployment rates similar or worse than predominantly white residents in rural counties, they face more demanding burdens.[78]

As with other aspects of the ACA, outreach for Medicaid varies from state to state.[79] The thirty-two states that have expanded Medicaid eligibility thresholds have engaged in relatively extensive outreach efforts to enroll newly eligible individuals into the program. Several factors are common across successful states.[80] First, states that have already established strong networks at the grassroots level among advocacy organizations, social welfare organizations, and health-care providers are well positioned to engage in outreach within the community. Second, most states use mass market campaigns to spread information about eligibility and enrollment with grassroots engagement targeted to specific populations, such as Spanish-language outreach in areas with large Latino populations. Third, application assistance is dispatched to sites with the most demand and need. For example, there are key demographic groups, such as non–English speakers, who need far more intensive support and assistance. Finally, successful states provide year-round assistance. Unlike enrollment in private insurance via the exchange, enrollment in Medicaid is not limited to a specific time frame.[81]

Although states varied in implementing elements of the ACA that could reduce administrative burdens, the average effect of the law clearly increased enrollment in the Medicaid program. The percent of eligible parents who are enrolled in Medicaid has risen. Between 2013 and 2014, the rate rose from 88.7 percent to 91.0 percent. The number of uninsured children eligible for Medicaid dropped by 741,000 between 2013 and 2014. Among those age thirteen to eighteen, the take-up rate rose by 4 percentage points to 88 percent. In states that expanded Medicaid, the increase was 3 percentage points, relative to 2.3 percentage points in states that did not expand Medicaid.[82]

Conclusion

The ACA was the largest expansion of government-supported health insurance since the passage of Medicare and Medicaid in 1965. Its prospects for success were shaped by the implementation process, which in turn was subject to both ongoing political attacks, as well as basic state capacity issues in administering the complex law.

Although the ACA passed during the only time when President Obama enjoyed Democratic control of Congress, the White House made significant concessions to private interests and removed the so-called public option to push the bill through. Building on an inter-governmental and public-private patchwork required making the machinery of the ACA complex. But once the policy was put in place, opponents could further impose administrative burdens as a tactic to undermine the law. By refusing to open exchanges, states opposing Obamacare increased the complexity of the task left to the federal government, which compelled an intergovernmental coordination with state and local actors to verify status and eligibility. This partially contributed to the disastrous rollout of Healthcare.gov. States could also impose burdens in other ways, such as hampering assisters whose job it was to reduce learning costs for a complex new federal program.

The ACA also illustrates how a president can influence administrative burdens. Realizing that take-up was essential to the viability of the ACA, the Obama administration reduced burdens by using technology and administrative data that allowed it to verify the eligibility of individuals and coordinate information with state counterparts. They used the same strategy to reduce burdens in Medicaid while drawing from state experiments to reduce burdens. Conversely, the ACA illustrates how a president can exacerbate administrative burdens. The Trump administration quickly slashed outreach funding and shortened the enrollment period. Both the Obama and Trump administrations leveraged executive power to constrain states that did not share their goals when it came to administrative burdens.

A major lesson from the rollout of the ACA is that the success or failure of big policy changes depends on administrative burdens. The actions of proponents and opponents of Obamacare support this view. Proponents, realizing the program's complexity, reduced burdens by educating the public about the program and making it as easy as possible for people to enroll. Opponents sought to create administrative burdens to undermine program enrollment. For both sides, the stakes were clear. Administrative burdens were seen as a key to either guaranteeing the long-term viability of the law, or ensuring its unpopularity and ultimate failure.

NEGOTIATING THE MEDICARE MAZE

5

The basic characteristics of a public program can make it easier or harder to shift burdens away from recipients. However, Medicare offers the lesson that these characteristics, such as nearly universal eligibility, are not always determinative. As a program that benefits nearly all older adults—98 percent of Americans will eventually receive Medicare—it should be easier to minimize burdens, illustrated by the history of Social Security in chapter 9.[1] But the recent history of Medicare shows that while means-tested programs such as Medicaid and the Supplemental Nutrition Assistance Program (SNAP) were innovating to reduce burdens, Medicare was changing in ways that actually increased burdens.

The increase in Medicare burdens arose because of the expansion of third-party actors, specifically private health insurers, into the program through a series of changes starting in the 1980s. Beneficiaries could enroll in an array of private health insurance plans, in addition to traditional Medicare. Today, one-third of beneficiaries are in a private health insurance plan instead of traditional government fee-for-service Medicare. Half of beneficiaries have additional private health insurance to supplement their traditional Medicare. Although popularly understood as a single payer system, Medicare is in fact a mixed public and private system.

Changes to Medicare illustrate how the inclusion of third parties can increase learning costs. This case also demonstrates how third-party actors can profit from increased administrative burdens, making efforts to reduce burdens less likely to arise or succeed. Pro-market voices argued that more competition would spur

Table 5.1 *Burdens in Medicare*

Learning costs	Determining whether to choose traditional Medicare or Medicare Advantage; choosing between variety of Medigap programs, Medicare Advantage, and Prescription Drug plans that change annually
Compliance costs	Low for eligibility; some costs related to annual reenrollment
Psychological costs	Stress, frustration of managing choice overload

Source: Authors' compilation.

improvements in health-care quality while driving down costs. More skeptical voices saw a Trojan Horse privatization of a Great Society program, a trade-off that others were willing to accept if it meant expanding benefits, such as prescription drug coverage. Debates over private insurers were contentious, but little attention was paid to their implications for administrative burdens. Greater choice has led to greater confusion and learning costs, resulting in poorer decisions and outcomes. More than four in ten beneficiaries find choosing among a wide array of plans to be confusing. This confusion helps explain why one-third of those enrolled in Medicare-supported private plans do not review their coverage options on an annual basis. As the mechanisms of competition between insurers are defused, individuals make suboptimal choices and face higher health costs, and the Medicare program fails to see the promised cost savings.[2]

Medicare imposes an ongoing set of learning costs on beneficiaries (see table 5.1). Unlike Social Security, signing up for private-plan options is not a one-off process; it is instead a decision revisited annually, during an open enrollment period, by an older population whose ability, on average, to manage learning costs gradually declines. Figuring out the right insurance as your health needs evolve later in life is difficult enough. Doing so as the insurance options themselves shift annually is even more challenging. The choice overload theory from behavioral economics proposes that people presented with more and more options become less motivated to choose and make poorer decisions. The risks of choice overload can be expected to become greater as older adults experience cognitive decline.[3]

In this chapter, we review the learning costs that older adults must manage for Medicare. The wrong choice can prove highly consequential. Incorrect assumptions about coverage can result in costly health-care bills. Perversely, private insurers stand to benefit from such bad choices, giving them little incentive to reduce learning costs.

Understanding the learning costs of Medicare is important because of a broader philosophical push to make health care more consumer directed, giving people more choice but also more responsibility to overcome learning costs. Because Medicare is a nearly universal program, psychological costs due to stigma are limited, but stresses do arise from managing complex and high-risk choices. Compliance costs are also less of an issue than in other cases, and again tied to managing choice, rather than establishing eligibility, which is straightforward for the program. Despite the potential for choice to generate benefits, we focus on the relationship between the choice and learning costs in detailing the administrative burdens in the Medicare program.

The case of Medicare shows how administrative burdens are a tool used by third-party actors during implementation to enhance their profits. Evidence is scant that policymakers who are proponents of privatizing Medicare have any interest in addressing the resulting burdens for beneficiaries. Indeed, with little pushback from Democratic policymakers, the Trump administration eased existing regulations and rules applied to private health insurers involved in the Medicare program that will further exacerbate the learning costs beneficiaries face.

What Is Medicare?

In some ways, Medicare is a strikingly effective, simple, and straightforward program. Historically, retirees faced high health-care needs with limited access to health insurance. Since its creation in 1965, Medicare has provided nearly universal health insurance to those aged sixty-five and older and to those who are disabled. If we are to judge Medicare by its goal of ensuring that older adults have reliable access to health care, it has been a success. Before the program began, just 56 percent of the aged had hospital insurance. In 2014, nearly 97 percent did.[4]

As a defined-benefit program, beneficiaries receive a standard set of benefits and services. Those who are eligible for Social Security are generally eligible for Medicare, which is a function of having either ten years of employment or being married to a qualified worker. At inception, Medicare had two parts. Medicare Part A, which is fully funded by the Federal Insurance Contributions Act payroll tax, covers hospital stays and short-term nursing home stays. Medicare Part B, which is financed by premiums—generally deducted from beneficiaries' Social Security checks—and general tax revenues, provides optional coverage of up to 80 percent of the cost of physician visits and services.

Two additional elements of the program were added between the 1980s and early 2000s. Both expanded the role of private health insurers in the program. Medicare Part C, passed in 1982 and implemented in 1985, offered beneficiaries the option of enrolling in a private managed care plan instead of in traditional fee-for-service Medicare. Part C, however, did not become a major part of the program until the 1990s. Part D, passed in 2004, subsidized beneficiaries' purchase of private health insurance plans to cover their prescription drug costs. The passage of Part D was especially controversial. Although many Medicare proponents wanted the program to cover prescription drugs, some were deeply concerned about, or even opposed to, Part D because of the inclusion of private health insurance providers. Ultimately, these changes added both choice and new complexities for beneficiaries to navigate.

The Emergence of Choice

When Medicare was first implemented, health-care costs were substantially lower, so out-of-pocket costs were smaller.[5] Individuals could go to any physician or provider that accepted Medicare and the federal government would then reimburse for services provided. By the 1980s, new medical technologies and interventions addressed key causes of mortality among older adults but also drove an increase in costs.[6] The gap between higher costs and what Medicare actually covered grew. To manage growing out-of-pocket costs, people turned to supplemental insurance. The private supplemental health insurance market, or Medigap insurance, emerged in the 1970s, selling a wide array of different policies to older adults to provide "wrap around coverage" for copayments and other costs not included in the Medicare benefit. The proportion of individuals relying on supplemental insurance rose from 36 percent in 1967 to 90 percent by 1994.[7] Today, nine in ten beneficiaries have supplemental coverage for the 50 percent of their health-care costs not fully covered by Medicare, such as long-term hospital, nursing home, and home care services.[8]

The rapidly growing Medigap market of the 1980s offered evidence of the problems with relatively unregulated choice. Older adults made poor decisions and were taken advantage of by insurance companies. For example, insurance brokers and agents would sell older adults multiple and unnecessary supplemental plans to garner additional commissions. More than one in ten Medicare beneficiaries had duplicative coverage.[9] Medigap made it clear that private insurers could benefit from confusion on the part of older adults.

The Omnibus Reconciliation Act of 1990 set out to better regulate Medigap plans in order to reduce the confusion beneficiaries faced and to eliminate fraud. Beneficiaries could now choose from a standard set of Medigap plans, labeled from A through J and now up to N (see table 5.2). The plans cover costs such as copayments (for example, Medicare Part A covers only 80 percent of hospital costs after twenty days), as well as products not covered (such as blood).[10]

Clearer labeling of different plans helped reduce learning costs. However, variation that beneficiaries need to navigate to enroll in a Medigap plan is still significant. First, prices vary considerably across these identical plans—in some cases by as much as 100 percent.[11] Second, beneficiaries need to pay attention to whether plans are community or age rated. Plans that initially appear affordable often become unaffordable over time if older Americans purchase age-rated plans rather than community-rated plans. The attained-age rated plans are less expensive to start with but increase in price as beneficiaries age, whereas community-rated plans are the same price for all individuals in a given geographical area regardless of age.[12] Moreover, individuals have only six months after they enroll in Medicare to select policies before they are subject to underwriting that factors in their health into the cost of their coverage. Such variation has led to higher costs for older Medicare

Table 5.2 *Choices Between Medigap Plans*

Benefits	Medicare Supplement Insurance (Medigap) Plans, Percentages									
	A	B	C	D	F[a]	G	K	L	M	N
Medicare Part A coinsurance and hospital cost (up to an additional 365 days after Medicare benefits are used)	100	100	100	100	100	100	100	100	100	100
Medicare Part B coinsurance or copayment	100	100	100	100	100	100	50	75	100	100[c]
Blood (first three pints)	100	100	100	100	100	100	50	75	100	100
Part A hospice care coinsurance or copayment	100	100	100	100	100	100	50	75	100	100
Skilled nursing facility care coinsurance			100	100	100	100	50	75	100	100
Part A deductible		100	100	100	100	100	50	75	50	100
Part B deductible			100		100					
Part B excess charges					100	100				
Foreign travel emergency (up to plan limits)			80	80	80	80			80	80
							Out-of-pocket limit in 2015[b]			
							$4,940	$2,470		

Source: U.S. Centers for Medicare and Medicaid Services (CMS) 2015.

Note: Plans K and L are the only plans to include catastrophic coverage. Out-of-pocket costs absorbed by beneficiaries are capped at the levels noted at the bottom of this figure underneath these plans.

[a] Plan F is also offered as a high-deductible plan by some insurance companies in some states. If you choose this option, this means you must pay for Medicare covered costs (coinsurance, copayments, deductibles) up to the deductible amount before your policy pays anything.

[b] For Plans K and L, after you meet your out-of-pocket yearly limit and your yearly Part B deductible, the Medigap plan pays 100 percent of covered services for the rest of the calendar year.

[c] Plan N pays 100 percent of the Part B coinsurance, except for a copayment of up to $20 for some visits and up to a $50 copayment for emergency room visits that don't result in an inpatient admission.

beneficiaries, leading to hundreds of dollars in unnecessary costs per person.[13]

Expanding Benefits and the Role of Private Insurer Third Parties

The addition of Medicare Parts C and D further enhanced the role of the private sector in providing insurance coverage for older Americans. But, unlike Medigap, Parts C and D actually introduced private health insurer involvement within the Medicare program.

MEDICARE ADVANTAGE (PART C)

One way for beneficiaries to navigate the coverage gaps in Medicare was to enroll in Medigap. The addition of Medicare Part C offered an alternative. Rather than directly reimburse payments to providers and suppliers, the government would provide a lump sum annual payment to insurance companies, which would then manage services and payments for the enrolled Medicare beneficiary. Medicare beneficiaries could enroll in a private managed care plan. Although beneficiaries could not freely choose which providers they would see, the plans would generally cover most of the copayments and services not included in Parts A and B. Insurance companies profit if the lump sum payment is larger than the beneficiary's health-care costs.

This market approach has been an option in Medicare since the early 1980s. In 1982, the Tax Equity and Fiscal Responsibility Act developed health maintenance organizations and preferred provider options under Medicare. Part C did not gain in popularity until the 1990s.[14] Until the mid-1990s, fewer than 5 percent of beneficiaries were enrolled in Part C, increasing to nearly 20 percent by the late 1990s but then dropping to just over 10 percent by the early 2000s. The variation in enrollments reflects variation in the annual lump sum payment per each beneficiary over time. The 2004 Medicare Modernization Act increased reimbursements, thus increasing enrollments to 30 percent of Medicare beneficiaries as of 2016.

Although the explicit goal of the market approach was to reduce health-care costs, Medicare Advantage is associated with higher costs. Congress, largely driven by Republican Party preferences, reimburses at higher rates than traditional fee-for-service Medicare.[15] One reason for the overpayments might be that Medicare Advantage participants are less healthy and therefore more expensive to serve. But the opposite is actually true. Medicare Advantage plans are deliberately designed to attract the healthiest enrollees, such as by offering plans only in areas that have a higher concentration of healthy beneficiaries.[16] Nevertheless, Congress currently pays 2 percent more for Medicare Advantage beneficiaries relative to those in traditional Medicare. This supplement for Medicare Advantage was even higher before the Affordable Care Act. Previously, Medicare Advantage plans had been reimbursed as much as 18 percentage points more per beneficiary than a comparable beneficiary in Medicare fee-for-service.[17]

When beneficiaries enroll in Medicare Advantage, they must choose from an array of plans—which vary based on what they cover, as well as their premiums, deductibles, and copayments. The variation in Medigap plans is much less than the range of choice in Medicare Advantage plans. Although Medicare Advantage plans are required to cover the standard Medicare benefits included in Parts A and B, plans vary enormously beyond these basic benefits in terms of what providers cover and the costs for beneficiaries. Just five years ago, beneficiaries were selecting from nearly 50 plans on average. As federal reimbursements declined, fewer providers stayed in the market. Nevertheless, current beneficiaries choose from among approximately twenty plans. Though in rural areas there are far fewer, and sometimes no plans, offered.

THE CONSEQUENCES OF CHOICE: EVIDENCE FROM MEDICARE ADVANTAGE

Although Medicare Advantage does not save money, it can be beneficial for enrollees. Because the plans are more heavily subsidized than traditional Medicare, they tend to offer more generous benefits for lower costs. However, as with Medigap plans, individuals are often overwhelmed by the choices and fail to enroll in plans that provide the best coverage for the lowest costs.[18] Vulnerable beneficiaries are especially likely to make bad financial choices, by, for example, being less likely to switch to plans with better benefits.[19]

Part of the challenge is the expectation that individuals will reenroll, ideally every year, with the goal of improving their personal cost-benefit calculation, thereby increasing competition and reducing program costs. That personal calculation shifts annually depending on the person's evolving health needs and changes across a wide array of plans. The enrollee is left with the complex task of factoring in the combination of the premium, what the plans do and do not cover, and the ultimate implications for their overall health care and costs. When faced with such difficult choices, individuals become more likely to stick with the status quo.[20] A growing body of evidence shows that consumers who faced more choice were less likely to switch plans.[21] Indeed, a series of focus groups found that older adults are overwhelmed and frustrated by the array of choices. As one recipient noted, "I went online. I had papers taped together, it was six feet wide, of the different companies and circles and arrows."[22]

THE 2003 MEDICARE MODERNIZATION ACT AND THE PRESCRIPTION DRUG BENEFIT (PART D)

The 2003 Medicare Modernization Act further increased the role of third-party providers in two ways. First, it dramatically increased payments to Medicare Advantage plans. The Balanced Budget Act of 1998 cut payments to managed care health insurance companies to accurately reflect the health-care costs of the beneficiaries they were enrolling. By 2009, companies were receiving a 14 percent payment supplement for each beneficiary they enrolled, which allowed them to significantly enhance the benefits on offer. Between 2003 and 2014, enrollment in the program grew from 13 percent of beneficiaries to 30 percent.[23]

The second way the act enhanced the participation of third-party providers was the addition of Part D, a prescription drug benefit. Policymakers sought to address the fact that 25 percent of Medicare beneficiaries had no prescription coverage whatsoever, and others had high out-of-pocket costs.[24] In doing so, they favored choice over simplicity. Instead of offering a single, universal benefit through Medicare, or allowing Medigap plans to include prescription drug coverage, beneficiaries must pick from an array of plans offered through the private insurance market.

The choice to structure the benefit this way was controversial. President George W. Bush and Republicans led the campaign to expand Medicare's coverage, in what was the largest expansion of the program since its implementation in 1965, but on the condition that private insurers played a central role in the program.[25] Many Democrats were split on their support for the policy, with some willing to accept private involvement and others actively opposed to it.[26] What was not on anyone's radar, however, were the implications for administrative burdens in the program.

The result of the new structure for those who choose traditional fee-for-service Medicare was that they needed not just a Medigap policy but also a second supplemental policy to provide coverage for prescription drugs. In short, beneficiaries needed to participate in three enrollment processes. Alternatively, they could simply choose to enroll into Medicare Advantage, which would effectively provide all of their insurance coverage. Essentially, the conditions of the Modernization Act added learning costs for those who wanted to stay in traditional Medicare to the extent that the relatively complex Medicare Advantage plans looked more and more attractive.

Unlike in the Medigap plans, standardization is minimal across the Medicare prescription drug plans—the drugs covered, premiums, deductibles, and copayments vary from policy to policy. Again, these policies can change from year to year. Enrolling in one plan in a given year that covers a particular prescription drug is no guarantee that plan will offer the same coverage the next year. Moreover, beneficiaries face many plan options. The number of plans varies depending on where one lives but nationally averages around thirty plans.

Given the lack of standardization, learning costs generate confusion and higher costs for beneficiaries. Finding accurate information about the coverage plans provided has proven remarkably difficult. In 2004, the Government Accountability Office placed nine hundred calls to the ten largest companies offering Part D prescription drug coverage, but received accurate and complete information in only 30 percent of the calls.[27] Real costs to beneficiaries were often underestimated by up to thousands of dollars.

Part D was constructed on the premise that older people would act as savvy consumers, making informed choices among dozens of competing plans.[28] But older adults, like the rest of us, are not always rational consumers. For complex products such as health insurance and prescription drug plans, our ability to make the best decision declines as more choices are added. The elderly are especially likely to make suboptimal decisions in the face of greater choice because they rely more on invalid heuristics or random choice.[29] One study showed that increasing the number of prescription drug plans from three to nine plans was associated with a 19 percent decline in the probability of picking the cheapest plan, given an individual's particular needs.[30] The lessons from these experiments align with evidence from administrative data showing that fewer than one-quarter of individuals enroll in the most efficient plan for their needs, resulting in an average of $300 per beneficiary additional out-of-pocket spending each year.[31]

The Aggregate Impact of Burdens on Beneficiaries

The consequence of how Medicare has developed over the past forty years, including the creation of the Medigap market and the growth of private insurance providers within traditional Medicare under Parts C and D, is that the process of enrolling in Medicare—and then choosing supplemental insurance—is strikingly complicated. There are now substantial administrative burdens, which are largely a function of learning costs. Figure 5.1, included in a guidebook for Medicare beneficiaries and developed by the Centers for Medicare and Medicaid Services (CMS), illustrates the learning costs that Medicare enrollees face. Strikingly, however, the figure actually understates the complexity of the process by not highlighting the range of options included within each box. To find the best coverage requires older adults to consider a wide array of plans in conjunction with each other. How do Part D plans correspond with Medigap plans and with Medicare Advantage plans? The options are seemingly endless.

FINANCIAL RISKS OF POOR CHOICES

Although administrative burdens sometime limit access to a service, Medicare shows how learning costs can affect whether a client selects the right service. The financial stakes of picking the wrong supplemental insurance plans are huge. The total median lifetime health-care costs for individuals aged sixty-five and older are $188,658.[32] Medicare covers only about half of these costs. For

Figure 5.1 *The Medicare Maze*

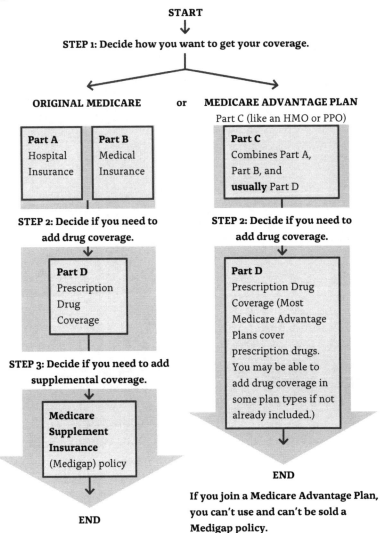

START

STEP 1: Decide how you want to get your coverage.

ORIGINAL MEDICARE or **MEDICARE ADVANTAGE PLAN**
Part C (like an HMO or PPO)

Part A
Hospital
Insurance

Part B
Medical
Insurance

Part C
Combines Part A,
Part B, and
usually Part D

STEP 2: Decide if you need to add drug coverage.

STEP 2: Decide if you need to add drug coverage.

Part D
Prescription
Drug
Coverage

Part D
Prescription Drug
Coverage (Most
Medicare Advantage
Plans cover
prescription drugs.
You may be able to
add drug coverage in
some plan types if not
already included.)

STEP 3: Decide if you need to add supplemental coverage.

**Medicare
Supplement
Insurance**
(Medigap) policy

END

END

If you join a Medicare Advantage Plan, you can't use and can't be sold a Medigap policy.

Source: U.S. CMS 2015.

example, it covers ninety days in the hospital annually, but the annual deductible in 2018 was $1,340. Days one through sixty require no coinsurance, but days sixty-one through ninety require a daily coinsurance payment of $335. Thus, a ninety-day stay in the hospital could lead to $11,390 in out-of-pocket costs if an individual does not have supplemental coverage.[33]

An uncovered medical liability could easily become a catastrophic cost. This is all the more salient given how much the elderly already spend on health care. Those age sixty-five and older spend nearly 20 percent of their incomes on out-of-pocket medical costs: in 2010, the average Medicare beneficiary spent $4,734 out of pocket. Out-of-pocket spending tends to increase with age: in 2010, beneficiaries age eighty-five and older spent three times more, on average, than those age sixty-five to seventy-four.[34] Between 2000 and 2010, average total out-of-pocket spending among beneficiaries in traditional Medicare rose from $3,293 to $4,734, a 44 percent increase.

People with low incomes have relatively high out-of-pocket costs. Individuals with less than $10,000 in annual income spend an average of $2,817 a year. Those with between $10,000 and $20,000 spend $4,467. To offer some context for these costs: between 2009 and 2010, individuals between eighteen and sixty-four had a median family income of $48,430, those between sixty-five and seventy-nine had $35,690, and those eighty and older had $23,370.[35]

Indeed, for many older adults, these financial risks are exacerbated by how close they live to the poverty line. Whereas 29 percent of those between eighteen and sixty-four live below 200 percent of the poverty line, 34 percent of those age sixty-five and older do. The risks are more pronounced for women, unmarried people, and minorities. Whereas 7 percent of men over sixty-five live below the poverty line, 12 percent of women over sixty-five do. Five percent of married and 16 percent of unmarried older adults live below the poverty line. These disparities increase when factoring racial and ethnic differences into account. Among unmarried individuals, the poverty rates are 9 percent for whites, 19 percent for blacks, and 18 percent for Hispanics.[36]

These numbers may be striking, but the official poverty line actually understates financial risks by not accounting for out-of-pocket health-care costs.[37] An alternative supplemental poverty level, which takes these costs into account, shows just how much health costs contribute to poverty. If those age sixty-five and older had no out-of-pocket expenditures, the percentage living below 100 percent of the supplemental poverty measure would fall from 15 to 9 percent.[38]

LEARNING COSTS AMID COGNITIVE DECLINES

Older adults face a complex array of choices, not only when they first enroll in Medicare but also every year they remain in the program. Such choices must be made at a point in life when, sooner or later, both cognitive and physical abilities decline. As one Medicare beneficiary remarked, "That's what gets me, they wait until we retire to make it complicated." Another noted, "There are days when I look at a plan, or look at my plan, and I think about the possibility of making a change.... I've reached the age of 78 and I'm saying to myself, 'I'm too goddamn tired to investigate this.'"[39]

As disability and cognitive decline become more prominent, so do the challenges of navigating the administrative burdens of Medicare. Approximately one in five older adults have a physical disability that limits their mobility.[40] More than 30 percent have heart disease and 8 percent have had a stroke—rates that are fifteen and eight times greater, respectively, than for those age eighteen to forty-four.[41] Estimates of mild cognitive impairment among older adults range from 10 to 20 percent and increase as individuals age.[42]

It is therefore not surprising that older adults with more cognitive limitations are less likely to have any supplemental coverage than those with more preserved cognitive abilities, and thus at substantial risk for extremely high out-of-pocket costs.[43] Those with low incomes, less education, and more cognitive impairments are less likely to be aware of prescription drug coverage via Medicare Part D.[44] Those with lower levels of cognitive ability are also significantly less likely to sign up for Medicare Part D or to sign up for financial assistance to help cover the costs of this coverage.[45] There is no reason to assume that individuals with cognitive decline are less likely to need prescription drugs; instead, it seems more likely that lower cognitive functioning reduces the likelihood of accessing needed services.

Even when older adults with low cognitive function do sign up for supplemental coverage they make poorer choices—picking plans that provide fewer benefits for higher costs.[46]

THE LIMITS OF CHOICE IN CONSUMER-DIRECTED HEALTH CARE

As consumers, we generally value choice. A restaurant that featured just one entrée would soon become very dull. But beyond a certain point, an abundance of choice becomes too much of a good thing, making us less able to make decisions, less happy about the decisions we make, and more likely to make bad decisions. Such behavioral insights matter as health care is reorganized to become more and more consumer-directed, when individuals are offered more choices but in turn are expected to manage burdensome decision-making processes. Such a model relies on certain assumptions about how applicants manage information. Former Maine Senator Olympia J. Snowe noted that "Any program that relies on choice must ensure that those choices are well informed." But having lots of information about lots of choices does not necessarily result in better decisions.[47]

In recent years, Republicans have proposed further increasing the role of private health insurers in the program by replacing Medicare's guaranteed package of benefits with vouchers, or what is termed *premium support*.[48] Older adults would be responsible for health-care costs beyond the voucher. In short, the program would switch from a defined benefit—when a set of services and products are guaranteed—to a defined contribution—when the government provides a set amount of money to subsidize the cost of individual beneficiaries choosing from a range of private health insurance plans in an Obamacare-like exchange.

Theoretically, if the value of the voucher or premium support is high enough, such changes to Medicare could be implemented without increasing out-of-pocket health-care costs. However, analyses of Republicans' proposed plans by the Congressional Budget Office estimate increased cost burdens for Medicare beneficiaries, leading to a total reduction in $129 billion from Medicare over ten years.[49] The notion that premium support plans will increase competition—and thus reduce the cost of health care—is belied by most existing evidence about Medicare thus far. Medicare Advantage, which was touted as increasing private-sector participation and competition, thus leading to reduced health-care costs, has produced the opposite effect, costing U.S. taxpayers far more than the traditional, single payer, fee-for-service portion of the program.[50]

Ultimately, if the mix of vouchers and cuts is to work, it depends on a belief that savvy health consumers will use a more limited pot of dollars to drive down the costs of health care. Any model that relies on increasing rather than decreasing the learning costs in Medicare is fatally flawed. Acting as informed consumers has proven difficult for older persons for a variety of reasons. Reliable information is hard to obtain; decisions are based on current health, but the cost-effectiveness of those choices will be decided by future health, which is difficult to predict. Older adults lack information on important aspects of their plan, providers, and treatments, which affects the choices they make.[51]

The hope that a consumer will use information to choose wisely becomes more distant as more information must be processed across a wider array of choices. A range of studies show that more choices can actually make Medicare consumers worse off. Fewer choices increase older adults' ability to pick the plans that best meets their needs for the lowest cost.[52] This is not relevant only for entry into the program. A large number of choices increase "stickiness"—that is, the tendency to stay with the default option.[53] Indeed, fewer than one in ten Medicare beneficiaries actually change plans during open enrollment.[54] As fewer people switch, the benefits of market-based competition erode.

Choice overload can reinforce a tendency to stick with the status quo.[55] A randomized experiment illustrated how learning costs matter in these processes. The experiment provided a letter to the treatment group that included personalized cost information. Everyone, both treatment and control, had access to this personalized information, but the control group had to seek it out. The results were striking. The group that received a letter detailing how varying plans affected their personal costs were significantly more likely to switch plans. Only 17 percent of the comparison group switched plans, but 28 percent of the treatment group did. This led to a savings of nearly $100 a year for the treatment group.[56]

Consumers also tend to make errors in thinking about costs and risks. For example, they focus on the sticker price of the plan premium rather than make the more complex calculation of how premiums reduce their out-of-pocket costs.[57] Out-of-pocket costs can be quite high for prescription drugs. The standard benefit in 2015 had a $320 deductible and 25 percent coinsurance up to an initial coverage limit of $2,960 in total drug costs, followed by a coverage gap. While in the gap, enrollees are responsible for a larger share of their total drug costs than in the initial coverage period until their total out-of-pocket spending reaches $4,700. The Affordable Care Act, however, reduced the costs in the "donut hole" from 35 to 25 percent of the cost of drugs. Thereafter, enrollees pay either 5 percent of total drug costs or $2.65 for each generic drug and $6.60 for each brand name. This is simply the base benefit, but plans typically cover more than this.

Finding the most cost-efficient benefit requires learning about all of one's existing prescription drug costs—as well as calculating how these drugs and costs might change in the coming year. Individuals need to consider as many as fifty plan options. The premium is actually the smallest—but simplest—part of this cost calculation for most individuals. Hence, that people are biased toward emphasizing the premium cost in their decision-making is not surprising. After all, the sticker price offers a simple heuristic. But failing to consider out-of-pocket costs leads to an estimated 27 percent loss in economic resources.[58]

The potential consequences of a maze of public services goes beyond efficiencies—it may also affect how consumers view the program itself and the government that created it. Despite the introduction of Medicare Part D and the significant new benefits to the elderly it provides, a majority of the first round of enrollees receiving these benefits reported themselves as less satisfied in response to the question, "Does your experience with Medicare Part D leave you more satisfied or less satisfied with the Medicare program?" Three-quarters of the same group were less satisfied with the "political process in Washington" that had just given them a large new entitlement. Once beneficiaries were signed up, the level of dissatisfaction declined over time to about one-third, and the "remaining dissatisfaction focused on the complexity of the program, formularies, the gap, and tedious appeals procedures."[59]

Policy Options to Reduce Learning Costs

The potential solutions to the learning costs in Medicare require government intervention. The private sector has little incentive to fix or address these burdens because it stands to profit from the poor decision-making of Medicare participants. Broadly, addressing these burdens entails three approaches: greater standardization and regulation of coverage options, more outreach and assistance, and use of administrative data and information technology. These are not mutually exclusive solutions.

The first approach is to reduce choice and simplify options.[60] The history of Medigap plans offers a model for how to standardize coverage options across plans. Medigap currently offers ten standardized plans. This approach could be replicated with both Medicare Advantage plans and Part D prescription drug plans. That prescription drug coverage must currently be sold separately from Medigap plans, though it can be included in Medicare Advantage plans, complicates the process. Even with standardization, individuals could potentially be comparing thirty (or more) standardized plan options (for example, ten for Medigap, ten for Medicare Part D prescription drug coverage, and ten for Medicare Advantage). Ideally, Medigap would be reformed so that these plans could include prescription drug coverage. Following this approach, individuals might compare across a standard set of Medigap plans versus Medicare Advantage plans.

Such an approach would likely require congressional approval. A second approach is to expand outreach to assist individuals in picking plans. Currently, support services include online tools on the Medicare website and assistance provided by nonprofit organizations. The online tools are good at taking into account particular health-care needs and filtering the options based on those needs. The problem, however, is that four in ten people age sixty-five and older do not use the internet.[61] Even if they do, online tools are challenging to use, especially for those with cognitive issues. The large majority of older adults need more direct help.

Resources could be generated to expand assistance in picking plans—even simple assistance with the online tool—and target places older adults are most likely to frequent. Current outreach provided by nonprofits and community groups varies considerably depending on where one lives. And though CMS offers telephone assistance in practice, this service has been ineffective because of extensive wait times and seemingly poorly trained service providers. These services could also be expanded to places where older adults are certain to frequent. The most obvious setting is physician offices. What experimental evidence makes clear is that information cannot be passively offered on the assumption that beneficiaries will seek it out. Instead, information provided proactively is more likely to lead to action.[62]

This brings us to a third approach, which is to combine information technology with administrative data. In the case of Medicare, this could entail using service and supply reimbursement records to generate customized recommendations regarding which plans would be most efficient, given their health-care use and geographic location, for individual re-enrolling in Medicare. Indeed, such an approach could direct consumers to what appears to be a better approach, automating much of the learning costs. Philosophically, this approach might make some uncomfortable given that it appears to reduce the role of the consumer. It becomes more palatable if technology were provided as a decision-aid rather than as a decision-maker, helping the consumer make smarter choices but allowing them to make the final decision. Richard Thaler and Cass Sunstein label such an approach as "intelligent assignment," where data on prior prescription drug use is used to switch individuals to plans that cover their drug needs at lower cost.[63] One study of the effectiveness of this approach for schizophrenia patients found that it saved $466 per patient per year.[64]

Using administrative data means overcoming some practical problems. Private providers are not required to provide utilization information to the federal government. The government therefore does not have detailed records for each individual beneficiary enrolled in Medicare Advantage, or for many individuals enrolled in prescription drug plans. As a result, administrative data can currently only be used effectively for those enrolled in traditional Medicare and for some of those with separate prescription drug insurance policies. If the government did require private insurers to provide data, however, it could be highly beneficial. The federal government would be able to use data to actively support all beneficiaries in their decision-making when picking plans. The result would be to increase probability of participants switching plans to one that best fits their need—which is critical for both keeping individual costs low and ensuring that competition actually reduces the overall costs of these plans.

Probability for Reform

What is the political feasibility of these options? Medicare has enormous popular support. But the learning costs of the program have largely flown under the radar. Reforms to enhance benefits, such as the addition of prescription drugs benefits, receive most of the attention and support from stakeholders at the expense of reforms that simply make the program work better. Moreover, private health insurance stakeholders have an active interest in ensuring these burdens are not reduced.

The Trump administration has instead pursued changes that will increase complexity. For example, the CMS opposed the Obama-era *meaningful difference* standard, which requires that new Medicare Advantage plans offered by a private insurer be sufficiently different from existing plans the insurer already offers. The standard was adopted, despite significant opposition from health insurers, with the explicit goal of reducing "confusion" among beneficiaries.[65] It had the intended effect, resulting in a significant reduction in the number of Medicare Advantage and Medicare prescription drug plans.[66] Removing this standard could significantly increase the number of plans from which beneficiaries choose, thus increasing confusion and learning costs—with no real advantage in terms of range of options offered to beneficiaries.[67]

The standardization of Medigap plans, which took place under President Reagan, offer some hope for another generation of reformers. The potential for reducing burdens in Medicare, however, requires that stakeholders start to better frame learning costs as a pressing political problem that grabs the attention of policymakers.

Conclusion

The role of third-party actors in Medicare reflects the complex public-private network that is the U.S. health system. The gradually increasing nature of that role has also raised the burdens faced by

Medicare beneficiaries. For older adults, these learning costs come at a time in life when people face increasing cognitive and health declines.

Private health insurers actively profit from these burdens, which lead older adults to make poor financial decisions when faced with an overwhelming array of insurance options. In essence, third-party providers use burdens as a tool for profit, just as politicians use burdens as a tool to make policy. The welfare loss that results from learning costs hurts not just the individual beneficiary but also society: as individuals fail to select the best plans for their needs, the pressure on health providers to pursue efficiencies is blunted.

Yet, policymakers pay surprisingly little attention to the role of burdens in Medicare. Democrats who opposed the gradual privatization of the program have done little to reduce the resulting learning costs. Republicans who supported privatization based on arguments that more choices reduce costs and improve beneficiary outcomes have also done little to reduce the learning costs that undermine these goals. Nonetheless, changes could be made. Assuming that private insurers will continue to play a prominent role in the program, a combination of more outreach and assistance, standardization and better labeling of Medicare Advantage and Medicare prescription drug plans, and smarter use of administrative data could help beneficiaries better manage this complex system, providing better outcomes both for individuals and taxpayers.

BIPARTISAN FIXES AND PARTISAN BLAME

6

CYCLES OF BURDENS IN SNAP

The Supplemental Nutrition Assistance Program (SNAP), colloquially known as food stamps, subsidizes food purchases for half of all
Americans over the course of their lives and an estimated one in
seven Americans in any given month. Many Americans receive benefits, but generally only for a relatively short time, two-thirds of participants for three or fewer years.[1] The effectiveness of SNAP, like
the Affordable Care Act (ACA), has been significantly influenced by
administrative burdens. Unlike the ACA, however, SNAP's recent history of burdens defies easy partisan categorizations regarding the
source of burdens. Instead, it reveals a more complex pattern, oscil-
lating between periods of bipartisan support for accessibility and
high take-up of benefits, followed by greater polarization and new
efforts to impose burdens.

Prior to the 1996 Personal Responsibility and Work Opportunity
Act (PRWORA), receipt of food stamps was tied to welfare cash assistance, meaning that most of those who were eligible automatically
received it. But PRWORA delinked the two, contributing to a dramatic
decline in participation. The Bush and Obama administrations found
ways to incrementally reduce burdens in ways that increased take-up:
by 2014, approximately 83 percent of eligible individuals received food
stamps.[2] Third-party actors, especially nonprofits, played a key role in
reducing learning costs by helping to get the word out about SNAP.

Indeed, the relative ease of access to SNAP helped the federal
government cushion the effects of the Great Recession, not just for
the long-term poor but for a much broader swath of Americans as
well. As the Great Recession pushed more people into poverty, they

became eligible for, and received, SNAP benefits. Recipients spend their benefits quickly. Every SNAP dollar is estimated to generate $1.70 in economic activity.[3] Beyond providing income and food for poor households, SNAP also generates long-term positive impacts on children's health and women's economic self-sufficiency and has even been found to reduce criminal recidivism.[4]

The recent history of SNAP illustrates the fragility of the bipartisan consensus to reduce burdens. The increasing use of SNAP became proof to its critics of the failings of the modern welfare state. For example, former Fox News host Bill O'Reilly described the "food stamp scandal: right now, 15 percent of the entire American population [is] receiving food subsidies" and suggested "that the Obama administration is encouraging parasites to come out and ... take as much as they can with no remorse."[5]

Such criticisms reflect a growing polarization around SNAP, making it vulnerable to a new round of administrative burdens. House Republican budgets in recent years have proposed drastically cutting SNAP allocations and giving states more discretion to add barriers to the program. The Trump administration welcomed state requests for waivers that would allow them to expand work requirements and impose drug tests on applicants and considered adding such requirements at the national level.[6]

SNAP also illustrates the potential for the disparate experience of burdens. Although take-up rates among the general population are high, older adults face substantial burdens in accessing the program. Estimates of take-up among eligible older adults range from 34 to 42 percent.[7] The low-income older adults who most need these benefits are also the most likely to face mobility and cognitive issues that limit their ability to navigate administrative barriers. We therefore detail the special challenges and issues facing older adults in the SNAP program.

Administrative Burdens in the SNAP Program

Created as a Great Society program under President Lyndon Johnson, SNAP was intended to address the scourge of malnutrition in one of the wealthiest countries in the world. Initially, the program targeted only the very poor who were not employed. The 1996 welfare reform, however, fundamentally altered the program by expanding eligibility to the working and near-poor. The goal of broadening access was undercut by a decline in participation rates: by 2001 SNAP take-up had fallen nearly 20 percentage points in less than a decade, to 54 percent of eligible individuals (see figure 6.1).

Much of the decline in participation reflected broader economic patterns. Changes in SNAP take-up are driven by unemployment rates, and the booming 1990s economy lifted many above the eligibility level.[8] The structure of SNAP benefits formula also likely reduced take-up: because less needy families receive lower SNAP benefits, some people may have opted to forgo the hassles of the application process given the relatively meager returns. By contrast to the 99 percent take-up rate for individuals in households who are eligible for the maximum benefits, only 47 percent of individuals in households who receive less than half the maximum benefits participate.[9] SNAP therefore is most used by those who are in the deepest poverty and have the most motivation to seek it out. Eligible recipients appear to weigh the costs in accessing the program against the benefits to be received.

An increase in administrative burdens also played a role in the decline of SNAP participation in the second half of the 1990s. Prior to PRWORA, the marginal burdens of applying for SNAP were minimal because benefits were automatically tied to cash assistance. Once SNAP eligibility was no longer linked to traditional welfare, the burdens associated with it became more apparent and more consequential (see table 6.1).

PRWORA replaced the Aid to Families with Dependent Children (AFDC) program with the Temporary Assistance to Needy Families (TANF) block grant. Families who had been enrolled in AFDC were automatically enrolled in SNAP. The creation of TANF severed this automatic link. Moreover, TANF featured more restrictive eligibility requirements, including time limits on the receipt of benefits. Between 1994 and 2000, the number of individuals receiving cash assistance dropped from 14 million to 5.6 million. Participation in SNAP declined in a parallel fashion.

Although federal welfare reform did not occur until 1996, more than half of states had already received waivers that resulted in the decoupling of SNAP from AFDC by that point. As people became

Figure 6.1 *Participation Rate in SNAP, 1995–2014*

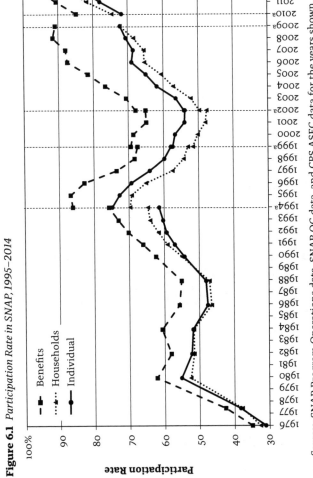

Sources: SNAP Program Operations data, SNAP QC data, and CPS ASEC data for the years shown.

[a] There are breaks in the time series in 1994 and 1999 due to revisions in the methodology for determining eligibility and in 2002 and 2009 due to revisions in the methodology for determining eligibility and the number of participants.

Table 6.1 *Administrative Burdens in SNAP*

Types	Reduced by	
Learning costs	· Finding out about the program and eligibility, which became more complex after the delinking of cash assistance to SNAP · Determining size of benefits · Identifying relevant deductions, especially health deductions · Identifying where can benefits be used	· Creation of call centers, online screening tools, clarity that food stamps can be used · Support from non-profits or groups such as SSA
Compliance costs	· Detailed interview process, extensive documentation requirements · Recertification process · Potential for work requirements, and drug testing	· Alternatives to in-person interviews, removing vehicle-asset tests, online applications · Standard medical deduction waivers
Psychological costs	· Sense of stigma in applying for and using benefits	· Reduced by EBT cards, welcome signs in grocery stores

Source: Authors' compilation.

ineligible or could not negotiate the barriers for cash assistance, they became less likely to access SNAP.[10] Studies have found that the exits of former TANF recipients from SNAP was higher than non-TANF recipients, suggesting that the administrative costs raised by the disruption with TANF contributed to the exclusion of many from the program.[11]

Even if eligible nonparticipants are aware of the program, surveys suggest that about half are unsure about their eligibility.[12] One field experiment confirmed that simply informing people about their eligibility for SNAP raised participation rates.[13] After

PRWORA, people now needed to know about SNAP as a separate program and application process—a new learning cost. Many who were no longer eligible for cash assistance did not realize that they *were* still eligible for SNAP benefits. Frontline employees at welfare offices felt that they appropriately conveyed eligibility information, but observations found they often left out key points, or even provided incorrect information.[14] Not surprisingly then, people were confused about their status.

An evaluation of the decline in take-up of SNAP benefits in the late 1990s documented such learning costs: "The majority of the ethnographic study participants who were interviewed either said that they didn't know about the current rules for food stamps and/or Medicaid or referred to time limits for these benefits."[15] Individuals who doubted their eligibility had little other reason to appear for TANF redeterminations. Rather than reaching out to those still eligible for food stamps, frontline officials instead systematically removed SNAP benefits from those who no longer came to TANF redeterminations.[16]

Confusion about eligibility affected some groups more than others. Welfare reform cut food stamp access for noncitizen adults. Many of their children remained eligible, however, because most are citizens, and some states also allowed legal-resident children of noncitizens to receive benefits. But access to SNAP declined among these children at a greater rate than among the children of citizens, perhaps in part because noncitizen parents had more reason to be confused about eligibility and faced a different and more pronounced form of stigma relative to citizens.[17] Even after the Bush administration liberalized SNAP access to noncitizen legal residents, their take-up rate of 56 percent remained much lower than that of citizens.[18]

A standard way for states to reduce learning costs is to work with community-based organizations to share information about SNAP.[19] Such partners can also help potential participants to understand the size of benefits. The calculation of SNAP benefits is not straightforward, making both eligibility and the size of benefits difficult for potential claimants to understand. Table 6.2 details the variety of financial factors that shape these determinations, highlighting the learning costs for applicants.

Table 6.2 *Calculating SNAP Benefits*

Step 1	Count household's gross income in the prior twelve months
Step 2	Subtract earned income deduction (20 percent of household earnings)
Step 3	Subtract standard deduction for household size
Step 4	Subtract dependent care expenses, if any
Step 5	Subtract medical expenses
Step 6	Determine household shelter costs
Step 7	Subtract half of net income (gross income minus deductions) from shelter costs to determine shelter deduction
Step 8	Subtract shelter deduction from net income
Step 9	Calculate 30 percent of household's net income to determine household's contribution to food costs
Step 10	SNAP benefit amount = maximum SNAP benefit amount for household size minus 30 percent of household contribution

Source: Center on Budget and Policy Priorities 2017.

The delinking of SNAP from cash assistance also created a new and separate set of compliance costs for applicants, including travel and wait times, forms to complete, income to document, deductions to identify and assets to verify. Federal policymakers recognized this problem, leading to a period of bipartisan policy learning when they sought to ease burdens. President George W. Bush's undersecretary for the Food, Nutrition, and Consumer Services at the Department of Agriculture, Eric Bost, noted this increase of compliance costs:

> Concerns have grown that the program's administrative burden and complexity are hampering its performance in the post-welfare reform environment. There is growing recognition that the complexity of program requirements—often the result of desires to target benefits more precisely—may cause error and deter participation among people eligible for benefits.... These burdens are particularly significant for the working families that comprise an increasing portion of the Food Stamp caseload. Caseworkers are often expected to anticipate changes in their income and expenses—a difficult and error-prone task, especially for working poor households whose incomes fluctuate.[20]

Bost led a series of changes by the Bush administration to improve access, focusing on reducing learning and compliance costs in particular, resulting in an almost 10 percentage point increase in the take-up rate.[21] Previously, the federal government had provided funding based on a formula that penalized overpayments rather than underenrollment. This policy was relaxed toward the end of the Clinton administration, when state governments were allowed to adopt streamlined eligibility determinations. Because food stamps bring federal support directly into a state economy (there is no requirement for the state to match funding), state policymakers generally have an incentive to expand access (though, as we discuss later, this might be tempered by ideological preferences).

The 2002 Farm Bill gave states more flexibility to reduce administrative burdens, which helped to increase participation even when the economy continued to grow. The federal government allowed states to extend recertification processes, that is, reestablishing eligibility for existing beneficiaries. Although an income-contingent program like SNAP requires procedures such as recertification, the programmatic goal of ensuring adequate access to food needs to be balanced against overly rigorous procedures intended to ensure eligibility. Each recertification is costly and creates an opportunity for claimants to lose their benefits.[22] Indeed, one study found that exits from the program were five to six times more likely during recertification periods.[23] Lengthening the recertification window substantially increases take-up and duration of food stamps.[24] By 2007, all fifty states had lengthened the recertification window from six to twelve months.

The central eligibility issue to be managed is changes in income, especially for those who are employed and had variable income throughout the year. By 2007, most states only required updates in reported income if it made individuals ineligible for benefits. Another substantial obstacle was the requirement of in-person interviews for both entry into the program and for recertification. This obstacle was especially burdensome for those working, those with children, and those without easy access to transportation. Encouraged by the Department of Agriculture, thirty-four states did not require an in-person interview for recertification by 2009, and twenty-one did not require an in-person interview to determine initial eligibility.[25]

Changes in how vehicle assets were counted also appeared to have increased participation, though perhaps largely because it reduced the compliance costs of applying rather than making previously ineligible applicants eligible.[26] Other initiatives included the establishment of call centers and online applications. As of 2016, forty-four states provide online applications and thirty-three provide online eligibility screening tools.[27] States that rolled out electronic applications earlier saw increases in SNAP take-up.[28]

Even with these changes, compliance costs continue to limit access to SNAP benefits. One field experiment found that providing application assistance led to an almost 80 percent increase in SNAP applications relative to those who were informed they were eligible but given no special assistance.[29] A particular problem is *churning* within the program—the degree to which individuals quickly cycle off and then back on the program. A recent report by the Urban Institute found that between 17 to 28 percent of beneficiaries in Florida, Idaho, Illinois, Maryland, Texas, and Virginia experienced at least one churning spell in 2011.[30] Some of this is due to actual income changes, but it is also the case that seemingly small issues—such as an unrecorded address change—could lead to individuals erroneously losing SNAP benefits.

The psychological costs of participating in the program remained an issue. Eligible nonparticipants for SNAP point to stigma in surveys. Some of this reflects a general reluctance to be on welfare. Sixty-four percent of eligible nonparticipants say they do not like to get by on government assistance.[31] SNAP may be especially vulnerable to such stigma, because, as one potential recipient put it, "I don't have a job but that program is not for me. That is the way I see it. I see it for people with kids and then the elderly."[32]

The government may not have full control over public perceptions of the program, but it does control the application process itself, which can give rise to its own psychological costs. One in four potentially eligible beneficiaries identified a reluctance to answer personal questions as a reason for not applying, and some who had previously been food stamp participants pointed to negative treatment in the past.[33] One previous recipient said, "As far as food stamps are concerned, after that last one incident, I'll probably have to hit pretty much rock bottom before I try again."[34]

SNAP eligibility procedures vary by state, but recipients can be expected to be asked questions not just about themselves but also about everyone else in the household, questions that range from the intrusive (the nature of the relationship with others) to the trivial (who buys and prepares food? Where is the food stored?) Qualitative studies find that potential applicants see the application process itself to be a greater source of stigma than receiving the benefits:[35]

> You go into the food stamp place and you do it and they pretty much look at you, like, what do you want? You're a scum, you're nothing, you want a handout from us? And it's like, no, I don't want a handout, I want some help and that just turns you off immediately. You want to just run out the door and say, the hell with you, I'll do it on my own, but I can't.[36]
>
> When I first inquired about food stamps I was referred to the office, it's like a welfare office, there is a lot going on, it's a long process you sitting there all day and the people are not really friendly and then they ask a lot of invasive questions. Basically, I feel like they go all up your record with a microscope. They are all into your life. I am just there for food stamps and I don't feel they need to know whether I have life insurance or things like that. They make me feel that I have to show everything that I have before I get food stamps.[37]

Another venue for psychological costs with food stamps comes with their actual use. In a survey of likely eligible individuals not receiving SNAP benefits, many reported a desire for others not to observe them shopping with food stamps.[38] The move to near universal use of electronic benefit transfer (EBT) cards to replace actual food stamps appears to have had a small positive effect on take-up, largely by reducing stigma.[39] The Obama administration also adopted a program to encourage retailers to advertise that they welcomed EBT, reducing both stigma and learning costs in the use of benefits.

Throughout this book, we describe the incidence of psychological costs as one-off negative experiences arising from discrete inter-actions, typified by a visit to the welfare office. However, the writer Kaitlyn Greenridge uses her childhood experience with food stamps to describe how the psychological costs accumulate and last, generating lifelong stresses in how administrative burdens are experienced:

> I remember the first time my mother used food stamps in the grocery store. This was before EBT cards, so when you used your benefits, you had to use a different checkout line than everyone else. We were at the same grocery store we'd always gone to, my mother had stepped into the same line we'd always used. But the cashier had looked at the envelope in my mother's hand and her expression changed, her voice became higher and her smile strange, as she told my mother that she couldn't take her in that line, that we would have to move over.
>
> When you move through life with a certain sense of security, forms are sacrosanct. You believe them to be a necessary, valid part of life. You know they're a pain—nobody likes to fill them out. But you have faith that they are there for a reason, and most important, they can contain the basic truth about you.
>
> If you have ever had to deal with the bureaucracy of poverty, of having to prove over and over again to those in charge how fundamentally unworthy you are, you understand that forms are not sacred.... There are government agencies that use their forms to try to help you. And there are those that seem to have designed their forms to remind you of the audacity of expecting your government to help you with anything.[40]

Making SNAP Less Accessible

As SNAP take-up reached historic highs, the program became the victim of its own success. Critics charged that the program grew because of an outreach effort that did little to manage fraud. For example, in December of 2016, a report on Fox News claimed that "Food Stamp fraud is at an all-time high and some of the worst offenders this year have included a state lawmaker and a millionaire. This year it is estimated $70 million in taxpayer money was wasted on food stamp fraud. Is it time to end the program altogether?"[41]

Official measures of fraud—error rates in paying an ineligible person or overpaying an eligible person—have actually declined over time, aided by the adoption of the EBT system. In fiscal year 2014, the error rates for overpayment was 3 percent.[42] Many of these errors are administrative rather than a function of deliberate fraud and are later corrected. Estimates of deliberate fraud—exchanging food stamps for cash—are even lower, and have also been declining, from 3.8 percent in 1993 to 1.3 percent in 2011.[43]

Another critique is that SNAP has evolved from its original purpose, becoming fungible enough that it effectively funds nonfood purchases. However, studies of consumption of SNAP recipients find that it leads to large increases in food spending. Each additional $1 results in a 53 cent increase in food spending for home, even higher for lowest-income and single-parent households.[44]

The attacks on SNAP are not new. The same arguments were used to attack—and ultimately dismantle—Aid to Families with Dependent Children in the 1996 welfare reform. This pushback against SNAP has made it politically feasible to adopt measures that will reduce participation. As unemployment rates declined, most states reimposed three-month limits for unemployed childless adults that were waived during the Great Recession.[45] Conservative lawmakers concerned about the growing scope of the program have also argued for making access more conditional. This could occur via changes in federal legislation, waivers provided by the federal government to states under a conservative White House, or by turning the program into a block grant.

Work requirements are not new for SNAP. Federal law requires that adults ages eighteen to fifty-nine be working part time or agree to accept a job if offered one. Those ages eighteen to forty-nine without dependents or a disability face additional requirements. Some states have gone further. In Wisconsin, Governor Scott Walker imposed a thirty-hour work requirement for parents of school-age children in 2018.[46] Requirements to document this work and employment training throughout the year could quickly become highly burdensome. Indeed, the evidence from Temporary Aid to Needy Families is that documentation requirements place high demands on both state administrators and beneficiaries.[47]

States have proposed that they should be given more latitude to place constraints on SNAP. The Obama administration declined such requests, but the Trump administration has signaled that it will allow states to make changes to encourage "self-sufficiency" and reduce "waste, fraud, and abuse," thereby green-lighting conditions such as work requirements and drug tests.[48]

Beyond state waivers, large legislative changes to the program could also significantly increase compliance costs. House Republicans approved additional work requirements and drug testing in 2013 but failed to win support from the Senate. The 2018 Farm Bill proposed by Republicans included a twenty-hour employment or employment training requirement to receive SNAP benefits for all individuals.[49] Notably, the bill required participants to document employment on a monthly basis. Failing to overcome administrative burdens would be met with severe punishment. An applicant who missed submitting documentation for a single month would lose benefits for twelve months. A second failure to keep up with paperwork demands would see the applicant banned from SNAP for three years.[50]

The chair of the Agriculture Committee, Republican Representative Mike Conaway, explained the rationale for such a punitive approach: those who fail to submit their paperwork are choosing to "self select" out of the program.[51] "If food stamps are not worth whatever the deal we put up—the array of opportunities we have for them—if it's not worth that, then fine. We're American. I'm not going to force food stamps on anybody."[52] Moreover, without broad-based eligibility, the automatic link between SNAP receipt and free school lunches or heating assistance would be gone, requiring even more paperwork.

Alternately, were Congress to treat food stamps as a block grant program, as successive House budget plans have proposed, states would have the flexibility to add burdens and limit the growth of the program. Such plans also envision a much smaller program, cutting it by about a third, or $125 billion, after the block grant is introduced, thereby creating strong incentives for states to curb access.[53]

To understand what a block grant approach might look like, we can examine how states now regulate traditional cash assistance, which is block granted. In many states, such welfare is provided via debit cards, as SNAP is. In Kansas, beneficiaries are prohibited from using benefit cards at sites deemed inconsistent with their status as supplicants to the state, such as movie theaters, liquor stores, or tattoo parlors. The state also limited withdrawals to a maximum of $25 per day, effectively reducing the size of benefits through the additional costs that arise from ATM fees.

Some conservative lawmakers in other states, such as New York or Missouri, have proposed a different kind of restriction of SNAP purchases, limiting purchases of "luxury" foods or unhealthy items such as such as cookies, soft drinks, seafood, or steak. Even if such bills are not enacted, they still contribute to a particular type of administrative burden, which is stigma; they convey to beneficiaries and to the general public that SNAP users do not deserve the autonomy that other citizens have in living their lives and cannot be trusted with government resources.

Providing more flexibility to states could result in the addition of new burdens through drug testing of applicants. For example, Republican governors in Wisconsin and Georgia have proposed imposing drug tests on SNAP beneficiaries. The argument for such limitations is not quite fraud—SNAP benefits cannot be used directly for drugs—but that the funds would indirectly subsidize a drug habit. What might these tests look like? Again, we can look at cash assistance programs. In 2015, fifteen states already had drug-testing requirements for TANF, but only when suspicion of drug use is reasonable.[54] Drug-testing protocols are expensive: a survey of ten states with such programs estimated $850,909 in costs in 2015, yielding only 321 positive tests.[55] The state can decide—as Florida did—to pass these costs on directly to the recipients, who have to pay for the drug test costs up front. Drug tests also increase stigma, communicating images of the irresponsible poor, even though welfare users do not appear to use drugs at a rate different from the general population. Another stigma is the test itself, which typically involve urine tests that reduce the individual's sense of personal autonomy.

A new front in the battle over administrative burdens with SNAP is to restrict how people use the benefit. Nutritionists concerned about obesity have petitioned policymakers to prohibit the use of SNAP benefits for unhealthy products, similar to restrictions placed on the Women, Infants, and Children (WIC) food supplemental program. Such proposals enjoy support from across the political spectrum, though are usually proposed by Republican lawmakers. A front-page *New York Times* headline declared, "In the Shopping Cart of a Food Stamp Household: Lots of Soda."[56] Such a critique gives the impression that SNAP encourages unhealthy consumption, when, in fact, the difference between families who use their own money or SNAP

BIPARTISAN FIXES AND PARTISAN BLAME | 157

when it comes to purchasing foods considered unhealthy is not significant.[57] Moreover, evidence demonstrates that increasing SNAP benefits actually increases healthy food consumption.[58]

Restrictions may have health benefits, but they would also result in administrative burdens that reduce take-up and increase food insecurity. A list of banned goods produces practical difficulties.[59] Foods would need to be classified as "unhealthy," which is complicated, given that sixty thousand food and beverage products are on the market and another twenty thousand are introduced each year.[60] Moreover, nutrition experts are wary of a nutrition plan that excludes foods from diets and instead advocate for a focus on the "total" diet or overall pattern of food consumption.[61]

Beneficiaries and stores would need to be aware of forbidden goods, creating learning costs. Such costs would fall heavily on small vendors, which are a key food resource in urban areas that lack easily accessible supermarkets. SNAP users would risk stigma if they were declined from using their benefits. Evidence also indicates that poor parents face particularly high levels of stress around wasting food.[62] They cannot afford to throw away food that their children do not eat. Restricting food choices that may be among the only options a child will eat could further increase stress and decrease food consumption in some poor households. Generally, it undermines individual agency and autonomy over one of the most basic human needs. Even if there were an easy way to distinguish between allowed and separate goods, the experience of purchasing only state-sanctioned products would form a perennial reminder of the limited autonomy SNAP users have over their lives.

The Special Case of Older Adults

Even with recent political setbacks, SNAP has succeeded in reaching more eligible recipients. Yet, for one group, this success has been elusive. Older adults stand out for their relatively low use of SNAP: only about one-third of those eligible actually receive benefits.[63] Unlike other supports targeted to the elderly, such as Medicare and Social Security, older adults may be more sensitive to the stigma of food stamps, especially if they had spent their life working and developed critical views of SNAP recipients. Administrative burdens related to gaining access and maintaining eligibility also loom larger for older adults, given their higher levels of disability. Health and cognitive limitations are especially relevant given the SNAP health documentation requirements.[64]

The low take-up of SNAP for older adults is striking given the level of income insecurity among this population. Social Security provides an income floor, but about 9 percent of older adults fall below the poverty line, though poverty rates that account for the high out-of-pocket spending for older adults' medical care place it closer to 15 percent.[65] The problem is even worse for subgroups. The poverty rate for single older adults is three times as high as for married older adults.[66] Given that poverty level income for single older adults was $899 a month, the average $148 monthly SNAP benefits can constitute a substantial share of their income.

As discussed in chapter 5, administrative burdens are generally more problematic for older adults because of their greater risk for cognitive declines. Estimates of mild cognitive impairment among those sixty-five and older range from 10 to 20 percent but increase as people age.[67] Those with low socioeconomic resources are also much more susceptible to cognitive declines. The risk of dementia doubles for those with low educational attainment.[68] A decline in cognitive skills is especially problematic for those needing to navigate complicated administrative procedures and choices when attempting to access, or keep, a social welfare benefit.

SNAP eligibility rules and rules regarding recertification are more generous, and more complex, for those age sixty and older. Older adults face no gross income limit. Instead, they must have an adjusted income below 100 percent of the poverty line. They also must have assets of less than $3,250, a somewhat higher allowance than for younger individuals. Older adults can include out-of-pocket medical care costs to adjust their income to qualify for SNAP. This deduction matters a great deal, given that older adults pay nearly twice as much in out-of-pocket costs than those under age sixty-five.[69] Moreover, out-of-pocket health-care costs for older adults have increased by nearly 50 percent over the past fifteen years.[70] The average older adult spends approximately $4,700 in out-of-pocket costs annually. Those with incomes of less than $10,000 a year spend an average of

$1,817 annually, whereas those with incomes between $10,000 and $20,000 a year spend an average of $4,467 annually.

A consequence of the health-care deduction is that a far greater proportion of older adults with incomes between 100 and 200 percent of the poverty level—about one in five older adults—are eligible for SNAP relative to those under sixty-five. For those receiving SNAP, the medical deduction can also increase the size of the benefit. For an individual with an income of $721 a month, medical expenses of $200 can increase their monthly SNAP benefit by $69.

The medical expense deduction makes SNAP accessible, but it also creates a high administrative burden. Many older adults are unaware of this eligibility provision.[71] Indeed, only 12 percent of aged beneficiaries take this deduction even though it is likely that the majority would have allowable medical expenses. Older adults also face significant compliance costs to document medical expenses. Case workers may require paperwork to show that a procedure was medically necessary. All applicants must provide bills, receipts, and provider statements. The caseworker must then determine whether these expenses are monthly or nonrecurring to factor in how they should be calculated into the deduction. For recertification, individuals must again provide documentation—even if the expenses have not changed.

A growing awareness of the significant burden that health-related paperwork places on beneficiaries has led nineteen states to adopt waivers that would allow applicants to apply a standard medical deduction (based on average medical costs) for those who can demonstrate at least $35 a month in medical expenses.[72] Other states are reducing burdens at the recertification stage by not requiring individuals to once again document medical expenses.

The combination of cognitive decline and a different and more complex set of rules can facilitate confusion among elderly food stamp recipients, illustrated in this anecdote.

Glenna Flournoy, 85, a retired teacher of English as a second language, said that when her $15 a month in food stamps stopped without warning two years ago, she did not know what to do, so she did nothing. "I didn't know about the system," she said. "I just thought it would go on until you dropped dead." After joining a neighborhood senior center, Ms. Flournoy said she has tried to reapply for food stamps. She said she spoke to program workers twice by phone, and went to a program office, only to be told that she still needs to be interviewed. The food stamps, though not much, were enough to buy milk and cereal for breakfast; without them, she often skips breakfast or goes to the senior center to eat.

Such confusion costs can be reduced by effective outreach, which in turn relies on networks of nonprofits whose quality varies across communities. An alternative way to reduce learning costs about SNAP among older adults already exists but is not being used. The Social Security Administration (SSA) has interactions with older adults on a regular basis and could offer a more systematic effort to inform those who might be eligible. SSA has ready access to benefit information for individuals and married couples, allowing them to providing reliable case-by-case information. If a total family benefit was below the food stamp eligibility criteria, the SSA could mail information about the SNAP program to potentially eligible older adults.

Medicare could also play a more active role. Because older adults have such high out-of-pocket medical care costs and Medicare has information on these costs, they could selectively mail out information about SNAP to individuals with significant health-care expenditures. Even more effectively, administrative linkages between Medicaid and SNAP databases could be more clear to assist caseworkers in verifying medical expenses.[73] More broadly, public-private partnerships could be enlisted to raise awareness of the program among older adults. For example, SSA could partner with the AARP to help raise awareness.

Ongoing efforts to expand SNAP access via internet applications work less well for older adults. Only four in ten older adults use the internet, and rates are even lower among low-income groups.[74] Most need hands-on assistance in the actual application process.[75] Again, the SSA is well positioned to play a role. Currently, SSA offices can accept SNAP applications and provide assistance to those eligible for the Supplemental Security Income (SSI) program but cannot help those ineligible for SSI. SSA offices could expand assistance to those with incomes above the SSI eligibility level. All older adults could apply at their local SSA offices, where they could receive assistance with the application and documentation.

In-person interviews are an especially burdensome part of the process for the elderly. Many are unable to drive, lack reliable transportation, or have trouble walking. Approximately one in five older adults have a physical disability that would make it difficult for them to be mobile.[76] More than 30 percent have heart disease and 8 percent have had a stroke—rates that are fifteen and eight times greater, respectively, than among those age eighteen to forty-four.[77] Older adults most likely to qualify for SNAP also have substantially poorer physical functioning than their peers. More than half of those below 100 percent of the poverty level have an activity limitation, versus only 17 percent of older adults with incomes above 400 percent.[78] Consequently, providing an option for a telephone interview is especially important to improve access for older adults.

A key barrier in keeping older adults enrolled is the need to recertify to continue receiving benefits. Although recertification for benefits is only every twelve to twenty-four months for older adults, relative to six to twelve months for other age groups, it causes significantly more problems for older adults. Indeed, the proportion of older adults who are temporarily removed from food stamps during recertification is 30 percent higher than any other group of beneficiaries.[79] Given that income, family situations, and even medical expenses for older adults tend to be relatively stable, one could further lengthen the period between recertifications beyond twenty-four months.

The challenges facing older adults point to a more general need to incorporate administrative data to get and keep older adults enrolled in SNAP. For example, state governments could simply auto-reenroll individuals with very low incomes who are receiving SSI. The closest they have come to this is the Combined Application Program piloted in eighteen states, which allows SSI beneficiaries in single households to apply for SNAP using a shortened application when they apply for SSI. It also does not require a separate interview or any documentation. These applicants also benefit from a forty-eight-month recertification window. In South Carolina, this change increased the percentage of SSI beneficiaries on SNAP by 12 percentage points.[80] States could also more closely track older adults enrolled in Medicaid with very high medical expenses, and target information and support to these individuals to see whether they are eligible for SNAP—and then provide support for that application process.

Conclusion

Improving social welfare policy does not always involve new programs or changes in benefits or eligibility guidelines. Given the numbers of eligible individuals who fail to receive benefits, a viable and straightforward path is to improve enrollment in existing programs. The post–welfare-reform era under SNAP shows both how delinking programs from cash assistance depressed participation and how incremental reductions in administrative burdens can improve policy outcomes. The federal government under both Republican and Democratic administrations found ways to increase the participation in SNAP while reducing fraud.

But this success is fragile. As the bipartisan consensus on SNAP falters, a welfare program with low burdens inevitably becomes a target for conservatives generally opposed to the welfare state. The attraction of adding new burdens increases as opponents to SNAP struggle to alter it via traditional legislation that alters eligibility criteria. The federal government could decide to impose a new round of administrative burdens, or to delegate the capacity to do so to states. If state oversight of other welfare programs is any guide, the result would be to constrain what individuals could purchase and layer more conditionality on the receipt of benefits. Such changes— even when they exist only as policy proposals—reinforce the notion that the poor must be closely policed in the use of public funds, more so than other beneficiaries of tax dollars. We do not demand drug tests of homeowners taking a mortgage deduction, students receiving subsidized loans, or corporate employees provided with tax subsidies.

The recent history of SNAP therefore illustrates the fragility of a purely technocratic approach to burdens. Political support is needed to reduce burdens. Administrative burdens, once discovered and eliminated, are not necessarily gone forever. Instead, policymakers can look at a successful record of reducing barriers and improving access and decide to make the program more burdensome once again. Such policy lessons are informed by partisan worldviews about the size of the program and the perceived qualities of those receiving the benefits.

Another lesson from the SNAP experience is that even when a program succeeds in engaging most eligible participants, some subgroups can fall behind. The costs this subgroup faces may be different from others, meaning that the strategies to engage them also need to be different. Older adults enroll at lower levels than younger SNAP participants, at least partly because of their greater propensity to have health problems and cognitive impairments, thereby limiting their ability to overcome burdens. A growing understanding of the particular burdens they face has encouraged experimentation with tailored techniques to reduce those burdens, but much more remains to be done.

MENDING MEDICAID 7

THE POLITICS OF SHIFTING BURDENS
AT THE STATE LEVEL

To provide a granular analysis of how changes in administrative actions are linked to evolving political preferences, this chapter tracks changes in administrative burdens in a single state (Wisconsin) for a specific policy issue (Medicaid) over two decades, from 1995 to 2015.[1] During that time two governors, one Republican and one Democratic, both sought to reduce burdens, albeit for different reasons, and one Republican governor took actions that increased burdens.[2]

To demonstrate the political construction of administrative burdens, we show how gubernatorial policy and ideological preferences align with attempts to alter administrative burdens. We also account for the preferences and importance of a sitting president, echoing the federalism discussion in chapter 4. Federal actors adjudicated waiver requests necessary for significant program reform, sometimes pushing governors to further reduce burdens or blocking efforts to increase burdens. Presidents and Congress also offered financial incentives that encouraged states to impose or reduce burdens. Medicaid offers an excellent example of the impact of the construction and reduction of burdens, given its size, and the large numbers of people eligible for the program who do not actually enroll, even when they lack any other insurance.

Medicaid is not just important for providing access to health care. It also matters for inequality. People who lack access to health care are more likely to struggle to break cycles of poverty. As young people gain Medicaid early in life, they are more likely to see long-term benefits to their health and educational attainment.[3] Medicaid can even facilitate intergenerational mobility: because Medicaid is made more available to low-income pregnant women, their children enjoy better economic outcomes as adults.[4]

Medicaid covers about one in five Americans at any given time, and is a key mechanism by which the Patient Protection and Affordable Care Act of 2010 (ACA) sought to expand health insurance coverage. Broadly, Medicaid provides health insurance coverage for low-income pregnant women, parents, and children, covering nearly 26 percent of all children and 37 percent of all pregnant women.[5] It also serves the elderly and disabled: indeed, two-thirds of Medicaid spending is devoted to these groups.[6] Eligibility for the program varies considerably by state, though minimum federal eligibility standards are in place. For example, every state must insure pregnant women at or below 133 percent of the federal poverty level.

The access of those with low incomes to health care via Medicaid is generally debated in terms of the eligibility levels and generosity of state policies.[7] But eligibility guidelines are not the only factors that affect access to the Medicaid program. Estimates of take-up of program benefits vary a good deal but typically find that anywhere from 30 to 50 percent of eligible beneficiaries do not access Medicaid.[8] Coverage also varies significantly across states, ranging from 48 percent in Texas to 96 percent in the District of Columbia.[9] Wisconsin's rates range from 80 to 90 percent, placing it among the ten states with the highest participation rates.

A growing body of evidence demonstrates how specific procedures affect Medicaid enrollment, but little research has examined how a state has systematically attempted to alter take-up of a program by administrative action. Many of these reforms hinge on each other, so it helps to consider them collectively, rather than as isolated interventions. The chapter also illustrates the subterranean nature of administrative burdens. Governors dramatically reduced learning and compliance costs for the individual via mechanisms such as auto-enrollment, simplified applications, online application systems, and application assistance. They also influenced burden by setting an expectation for administrators and caseworkers that administrative practices should not unnecessarily impede access to a program for which people were eligible. These changes were significant and meaningfully increased enrollment but were largely unobtrusive and enacted with little broad political discussion.

We trace the evolution of administrative rules and practices during the expansion of the Medicaid program administered by the Wisconsin Department of Health Services.[10] Wisconsin became a leader in reducing administrative burden in Medicaid and, more broadly, in shifting administrative burden away from citizens and onto the state during the governorships of Tommy Thompson (1987–2001) and Jim Doyle (2003–2011).[11] Republican Governor Scott Walker, who succeeded Doyle, sought to reduce some learning and compliance costs but largely pursued changes that placed burdens on applicants.

Governor Thompson: Making Work Pay

Governor Thompson was a pioneer in the movement to tie welfare benefits to work, passing a version of welfare reform that informed later federal policy changes. Welfare reform was a defining political issue for him. He saw changes in public health insurance as inextricably tied to his policy goal of "making work pay"—a way of encouraging individuals to move off welfare, as well as a basic matter of fairness, arguing that those on public assistance should not enjoy better health insurance than the working poor.

The making-work-pay frame shaped how the Thompson administration wanted health insurance to work. Even if the program was technically welfare, those in the governor's administration saw it differently.[12] One said, "a simple message needs to be marketed— Medicaid and BadgerCare are health insurance for working families."[13] Another noted, "They wanted it not to be an entitlement. They wanted it more like an employer plan, and they really wanted to cover families."[14] That the governor saw it as a benefit earned, rather than welfare, shaped strategies to limit the administrative burdens that participants faced.

When welfare reform was originally passed in Wisconsin, Thompson tried unsuccessfully to include a health insurance plan. After Congress passed the Children's Health Insurance Program (CHIP) in 1997, Thompson saw another opportunity to link health insurance to work, in the form of a new program. BadgerCare (named after the state symbol) expanded Medicaid to the working poor using a mixture of funds from federal Medicaid and CHIP. CHIP was targeted at children, but Wisconsin officials used its funding to extend coverage to parents, a simple program structure that allowed BadgerCare to cover all family members under one plan.

BadgerCare required a waiver from the Department of Health and Human Services.[15] The waiver process gave the Clinton administration an opportunity to influence the design of the program. President Clinton was troubled by the estimated 1.37 million decline in Medicaid coverage for eligible children across the United States after the 1996 federal welfare reform.[16] This decline occurred when Medicaid eligibility was delinked from receipt of traditional welfare programs, making it more burdensome for poor people to seek it out as a separate program.

The Clinton administration offered guidance to state health and welfare agencies on ways to reduce learning and compliance costs, such as eliminating asset tests, making eligibility workers more accessible, and introducing shorter joint forms for Medicaid and CHIP.[17] The Clinton administration's desire to reduce burdens was reflected in the conditions placed on Wisconsin's waiver request, including the elimination of its asset test (a change Thompson had previously vetoed when proposed by the state legislature), a simplified application form, and a mail-in application process for Medicaid and BadgerCare. Although the asset test was, strictly speaking, a marker of eligibility, the documentation required significantly increased compliance costs among a population with few assets, to the point that it was considered counterproductive.

Thompson accepted the conditions, received the waiver, and BadgerCare was implemented in July 1999, covering parents and children living below 185 percent of the federal poverty level. Enrollment was restricted to those ineligible for Medicaid funds, but BadgerCare was designed to be integrated with Medicaid for applicants and participants. From the perspective of participants, there was only one program, which reduced learning and compliance costs. BadgerCare participants with higher incomes had to pay premiums, but all received the same benefits as other participants in Wisconsin's relatively comprehensive Medicaid program.

Table 7.1 summarizes the administrative actions of the Thompson administration and how they relate to learning, compliance, and

Table 7.1 *Changes in Administrative Burden in Wisconsin Medicaid Programs During Thompson Administration (1987–2001)*

	Learning	Compliance	Psychological
Information and outreach efforts			
BadgerCare marketing		X	X
Expanded placement of eligibility workers at various local governments	X	X	
Placed outstationing sites at local community centers, health clinics, and schools	X	X	X
Creation of hotline to help applicants		X	
Administrative data and information technology			
Scanned state databases for family members of Medicaid recipients likely eligible; screen those who lost Medicaid eligibility for BadgerCare	X	X	
Used private data company to verify access to employer-provided insurance	X		
Documentation requirements			
Created short application form[a]	X		
Extended redeterminations from six to twelve months, allowing for a single annual redetermination for Medicaid, BadgerCare, and SNAP	X		
Allow phone and mail-in application forms[a]	X	X	
Eliminated asset test[a]	X		
Presumed eligibility while waiting for confirmation of lack of employer-sponsored health insurance	X		

(continued)

Table 7.1 (*continued*)

	Learning	Compliance	Psychological
Instructed employees to seek verification data rather than deny assistance if client could not provide it, prohibited employees from asking for nonrequired data and encouraged the acceptance of many types of documentation	X		X
Instructed employees to make assumptions about eligibility to complete forms		X	

Source: Authors' compilation.
[a]per federal requirement.

psychological costs. Outreach efforts reduced learning and psychological costs. The Wisconsin Department of Health Services sent a direct mailing with information about BadgerCare to eighteen thousand families who had lost means-tested income support after welfare reform. In Milwaukee, National School Lunch Program applications also contained an additional form for those interested in applying for Medicaid or BadgerCare, resulting in the enrollment of several hundred new families. Advertising campaigns by the state specifically targeted low-income populations with a message meant to reduce the stigma traditionally associated with public health insurance. A television commercial featured Thompson promoting the new program, a back-to-school initiative promoted BadgerCare and Medicaid among schoolchildren, and public health officials educated parents whose children were participating in an immunization program.

Department of Health Services operations plans instructed all direct marketing materials to be "written in prose that is easily understandable," and at no higher than a sixth-grade reading level. Department of Health Services also targeted outreach to non–English speakers. Health-care providers, public health departments, community organizations, and school systems received 850,000 brochures in English, Spanish, and Hmong, and the state offered translators who could provide program information. A toll-free hotline was set up to aid potential applicants.

Governor Thompson tapped into active community outreach to increase enrollment. The state benefited from the Robert Wood Johnson Foundation's Covering Kids Expansion project in Wisconsin, supplemented by additional funding from the Department of Health Services. Working with community organizations, health-care providers, and translators, these outreach efforts trained hundreds of workers from schools, public health agencies, dental providers, utility companies, legal service agencies, food pantries, and homeless shelters in BadgerCare and Medicaid eligibility.[18]

Outreach matters in three ways. First, the provision of information can reduce the learning costs of finding out about the existence of the program and understanding eligibility. Second, the ability of outreach workers to directly provide a helping hand to individuals completing applications reduces compliance burdens and raises application completion rates.[19] Third, if done well, outreach that uses nonprofits and health-care providers who are known to and trusted by the target population can reduce psychological costs. Outreach workers are more likely to be recognized as advocates for the individual, and applicants are likely to encounter peers also seeking to receive benefits.

To begin an application, clients had to sign and date the form in the presence of an eligibility worker. To reduce this compliance burden, workers were located at county, tribal, social, and human services departments; state agencies; local community centers, health clinics, and schools; and various outstation sites like federally qualified health centers. Out-stationed eligibility workers had laptop computers with dial-up capacity to link them to state databases. Allowing participants to sign up at out-stationing sites, rather than welfare offices, was also meant to decrease psychological costs by making BadgerCare look more like private insurance and less like welfare.

A change in state law in 2000 reinforced that the role of eligibility workers was to help clients. Case workers generally have discretion in how they interact with beneficiaries. The state law set an expectation that agency workers should prioritize access over verification. This provided a frame for how agency workers saw applicants and how they used discretion during the application process. If applicants were not able to obtain the required verification on their own, the law stated that "the agency may not deny assistance but shall proceed immediately to verify the data elements." In an internal operations memo, eligibility workers were instructed to "only verify those items required to determine eligibility and benefits," not to oververify by "requiring excessive pieces of evidence for any one item," or "exclusively require a particular type of verification when various types are possible."

Linking CHIP and Medicaid via BadgerCare reflected a belief in the Thompson administration that expanding an existing program would reduce learning costs relative to creating a separate program for CHIP. Indeed, BadgerCare avoided the struggle with take-up that other states with standalone CHIP programs experienced.[20] BadgerCare quickly became widely known in Wisconsin. By 2002, a survey of families who were eligible for BadgerCare but not participating in the program found that even among those who had never had any member of their family enrolled in the program, four in five had heard of the program.[21]

By putting multiple state medical assistance programs and funding sources under the umbrella of a single program, the state was able to streamline the marketing message and make it easier for individuals to understand if they were eligible. The efforts to increase access appear to have been successful. Between its implementation in 1999 and 2008, before BadgerCare Plus enrollment in the program more than doubled from approximately 215,000 to 510,000.

Governor Doyle: All Kids

Unlike Governor Thompson, Democratic Governor Jim Doyle did not view health insurance as a benefit tied to work but as a basic right. Doyle set a goal of 98 percent of citizens having access to health coverage. Doyle pushed this goal through policy changes that emphasized covering all kids, expanding BadgerCare and consolidating it with Medicaid and Healthy Start effective February 2008, creating BadgerCare Plus.

BadgerCare Plus significantly expanded eligibility to all children and pregnant women up to 300 percent of the federal poverty level, and all other covered groups up to 200 percent of the federal poverty level, including a large expansion to *caretaker adults*, defined as either parents or relatives of the child. Although BadgerCare had been designed to be an expansion of Medicaid, programs formally retaining separate names, the creation of BadgerCare Plus treated Healthy Start, Family Medicaid, and BadgerCare as one program from the point of view of the applicant, thereby reducing learning costs. BadgerCare Plus also led to the implementation of several changes to administrative procedures in the program that were intended to reduce administrative burden for recipients and increase enrollment (see table 7.2).[22]

Wisconsin again needed a federal waiver to expand BadgerCare to BadgerCare Plus. Winning this waiver required negotiating with the Bush administration, which had become increasingly concerned about the growing size of CHIP and Medicaid, and resistant to waiver requests that would expand these programs. Under President Bush, the federal government had put stronger pressure on state governments to reduce take-up error rates in Medicaid—and consequently increase administrative burden.[23] Even as the Bush administration policed errors in a way that discouraged take-up, they put states in a catch-22 by making expansion of the program contingent on unrealistic take-up goals. In a letter dated August 17, 2007, the Bush administration told states that they had to demonstrate a 95 percent take-up rate for eligible CHIP beneficiaries before they could expand it to citizens above 250 percent of the federal poverty level (FPL). This target was so unrealistic as to discourage efforts to expand CHIP. Wisconsin sidestepped this requirement by agreeing to use state money to cover those above 250 percent of the FPL. Ultimately, the Obama administration withdrew the letter amid threats of litigation from states over the failure of the Bush administration to follow the rulemaking process for this relatively dramatic reinterpretation of law.

Governor Doyle also pursued higher insurance coverage through a reduction of administrative barriers. Even with this reduction, a survey before BadgerCare Plus was implemented found that burdens still discouraged participation: one in three said they found it too hard to get paperwork; one in five said that the application process was too hard; and one in four pointed to difficulties in applying in person.[24]

According to one advocate for low-income families, the Doyle administration "was genuinely committed to coverage for kids and he gave them [state employees] the green light. And then they felt they had a license to remove all the barriers they could." These efforts were encouraged by a federal environment that became friendlier to the goals of the Doyle administration after the election of President Obama in 2008, coupled with Democratic control of Congress.

Table 7.2 *Changes in Administrative Burden in Wisconsin Medicaid Programs During Doyle Administration (2003–2011)*

	Learning	Compliance	Psychological
Information and outreach efforts			
Expanded BadgerCare Plus marketing and outreach, using a simplified all-kids message	X		X
Trained third-party actors to express-enroll applicants at outstation sites		X	
More simple and specific communications to client about renewals	X	X	
Administrative data and information technology			
Used ACCESS to provide program information, individual benefit information, and preliminary assessment of eligibility	X		
Made online applications available	X	X	
One-time auto enrollment of individuals who appeared eligible based on state data	X	X	
Used data matches to verify citizenship status, allowed variety of documents for verification, maintained client in program if making good-faith effort to provide documentation		X	
Used private database to verify lack of employer-provided health insurance	X	X	X
Made online applications available	X	X	
Documentation requirements			
Simplified application form and notices	X	X	
Required employees to provide documentation of lack of access to employer-provided health insurance[a]	X	X	X

Table 7.2 (*continued*)

	Learning	Compliance	Psychological
For renewal, provided applicant with previously collected personal information (either via ACCESS for online applications, or preprinted forms for mail applications)		X	
Single application form for multiple programs	X	X	
Extended presumptive eligibility to certain groups		X	

Source: Authors' compilation.
[a]change expected to increase burdens.

The new Congress quickly passed the CHIP Reauthorization Act in 2009, which put in place a series of financial incentives to increase access. To qualify for federal bonuses, states had to increase enrollment with active outreach programs and implement features explicitly designed to reduce learning and compliance costs. Features included reducing the frequency of renewal of status requirements for children, liberalizing asset requirements, combining Medicaid and CHIP application forms, eliminating in-person interviews, providing presumptive eligibility for children, and using auto- or administrative enrollment. One hundred million dollars was allocated to outreach, the vast majority provided to state and local governments and community organizations. Error-reporting requirements passed under Bush were restructured to avoid discouraging efforts to increase take-up.[25]

As detailed in the following section, these incentives aligned with initiatives that Wisconsin was already pursuing, allowing it to win bonus funds of $23,432,822 in 2010 and $24,541,778 in 2011.

SHIFTING INSURANCE/ID VERIFICATION
CHECKS TO THE STATE

Although BadgerCare eventually became a key focus of his administration, Governor Doyle did not treat it as a top priority in its early years. Indeed, Doyle responded to legislative concerns that the availability of public health insurance would discourage low-income workers from using available employer-based insurance. To avoid this problem, the state required workers to have their employers complete forms to verify that affordable insurance was unavailable. A subsequent dramatic decline in enrollment became an early and important lesson for the Doyle administration officials regarding how seemingly minor burdens can generate large effects.

After May 2004, BadgerCare applicants were required to verify income and health insurance status before they enrolled, and again at every renewal (or when their employment changed). Additionally, each of the applicant's adult family members had to provide verification of income and health insurance status. Applicants were sent forms, which they were expected to take to their employers to verify insurance information. They also had the option of verifying income information through pay stubs or a letter from the employer. Before implementation, the Department of Health Services estimated that the new requirement would reduce enrollment by 2 to 3 percent, and state officials "thought it was just an innocuous change." But, between May of 2004 and January of 2005, enrollment dropped by 23 percent.[26]

The evidence suggests that the new requirement mostly affected eligible claimants, rather than weeding out the ineligible. The Department of Health Services surveyed BadgerCare applicants who were denied and recipients whose eligibility had been terminated to determine why verification materials were not returned. This evaluation found that procedural ineligibility was usually due to failure to verify health insurance status, and that the main reasons for failure included too little time, misunderstandings about the instructions and process by both applicants and employers, and employer inability to complete the form in a timely manner.[27] It is possible that some employees, who received many notices not directly relevant to them, simply ignored the forms. Even enrollees who understood the change may have been embarrassed to approach their employer to ask for help in seeking public benefits. Employers also had little incentive to complete and return the forms.

In response, the Department of Health Services first sought to simplify the form, adding instructions, revising questions, and clarifying when and how it would be accepted. The department also began accepting verification materials from employers via fax. When working with eligibility workers, it began emphasizing the policy to accept alternate forms of verification (such as paystubs). But enrollment problems persisted. The state then sought to shift the burden of form completion to employers, who had to complete verification forms or face a fine.[28] But insurance verification forms continued to be completed at low rates.

Ultimately, the implementation of BadgerCare Plus in 2008 fully shifted the burden associated with earnings and employment verification from the applicants and employers onto the state, using a new database of employment information that eliminated the need for paper verification. The experience with employee verification also influenced how Wisconsin officials responded to federal directives that would have increased burdens. In 2005, Congress required Medicaid applicants to provide citizenship documentation. Prior to this, self-declaration of citizenship status was deemed sufficient unless the claim was questionable, in which case eligibility workers could require documentation. The Wisconsin Department of Health Services sought to buffer the impact of these requirements, creating a series of policy guidelines that gave applicants flexibility in providing information. Further, state workers were instructed to collect the information from other sources if it was possible to do so. The CHIP Reauthorization Act of 2009 maintained these verification requirements but allowed states to create a data exchange with the Social Security Administration, which in turn reduced the need for states to seek verification from applicants.

AUTO-ENROLLMENT

In the month prior to implementation of BadgerCare Plus, the Department of Health Services carried out a one-time auto-enrollment effort of people who state data suggested were eligible. Auto-enrollment is a technique that uses information technology and administrative data to more efficiently capture eligible beneficiaries. For example, Massachusetts used it to enroll a pool of uninsured individuals into a state-run insurance program, allowing the state to claim the lowest uninsured rate in the country.[29]

The Wisconsin auto-enrollment was not initially planned, but, when gearing up for the implementation of BadgerCare Plus, the Department of Health Services reviewed its administrative files and discovered a large group of individuals who were eligible for the program. This included people who had been eligible for the original BadgerCare program, as well as those who would be eligible under the new, more generous eligibility guidelines established by BadgerCare Plus. The one-time auto-enrollment took place on February 1, 2008.[30] Essentially, the state decided to enroll all citizens as long as it had credible information about their eligibility. People were automatically enrolled in BadgerCare Plus, and caseworkers followed up with verification notices if needed.

A total of 44,264 people were enrolled as a result of this one-time auto-enrollment. Auto-enrollees looked similar to other enrollees in terms of income—indeed almost three-quarters were already income eligible—and stayed enrolled at about the same rates as those not auto-enrolled, suggesting that they valued and needed health insurance as much as other enrollees.[31] The results are consistent with behavioral economics research, discussed in chapter 1, that simply changing the default from opt-out to opt-in dramatically increases participation.

PRESUMPTIVE ELIGIBILITY

BadgerCare Plus expanded *express enrollment* (also known as presumptive eligibility) to children below 150 percent of the federal poverty level and pregnant women below 300 percent. Presumptive eligibility provided immediate access to Medicaid to those deemed eligible by qualified enrollment organizations, such as hospitals. Beneficiaries then received assistance from the state to finish the application process in the month following enrollment, reducing compliance costs.

PROGRAM AND FORM SIMPLIFICATION

BadgerCare Plus incorporated many family Medicaid programs under one program name and one set of rules, making it easier for people to understand whether they were eligible and reducing the need to apply for multiple programs with multiple applications, thereby reducing learning and compliance costs. This change was a response to the complexity that resulted from decades of adding programs on top of one another—from AFDC to Medicaid to Healthy Start to BadgerCare. "We had this very organic, but very disorganized, chaotic system," one state employee said. Another remarked, "we were conscious that the system that had evolved had complexity in it which we wanted to streamline. We weren't deliberately trying to make the system difficult, but as you build system and add pieces, that happens."

Each program had different eligibility criteria, so members of the same family were often subject to different rules. "Before we did BadgerCare Plus, a family could be on Medicaid and BadgerCare and different members of the family were subject to different eligibility, different criteria, different benefit packages," a Department of Health Service's staffer noted, "so under BadgerCare Plus, we were trying to simplify that."

Program simplification made the application process easier in tangible ways. The Wisconsin Family Medicaid, BadgerCare and Family Planning Waiver Program Application and Review Packet thus became the BadgerCare Plus Application Packet. Individuals could fill out just one form to apply for multiple programs. The application did become somewhat longer but was made user-friendly with larger typeface, clearer formatting, and more space for applicants' responses. Several groups of questions relevant for only some applicants—such as questions about employment, pregnancy, and absent parents—were moved out of the basic form and into attachments at the end of the packet. The state later added information and attachments to the BadgerCare Plus form to allow users to also apply for food stamps and Medicare Premium Assistance.

Program simplification also allowed the Department of Health Services to simplify its communications with beneficiaries. For example, rather than informing enrollees when their cases switched from one funding source to another—such as Healthy Start, Family Medicaid, or BadgerCare—the department tried to provide only relevant information to enrollees. "We were working on notices at the time and we realized we were telling them things that didn't matter to them," said a manager, "So we decided to take all of that stuff and sweep it behind a curtain and say we have one program, BadgerCare Plus." By simplifying the rules and explanations,

Department of Health Services made BadgerCare Plus easier for applicants and enrollees to understand, reducing learning costs.

ONLINE ACCESS

Prior to the passage of BadgerCare Plus, the state sought to significantly streamline the application process via a new website named ACCESS. By making it easier for potential applicants to determine whether they were likely to be eligible, and what eligibility information they needed to provide, the website reduced learning costs. By making it easier for outreach workers to enroll applicants, and facilitating single applications for multiple programs, ACCESS reduced compliance costs.

In July 2003, Wisconsin received a $1.7 million grant from the U.S. Food and Nutrition Service to develop ACCESS. Launched in 2004, the website included information in both English and Spanish about food stamps, Medicaid, and BadgerCare. An innovative aspect of ACCESS is that it allowed potential applicants to enter basic information to do a preliminary check of their eligibility. In a 2004 operations memo, the Department of Health Services wrote that the screener tool would give applicants greater confidence of their eligibility: "They may choose not to apply because of incorrect assumptions about their potential level of benefits or specific policies—such as the vehicle asset rule—that have changed over time. Many people believe the application process would involve too much time and effort unless they feel reasonably confident that they will be eligible for benefits."[32] In September 2005, ACCESS added a Check My Benefits feature to address this problem.

ACCESS supplemented but did not replace notices and other communication with caseworkers and allowed users to find the date their benefits began, the date of their next review, information on cost-sharing, reasons for denials of benefits, items needed by their caseworker (such as verification documents), contact information for their caseworker, a history of changes in benefits, and answers to frequently asked questions.

By June 2006, applicants could fill out an application online for food stamps and BadgerCare, thereby reducing compliance costs. The online form could also be combined with a phone interview with an eligibility worker to finalize the application, and eligibility workers could call to request more information in case of inconsistencies.

The Department of Health Services made ACCESS more user friendly, simplifying the language in the online screener and application to a fourth-grade reading level. The department conducted twenty-five focus groups with eligibility workers, supervisors, service providers, and low-income residents to survey what type of questions recipients had about their benefits and to make the design of ACCESS as user friendly as possible. ACCESS also became a mechanism by which participants could report changes that had material relevance to their benefits, including employment status, contact information, and change in family status.

By 2010, the online system had become the most popular method of applying for the program. Walk-in applications made up just 20 percent of applications in rural areas and 14 percent in urban counties.[33] ACCESS clearly eased the application process. One eligibility worker describing the process said,

> Now, it's much faster.... I use the application so much now that I can kick out an application in 15 minutes versus somebody doing it on their own could take them an hour. In the beginning it was more like 30–50 minutes. It's much less time than it was before BadgerCare Plus, which I attribute to the online ACCESS program. It's so convenient and it doesn't matter where you're at ... So tonight when I leave here, I'm taking my printer, copier and scanner—I'm going tonight to meet with a pregnant woman and I'll be able to give her the application and do her express enrollment all at once with her.[34]

MARKETING AND ALL-KIDS BRANDING

By putting the many state medical assistance programs and funding sources under the umbrella of a single program, the state was also able to streamline the marketing message around the all-kids theme. This mattered in two ways. First, it communicated broad eligibility for the program, reducing learning costs. Second, the marketing sought to reframe the negative conceptions of welfare, thereby reducing psychological costs.

Department of Health Services administrators believed the all-kids frame allowed for broad-based marketing which made it less likely that eligible parents would be confused about their status. As one administrator noted, "the 'All Kids' message is very helpful for marketing even for people who are otherwise eligible for the program. I think that was one of the things that we hoped and talked about is that we wanted to end the stigma."[35] One parent in a suburban school district said, "I've always been under the impression that it was for a certain income group. When I was newly divorced and I had my son, and even then when I was not making much money, I was still under the impression that I had to be receiving some other state benefit. Which may not be the case, but it was at the time what I was thinking."[36] In short, this marketing may have created a welcome mat effect by expanding applicant understanding of eligibility, and reducing stigma that have limited take-up of Medicaid.[37]

BOOTS ON THE GROUND: COMMUNITY OUTREACH AND ENROLLMENT

The lessons of community outreach from BadgerCare Plus point to the importance of using a diverse mix of third parties who have robust incentives to enroll participants yet still provide strong state oversight. The state contracted with county income maintenance or tribal offices to process Medicaid enrollment forms and to help individuals apply for the program. Income maintenance offices continued to play a central role, but the state broadened the number of agencies on the ground to help people apply for the program, even allowing presumptive enrollment. Indeed, states that have increased enrollment of Medicaid beneficiaries typically engaged in active outreach with partners in the nonprofit and health-care community.[38]

The implementation of BadgerCare Plus built on the Thompson administration's practice of third-party outreach. The state relied heavily on community-based organizations to assist enrollment efforts. In these strategic partnerships, the Department of Health Services provided community organizations with monetary incentives and training, as well as bilingual and culturally specific marketing materials. The Department of Health Services encouraged cooperation by offering a $50 finder's fee for organizations and providers for every person they enrolled in BadgerCare Plus. In addition, it awarded mini-grants of up to $25,000 to thirty-two organizations to help finance locally based outreach efforts. Approximately three thousand people from almost two hundred community organizations and health-care providers were trained by state officials to provide outreach about the new program and enroll eligible individuals.[39] These included community groups likely to have direct interaction with eligible applicants, such as groups providing Head Start, and Women, Infant, and Children programs, as well as community health clinics, schools, and faith-based groups. These relationships with community groups reflected the Department of Health Services' broader efforts to use local partners to locate and help solve problems.

Both the mini-grants and the training helped foster high enrollment levels in BadgerCare Plus. The mini-grant funds allowed county eligibility workers to accommodate the large number of applicants received after the transition to BadgerCare Plus. One said, "The mini-grants were really effective. We're getting referrals from everywhere and if we didn't have that mini-grant, I don't know how much time we would be able to allow or allot for that. But because of that funding, we are doing as much as we can as soon as we can based on the needs of the community."[40] Another county eligibility expert said of the community partnerships, "I would say that media attention has been good but I don't think that's the most significant factor, I think it's the involvement of so many external partners that has generated a level of buzz that is unprecedented."[41]

Governor Walker: Increasing Burdens

The reductions in burden under the Doyle administration increased program enrollment, even among those who were previously eligible before the introduction of BadgerCare Plus.[42] However, Doyle's successor, Republican Scott Walker, challenged the underlying assumptions of BadgerCare, and especially BadgerCare Plus. The Walker administration saw the program as too large, covering individuals who were not truly poor. By covering children up to 300 percent of the poverty line, around half of state households had become income eligible under Doyle. The Walker administration also argued that innovations that had reduced administrative burden made the program vulnerable to widespread fraud and therefore should be reversed.

Under Thompson and Doyle, most criticisms of Medicaid focused on the affordability of the program for the state and the risks of crowding out of private insurance, but "at that time [policymakers] weren't making the fraud argument," a Department of Health Services employee said. Walker was reluctant to call for cuts in a popular program, instead suggesting that the program was rife with fraud and abuse. Walker's Department of Health Services sought to reduce the size of the program, partly by using administrative procedures to limit access in the name of curbing fraud.

As one of his first acts as governor, Walker created a Commission on Waste, Fraud and Abuse. The commission criticized "an explosion in public assistance spending and program expansions over the last decade with no corresponding investment in program integrity," identifying the efforts of the prior administrations to reduce burden as part of the problem.[43] It argued that ex-post facto punishments for fraud were ineffective and called for moving the burden of proof back on the citizen at the front-end of the application process, increasing the frequency of program eligibility recertifications, and requiring face-to-face interviews for eligibility verification when possible. Walker also created an Office of Inspector General within the Department of Health Services to pursue fraud and abuse. From 2011 through 2013, the Wisconsin state budget set aside $2 million to pay for nineteen new positions to support fraud prevention.

The actual evidence of applicant fraud was largely anecdotal, and the impact that administrative burden would have on eligible beneficiaries was not discussed. The commission claimed its recommendations would save $455 million annually, or $3.1 billion over ten years (see table 7.3). The implication was that all of these savings could come from preventing fraud rather than from a loss of eligible claimants. This willingness to ignore the burdensome effects of proposed requirements may have been enabled by Governor Walker's generally skeptical view of government-provided welfare supports. He argued that the program had grown unnecessarily large, as was articulated on the retooled Department of Health Services website: "Medicaid is no longer exclusively for individuals living below the

Table 7.3 *Changes in Administrative Burden in Wisconsin Medicaid Programs During Walker Administration (2011–)*

	Learning	Compliance	Psychological
Information and outreach efforts			
Coordinated regional outreach networks to redirect individuals to the ACA federal marketplace	X		
Mandated regulatory requirements for federal navigators[b]	X		
Administrative data and information technology			
Autorenewal for groups unlikely to lose eligibility	X	X	
Policy changes			
Reduced eligibility for BadgerCare Plus pushed individuals to look for other forms of health insurance[b]	X		
Processing fee for renewal[ab]		X	
Premium increases[ab]		X	
Annual (rather than six-month) waiting period for failure to pay program premium[ab]		X	
Proposed drug testing for Medicaid beneficiaries[ab]		X	X
Work requirements[ab]		X	

Source: Authors' compilation.
[a]requires federal approval via waiver process.
[b]change expected to increase burdens.

poverty level.... Medicaid provides a richer benefit package for children than what is typically offered in the private sector."[44]

At a time that the federal government drew lessons from Wisconsin and other states to reduce administrative burdens via the Affordable Care Act (see chapter 4), Wisconsin was walking away from its commitment to reduce burdens on participants. In a waiver application, the state proposed a series of changes that would have increased administrative burden and beneficiary costs. For example, it sought to remove presumptive eligibility for children. It also proposed redefining household income to require the provision of evidence of income from all residing in the house for more than sixty days, excluding grandparents but including boyfriends, girlfriends, siblings, friends, and other relatives with no legal obligation to support the mother or child actually claiming benefits. Finally, the state sought to require verification of state residency before providing aid, having an effect similar to an identification requirement.

In line with its support for Medicaid and CHIP, the Obama White House largely rejected Walker's proposed changes, consistent with prohibitions on states in the ACA from making their medical assistance "eligibility standards, methodologies, or procedures" more restrictive. Some proposed waiver changes for adult applicants were allowed. Premiums were increased, and eligibility changed. This did alter administrative burden. Increases in premiums in Medicaid and CHIP, even small ones, have been shown to reduce participation, especially among those with the lowest incomes.[45] Although Medicare also features premiums, they are deducted directly from Social Security payments, so no one loses coverage because they were unaware of or unable to pay. Recipients who failed to pay a premium were required to wait an additional six months to reenroll. New income reporting requirements were added, failure to verify these changes resulting in the loss of eligibility. Clients faced a new $60 processing fee to pay for their renewal in the program, which previous evidence suggests will reduce Medicaid take-up among individuals with low incomes.[46] These kinds of fees are both burdens and actual additional financial costs that have to be absorbed by applicants.

Walker's need to rely on administrative burdens to reduce access to Medicaid was made less pressing by the 2012 Supreme Court decision in *National Federation of Independent Businesses v. Sibelius*, which gave states more discretion in determining eligibility levels than was allowed in the ACA. Rather than adding administrative burdens to restrict access to the program, they simply altered eligibility criteria to restrict access. Governor Walker rejected new federal funding from the ACA, reducing Medicaid access to citizens above the federal poverty line. The state's 2013–2015 budget reduced maximum income eligibility levels for BadgerCare Plus from 200 to 100 percent of the FPL for parents (approximately ninety-seven thousands parents would lose coverage), and would not expand the Medicaid program to cover childless adults above 100 percent of the FPL.[47]

These changes quickly had an effect. In 2008, Wisconsin was sixth in the nation in insured children. By 2014, it had dropped to sixteenth. Other states caught up and surpassed Wisconsin's participation rate in Medicaid and CHIP. After the passage of the 2013 budget, Wisconsin's participation rate actually fell, even as all neighboring states who had accepted the ACA saw increases in coverage.[48]

A decline in health insurance coverage created a political risk for Walker in the 2014 election year. The creation of a federal health insurance marketplace through the ACA offered an opportunity to offset losses in state-provided insurance. Although his predecessors had used outreach to expand BadgerCare and BadgerCare Plus, Walker now used this tool to direct Wisconsinites to the federal marketplace. Walker's Department of Health Services maintained relationships with third parties who helped individuals gain coverage via the federal marketplace, and ACA navigators were given support by the federal government for outreach. Walker benefited from existing networks of public and private health-care providers, local governments, community organizations, tribal representatives, and others. These groups formed regional enrollment networks dedicated to maintaining outreach. The Milwaukee network alone involved a hundred public and private organizations. The Department of Health Services disseminated Milwaukee's network as a model for other parts of the state to follow and helped to coordinate other networks.[49]

However, other parts of the Walker administration sometimes worked at cross-purposes with the outreach goal. The Office of Consumer Insurance placed extra requirements on navigators, increasing learning costs, and publicly stated that it believed that the costs of marketplace plans would soar in the future. Doyle and Thompson tried to simplify branding and send positive messages about health insurance, but the Office of Consumer Insurance described the federal exchange as the provider of "public assistance" products.[50] The different actions by the Department of Health Services and the Office of Consumer Insurance reflected the paradox of Walker's position: he was a vocal critic of Obamacare yet relied on it to maintain health insurance coverage for many in his state.

The Walker administration did reduce administrative burdens for some groups, allowing administrative renewal for select low-risk BadgerCare Plus, SNAP, and Medicaid cases. According to a Department of Health Services operations memo, "the primary purpose of the administrative renewal project is to increase program integrity by focusing eligibility workers on higher-risk renewals."[51] For administrative renewals, department staff identified cases that are highly unlikely to lose eligibility and allow them to renew based on state data. Perhaps because they faced lower burdens, the participation of children in families with income below the FPL actually increased in the fifteen months after the Walker administration implemented new eligibility standards, but this gain (15,500) was more than offset by declines of children with families with income above the new eligibility levels (24,900).[52]

The election of President Trump offered Governor Walker a more friendly audience for waiver requests that would increase burdens. Walker proposed that some Medicaid recipients be subject to drug testing. No other state has done this with Medicaid recipients, but it is consistent with Walker's prior efforts to add drug-testing requirements to other public benefits such as SNAP (for detail on problems with drug testing in SNAP, see chapter 6). In Wisconsin, drug testing is required only if an applicant admits to using drugs. The proposal for small premiums, ranging from $4 to $8 a month for those with incomes approximately between $6,000 and $12,000 a year, will likely prove more burdensome.[53] Individuals with such low incomes often lack checking accounts or credit cards making payment practically difficult. In addition, it opens the door to losing coverage via nonpayment.[54]

Finally, Governor Walker sought a work requirement for Medicaid recipients who do not qualify based on age, pregnancy, or disability. It would require childless adults below 100 percent of the poverty level to be employed at least eighty hours each month. This requirement would be implemented after those subjected to the requirement had not been employed for four years. Such employment requirements are, strictly speaking, a new condition on eligibility, but they also add significant compliance costs for all participants who must verify they are fulfilling the requirement.[55] Even exceptions from work requirements for those unable to work because of illness or disability impose new compliance costs to verify that status. The process of clarifying who is subject to these changes and then ensuring compliance could create "a rat's nest of paperwork, red tape, bureaucracy for people," according to Bobby Peterson, executive director ABC Health, a public-interest law firm.[56]

All such changes are ultimately subject to approval by the Centers for Medicare and Medicaid Services (CMS) via the waiver process. The Trump administration proved willing to allow governors to add new burdens to Medicaid. President Trump's CMS quickly approved Medicaid work requirements in Kentucky, Arkansas, Indiana, and New Hampshire.[57]

The addition of work requirements face legal challenges. Opponents argue that the CMS is using the waiver process to undermine the statutory intent of Medicaid, which is to improve health outcomes by providing health insurance to those who cannot afford it.[58] The Trump administration claimed that the work requirements would improve health outcomes because those who are working tend to enjoy better health.[59] This argument, however, ignores underlying health issues among those who are already on Medicaid. Moreover, no evidence suggests that if administrative burdens result in people losing public health insurance, those people enjoy better health. Alice Hoffman, a professor of law at the University of Pennsylvania and expert in health-care issues notes, "There is . . . good evidence that such requirements add enrollment hurdles that cause people to lose eligibility."[60] In short, a central part of the legal challenges is that administrative burdens have such policy importance that they undermine the core goals of Medicaid.

Conclusion

Wisconsin's implementation of BadgerCare Plus was the culmination of a steady pattern of state innovation to shift administrative burdens in Medicaid and other state health insurance away from beneficiaries and onto the state. The Wisconsin case not only shows that administrative burdens can reduce access to health insurance but also points to concrete ways that states can reduce burden on citizens to increase enrollment, including auto-enrollment, simpler forms, online information and application systems, and better outreach.

The case also illustrates the interactive nature of efforts to reduce burdens. For example, an online enrollment tool worked hand in hand with aggressive outreach and presumptive eligibility to capture difficult-to-reach citizens. The shifting of burdens onto the state required more government capacity but led to reduced administrative burden for applicants and beneficiaries. In sum, if states want to maximize enrollment, they need to find ways to shift burdens away from beneficiaries.

This case also illustrates ways in which the politics of burdens play out away from the legislature, within the executive branch. Consequential decisions were made with minimal external consultation. Actors at the state and federal level sought to alter the level of burden to pursue broader policy goals. Although delinking Medicaid from other welfare programs allowed Republicans like Governor Thompson to embrace Medicaid as a form of health insurance rather than welfare, partisan attitudes hardened over time.[61] Governor Doyle favored broader access like Governor Thompson. Governor Walker identified program size and fraud as a rationale to increase burdens on state residents. A cross-state analysis reflects this trend: compliance burdens in Medicaid application forms are higher under unified Republican control.[62]

Any discussion of the politics of administrative burden in an intergovernmental program must also consider the role of the federal government.[63] The creation and expansion of BadgerCare occurred under federal waivers from standard rules. Federal regulators pushed Governor Thompson to reduce burden with the creation of BadgerCare and supported Governor Doyle's reforms. Governor Walker was largely stymied to implement the changes he wanted by the Obama administration but found a more willing partner with the Trump administration.

THE EARNED INCOME TAX CREDIT

8

BENEFITING BUSINESS BY REDUCING BURDENS ON THE WORKING POOR

Milton Friedman, the Nobel Prize–winning champion of the Chicago school of free market economics, was the unlikely proponent of what became the largest income support policy for the poor in the United States. Friedman first proposed a negative income tax in *Capitalism and Freedom* in 1962, seeing it as a tool to displace other welfare programs while encouraging labor market participation.[1] The negative income tax became the inspiration for the first attempt to pass a wage subsidy, President Richard Nixon's failed Family Assistance Plan (FAP). From the ashes of this failure, the Earned Income Tax Credit (EITC) was born.

The EITC is a government-funded wage subsidy for low-income workers. The program defies many of the expectations about administrative burdens laid out in the preceding chapters. Whereas other programs targeted at the poor have fraught histories layered with barriers that reduce take-up, the EITC is a large program, especially generous for recipients with children, with high take-up. In 2015, almost thirty-two million people benefited from the EITC, claiming $67 billion. The EITC achieves an estimated take-up rate of 80 percent of eligible beneficiaries, higher than the 30 to 60 percent typical of means-tested programs.[2] We describe the benefits of the EITC for employment, poverty, and child well-being and explain why the program has low burdens relative to many of the other policy areas we examine.

Although not immune to partisan criticism and facing a growing concern about fraud, the EITC enjoys strong bipartisan support. As a result, one party has not systematically tried to layer unnecessary burdens onto the program to hamper access in a way that is evident in nearly all the prior cases discussed in this book. The chapter explains why, supplementing standard explanations for the success of the EITC. One common explanation for the EITC's trenchant bipartisan support is that it reinforces political values that appeal across party lines. By tying aid to work, the EITC largely avoids traditional conservative critiques of welfare.[3] Another common explanation is that the EITC is concealed within the tax system, which reduces its visibility—the public simply does not understand it as well as other policies and does not equate tax reimbursements with direct cash payments to poor people.[4]

Although useful, these arguments are incomplete, failing to appreciate the degree to which path dependency and the political influence of third parties have shaped the program. To understand these factors, we need to trace the history of the program and focus on the politically powerful stakeholders, beyond direct beneficiaries, that it serves.

From an employer perspective, the EITC is a subsidy for low wages paid for by taxpayers, whereas increases in the minimum wage are borne directly by business owners. As business interests realized that the EITC offered an attractive political alternative to minimum wage increases, they became strong supporters, helping ensure a level of bipartisan support that eluded other targeted programs. In this respect, the EITC illustrates how program stakeholders played a role as policy influencers to protect the program.

Employer benefits from the EITC depend on its being accessible to their workers. Employers and groups such as the Chamber of Commerce have therefore worked to expand the reach of the program by reducing learning and compliance costs for beneficiaries. Another vital interest group is the tax preparation industry, which has structured its business model to take advantage of the EITC and has argued for its expansion. Tax preparers shift EITC burdens away from recipients and onto themselves in exchange for a fee. At the same time, the tax preparation industry has lobbied to maintain enough documentation requirements to ensure that the EITC remains burdensome enough that low-income workers seek professional tax preparation help.

The efforts of third parties therefore make the program feel less burdensome than other programs aimed at the poor, especially when beneficiaries are willing to pay for help. An administrative explanation also helps explain why the burdens for the EITC are not higher. The EITC is federally controlled program, its benefits distributed through the Internal Revenue Service (IRS), covered by clear rules that do not vary by state or locality. The federal character and standardized approach prevents states from layering additional compliance costs on the program, thereby closing one route to administrative burdens observed in intergovernmental programs such as Medicaid. The IRS uses the tools of tax compliance to deal with risk of error and fraud. These include cross-checks, reliance on administrative data, and ex post compliance, tools that are less burdensome than ex ante requirements that typify programs delivered by welfare agencies. Over time, the IRS has been criticized by conservatives for being too lax in its implementation and has added other tools to address fraud, but it has largely maintained a tax compliance and—by extension— a low-burden approach even as the program has become larger.

A Policy Silver Bullet

More work means a higher EITC refund up to an income ceiling, after which the value of the credit declines. In 2017, the ceiling ranged from between $39,300 to $53,500 depending on family status. It is primarily targeted at families with children, but a small credit is available for low-income individuals without dependents, and the income ceiling ranges from about $15,000 to $20,000. The EITC has historically been a refundable tax credit, claimed via tax returns; it is different from tax breaks such as home mortgage deductions because individuals can, and most do, receive back more than their federal income tax bill.[5]

In many respects, the EITC seems like a policy silver bullet. Its administrative costs are less than 1 percent, rivaling Social Security for efficiency. EITC spending has been shown to generate multiple benefits: increased labor market participation, poverty reduction, and, improved health and education outcomes for participating families.

Economists have studied the EITC for a generation, repeatedly documenting a large positive effect on employment outcomes.[6] Conservatives generally criticize welfare for discouraging work but cannot raise the same objection to the EITC, which significantly increases labor force participation, especially among poor single mothers.[7]

The EITC has more effectively pulled poor women into the labor market than the elimination of Aid to Families with Dependent Children (AFDC) or other changes to welfare rules. Between 1986 and 2000, the labor force participation of single mothers who dropped out of high school rose from 46 percent to 73 percent. The labor force participation of high school graduate single mothers rose from 76 percent to 89 percent.[8] Between 1986 and 1996, EITC expansions accounted for more than half of the increase in single mothers' employment.[9] Between 1993 and 1999, the EITC explains 34 percent of the increase in single mothers' labor force participation, whereas cuts to other forms of welfare account for just 19 percent of that change.[10] One study found that every additional $1,000 in EITC generosity results in a 7 percentage point increase in employment for single mothers.[11]

The EITC reduces poverty on a grand scale. Between 1999 and 2016, spending on the EITC increased from $32 billion to more than $67 billion.[12] At its peak, between the 1970s and the mid-1990s, federal and state spending on AFDC—also targeted at working-age Americans—averaged around $30 billion annually. The EITC has reduced income insecurity for many of the poorest Americans. In 2014, the national poverty rate was 15 percent. Without the EITC (along with the refundable portion of the child tax credit), the poverty rate would have been more than 18 percent. The effect on children is even higher—without these tax credits, the child poverty rate would be a third higher, 24 percent rather than 18 percent.[13] Every $1,000 increase in the EITC benefits leads to 9 percentage point reduction in poverty among the poorest families.[14] A growing literature suggests that by supplementing the income of the poor, the EITC also has measurable effects on child health, cognitive abilities, and educational performance.[15]

Burdens in the EITC

Saying that the EITC has low burdens does not mean that it has no burdens. Estimates of take-up of the EITC vary moderately. An early estimate is that between 80 and 86 percent of eligible families received the EITC in 1990.[16] The IRS has calculated that between 82 and 87 percent of those eligible claimed the benefit in 1996.

Table 8.1 *Administrative Burdens in the EITC*

	Types of costs	Reduced by
Learning costs	· Awareness of program, information on eligibility, and size of benefits · Awareness of information needed for audit process	· IRS reminders on eligibility · Employers, nonprofits, and tax preparers, increase awareness of program, provide support during audits
Compliance costs	· Paperwork requirements no more extensive than traditional tax return · Financial costs of paying for tax preparation services · Documentation required for audits	· No state variation · Little risk of arbitrary decisions or discrimination by caseworkers · Voluntary and paid tax preparers help with compliance and audits
Psychological costs	· Minimal	· No requirement to engage with welfare workers

Source: Authors' compilation.

Other estimates suggest that nonparticipation is higher, between 20 and 25 percent.[17] In 2012, the IRS estimated an 80 percent participation rate.

Table 8.1 summarizes the basic costs EITC claimants face. The level of learning costs are reflected in the fact that surveys have found that 43 percent of those eligible were unaware of the program, that 33 percent believed incorrectly they were ineligible, and that respondents significantly underestimated the benefits they would receive.[18] These costs limit participation in the EITC, because field experiments show that the provision of reminders with information—such as an estimate of potential benefits—increases take-up.[19] The EITC form itself is only a page long, minimizing compliance costs, but the explanation of how to determine eligibility is thirty-seven pages. Even among those who are aware of the program, many do not understand how it works or how changes in their status might affect benefits.[20] One field experiment that provided a two-minute personalized explanation of the EITC led to a small increase in benefits claimed during their next refund.[21] Learning costs are likely most demanding for households in which the parents of a child are not living together and parents need to determine eligibility for claiming the qualifying child. About one in three EITC claimants are new each year—meaning that they face greater learning costs than those already familiar with the program.[22]

Given these learning costs, how does the EITC maintain such a high participation rate? When the program was relatively small, the IRS simply provided the refund for filers who appeared eligible.[23] Such an approach offered a de facto form of auto-enrollment for at least those who completed a tax form, placing a minimal burden on claimants to learn about the program. But even as the IRS moved away from this approach in the early 1990s, participation has remained high. In part, this is because a variety of actors work to reduce learning and compliance costs. The IRS sends reminders about the EITC to those who appear to be eligible, which has been shown to generate a 41 percent jump in take-up among initial nonclaimants.[24] It has worked to improve those reminders, learning from experiments that show that reminders featuring simplified language, with estimated benefits, generate greater take-up (see figure 8.1). The IRS helps in other ways too, sponsoring voluntary programs that provide free tax help, thereby reducing compliance costs. Regional offices feature a Stakeholder Partnerships, Education, and Communication Office that works with outreach coalitions.

Nongovernmental third parties have played an important role in further minimizing burdens. Nonprofits and advocacy groups have worked to publicize the program, thereby reducing learning costs. The Center on Budget and Policy Priorities develops outreach materials that can be used for marketing campaigns. At a local level, successful outreach involves a coalition of IRS staff, local government leaders, nonprofits, employers, faith-based organizations, foundations, and voluntary tax preparers.[25] Coalitions that feature free tax return services can also reduce the compliance costs of completing a tax return.

The basic design of the program helps to minimize psychological costs. That the EITC is a tax credit resulting from work minimizes the stigma of participating in the program. Field experiments that sought to reduce the stigma of the EITC—by sending mailings to eligible

Figure 8.1 *IRS Simplified Reminders to Potential EITC Beneficiaries*

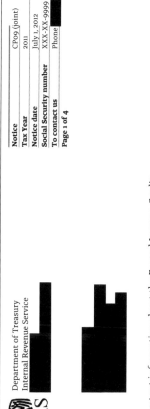

Department of Treasury
Internal Revenue Service

IRS

Notice	CP09 (joint)
Tax Year	2011
Notice date	July 1, 2012
Social Security number	XXX-XX-9999
To contact us	Phone
Page 1 of 4	

Important information about the Earned Income Credit

You may be eligible for a refund of up to $ 5,751

Our records show that you may be eligible for the Earned Income Credit (EIC), but didn't claim it on your 2011 tax form. Depending on your earnings and eligibility, your benefit can be up to $5,751.

Do not discard or overlook this notice because you may be entitled to some additional money.

Summary

The credit, which can be up to $5,751, is for certain people who have worked and earned income. Please complete the worksheet on Page 3 to determine if you're eligible for the credit.

What you need to do

Complete the Earned Income Credit Worksheet on page 3.

If the worksheet confirms that you're eligible for the credit
- Sign and date the attached worksheet, and mail it to us in the enclosed envelope.

Source: IRS 2018.

respondents emphasizing higher peer use or by framing benefits as a reward for hard work—found little effect, suggesting, perhaps, that there is little stigma to reduce.[26] Indeed, the primary sponsor of the EITC in Congress, Louisiana Senator Russell Long, framed it as a "work bonus" for the "deserving poor."[27] Qualitative research shows that beneficiaries also adopt this framing: those who have been both on welfare and the EITC see welfare "benefits are distributed via a stigmatized system in which clients are, by definition, violating social norms of work and self-sufficiency.... In contrast, respondents believe the EITC is a deserved reward for hard work."[28] EITC recipients value not just the financial relief that comes with their refund check but also the sense of social inclusion it provides. It is seen as an earned reward that allows recipients to spend on special treats or indulge their children like "real Americans."

The structure of the EITC reduces the potential for psychological costs in other ways. As a federal program, the rules are consistent and recipients cannot be denied benefits based on arbitrary decisions by caseworkers (also reducing the potential for state-by-state variation in compliance costs). Traditional forms of welfare have long been used to control family and sexual morality.[29] For example, at varying points, AFDC receipt could be rescinded if single mothers were found to have men living with them, and some states require recipients to provide paternity declarations to receive welfare.[30] Such intrusive questioning is absent from the EITC. For EITC claimants, there is no welfare office to visit, no concern that bureaucrats will treat them unfairly, and no incentive to play a role perceived to engender more sympathetic treatment. Claimants either fill out their own tax returns, or work with tax preparer, where they are more likely to be treated with the courtesy of a paying customer rather than the suspicion of an unwanted claimant.[31]

The History of the EITC

The roots of business support for the EITC, especially in the low-wage labor sector, can be found in its pro-employment origins. A negative income tax was discussed during the Johnson administration, though Johnson himself preferred more explicit pro-work polices such as job training.[32] President Nixon enjoyed initial public support for a negative income tax in his proposed Family Assistance Plan but was stymied in Congress. One of FAP's most vocal opponents, Louisiana Democrat Senator Russell Long, became the architect of the EITC. The critical difference between the two approaches for Long was that the EITC included no minimum income guarantee and served only as a wage subsidy.[33] In this respect, the failure of FAP and creation of the EITC represented a turning point in legislative debates about aiding the poor in America, "a transitional period between the perceived social ills of poverty on the one hand and welfare dependency on the other."[34]

Southern congressmen like Long were among the strongest opponents of FAP. Their opposition, to some extent, reflected the structural or indirect influence of business. FAP's demise started in the Senate Finance Committee, chaired by Long. He and other Southern Democrats never allowed FAP to exit the committee and reach the Senate floor. This was partly a function of racism, given that many blacks would stand to receive the benefits. But just as early versions of Social Security excluded agricultural and household labor, the opposition to the FAP reflected a desire to maintain the structural pattern of labor in the South. The majority of black Southerners were employed in jobs with such low wages that the minimum income guarantee, set at half of the poverty level, would be roughly equivalent to their wages.[35] FAP would either push them out of the labor market or pressure employers to raise wages. As Representative Phil Landrum, a Georgia Democrat, argued, "There's not going to be anybody left to roll those wheelbarrows and press those shirts."[36] Senator Long concurred, arguing, "35 percent of the entire population of the State of Mississippi would be drawing welfare payments from the federal government.... I do not see any enthusiasm coming from Mississippi for this program. The reason is that those people ... fear that they are going to have grave difficulty ever getting people to work in Mississippi once one third of the whole population is on welfare, with the rest of them saying, why do we not quit work and go on welfare too?"[37]

In opposing FAP, Long distinguished between the "deserving" and the "undeserving" poor. The undeserving engaged in both fraud of the welfare system and "malingering" that could be cured by "workfare rather than welfare."[38] They robbed the truly deserving poor—those who were unemployable, or those engaged in gainful employment. Long was particularly worried about the impact of FAP on the supply of domestic laborers and proposed a tax deduction for those who employed domestic servants.[39]

Business had a mixed perspective on the FAP. Manufacturers did not oppose it because their unionized employees were paid well above the minimum guarantee.[40] On the other hand, the minimum income guarantee drew opposition from the Chamber of Commerce. The Chamber represented the growing small business and service industry, which was becoming more important as manufacturing declined. These businesses largely employed low-wage labor, and were convinced that the minimum income guarantee would dramatically reduce work incentives and "put 50 percent of the population on welfare."[41] The work subsidy components of FAP that looked most like the EITC were largely unexamined because businesses had not determined the likely impact. The idea of a negative income tax was relatively new, not well understood, and accepted only to the extent that it did not hurt existing interests.

After defeating the FAP, Long created a proposal for what would become the EITC.[42] Long argued that the solution to the working poor was "if we simply supplemented their wage by passing it through their employer to get it to them.... we would know then that the people we are helping are people who are working and we are actually getting these people to work."[43] Long crafted the EITC as an incentive to work, hoping that it would replace welfare, in particular the AFDC.[44] He wanted to "prevent the taxing of people onto the welfare rolls."[45] The EITC provisions were included in a routine tax bill that passed in 1975 with little fanfare and almost no opposition. Long cut the aspects of the FAP that most concerned fellow Southern Democrats and businesses.[46] The EITC was originally a temporary measure, not becoming a permanent part of the tax code until 1978. The modest size and temporary nature of the original version of the EITC, embedded in the tax bill, drew much less attention than the FAP proposal.

EITC EXPANSIONS

If businesses were not initially champions of the EITC, they soon became so. What accounts for this transformation? To answer this question—and by extension to understand how the EITC has been able to resist red tape—requires looking closely at how it has built its broad base of political support.

Policies are often path dependent—as they are implemented, beneficiaries fight to defend and expand them.[47] The EITC provides an example of where business beneficiaries belatedly grasped benefits but became powerful supporters of the program once they did. Although business interests had strong beliefs about the costs of the minimum wage, they had little sense of how a wage subsidy would work. Thus, when the small-scale EITC was finally implemented, market actors and policymakers began to learn about its benefits. The 1980s and 1990 saw a shift in business understanding of the EITC and its potential to further their interests. Policymakers first began to see the EITC as an alternative to raising the minimum wage, which—though immensely popular among the general public and cheap for government to implement—was fiercely opposed by business. Businesses, and particularly their lobbying organizations, came to understand that the EITC could be used as a way to fend off minimum wage increases. In short, as path dependency predicts, the policy created its own supporter.

After Nixon, the Carter administration saw the EITC both as a tool to reduce poverty and as an alternative to traditional welfare, and so proposed expanding the program as part of a larger welfare reform package.[48] The broader reform struggled, but the EITC saw a modest expansion and was made permanent under Carter, demonstrating a bipartisan appeal that exempted it from welfare retrenchment efforts pursued by Carter and Reagan.

The first major expansion of the EITC occurred in 1986, as part of the Tax Reform Act. Analyses pointed to the tax burden on the working poor, and recommended expansions of the EITC. Conservatives who opposed the minimum wage were able to support the EITC in the name of tax fairness. The act indexed the EITC to inflation, while raising the maximum value to just above the 1975 value. Overall, six million low-income people benefited from the policy change, which doubled the number of beneficiaries.[49]

As Democrats pushed for greater increases in the minimum wage, which was losing value due to inflation, the EITC increasingly became the go-to business-friendly alternative. Republicans

202 | ADMINISTRATIVE BURDEN

fought off minimum wage increases until President George H.W.
Bush promised an increase in his 1988 election campaign. His proposed increase was far less than Democratic proposals, but he
also argued for a significant expansion of the EITC. After vetoing
a $4.55 minimum wage, Bush got largely what he wanted—a more
modest increase to $4.25 per hour, followed by a $12 billion expansion
of the EITC over five years.[50]

When President Clinton came into office in 1993, two major items
on his agenda were the expansion of the EITC and a further increase
in the minimum wage.[51] The National Association of Manufacturers,
the National Restaurant Association, and the National Federation
of Independent Businesses quickly began organizing their members
for a fight over the minimum wage.[52] Part of their lobbying strategy
was to argue that the EITC was a better, more targeted approach than
increasing the minimum wage.[53] As a result, by early 1993, Clinton
continued to discuss the EITC as part of his economic plan, but the
minimum wage had been relegated to the back burner. Clinton succeeded with a compromise proposal that added six million people
to the program and raised the maximum credit from $1,300 a year
for families with two children to $3,554 by 1996, when the changes
had been fully phased in.[54] Childless earners also became eligible for
the credit. Total spending would be $20.8 billion over five years.[55]

THE ROLE OF BUSINESS INTERESTS

By the time Clinton promised to "end welfare as we know it," the
EITC had become larger than the AFDC. The rise of the EITC and subsequent decline of the AFDC reflected a shift to a workfare approach
envisioned by Senator Long, redefining welfare away from meeting
needs and toward rewarding work.[56] Businesses helped this process
with their opposition to the minimum wage. The EITC allowed
politicians to address the needs of low-income workers without
aggravating business interests. By the early 1990s, however, lobbyists
for business groups were directly supporting the EITC, particularly
those that employed many low-wage workers. They began to see
it not only as a tool to counteract the minimum wage but also as a
policy that directly benefited them.

Employers have a strong incentive to encourage employees to sign up for the EITC, and by extension have an incentive to make sure they know the program exists. The Institute for a Competitive Workforce, a nonprofit affiliate of the Chamber of Commerce, has promoted the EITC to its members. The institute argues that the primary problem with the EITC is that too few are receiving it because of the learning costs: "The biggest challenge of any campaign centered on EITC continues to be awareness. Nationally, 15 percent to 20 percent of eligible filers simply do not know about the credit, don't understand how it works or how to file for it, or have an incorrect understanding of its benefit."[57] To increase take-up, the institute encouraged members to work with an outreach coalition that would help them reach low-income workers, including local IRS officials, free tax preparers, local nonprofits, church groups, and labor unions. With such partners, an outreach campaign "can range from a simple effort to raise public awareness to an in-depth initiative that not only informs families about EITC but also helps them claim and make the most out of this benefit."[58] Put another way, employers can use outreach to reduce both learning and compliance costs by helping eligible claimants complete the application process.

Low-wage employers drew on research and support from think tanks to argue for the EITC and against the minimum wage. For example, the Employment Policies Institute (EPI) is a ready source of information for reporters or politicians looking for a critical perspective on minimum wage.[59] EPI has written hundreds of editorials for national and local newspapers arguing for the EITC as a direct alternative to the minimum wage. A sample headline reads, "Expand tax credit instead of raising the wage." EPI's research director appears on national television and the organization is effective at putting research reports with the patina of scholarly credibility into the hands of policymakers. In some cases, it hires academic researchers whose findings align with EPI's perspective.

To suggest that the restaurant industry and other low-wage employers are fortunate to have such aggressive and capable advocates would be to understate their involvement and investment in the creation of such advocates in the first place. EPI simply would not exist without industry support. EPI describes itself as a "non-profit research organization dedicated to studying public policy issues surrounding employment growth. In particular, EPI, focuses on issues that affect entry level employment."[60] The nonprofit status offers a helpful tax subsidy, but it also offers its funders anonymity.

EPI was created in 1991 by Richard Berman, a longtime lobbyist for restaurant, hotel, alcohol, and tobacco companies. Although nominally independent, EPI remains a creature of, and financial resource for, Berman and Company, Berman's public relations firm. EPI is only one of many nonprofit think tanks that Berman has created to generate pro-industry research for the agricultural, restaurant, and beverage industries. The nonprofits, in turn, funnel industry contributions for their work back to Berman by paying his firm for basic services such as staff, administrative help, and rent. For example, in 2012, EPI paid Berman and Company $1.1 million, or 44 percent of its total budget.[61] EPI has no actual staff, or offices; even its research director is an employee of Berman and Company. Berman has estimated that 70 percent of his public relations firm's revenue comes from the nonprofits he has created.[62] In op-eds, EPI sometimes notes that it receives funding from "businesses, foundations, and individuals," but offers little additional acknowledgment that their funding depends on pursuing an industry perspective. In 2012, EPI's $2.4 million in donations came from just eleven contributors.

One lobbyist asked to comment on EPI noted, "Once you have the study, you can point to it to prove your case—even if you paid to get it written."[63] In an irony so delicious that only a restaurant industry lobbyist could have cooked it up, EPI specializes in attacking the biases of researchers who have argued for the minimum wage. For example, in the 1990s, EPI ran attacks on the Princeton economists David Card and David Kreuger, whose work showed that increases in the minimum wage had little effect on employment. A sample op-ed was titled "Minimum Honesty on the Minimum Wage." As late as 2011, EPI was still taking the time to call reporters to attack Krueger's record when he was nominated to chair the Council of Economic Advisers.[64]

The largest business proponent of the EITC is the Chamber of Commerce, also citing it as a better alternative to the minimum wage. The Chamber of Commerce has actively encouraged members to help their employees sign up for the program. In testimony for the

Immigration, Border Security and Citizenship Subcommittee of the Senate Committee on the Judiciary, the president of the Chamber of Commerce, Thomas Donohue, stated that one of the Chamber's activities was "informing businesses on using the Earned Income Tax Credit as a retention tool to support entry-level workers."[65]

Regional Chamber of Commerce leaders point to the EITC when writing op-eds in local papers that oppose minimum wage increases.[66] The Chamber of Commerce has also promoted the EITC to its members. An affiliate of the Chamber of Commerce, the Institute for a Competitive Workforce, shares publications and runs courses to provide information about the EITC. In one report, it noted that most hourly workers are paid $10 or less: "To have unhappy and unstable employees is to have unproductive and unstable workplaces. And no employer wants that."[67] In explaining "the case for business involvement" with the EITC, the institute pointed to the usefulness of the EITC in expanding the workforce and reducing turnover: "Through EITC, employers can potentially raise their employees' wages by $1 to $2 per hour at no cost. . . . By introducing employees to these benefits, businesses help their employees—and help themselves."[68]

More traditional lobbying organizations have also come out in favor the EITC. In a House Committee on Ways and Means hearing on the EITC, the American Hotel & Motel Association, which represents most of the hotel industry, strongly endorsed the EITC: "We believe the EITC has been a valuable tool, targeted to low-wage workers to provide a supplement as they learn, train, and begin their climb up the economic ladder. . . . As opposed to an increase in the minimum wage, which is spread broadly across workers whether or not they may need the increase, the EITC specifically helps workers whose earning level and family status warrant support."[69]

The incentives for employers and their interest groups are clear. Employers must cover the costs of minimum wage increases, but citizens bear all the costs of the EITC. Further, the EITC generates some distinct benefits for businesses. Nearly 20 percent of beneficiaries use their EITC refunds to facilitate their labor force participation—such as buying clothes and cars for employment.[70] To the extent that the effects of the EITC on wages has been studied, they confirm a pattern of restraining real wages, effectively subsidizing employer's contributions. A 10 percent increase in EITC generosity is associated with a 5 percent fall in wages for high school dropouts, a 2 percent loss for those with just a high school diploma, but negligible effects for those with higher education.[71]

THE ROLE OF THE TAX PREPARATION INDUSTRY

In addition to low-wage employers, private tax preparers have been instrumental in facilitating access to the EITC. The tax preparation industry has championed the EITC as a policy and facilitated access to the benefits. Its motivation is not based on any overriding conviction about the burdens citizens should face in the tax system but instead reflects simple profit incentives. This motivation has also resulted in the introduction of burdens to maintain and maximize revenues from EITC beneficiaries.

Even if the beneficiary does not know the EITC by name, tax preparers can help ensure they receive the credit. The tax preparation industry has designed a business model based on reducing the burdens that citizens face in accessing the EITC. They have marketed the program to clients, built new offices in low-income neighborhoods, and partnered in outreach campaigns to educate individuals about their eligibility.[72] The tax industry reduces learning costs by marketing the EITC as a benefit and ensuring that eligible claimants are aware of it. The industry reduces compliance costs by helping the claimant work through the documentation. The availability of electronic applications expanded the use of the EITC and reduced compliance costs. States that allowed electronic forms saw a spike in the use of the EITC, especially benefiting individuals who might otherwise not file tax returns.[73]

The EITC broadened the customer base for tax preparation firms. The tax industry developed partnerships with the IRS to pioneer electronic returns in 1985, and electronic filing was first made available only through professional tax preparers.[74] The fees charged for tax preparation represent a monetary compliance cost that many applicants bear in order to navigate the EITC.

Another profit opportunity for tax preparers is to broker loans from banks that they can sell to filers based on their anticipated return. The IRS initially shared filer debt information to tax preparation firms. This allowed these firms to offer refund anticipation loans to customers without the risk that other creditors could claim the refund. Although refund anticipation loans might be repaid in just a couple of weeks, the associated fees made them highly profitable. At one point, such quick-refund products accounted for 30 percent of the total revenue for Jackson Hewitt Tax Service. IRS pronouncements on their willingness to facilitate such programs caused enormous swings in the stock market value of these firms.[75] In 2009, 64 percent of EITC recipients relied on such loans.[76]

The IRS stopped providing taxpayer debt information in 2010, making refund anticipation loans less attractive. Tax preparation firms still sell a similar product called refund anticipation checks, where they set up a temporary bank account in which the refund is deposited. In addition to the preparation fee, filers also pay for this service and may face additional check-cashing fees.

The industry has lobbied to keep or even expand the compliance burdens in the EITC. It has actively opposed proposals for return-free filing that would eliminate the need for most citizens to prepare taxes, as described in the introduction. The tax industry has also argued for keeping EITC complex enough that their services are necessary. H&R Block has lobbied Congress to increase the length of the form, despite the fact that the additional questions proposed are redundant, seeking information already provided elsewhere in the tax returns. Such changes are a definitional example of red tape—adding burdens without any clear benefit, making forms longer and more challenging without providing additional value. In a letter to the IRS, H&R Block identified a fundamental concern to justify more complex forms: "in tax season 2008, 28 percent of EITC filers self-prepared their returns, but just four years later, in tax season 2012, 38 percent of EITC filers self-prepared their returns."[77] More and more EITC filers are forgoing professional tax preparation services, but the prospect of facing a daunting array of compliance costs might bring some of them back.

Balancing Fraud and Access

H&R Block has justified making the EITC more complex by promoting the impression of fraud in the EITC. It has created a research institute, the Tax Institute, which offers pseudo-scientific analyses that reinforce the notion of fraud in the program.[78] For example, one report relied on a telephone survey to offer a series of claims about citizen beliefs: that self-filers were more likely to commit fraud than professional tax preparers; that individuals should be willing to provide more documentation to combat fraud; and that professional tax preparers and self-filers should be held to the same standards. Relying on citizen's beliefs to document the risk of fraud is simply a poor evidentiary base to make such judgments when actual fraud can be directly studied based on tax records. Such analyses show more errors on the part of tax preparers than self-filers, with over-claiming of returns especially high for tax preparers not associated with national firms.[79]

It might seem puzzling that the same industry that has championed the EITC is also raising the specter of fraud, but the tactic is designed to appeal to a growing Republican critique of the program. Although the EITC originated as a work bonus that Russell Long would see targeted to the deserving poor, it came to face the criticisms that Long had directed toward welfare programs: that it is too large and beset by fraud. One often-cited example is a 2002 *Wall Street Journal* editorial that lampooned EITC recipients as "Lucky Duckies" who not only paid no income taxes but received money back from the government. In 2012, presidential candidate Mitt Romney was also implicitly criticizing the EITC when he complained that 47 percent of Americans paid no income taxes.

How serious is fraud? Before we address this question, it is important to offer some context. Misreporting in the tax system is not limited to the poor. About 6 percent of tax revenue lost due to individual tax noncompliance is due to EITC overpayments, relative to 52 percent lost due to individuals' underreporting business income.[80] Any serious attempt to deal with the tax gap—the gap between actual and reported liabilities—would focus on both these areas, or at least start with the area of largest noncompliance. Instead, despite repeated calls for additional resources to address the tax gap, the IRS has seen its funding cut and efforts to curb the tax gap derailed. At the same time, it has faced marked pressures to focus on the EITC relative to other areas of noncompliance, the director of the IRS stating in 2014 that "One of the biggest enforcement priorities for us in this area is the EITC."[81]

The IRS has reported overpayment rates above 20 percent based on random audits of EITC claimants. But these numbers give an exaggerated impression of the extent of the problem. An overpayment is determined if the claimant cannot provide adequate documentation for the audit. The audit process is one more venue where administrative burdens come into play in the EITC, and indeed is more burdensome than other aspects of the program.

The IRS uses automated filters to identity potentially erroneous or incomplete assessments.[82] The audits occur by mail, the IRS sending multiple letters to seek more information. That the audited population often has limited literacy and transient housing makes the risk of nonresponse quite high, as well as making it difficult for this population to provide sufficient documentation about questions such as residency.[83] A study of those audited found that 25 percent did not understand they were being audited and 40 percent did not understand what the IRS was asking them.[84] The Government Accountability Office estimated that it takes an average of thirty hours for individuals to respond to the audit, costing them about $500 of their time.[85] Claimants can seek an in-person trial, but courts may be far from them—they are located in seventy-four cities, and the trial could take more than a year to resolve. The stakes are high: if they are judged to improperly make a claim, or fail to respond to an audit, claimants are barred from receiving the credit for two years.[86]

Claimants who fail to negotiate these burdens may be eligible but simply have a hard time understanding and managing the documentation requirements. The National Taxpayer Advocate argues that audits "clearly places the burden of proof on the taxpayer, but if the taxpayer cannot sufficiently understand the rules or negotiate the audit process, reaching the goal of a correct audit outcome is brought into question."[87] There is no individual examiner assigned to a case, meaning that if the person audited can get through the IRS phone lines, the employee they speak to will be looking at the case for the first time, most likely with another call waiting for their response.

When EITC filers with denied claims were provided with assistance from an advocacy service, more than 40 percent of the denials were reversed.[88] The striking difference in audit outcomes for claimants with and without support points to the distributive effects of burdens. Poorer tax filers lack the support of professional accountants or lawyers to help them negotiate the demands of the audit. Given the limited literacy rate and high churn of EITC claimants on and off the program, audit mechanisms need to come with greater outreach to claimants and offers of personal assistance rather than relying on written correspondence alone.

Describing the audit process as "an unnavigable labyrinth," the National Taxpayer Advocate has also proposed the adoption of virtual person-to-person support that would help the claimants by reducing learning and compliance costs. Such technology is used in telemedicine, by tax systems in other countries, and other parts of the U.S. government (such as Veterans Administration benefit hearings).[89] But such a shift of administrative burdens onto the state requires an investment in state capacity to update IRS technology, at a time when Congress has instead dramatically reduced the IRS budget, by 18 percent between 2010 and 2017, even as it processes 7 percent more tax returns.[90]

By the early 1990s, the IRS estimated high rates of overclaimed benefits, and Republicans began to argue that the agency was incapable of managing the program. In 1995, Don Nickles, a Republican senator from Oklahoma, referred to the EITC as "the fastest growing, most fraudulent program that we have in Government today."[91] By the mid-1990s, the EITC was subject to multiple congressional hearings. Proposed policy changes included increased verification checks and a reliance on traditional welfare workers to determine eligibility.[92] These choices would fundamentally change the nature of the burdens faced by applicants, resulting in a lower participation rate associated with traditional welfare programs. More burdens might have reduced fraud but added administrative costs that would have consumed most, if not all, of the resulting savings. The administrative costs for the EITC are estimated to be about 1 percent but can be up to 20 percent for traditional means-tested welfare programs such as the AFDC and TANF.[93] More ex ante verification of income becomes more onerous as more people move into the gig economy, where income may not be subject to third-party reporting, and claimants would face the compliance costs of tracking transactions.

Despite pressure, the IRS has largely resisted adding burdens typical of traditional welfare programs onto the EITC, pointing to another reason the program has relatively low burdens. A basic truism of public administration is that different organizations with different histories, different expertise, and different professional backgrounds will approach the same problem in different ways. The IRS did not approach EITC compliance in the same way that traditional welfare agencies would, seeking more documentation before providing benefits. Instead, it approached EITC compliance as another form of tax compliance, which could be best addressed postpayment via cross-checks with other sources of information.

The professional culture of the IRS led it to deal with a large population of tax filers by placing much of the verification burden on the government rather than on the individual. As compliance problems were identified, the IRS continued with this approach, with more aggressive cross-checks and use of administrative data to verify participant eligibility. The IRS also sought to change the rules in ways that favored simplification rather than complexity. Such rules both made verification checks easier and reflected an assumption that errors in reporting were at least partly because of confusion arising from the complexity of reporting requirements.

Simplified child qualifying criteria were adopted in 1990, and the IRS was given authority by Congress to use Social Security numbers to cross-check dependent claims.[94] The IRS was also given more tools to deal with fraud, some of which were ex ante (more discretion to decline applications) and some were ex post (ability to reclaim excess payments and to suspend filers who had abused the system).

The Bush administration argued unsuccessfully for further simplification of categories but faced opposition from the tax preparation industry and Congress. Such simplification could further reduce errors. Errors with the EITC are at least partly a function of the complexity of determining eligibility, especially for the growing number of families with complex family situations.[95] Multiple working adults might qualify to claim the same credit. Noncustodial parents may not be aware that they cannot claim the credit even if they pay child support. The same cuts that prevent the IRS from investigating fraud elsewhere also prevent it from undertaking better matches with existing administrative data, following up on those matches when potential errors are identified, and investing in information technology that will allow better data matching in the first place.

More resources could shift burdens onto the federal government and simultaneously address the threat of fraud.

Conclusion

The EITC is, in part, a case of policy path dependency. The program originated as an alternative to traditional forms of welfare or minimum income proposals but survived because it evolved into an alternative to the minimum wage. Although some conservatives criticize the program, its value in undercutting minimum wage proposals has meant that it enjoys reflexive support among business interests, their lobbyists, and conservative think tanks. For example, President Obama's 2014 State of the Union address called for both increases to the EITC and minimum wage. Stephen Moore, member of the *Wall Street Journal* editorial board, founder of the Club for Growth, and Trump economic advisor, said, "Raising the earned income tax credit isn't a bad idea, because it is tied to work. But this should be done INSTEAD of raising the minimum wage, not in addition to it. The idea of EITC was to reduce the need for raising minimum wage so that all of the burden doesn't fall on employers" (emphasis in original).[96] Reports by conservative foundations such as the American Enterprise Institute and American Action Forum explicitly contrast the two policies, arguing for the greater effectiveness of the EITC in expanding the labor pool and reducing poverty.[97] It has become difficult to raise the issue of the minimum wage to the conservative intelligentsia without hearing about the virtues of the EITC.

The EITC also demonstrates how interest groups play multiple roles in administrative burdens. First, they lobby for a program and the level of burdens in program design. In this respect, business groups have been supportive of a simple program, although the tax preparation industry argues that the EITC should remain just complex enough that their services are needed. Second, interest groups also change the costs beneficiaries face once a policy is adopted, helping to reduce learning and compliance costs. The Chamber of Commerce does this by helping its member organizations take advantage of the program to boost their employee earnings. Employers do this by providing information and even helping link employees to tax preparation services. The tax preparation industry, private actors with strong business incentives to aid access to the EITC, also reduces the information needed by clients about the program, reduces compliance costs by helping tax preparation, and reduces psychological costs (relative to other services) by treating citizens as clients to be served rather than claimants to be adjudicated. This unlikely coalition between business interests and those supporting the working poor has been a key protection for the EITC against retrenchment.

SOCIAL SECURITY 9

It is hard to point to a more successful income support policy in the United States than Old-Age and Survivors Insurance (OASI)—more colloquially known as Social Security. The program has dramatically improved income security and reduced poverty among older adults with its large redistributive nature masked within a near universal framework. A less-known achievement is that Social Security has also provided life insurance for the surviving families of those eligible based on their employment histories. In addition to constituting 40 percent of older adults' income, Social Security provides nearly $30 billion a year to the children of deceased beneficiaries. It is immensely popular with the American public, even among those who are otherwise harshly critical of government or welfare.[1]

Across the range of policies explored in this book, Social Security stands out for its success in shifting burdens onto the state that could otherwise easily fall onto beneficiaries. As a consequence, almost all of those eligible—that is to say, almost all Americans—receive benefits with little difficulty.[2] The Social Security Administration (SSA) has kept track of their earnings over the course of their working lives and automatically determines eligibility and benefit levels. Beneficiaries simply enroll online or in person at one of the more than 1,200 SSA field offices around the country. Within a month, they start to receive direct deposits in their bank account.

The design of the program has made for largely positive interactions between the SSA and its beneficiaries. At a time when people find government cumbersome, Social Security is experienced as simple and accessible. It is tempting to assume that the success of Social

Security is because it is a relatively easy program to administer. Eligibility is linked only to earnings, and nearly everyone benefits from the program.[3] Given that, how hard can it be to cut checks? In his typology of bureaucracies, James Q. Wilson characterized the SSA as a "production" agency—an organization that is easy to manage because its processes are easy to observe and its outputs measurable: "SSA was given a relatively simple task that was carefully defined by law."[4]

We argue, however, that task simplicity on its own does not fully explain Social Security's success. Indeed, Wilson's characterization understates the daunting challenges that faced the program at its origin. The triumph of Social Security's administrative design reflects the degree to which we now take the program's low administrative burdens to be the natural order of things. Administrative capacity and expertise were also necessary in managing burdens and, by extension, protecting the long-term viability of the program.

Early program administrators faced an unprecedented—some said insurmountable—task. The U.S. government had never implemented such a large social program. In addition to developing a large, reliable, and efficient administrative structure to serve twenty-six million Americans in its first few years, the SSA had to ensure that it was free of the corruption that plagued the Civil War pensions system. Many experts, including those from European countries who had implemented old age pensions decades before the United States did, deemed the task impossible.[5]

Moreover, early administrators had to build the largest social welfare administrative structure in the developed world in an unpromising environment that featured ongoing political opposition, politicians who saw the program as a patronage goldmine, and legal challenges that questioned the very constitutionality of the program. These challenges made a positive outcome more unlikely than inevitable.

What then explains the success of early administrators? They were motivated by political goals, adept at the art of bureaucratic politics, and highly skilled in the basic requirements of administration. They badly wanted the program to succeed and worked with President Franklin Roosevelt to engineer ingenious workarounds in the face of seemingly impossible administrative challenges. Ultimately, they won a measure of bureaucratic autonomy from political interference. Rather than play the role of neutral bureaucrats, they were outspoken in arguing for expansions of the program to cover spouses, survivors, and agricultural and domestic workers—who were initially excluded from the program.

Retracing the origins of Social Security shows how fundamental administrative design choices are—not just to reducing burdens but also to building durable and popular public programs. In addition to the sheer scale of the administrative task at hand and the ongoing political opposition, early administrators did not have the advantage of administering a program that immediately delivered benefits. Indeed, the first benefits did not arrive until 1940. The initial interactions most Americans had with Social Security, in 1936, were to pay taxes and provide personal information—not exactly the aspects of government that are best loved by the public. For this reason, early program administrators, in those first interactions, saw the need to avoid burdens as much as possible in order to enable the programs survival. One noted, "the techniques of administration … could not impose such burdens on individuals, both employers and employees, as to cause [political] opposition."[6]

At a time when we question whether government can do big things, these lessons could not be more relevant.[7] The OASI program is not only the largest federal benefit program, it remains one of the few programs under which no third-party entities are involved in administering or distributing benefits. Yet, the history of Social Security is also relevant for the SSA today. Just as the low burdens associated with the program were a function of administrative choice, those choices can be at least partly reversed. The program has been able to resist calls for privatization, but other recent choices have caused burdens to increase. Ongoing budget cuts by Republican lawmakers have led to a decline in resources for staff support to help new beneficiaries, just as a wave of baby boomers are becoming eligible for benefits.

Political Obstacles

The passage of the Social Security Act is generally recognized as one of the greatest political feats of the twentieth century, both because it created the foundation for the U.S. welfare state and because of the intensity of its political opposition.[8] The act was signed into law on August 14, 1935. The portion that included Old-Age Insurance was particularly fertile ground for conflict. After fierce debate, the final design emphasized a social insurance model. Individuals would contribute to the program through their earnings; their benefits would be based on those earnings and would "insure" them against the vicissitudes of poverty in old age.

Opposition came from both the Right and Left. Republicans who favored limited government saw Social Security as an unwarranted expansion of the state, and were supported by organized business interests concerned about their taxes and the potentially deincentivizing effects of Unemployment Insurance on labor force participation. Southern Democrats were concerned that generous benefits might undermine the availability of low-wage black labor.[9] The left wanted a more generous flat income guarantee not tied to labor force participation.[10] As we explain, opposition did not end with the passage of the bill. Attempts to undermine and repeal the Social Security Act continued throughout its implementation.

In such a context, the early administrators of the program were very much aware that any misstep would be pounced upon. In a tense political environment, they faced an immense task: to create a massive social welfare program unprecedented in U.S. history.

The Social Security Board was created to implement and oversee not only Old-Age Insurance, but also Unemployment Insurance, Maternal and Child Welfare, Public Health programs, and Aid to Dependent Children. The Social Security Board's Bureau of Federal Old-Age Benefits (which would become the Bureau of Old-Age Insurance in 1939) was tasked with dealing with what would become OASI. From the start, the Bureau of Federal Old-Age Benefits faced an extraordinary deadline: by January 1, 1937, the program had to enroll twenty-six million citizens.

In the meantime there was the small matter of the 1936 presidential election, which many saw as a referendum on the Social Security Act.[11] Alf Landon, the Republican candidate, actively campaigned against the program, as exemplified by a campaign speech in Milwaukee:

The administration is preparing a plan, the exact nature of which we shall not know until after the election, for keeping the life records of 26,000,000 of our work people. Imagine the vast army of clerks that will be necessary to keep these records, check up on the people whose records are not clear…. And so bureaucracy will grow and grow, and Federal snooping flourish.[12]

Political rhetoric about government incompetence has become a staple of presidential campaigns, but it is unusual to have such an explicit focus on the administrative machinery required to provide services. In most respects, Landon's characterization was accurate. Social Security would indeed require a new army of clerks and closer federal oversight on the work lives of Americans. But Landon's warnings proved unpersuasive. Roosevelt was reelected with the largest victory since the inception of the two-party system in the mid-nineteenth century, winning every state except Maine and Vermont.

Congress offered its own opposition, which included not just formal repeal efforts, but other legislative maneuvers to stymie implementation such that the enrollment deadline could not be met. The most pressing effect of this opposition was that the Bureau of Federal Old-Age Benefits had no budget. Democratic Senator Huey Long of Louisiana blocked the appropriation bill that was to provide funding for implementation and administration.[13] Long represented the more liberal perspective that saw Social Security as a chance to establish a minimum basic income; moderates like Roosevelt instead argued for a link between work and benefits.

Normally, an absence of appropriated funds would effectively either kill a program or at least delay implementation. But Roosevelt demonstrated the persistence and ingenuity that would characterize the early years of Social Security, cobbling together personnel and funding from the Works Progress Administration, the demobilizing National Recovery Administration, the Federal Emergency Relief Administration, and the National Youth Administration.[14] In February of 1936, the funding appropriation was signed. By March 15, the Federal Bureau of Old-Age Benefits was finally in place and quickly set up processes to enroll beneficiaries, and collect and track payroll taxes, by the January 1 deadline.[15] The bureau followed Roosevelt's tactic of repurposing other parts of the federal government to help them.

Uncertainty over the constitutionality of the Social Security Act also clouded the implementation process. Some employers simply refused to report earnings, at least partly on the basis of ideological objections, and their resistance was encouraged by the prospect of Roosevelt facing a Supreme Court defeat on the constitutionality of Social Security.[16] The Court had already struck down much of the policy architecture of the New Deal. Indeed, Roosevelt was able to draw staff to support Social Security from the National Recovery Administration only because it had been declared unconstitutional and needed to be disbanded. Most ominously for Roosevelt, the Agricultural Adjustment Act was ruled unconstitutional on the basis of a revenue-raising and spending structure quite similar to Social Security. It was not until May 1937, just seven months before all beneficiaries needed to be enrolled, that the Supreme Court ruled the program constitutional.[17] The favorable judgment was part of the "switch in time that saved nine" when Justice Owen Roberts switched from conservative to the liberal bloc of the Court in the aftermath of Roosevelt's court-packing proposal.

A final political obstacle to successful implementation was the threat of patronage. At a time when jobs were scarce and the vestiges of the spoils system remained, the "vast army of clerks" Landon warned against represented an opportunity for members of Congress to build political capital.[18] The Social Security Board viewed the quality of the new employees as central to the program's success. The last effort to build a large-scale pension system—for Civil War veterans—was undone as a result of patronage and poor administration.[19] The Social Security Board therefore devoted considerable effort to overseeing staff hired around the country.

To prevent patronage, it also battled the Civil Service Commission to gain exemptions from the civil service system for the purpose of hiring "especially talented persons, who shared the liberal commitment to a universal retirement system in which benefits would be guaranteed to all contributors as a matter of right and without a means test."[20] After hiring qualified candidates—made somewhat easier by the poor economy—the board also prioritized investments in training to generate both better quality and consistency in field office service.

The first three members of the Social Security Board, tasked with implementing all of the programs created under the 1935 Social Security Act, included John Winant, a former Republican governor of New Hampshire; Arthur Altmeyer, a La Follette Progressive from

Wisconsin who had significant administrative experience; and Vincent Mills, a Democratic Party insider.[21] Of the three, Mills was the least concerned about the dangers of patronage. He was not alone. Roosevelt himself was a skillful tactician both in providing patronage and then in protecting those he had favored by later blanketing them into the civil service system.[22] But Altmeyer and Winant formed a majority and were able to overrule Mills.

The board faced considerable pressure from Congress. For example, members of Congress lobbied aggressively to locate field offices in their districts. One senator, on finding that his hometown would not be a field office site, and that his unqualified protégé would not be hired, attached an amendment to the board's 1937 appropriations that put salary caps on those hired as experts, and specifically cut the salary by 5 percent of the specific board executive who had denied him.[23] Despite such pressures, the board fended off most patronage efforts. One of the early leaders at the Bureau of Federal Old-Age Benefits characterized the board as a "shield" against political interference.[24] For example, the board would frequently back up the bureau if a member of Congress challenged an appointment in a given state.

Inclusive Design and Psychological Costs

Today, the near universal nature of Social Security is taken for granted; nearly 98 percent of U.S. residents will receive OASI benefits in old age. At its inception, the Social Security excluded many groups, but the goal of administrators and proponents was to expand to bring more people into the program.

Natural advantages are inherent in Social Security's more universal design, most obviously a limited range of eligibility rules. Individuals are eligible based on marriage (individuals married to eligible workers) or earnings (a ten-year earnings requirement), and residency (of at least ten years in the United States). Eligibility based on marriage was added just as the program first started distributing benefits in 1940. Indeed, this near-universality is often used to explain why the program has such low burdens. Universal programs tend to encourage social trust among program beneficiaries. Social Security, particularly OASI, stands out as a form of government benefits that faces few accusations of fraud or mismanagement.[25]

Early administrators also leveraged the more universal nature of Social Security to reduce psychological costs arising from intrusiveness and consequential loss of autonomy tied to eligibility determinations, and stigma typically associated with welfare. John Corson, who oversaw the bureau from 1938 to 1941 and again from 1943 to 1944, contrasted Social Security and means-tested public assistance, which

> requires investigation of the individual's need and the exercise of judgment as to the eligibility of the applicant and the evaluation of the applicant's need. Under the insurance method eligibility and the amount of benefit are determined automatically on the basis of wage records and other objective factors. In the great majority of cases personal judgment is not required.... This reliance on objective impersonal facts and the consequent absence of individual judgment are, I believe, elements which tend to preserve and enhance the self-respect and independence of the beneficiary.[26]

Early administrators framed Social Security as insurance and an earned benefit rather than as welfare, a framing that became accepted by the public, preventing the program and its population from being stigmatized at a broader level. The success of this framing was not inevitable. Indeed, as a pay-as-you-go system, the taxes an individual paid were not deposited into an actual account that the individual eventually collected, meaning that the relationship between earnings and benefits was far less direct than many believed. The emphasis on the earned nature of Social Security was partly an attempt to distinguish Social Security from the Old-Age Assistance (OAA) program, a means-tested program also included in the Social Security Act.[27] The size and reach of the OAA program was comparable to Social Security until the 1950s.

Corson explained that the "fact that the individual has made contributions—paid specific taxes, if you insist—justifies, in the minds of contemporary society, efforts on the part of the Bureau of Old-Age Insurance to seek out beneficiaries and to help the survivors of workers who die. Similar efforts to seek out families who are in need would not be condoned as a part of a public assistance program."[28] This belief was very much consistent with Roosevelt's. Indeed, Altmeyer recalled Roosevelt's "desire to place chief reliance on a system of contributory social insurance was due as much to his belief that it was a financially safe system as to his belief that it provided protection as a matter of earned right."[29]

Roosevelt himself said, "We put those payroll contributions there to give the contributors a legal, moral and political right to collect their pensions." When faced with criticisms that the program was creating accounts when it did not have the money to pay for the obligations, Roosevelt responded, "your logic is correct, your facts are correct, but your conclusion is wrong.... That account is not useless. That account is not to determine how much should be paid out and to control what should be paid out. That account is there so those sons of bitches up on the Hill can't ever abandon this system when I'm gone."[30]

Individual contributions created a sense that all had a stake in the program and were benefiting directly from their own labor rather than via welfare. This design element disguised the redistributive element of the program, shielding it from popular stigma of targeted welfare. This belief that benefits were earned became a norm inculcated into the administrators and bureaucrats who populated the rapidly growing bureau. Employees saw their mission as to serve beneficiaries rather than distributing benefits to the needy and perhaps undeserving. In this, employee beliefs reflected an organizational culture that Corson and others built: "Three hundred field office managers, who would interpret this program to citizens throughout the entire country, had to be enlisted and educated as to the meaning and purpose of old-age insurance.... [They] must understand the spirit, as well as its letter."[31]

The spirit of the new organization was built on three broad principles. First, as articulated in the 1941 Social Security Board's Annual Report, the relationship between the agency and program participants was cooperative: "Social Security represents the collaboration of workers and their employers and the Government of the people." Collaboration reflected the idea that beneficiaries were not supplicants, but had earned their standing as a partner to government. A second key principle was that participants were deserving of benefits, that "the sacrifices made by these workers in their country's behalf are manifestly adequate social contributions."[32] Finally, the principle that Social Security was an insurance program was critical. Although the bureaucrat who was administering traditional public assistance might view the claim of the recipient through the lens of deservingness, insurance suggests compensating a broad population that had collectively contributed to minimize a shared risk.

RACE AND UNIVERSALISM

Nonetheless, the inclusiveness of Social Security's design had limits. Until 1950, agricultural and domestic workers, who were predominantly black, were not a part of the program. The effect was that whereas one-quarter of whites were excluded from benefits, two-thirds of black Americans were.[33] This exclusion ensured that relatively few black Americans benefited from Social Security for nearly a decade—and failed to benefit during the period when the return in benefits far exceeded the contributions that individuals made to the program.

Scholars still debate the reasons black Americans were excluded. Some argue that racism was not the primary cause.[34] Instead, they point to the administrative difficulties of capturing earnings records for this group of workers.

Nonetheless, it is difficult to imagine that race did not a play a role in the decision given Jim Crow laws and the extreme, and often violent, measures undertaken to maintain the racial order, particularly in the South, but also in the North. Moreover, evidence of racial discrimination is considerable in the Old-Age Assistance program, which was the means-tested portion of the Social Security Act. Black beneficiaries were systematically excluded from benefit receipt by local welfare offices in the South.[35] Until 1950, the OAA program was actually larger than Social Security, distributing larger benefits to a greater number of beneficiaries.[36]

Moreover, putting aside the initial passage of the 1935 act, racism likely played a role going forward. In particular, it is not credible to claim that the delay adding agricultural and domestic workers was solely due to administrative capacity issues. As early as 1938, the Social Security Board itself actively advocated for including domestic and agricultural workers.[37] In the hearings prior to the 1939 Amendments to the Social Security Act, the board requested the inclusion of both agricultural and domestic workers, stating that "the principal administrative difficulties with respect to domestic service will be overcome, just as they will be in the case of agricultural labor when the individuals affected become generally informed as to the benefits and obligations incident to coverage."[38]

In short, the administrators responsible for implementing the program were clear that they had the capacity to add agricultural and domestic workers. Instead, the 1939 amendments added survivor and spousal benefits that largely benefited white married older adults. It took another decade for the inclusion of agricultural and domestic workers. By 1956, approximately three-quarters of all agricultural workers were included in the program. Coverage of domestic workers expanded over this period as well, though estimates are that only about one-third were actually covered.[39] Social Security was, at its origins, a truncated model of universalism that would took decades to correct.

The Biggest Bookkeeping Organization in the World

Universalism brought benefits and lowered burdens, but it also posed such an unprecedented challenge for the U.S. administrative state that it was initially seen as an argument against Social Security. Arthur Altmeyer argued that the administrative capacity to resolve this challenge ultimately mattered as much to Social Security's success as the design of the program itself:

> "Administration is legislation in action." It is hoped that the importance of Administration will be demonstrated in such matters such as selecting and training qualified personnel; establishing proper organization and procedures; coping with the unique problems involved in the creation of the gigantic old age [and] survivors' insurance system; and, above all, exercising, in an intelligent and responsible manner the power that lawyers call "administrative discretion."[40]

Before the 1930s, nearly all social welfare was administered at the state level. The federal government had almost no capacity or experience administering large social welfare programs. The closest parallel was hardly a model for success. The Civil War pension system was so undermined by patronage, corruption, and dysfunctional administration that it became an archetype of fraud and waste in public services.[41]

The administrative obstacles to building a large federally run program were large.[42] Some experts from Europe, where social insurance schemes had been common for decades, as well as numerous efficiency experts in the United States, thought that the law should be repealed because it was impossible to implement.[43] As the Committee on Economic Security noted in 1937, "The volume of individual contribution records that must be kept would involve administrative techniques on a scale which is new to this country."[44] The closest the federal government had come to building administrative records of such scale was running the draft in World War I, but even this endeavor paled in comparison.[45] Enrolling twenty-six million individuals meant keeping track of their earnings over their entire working lifetimes. Newspapers at the time called the new bureau the "biggest bookkeeping organization in the world."[46]

REDUCING COMPLIANCE COSTS FOR BENEFICIARIES AND EMPLOYERS

Administrators today rely on SSA administrative data to reduce compliance costs. But the creation of these data was never guaranteed. The founders of Social Security had to figure out how to construct such data in the first place. How could they design and build the procedures to enroll individuals and track their earnings in a way that would determine eligibility and benefit size? To fully appreciate the design choices, we need to understand the policy alternatives that were not chosen.

One path not taken was to rely on stamp books to track earnings, used in many European countries that already had social insurance systems. It was a feasible enough option that an early administrator, Edwin Witte, proposed it in 1935 as the best way to include agricultural and domestic workers.[47] Employees would receive stamps from employers and then turn in the books at retirement age. Compliance costs were borne largely by employees, who would have been responsible for tracking these stamps across their entire working lives. Employees would also shoulder considerable risks if stamps were lost or in dispute, a relatively frequent problem.[48]

Concerns about fraud—employees could try to forge stamps or purchase them from corrupt employers—ultimately doomed the stamp book option.[49]

Instead of a stamp book, the Social Security Board chose to employ a Social Security number, which would allow the federal government to track individual earnings over the entire work life. Social Security numbers are now so deeply embedded in American life that we take them for granted. They are the closest thing to a national identification in a country that has long resisted such a form of identification. But at the time, the idea of providing beneficiaries with a number that would track them across their lives was revolutionary, another example of the ingenuity of the designers of Social Security as they sought to minimize compliance burdens while increasing access to benefits and protecting against fraud.

A major logistical challenge to enrolling millions of people was that thousands of planned regional Social Security offices were not yet in place. The Bureau of Federal Old-Age Benefits improvised. In November of 1936 it employed the Postal Service to enroll employers and employees. With forty-five thousand offices on the ground, daily contact with the public, and a generally positive reputation, the Postal Service offered an efficient and trusted choice that reduced both learning and compliance costs.[50] The Postal Service circulated and collected applications and then distributed Social Security cards. The eligibility process was brought to beneficiaries and employers via a familiar face—their local mailman. Within twenty-eight days of starting, the Postal Service had collected more than twenty-two million of the twenty-six million applications.[51] The success of the Postal Service gave the Bureau of Federal Old-Age Benefits some breathing room to train field office staff that were being hired as the initial enrollments took place.

During the early reporting periods in 1937—when employers started paying and reporting payroll taxes and earnings—the Bureau of Federal Old-Age Benefits acted to reduce burdens and foster participation with employers. For example, one challenge was that employers sometimes failed to provide Social Security numbers and instead provided employee names or failed to report any information.[52] The bureau sought to distinguish itself in the mind of employers from the Internal Revenue Service (IRS), which policed nonpayment of taxes. Consequently, the bureau relied on an educational rather than a punitive approach, featuring large and ongoing information campaigns as well as training additional staff to reach out and address reporting issues.

Unlike the IRS, the bureau and the Social Security Board had, according to one of its administrators, "an interest in good relations with the public. The attitude of the workers and employers who make the contributions is the measure of current cooperation and thus a factor in the long-range stability of the system."[53] In other words, the board viewed employers as coproducers in generating the new program. Without widespread participation, the program would have failed. A more forgiving approach reflected the need to build a nonadversarial relationship with recalcitrant employers.

The bureau also paid close attention to compliance costs faced by both employers and employees in completing forms that needed to be submitted for payroll taxes. They deliberately designed the forms to be simpler and clearer than standard IRS tax forms. When in the first year they realized that some employers were still having trouble with the forms, they engaged in further simplification.[54]

The Social Security Board spent considerable time and political capital ensuring that they had developed long-term administrative capacity to process, check, and store earnings records. A key decision that reflected their approach was how to structure the broader processing and storage of data: should there be regional centers or one centralized center? Experts pressured the board to proceed with regional centers, observing that the sheer task of storage would be more easily managed if it was distributed among many sites.[55] The board, however, foresaw problems that would happen when workers moved for employment, and the consequential potential for error when either moving records, or attempting to merge them, at the time of benefit collection. The board thus commissioned pilot studies of the regional approach, and the findings reinforced the board's desire for a single national center. Although more ambitious, the national center improved the long-term efficiency of the program, ensuring that beneficiaries avoided additional compliance costs in resolving errors that might have been created by multiple regional centers.[56]

REDUCING LEARNING COSTS

The novel nature and scale of Social Security required a need to educate the American public. The board created the Information Service in January of 1936 to manage public relations and outreach. The presidential campaign, and vitriol surrounding the Social Security Act, raised problems for the Information Service. As it was attempting to inform employees about the act, opponents of Social Security started distributing pamphlets to employees discrediting and challenging the program.[57] In particular, just prior to the 1938 election and during the period when the board was attempting to enroll employees into the program, the Republican National Committee, in collaboration with business owners unhappy with the payroll tax, distributed a flyer in employee pay envelopes. The flyer read: "PAY DEDUCTION: Effective January 1937, we are compelled by a Roosevelt 'New Deal' law, to make a 1 percent deduction from your wages and turn it over to the government. Finally this may go as high as 4 percent. You might [get] this money back in future years—but only if Congress decides to make the appropriation for that purpose. There is NO guarantee. Decide, before November 3—election day, whether you want to take these chances."[58] Some leaflets were actually signed by the "Social Security Board, Washington, D.C." The leaflet campaign was combined with a larger advertising campaign jointly with the Landon campaign that emphasized the theme of pay deductions (see figure 9.1). Roosevelt, however, ultimately won in a landslide, helping ensure that Social Security went forward.[59]

Outreach was intended to familiarize the public with the program, rebut efforts to discredit it, and—most important—reduce learning costs to facilitate the employer and beneficiary enrollment necessary for the program to function.[60] Robert Huse, who oversaw outreach efforts, explained its purposes:

A first requisite in administration of any legislation, and more particularly of social legislation, is the careful cultivation of a widespread and thorough understanding of the legislative intent, of the needs out of which the legislation grow and the objectives which it seeks to accomplish, as well as the specific administrative procedures through which the objectives are to be sought. In

Figure 9.1 *Flyer Distributed by Information Service*

Source: Social Security Board 1935.

short, a program of adult education on a very large scale is necessary, and the administrative agency will fall short of its objective
unless it takes reasonable steps to promote popular understanding of the law.[61]

The broader objective of the Information Service, in addition to
explaining the goals of the program, was to provide practical details
regarding its implementation.[62] Such explanations were designed to
meet the interests and capacities of different groups. Public organizations are more successful at building and maintaining a positive
reputation if they understand that they have multiple audiences and
tailor their message differently for each.[63] To meet these aims, the
Information Service included multiple divisions tasked with interacting with specific groups. The goal was to conduct outreach to employers and employees through trade, labor, civic, veteran and educational
organizations.[64]

One group dealt with the general media. Another focused on labor
organizations and the labor press. Another division was focused on
the business press, as well employers more broadly. An entire publications division existed to generate promotional and educational
materials. These were done so well that the *New Yorker* praised the
materials as "a triumph of clarity and simplicity."[65] The educational
division focused on colleges and the educational sector more broadly.
An inquiry division answered letters and questions from individuals
all over the country. There was even a motion picture division devoted
to creating films about the program. Board members themselves were
active on the radio giving speeches and doing interviews about the
program.[66] The positive messages conveyed by this onslaught of messaging helped to communicate the notion of Social Security as an
earned right, thereby reducing psychosocial costs.

The final piece of the puzzle—and most lasting in terms of programmatic outreach to maintain low levels of administrative burden—
was the creation of the Social Security field offices throughout much
of the United States. These offices would take over the tasks performed by the Postal Service for the initial enrollment. The Social
Security Board envisioned that it would create twelve regional and
108 field offices to be responsible for everything from answering beneficiary questions to processing program enrollment.[67] The bureau

continued to ramp up throughout the end of the 1930s, filling out field offices and fine-tuning its data archiving and processing procedures. As noted, the employees were selected, trained, and acculturated toward a "client-serving ethic" that encouraged helping beneficiaries.[68]

Perhaps the most striking evidence of the almost immediate administrative success of the program was the passage of the 1939 Social Security amendments. Just four years after the original act, and two years after it was implemented, policymakers expanded Social Security and sped up its implementation. The amendments dramatically broadened the program to cover the spouses, children, and survivors of those eligible based on work history, and moved up the initial date of benefit distribution by two years to 1940. This was a huge expansion: currently, more than one-third of new beneficiaries to the program receive benefits as a function of the 1939 amendments.[69]

The underlying rationale for the 1939 amendments was to increase the political popularity of the program. But the Social Security Advisory Council that recommended the policy, as well as the congressional committees through which it would need to be approved, were explicit about wanting clear confirmation that it could actually be administered. The passage of these critical 1939 amendments would have been impossible if not for the rapid speed—and high level of success—of the initial administrative structures that had been put in place since the initial 1935 legislation.[70]

Contemporary Threats to Administrative Simplicity

The early history of the program illustrates how the administrative simplicity and low levels of burden that characterize Social Security are a function of deliberate administrative choices and cultivation of administrative capacity. Many of these choices were made not by the legislators who passed the law but by the administrators tasked with implementing it. So tasked, they are vulnerable to reversal in ways that the statute is not. The field offices remain a key way to minimize administrative burdens for beneficiaries. Nonetheless, new political threats may undermine SSA's effectiveness by increasing administrative burdens on participants in an efficiency-driven effort to reduce administrative spending.

Table 9.1 *Social Security Administration's Workload and Volume, 2012*

Maintaining earnings information	
Earnings posted to worker records	220 million
Making eligibility determinations for program benefits	
Retirement, survivor, and Medicare applications reviewed	5 million
Making changes to beneficiaries' accounts that affect benefit payments	
Overpayment actions completed	3.2 million
Issuing Social Security numbers	
New and replacement Social Security cards issued	16 million
Other functions	
Automated Social Security number verifications performed	1.5 billion
Transactions completed on the 800 number	56 million
Visitors assisted	45 million

Source: Authors' compilation based on U.S. GAO 2013.

FIELD OFFICE TASKS

The Social Security field offices are the interface between beneficiaries and the SSA and provide a wide array of services. These include processing Social Security numbers, replacing lost Social Security cards, taking applications, and determining eligibility for Old-Age, Survivors, Disability Insurance, and the Supplemental Security Income program. These offices also perform other general tasks, such as ensuring payment accuracy, general customer service, and updating beneficiary records. Finally, SSA staff help individuals enroll in Medicare, its associated programs to help participants pay for out-of-pocket health-care costs, and in the Supplemental Nutrition Assistance Program.

Approximately 1,200 field offices are spread across the United States, staffed by eighty thousand employees. They vary significantly in size, smaller offices in rural areas serving fewer than twenty people a day to larger offices in cities serving over five hundred.[71] In aggregate, demand for help either in-person or via phone inquiries remains strong. In 2015, field offices served forty million visitors.[72] In 2013 alone, SSA field offices fielded more than sixty-eight million phone calls.[73] The national phone line fielded fifty-six million calls in 2012.[74] Table 9.1 provides a more detailed overview of field office workloads.

TIGHTENING BUDGETS

Social Security already has low administrative costs as a percentage of its expenditures. This is partly a function of the sheer size of expenditures, and the universal nature of much of the program (excluding disability insurance), requiring lower resources to determine eligibility. But, by any reasonable standard, it is an efficient program that has only become more efficient over time. Back in 1959, administrative expenses were 2.2 percent of expenditures and have steadily dropped since then. Twenty years later, they were just 1.4 percent and declined further to 1 percent by 1989. They stayed at about that figure until 2012, when they dropped to 0.8 percent, and have been at 0.7 percent since 2013.[75] On the one hand, this efficiency is to be praised. On the other hand, such declines can only continue if more and more burdens are shifted away from the SSA and onto beneficiaries.

A closer look at the effect of recent budget cuts offers some support for the concern that cuts will lead to an increase in burdens for beneficiaries. Between 2010 and 2016, Congress reduced SSA's administrative budget by 10 percent even as the number of beneficiaries rose by 12 percent.[76] In 2017 the House proposed freezing the SSA budget, and the Senate Appropriations Committee proposed a $400 million cut, which would reduce the budget by 4 percent, bringing it to a 16 percent inflation adjusted cut since 2010.[77]

The consequences of a reduced administrative budget grew apparent between 2011 and 2014, when field offices began reducing their hours. It started gradually. Offices closed thirty minutes earlier each day. By 2014, they were closing a full hour earlier four days a week and taking a half-day on Wednesdays. Within a few years, field office hours dropped from 35 to 27 hours per week.[78]

Ongoing cuts ultimately means reducing staff and closing field offices. Since 2010, the SSA has cut 6 percent of its staff and eliminated sixty-four field offices, paralleled by significant regional variation in the loss of coverage.[79] Alaska, Iowa, Kansas, Nebraska, and West Virginia have lost more than 15 percent of their staff.[80] All five hundred mobile offices, which targeted older adults in more remote rural areas, have been shuttered. As a result, clients have to travel farther to get help. In testimony to the Senate Select Committee on

Aging, the commissioner of Florida's Gadsen County detailed how after the closure of the county local field office, beneficiaries had to travel forty-five minutes to their closest office in Tallahassee. This travel is especially problematic for older adults with health or financial limitations that restrict their mobility.

Beneficiaries were often unaware of the reason for these changes, even as they felt the impact. The SSA Office of Quality Review found that the percentage of the public satisfied with the field office hours dropped from 97 to 93 percent between 2011 and 2012. The number of individuals served by field offices declined by approximately 1.5 million between 2011 and 2013. An evaluation found that at 80 percent of eighteen field offices surveyed, individuals reported arriving during the hours when the office had been previously open but were now closed.[81] The SSA Office of the Inspector General interviewed approximately seventy such people, who complained that they had left work early, taken convoluted public transportation, or paid for cabs only to find the offices closed.

In 2013 and 2014, the Office of Inspector General also surveyed 1,172 managers of field offices.[82] Managers reported a significant impact of budget cuts. The hours the offices were open were far busier, which in turn increased wait times from fourteen minutes in July of 2011 to more than thirty minutes by November of 2013. Managers reduced the number of scheduled appointments by 30 percent to redirect staff to service windows to manage the increasing demand. Wait times for appointments grew to approximately three weeks.

The public directed its anger at staff, who came to dread Thursday mornings. Clients who turned up at the field office the previous day only to find it closed would often return the following morning, adding to a backlog of frustrated citizens.[83] Lobbies were often so full that some had to wait outside. Field offices began to feel less like a doctor's office and more like an emergency ward. Not surprisingly, service complaints have increased substantially.

Declining budgets and administrative capacities need to be understood in the context of two big trends. First, SSA's workload is growing dramatically. In 2002, the SSA served fifty-one million OASI beneficiaries. That increased to sixty-two million by 2015 and is anticipated to jump even higher—to seventy-seven million in 2020 and eighty-five million in 2025.[84] The second trend is that the

SSA work force, like the clients they serve, are aging, the majority of supervisors eligible for retirement. In contrast to the early SSA investment in training, budget cuts have prevented leadership development programs that could offer a pipeline for future management personnel or succession planning. The SSA has been under a hiring freeze since 2010.[85] Given that it takes nearly two years to fully train new staff in the broad array of responsibilities ranging from eligibility determinations to claims reviews, long-term hiring freezes place the agency in a challenging position.

How can the SSA cut hours, staff, training, and field offices even as the population it serves is growing rapidly? One possible answer is that information technology makes hands-on human help less necessary. The SSA is being pushed to increase the use of its national phone line, which involves some "real person" contact, but also has a large automated component. It is also expanding online support. Another interpretation is that SSA is responding to budget cuts by shifting burdens back onto individuals. A shift to information technology does not help the nearly 40 percent of older adults do not use the internet. Among those with less than a high school degree, or living in rural areas, where broadband access is limited, 60 percent do not use the internet. Other technological interventions include incorporating video units in local libraries near closed rural field offices. But, as one Florida County Commissioner argued of library technology,

> It is a fine resource, but it is no replacement for a field office, with staffers who can walk our residents through a host of issues they may be having. We have a lot of special needs citizens here, so that unit won't work for everyone. We have people who can barely read because of vision problems. Or people with hearing problems, or poor comprehension problems. The computer is not the answer for many of these people. In fact, many of these people do not have phones. Many of these people have worked hard their whole lives, but are still financially restricted. These issues are not going away any time soon. We still have a direct need.[86]

Moreover, although the number of in-person visitors may be declining, people are still turning up at SSA offices seeking help—they are just waiting longer. In 2015, more than 4.5 million field office visitors faced waits for longer than an hour, compared with 2.3 million in 2010.[87]

Republicans have led the charge for administrative cuts, arguing that the SSA can improve its efficiency using new technologies and better administrative practices. Democrats counter argue that these cuts reflect underlying Republican antipathy to the program. In a 2011 hearing focused on fraud and abuse in the Social Security program, Representative John Lewis, a Democrat from Georgia, argued that the cuts were a "self-fulfilling prophecy" aimed at putting the SSA "in a very bad light." He made the case that the agency needs "more funding, more money, more staffing, more resources. It is that simple."

Although Republican lawmakers have been unwilling to increase the SSA's general administrative budget, which can be used to improve outreach services for beneficiaries, they have supported new funding for collecting erroneous overpayments and recertifying eligibility for the broad array of programs housed under the Social Security program (such as Disability Insurance and Supplemental Security Income). This "dedicated program integrity funding" began in 2009 with an annual appropriation of $504 million. Since the 2010 funding freeze, the diversion of resources to this fund have increased annually. In 2014, this funding was approximately $1.2 billion.[88]

Conclusion

Social Security remains perhaps the most successful and durable U.S. policy experiment to date. The poverty rate among older adults would be more than 40 percent, versus 9 percent, if Social Security were not included in their income.[89] Moreover, nearly one in three beneficiaries rely on it for 90 percent or more of their entire income.[90] We take this for granted, but in many ways Social Security was the Affordable Care Act of its day—though on a much larger scale. It expanded benefits to a large population of people in an unprecedented way, despite ongoing political opposition exercised in elections, court appeals, and direct targeting of the resources administrators needed to implement the program.

Social Security's success—both in terms of poverty reduction and political popularity—is in part a function of the program's low levels of administrative burden. The program could not be successful if it could not get off the ground. Many experts believed the program was impossible to administer effectively. The rapid speed—and high level of success—of the initial administrative structures that were put in place after the initial 1935 legislation paved the way for the 1939 amendments, which in turn were critical to ensuring the program's long-term viability by dramatically expanding the number of beneficiaries.[91]

The sheer scale of SSA's achievements make it easy to discount how much its popularity is tied to administrative design. But imagine if eligibility procedures for Social Security were similar to a program like SNAP. People would submit pay stubs—properly dated because credits for Social Security are earned based on a minimum set of earnings calculated during four periods during each year—that covered the full course of their work lives. They would also need to fill out a plethora of forms that relayed that same information. All of this would have to occur at a minimum of once a year, among an older population, some of whom are battling health and cognitive problems. Moreover, these burdens would not be offset by the support of thousands of local field offices filled with highly trained staff. The experience of SNAP suggests that such burdens would reduce take-up while increasing negative interactions beneficiaries had with the state. By contrast, Social Security is credited with positively engaging older adults and facilitating greater political participation.[92]

The low level of burden for Social Security beneficiaries was to a great extent a function of administrative choices, especially during the early years of the program. The focus on minimizing burden was maintained despite unpromising conditions: a huge task to achieve in a short time, with limited resources, facing political opposition, and with no clear model to emulate. Arthur Schlesinger's history of Roosevelt's New Deal points to the extraordinary administrative skill involved: "Facing an administrative challenge of staggering complexity, it operated with steady intelligence and competence. No New Deal agency solved such bewildering problems with such self-effacing smoothness. No government bureau ever directly touched the lives of so many millions of Americans—the old, the jobless, the sick, the needy, the blind, the mothers, the children—with so little confusion or complaint."[93]

As much as we credit the administrative capacity of these early Social Security staff, we should also credit the values that motivated their ability to deal with complex problems. These officials viewed Social Security as an earned right. If it was to be real, this right depended on the actions of administrators and street-level bureaucrats. A 1944 Social Security Board report based on interviews with nearly two hundred workers in field offices in nine states reflects how this motivation was part of the culture of the new organization all the way down to the front lines, even in its early years:

> Rights, however, are not self-maintaining. They are dependent for their realization upon the way in which they are administered. Here two basic considerations are involved: the one is clarity and predictability in the operation of the system and in its relationships with individuals; the other is the spirit of the organization and the attitude of the individual administrator. Rights to be available must be understood. This means that laws and regulations must be clearly expressed. More than that, it must be possible for the person who applies for insurance or assistance to know in advance to what he will be entitled and in what circumstances. This calls for the development and use of regulation and policy. The second consideration, the spirit of the organization and of the administrator, involves intangibles in atmosphere which are expressed in many different ways, from the arrangement of the office to the manner in which the applicant is received.[94]

The history of Social Security should also make clear why undoing its carefully developed model for minimizing administrative burdens is inherently risky. Worrying trends in the gradual reduction in the program's administrative capacity is weakening field offices, thereby undermining a historical cornerstone of the program's success.

TOWARD AN EVIDENCE-BASED APPROACH TO ADMINISTRATIVE BURDEN 10

As the cases in this book demonstrate, burdens frequently impede access to benefits and rights needed to ensure our social and political welfare. Administrative burdens can also undermine and subvert the intended purpose of a wide array of policies. Even so, the cases also demonstrate that this dysfunctional role of burdens is often no accident. Rather burdens serve as a form of policymaking by other means. In this, they are therefore governable. With enough political will, appropriate professional norms, and administrative capacity, the experience of burdens can be managed and reduced.

Too often, however, burdens are used to advance partisan goals at the cost of making citizen interactions with government more onerous. Progressives, who have largely focused on policy design, such as expanding the Medicaid program to larger numbers of Americans, need to pay closer attention to the role of burdens in undermining larger policy goals, such as reducing poverty and inequality.

In this final chapter, we take a pragmatic approach to considering how the concept of administrative burden can link to the practice of governance. Burdens matter to basic values of governance, such as transparency and rationality. Because the creation, nature, and effects of burdens are often opaque, they undermine transparency. Because debates about burdens usually fail to fully consider value trade-offs, they result in outcomes that are not just less than rational but also sometimes irrational. Put together, such basic failings undermine people's trust in government.

Can we fix these problems? A transparent and rational treatment of administrative burdens requires a professionalized approach that balances valid political goals with a systematic consideration of evidence. Public employees should be expected to be aware of administrative burdens as a standard professional norm. They need, however, the concepts and language outlined in this book to recognize and evaluate when burdens are necessary and when they are not, and how to minimize them while honoring important political values. Such an approach is anchored in four general principles:

- *Evidence based.* Both the costs and benefits of burdens must be considered in the context of a broad range of political values. Policymakers and public managers need to weigh the relative benefit, for example, of fraud reduction, with the relative costs of limiting access to benefits for which individuals are eligible. Such considerations must be informed by empirical evidence to the greatest degree possible.
- *Professional norm of assessing burdens.* In some cases burdens will be important and need to be maintained, but many burdens provide little value, or can be reduced without sacrificing other values. Policymakers and public managers should regularly evaluate the benefits of burdens with a bias toward reduction.
- *Regulatory.* The imposition of burdens on citizens by third parties is monitored and regulated by government in a manner akin to how financial and performance standards are set for private and nonprofit providers of public services.
- *Capacity.* Shifting burdens away from citizens requires a well-functioning administrative state.

How the Politics of Burdens Affect Policymaking

Administrative burdens interact with politics and policymaking in a number of ways. Political frames structure how policymakers perceive the value of burdens. Across a wide range of cases, we have shown that burdens that limit access are seen as more acceptable to the opponents of that policy. For example, policymakers skeptical of an expansive welfare state will place administrative barriers in front of claimants they would normally oppose if applied to businesses. The same holds true for abortion opponents who advocate for tightly regulating abortion providers in ways they would typically oppose for other health-care providers. Indeed, although terms that directly describe burdens on businesses are explicitly used in politics—*red tape, regulatory overreach, regulatory reform*—no such vernacular exists to critique comparable burdens in the social policy areas we have examined.[1]

Understanding administrative burdens helps us better understand politics and policymaking in contemporary America. In particular, such an understanding challenges a basic dividing line used to differentiate conservative and progressive political ideologies, which is that conservatives more aggressively oppose intrusive government regulation on individuals than their progressive counterparts. Such a view confuses the romance of libertarianism with the practice of contemporary conservatism by Republicans. The idea that conservatives are less averse to imposing burdensome rules and regulations on citizens depends, at best, on the policies in question. In the policy domains we examine, Republicans prove more willing and able to motivate their voters to actively support the imposition of administrative burdens.

Conservatives have succeeded by repeatedly and viscerally connecting burdens to underlying political values that their voters care about. Burdens in welfare and health policy are justified by the specter of wasteful spending on undeserving groups. The risk of election fraud is evoked to defend burdens in voting. Protecting the unborn motivates burdens in abortion. The danger of a governmental leviathan robbing people of their freedom—for example, Obamacare—has been used to make the case for making Americans' interactions with government more onerous.

A frontal assault on policies such as Social Security, Medicare, or even Medicaid is politically risky; new administrative requirements or reductions in administrative support much less so. The erosion of funding for the Social Security Administration is an excellent example. Few politicians are willing to call for cuts to the program, even as they gradually weaken the administrative structure that makes it so accessible to beneficiaries.

Conservatives have sometimes portrayed burdens in positive terms: as a way to protect women's health or ensure electoral integrity. Burdens have been justified as helping those they are imposed upon. For example, Governor Walker of Wisconsin has repeatedly argued that "public assistance should be a trampoline, not a hammock" when arguing for drug tests and additional work requirements for welfare.[2] In justifying state work requirements for Medicaid, and the mountain of additional documentation needed to satisfy these requirements, the Center for Medicaid and Medicare Director Seema Verma wrote that "True compassion is lifting Americans most in need out of difficult circumstances. The new flexibility requested by states will allow them to partner with us to help program beneficiaries live healthy, fulfilling lives as independently as possible."[3]

Such formulations reflect a desire to replace a punitive framing when imposing burdens with the gauzy language of empowerment. It proposes that true freedom is not freedom from want but freedom from government support. Although value-based, such language implies empirically testable claims. People either are or are not materially worse if they cannot gain access to certain programs because of administrative burdens. As we argue, evidence on the costs and benefits of burdens must be brought to bear on such claims.

Conservative skill in marshaling administrative burdens is not mirrored on the Left. Progressives who seek to reduce burdens either do so as a defensive response to conservative efforts (such as with voter ID), or as a technocratic approach that fails to make a broad political case for such changes (such as reduction of burdens in SNAP or student financial aid forms). Progressives prefer to campaign on policy expansions, such as "Medicare for All" or "free college." Our point mirrors Suzanne Mettler's concern about the failure of progressive politics to reveal the ways in which "submerged" public policies help people.[4] The parallel failure to build a progressive politics around the goal of reducing administrative burdens puts liberals in a reactionary or technocratic mode when it comes to defending the capacity of the state to help its citizens.

In short, Republicans figured out how to build a politics of burdens that Democrats have been unable or unwilling to develop. Republicans have done so despite the fact that in other areas—such as the regulation of businesses, campaign donations, or firearms—they have also been successful in opposing governmentally imposed burdens in the name of liberty. Their success is not built on an ideological consistency, but in a situational capacity to connect burdens to political values shared by their supporters. Christian conservatives who oppose abortion might support mandatory ultrasounds for women seeking abortions, but bristle at government requirements that employers cover birth control in their health insurance plans.

We can easily overlook conservative use of burdens as a policymaking tool because our received wisdom of what constitutes conservatism and liberalism condition us to do so. The imposition of burdens on individuals may also be easy to miss because they are less formalized and less regulated than burdens on businesses. But in the trench warfare of policies we discuss—social policies, health care, election administration, and access to abortion—administrative burdens have been a key weapon to pursue Republican goals and one that has been skillfully deployed.

Our observations about the politics of burdens are not intended to score a partisan point but to correct an existing misconception about how partisanship relates to burdens. In aggregate, both parties use administrative burdens as a complement or alternative to traditional forms of policymaking to pursue their political goals. Liberal politicians are fully capable of using burdens, of course, though this point is less surprising because it fits with the stereotype of liberals willing to regulate behavior, especially corporate actions. The concerns of businesses about government regulation are well articulated. Policymakers have been aggressively targeting burdens faced by businesses, which now have to overcome a barrage of cost-benefit analysis and rulemaking comment periods required by federal law.

Liberals are also willing to use burdens to constrain individual activities. An obvious example is access to guns. Here, as is true of voting and abortion, states and localities governments vary in their use of burdens to limit a right derived from the Constitution. Those wanting to buy a gun face a range of possible compliance costs ranging from identity and background checks, licensing and registration requirements, delays before purchases, and mandatory training. As in many of our cases, third parties play a powerful role. Gun rights groups, most obviously the National Rifle Association, help members understand their rights, provide legal challenge to burdens deemed overly restrictive, lobby policymakers to reduce compliance costs, and engage in outreach that has gradually altered how people conceive of gun ownership. The success of such groups has come gradually and is tied to a strategy that more aggressively polices and opposes restrictions on individual rights. As in other cases, the courts have played a pivotal role in refereeing what burdens are and are not overly restrictive.[5]

The connection between partisan politics and burdens is therefore not automatic. Although partisan identity tells us little about an aggregate willingness to make interactions with the state burdensome, it tells us a good deal in specific policy domains. Distributions of political power and conceptions of deservingness are also important to understand how burdens are imposed on citizens. Citizens who are poor, powerless, and seen as undeserving can expect to spend their lives struggling against burdens in their encounters with the state. Such encounters teach people that they are supplicants, not entitled to the protections and help that their richer and more powerful fellow citizens enjoy.[6]

The policies we identify where burdens are designed to not send negative messages to citizens—the EITC and Social Security— demonstrate two ways to break this general pattern. In the case of Social Security, nearly all Americans benefit from a near universal design, a prioritization of access in implementation, a general conception that the benefits are earned, and an emphasis on rights.[7] In the case of the EITC, burdens were limited partly because the benefit supported the working poor who are classified as deserving, but also because they offered a subsidy to those that employed them, and a market to the tax preparation industry. The "who" in "who gets what, when, where, and how" matters a good deal. Alliances that expand the "who" to include all citizens or powerful business actors facilitate making the "when, where, and how" less burdensome.

Although it is tempting to conclude that burdens are "just politics" that both sides engage in, we are also concerned with how the use of burdens undermines two basic values of policymaking and good governance: transparency and rationality.

TRANSPARENCY IN POLICYMAKING

In chapter 1, we note how the qualities of opacity, controllability, and political neutrality make administrative burdens attractive as a form of policymaking. Such qualities are also detrimental to transparency in policymaking. They allow policy choices to be made without widespread consultation, understanding of the consequences, and in some cases with a weak relationship between stated aims and actual intent. They help bridge the gap between political promises—to give generous welfare benefits or provide access to deserving refugees—and constraints that make those promises unrealistic—a limited budget, or a political concern about security.

This book uncovers one way that the hidden politics of the welfare state plays out: the construction of burdens within the executive branch.[8] As chapter 7 documents, administrators within the Wisconsin executive branch followed gubernatorial priorities on expanding or restricting access to Medicaid. In the same way, administrators were attentive to issues of simplicity and access when creating Social Security, in large part because they wanted to ensure ongoing and robust support for the program. These choices were made largely without legislative direction or any public fanfare, but they changed who got what, when, and how.

If burdens serve as a tactic in hidden politics, a related question is under what conditions such hidden politics become visible, subject to explicit political debate and overt political action such as legislation. For example, chapters 2 and 3, on election laws and abortions, show clear and public partisan divides. The answer likely has to do with growing awareness within a policy domain that burdens are consequential—and that stakeholders have a large role in arguing for or against burdens to further their policy interests.

As administrative burdens become more important as a political tool, the qualities that made them attractive will erode. In open democratic regimes, the effects of burdens will draw attention from stakeholders and policy analysts who make visible what was once hidden. Now aware of these burdens, opposition parties will mobilize to reduce burdens for their supporters. Assuming party disagreement about policy outcomes, policymaking by other means will look more and more similar to normal policymaking, with burdens managed through the legislative process. The 2002 Farm Bill included specific provisions to reduce burdens for SNAP beneficiaries, just as a proposed 2018 version imposed new burdens. Design innovations that reduced burdens in Medicaid migrated into the Children's Health Insurance Program Reauthorization Act in 2009 and the Affordable Care Act of 2010. Details such as the width of clinic corridors ended up in state laws to regulate abortion providers. Such transparency does not mean the end of burdens, but it does allow greater contestation of evidence about trade-offs via public legislative processes overseen by elected officials relative to decisions made in the recesses of the executive branch.

As burdens migrate to the legislative setting, the executive branch can no longer control them, and the qualities of opacity and political neutrality are reduced. But even in a diminished form, these qualities still provide value, as demonstrated in the areas of elections and abortion. For elections, politicians can justify burdens out of a need to prevent fraud, a value more broadly accepted than simply reducing the turnout of those likely to vote against your party. For administrative burdens in abortion, the standard justification of protecting the life of the mother is less politically divisive and more legally defensible than an explicit call to limit access to abortions. Maintaining public support for administrative policies that limit access to abortions depends on the public's not understanding how reasonable-sounding regulations create real barriers.[9]

Misleading statements about the motives behind administrative burdens are damaging because they undermine support for policies and programs and change how bureaucratic discretion is used. For example, politicians declaring that welfare programs are rife with fraud weakens support for a program and sends a cue to administrators to impose more demands on the citizens they encounter. The sincerity of how problems are framed also has implications for policy solutions. As we argue in the following section, there may be ways to structure burdens to offer equal or better outcomes on competing values that policymakers sincerely care about maximizing. For example, if done well, auto-enrollment can reduce burden, increase access, and also minimize fraud by providing more reliable information than self-reported data. The same is true of automated tax returns. But these solutions are attractive only if policymakers sincerely care about fraud, rather than see fraud as a convenient justification to reduce access.

RATIONALITY IN POLICYMAKING

In addition to transparency, another core value for policymaking and good governance is rationality: the idea that facts, logic, and reason play a role in governing. That we frequently fall short of this standard does not mean it is not worth aspiring to. Even in a time of unprecedented political polarization, calls for results-based or evidence-based approaches to governing have never been louder.[10]

A better understanding of administrative burden is the basis for a more rational government. The previous chapters show that when administrative burdens were poorly or partially understood, changes were imposed that were not based on a rational understanding of value trade-offs or the consequences of these changes on policy outcomes. Instead, we see policy actors motivated by beliefs that are weakly related to evidence. Political messaging about voter fraud has been successful despite an absence of evidence either that widespread fraud occurs or that the measures adopted actually do much to address the supposed problem. Examples of fraud in SNAP are given a privileged position in policy debates, offering credence to beliefs that such fraud is rampant. Meanwhile, evidence is substantial that putting burdens on access to programs like SNAP hurts those who are eligible, but this evidence is largely ignored. In short, we pay far more attention to the less than 3 percent overpayment rate than to the 15 to 20 percent of individuals qualifying for the program who are not accessing those benefits.

A rational approach to policymaking would consider both the costs and benefits of burdens. For new policies, this means mapping out both the potential costs and benefits. For existing policies, policymakers generally assume that the policy already generates benefits— why else have it?—and a rational approach therefore means better documenting unrecognized costs that offset those benefits, as we do in this book.

Understanding administrative burdens improves rationality because it highlights that the design and implementation of programmatic details—the length of a form, the location of an office, the amount of help available—are relevant to competing political values and policy outcomes. An explicit discussion of burdens should compel policymakers to spell out the political values in play, not just the particular ones they care about. In social policy, the debate has historically focused on the danger of waste, fraud, and abuse and given less consideration of how burden affects access to benefits.[11] An evidence-based approach would pay attention to how burden relates to both sets of values.

To return to the SNAP example, an evidence-based approach should compel policymakers to understand that rules to reduce fraud may also reduce access. Perhaps policymakers already understand this trade-off, but must now formally acknowledge it and consider the scale of the trade-off. A government with formal mechanisms of considering burdens, or informal values of appreciating them, will more rationally assess how policy design and implementation will affect its citizens.

If this all sounds unrealistic or excessively convoluted, consider the history of other administrative concepts, such as program evaluation, cost-benefit analysis, performance management, or evidence-based policymaking.[12] Each of these concepts aims to improve the rationality of governing by providing information about how well governments are designing and implementing policies using some evaluative criteria, preferably informed by evidence. Each has been developed into a set of professional norms.

Perhaps the most obvious parallel is cost-benefit analysis, a once-obscure analytic technique that seeks to estimate the likely effects of a program or regulation. It has generated a profession, with technical training for students in economics, public policy and administration, and its own society and journals. It was adopted by governments, in particular by conservative administrations, seeking a rational tool to support what they saw as a tendency for overregulation of private business. Now, every major regulation in the federal government must satisfy a cost-benefit analysis.

Currently, we do not have an equivalent awareness of burdens, meaning that they are not given systematic attention in governing.

Although the basic principles of cost-benefit analysis can be transferred to administrative burdens, the ways in which in which U.S. courts have wrestled with the issue of burdens are instructive to building an evidence-based approach.

An Evidence-Based Model to Emulate?
How the Courts Deal with Undue Burdens

The judicial branch has developed a set of principles to systematically assess state-imposed burdens on individuals. The role of courts is important for multiple reasons. The courts play an intrinsically important role in determining whether burdens are recognized and allowed to stand. For both abortion and voting, a legal standard of undue burden applies, meaning that the state cannot place excessive barriers on a recognized right.

Even if constitutional rights are not directly in play, courts can determine whether burdens violate the original intent of law. For example, if the federal executive branch allows new restrictions on Medicaid via a series of waivers to states, it may be required to prove in court that the waivers do not undermine the statutory intent of Medicaid—providing access to health care to poor people. In doing so, the court can block the use of burdens as a form of policymaking by other means. Courts also matter because they offer a potential model for other policymaking bodies to emulate as they evaluate burdens.

Perhaps not surprisingly, judges vary in their interpretations of what is an undue burden, and about whether and how evidence is considered in weighing burdens. In some cases, courts follow an evidence-based approach, which allows that burdens can produce benefits but requires evidence on the likelihood of those benefits. In the case of elections, do voter ID laws actually reduce fraud? In the case of abortions, do restrictions actually improve women's health? Simply claiming that such benefits will occur is not enough if reasonable evidence can be brought to bear on the question. An evidence-based approach also considers the likely consequences of burdens on other values, such as the right to vote or access to abortion. As an empirical question, do the burdens make it more or less likely that access to these rights or benefits will be weakened? If so, are those costs outweighed by the likely social benefit the burden will offer?

The evidence-based approach is not uniformly applied. Some courts take an alternate, deferential approach that illustrates what happens when an expert policymaking body submit to political judgments at the expense of evidence. Here, judges first examine whether there is a rational basis for the law. For example, are voter ID laws rationally related to reducing fraud? If such a rational basis is found, judges do not pursue the question of whether the laws actually achieve these goals, and at what cost, instead deferring to legislative judgments. For example, in upholding Texas abortion restrictions, the Fifth Circuit Court chided a lower court for "substituting its own judgment for that of the legislature" because "medical uncertainty underlying a statute is for resolution by legislatures, not the courts."[13]

The deferential approach raises four problems. First, it assumes that legislative claims are sincere. In the case of both abortion and voting, the state may have a rational interest in women's health and voting, but elected officials may be motivated more by an ideological interest in limiting abortions and a strategic interest in maximizing their party's vote share. The second problem with a deferential approach is that it ignores whether those claims hold up in the face of evidence. A claim can be rational in a narrow sense—it is logical to assume that voter IDs reduce fraud—but the empirical reality is that an additional regulation does little to discourage an activity that is increasingly scarce. Third, a deferential approach privileges the claims of legislators over the lived experiences of citizens, causing judges to ignore the degree of difficulty the burdens pose for citizens or the likely impact on accessing some right. Instead, they focus on whether it remains possible to access the right. Under this standard, laws that create substantial burdens are allowable even if they have no demonstrated value in achieving their stated purposes. In effect, the deferential approach frames the legal concept of undue burden to focus only on the burden and the feasibility of overcoming it, not on whether it is undue. This focus creates the final problem: it structurally ignores costs imposed on citizens.

The deferential model may be admired as an effort at judicial minimalism, but under this stance the court is not neutral. It does less to protect citizens against burdens, privileging what may be a relatively thin political logic as rational even if it is contradicted by evidence. The deferential approach does not completely ignore evidence but is asymmetric in how it demands it. Citizens bear the burden of proof when it comes to demonstrating the negative consequences of burdens.

Under a deferential standard, defenders of abortion restrictions are not required to provide any evidence of the merits of the laws or answer difficult questions such as why abortions are the only form of medical service subject to a higher standard of medical care than those that have much greater risks. However, citizens making the case for the impact of burdens are held to a higher evidentiary standard. Despite the rapid closure of abortion clinics after the implementation of the Texas's abortion law, the Fifth Circuit Court and Judge Alito in Supreme Court oral arguments demanded better evidence that the law caused the closures of clinics and better evidence that the existing clinics could not take up the four- to fivefold loss of capacity from those closures.[14] The deferential standard creates a legal zone in which some costs are counted and some are not; where some evidence is considered relevant, and some is ignored.

By contrast, an evidence-based approach allows both sides to offer empirical support for its perspective and considers both the costs and benefits of burdens. Within the courts, the evidence-based approach has been articulated most eloquently by Judge Richard Posner. An appointee of President Reagan, Posner's pioneering application of an economic approach to the law has made him the most cited legal scholar of the twentieth century. In weighing Wisconsin's abortion law, Posner noted that other courts had deemed it necessary only that the state have a rational law, not that empirical evidence had to support its goal: "But a statute that curtails the constitutional right to an abortion, such as the Wisconsin and Texas statutes, cannot survive challenge without evidence that the curtailment is justifiable by reference to the benefits conferred by the statute. The statute may not be irrational, yet may still impose an undue burden—a burden excessive in relation to the aims of the statute and the benefits likely to be conferred by it—and if so it is unconstitutional."[15]

These principles were applied by Supreme Court Justice Stephen Breyer in his majority opinion striking down a similar law from Texas in *Whole Woman's Health v. Hellerstedt*. In oral arguments, Breyer said,

"Where we have a judicial duty to say whether this is an undue burden upon the woman who wants the abortion, there are two parts: Is she burdened and what is the benefit?"[16] Justice Clarence Thomas, in his dissent, lamented the "benefits-and-burdens balancing test" used by the majority. With such a test, states must meet a higher evidentiary bar before they impose new burdens on their citizens than if the court were to take a deferential approach.

In policy situations when legislatures assert empirical claims that are demonstrably false or when the benefits are trivial, an evidence-based approach allows the court to fulfill its constitutional role of using reason and evidence to protect individuals from unwarranted use of burdens. It compels governments to show that their regulation of citizens' lives has some positive effect and to acknowledge the costs that are imposed in the process. In a practical sense, this approach merely puts citizens on similar footing in terms of access to their constitutional rights that corporations enjoy in protection against burdensome regulation.

Although much of this book has focused on burdens that provide more costs than benefits, an evidence-based approach can also justify when burdens are needed and providing demonstrable value. In some cases, burdens impose costs, and those costs are justified. In some cases, costs are justified, but the state can find alternative technologies to reduce burdens while not sacrificing other values.

A Professional Norm of Assessing Burdens

Burdens are inherently neither good nor bad but instead tools to other ends. Left entirely to the political domain, burdens become political tactics. For evidence on burdens to matter in policymaking, they need to be considered in a professional domain, where competing political values can be acknowledged rather than selectively dismissed and their consequences rationally examined. The courts are one such domain. The professional management of public organizations is another.

How can public managers tackle the practical questions of how to reduce burden and when such efforts are appropriate? To ask these types of questions within public organizations requires establishing a professional norm of being attentive to burdens. Public management is a profession, in which norms are established and embedded through professional education, workforce training, precedent, organizational culture, the popular media, and political guidance.[17] Through such mechanisms, public employees are urged to adopt, for example, norms of transparency, performance, and efficiency to guide their daily decisions. Such norms are exceptionally important to governing the public sector precisely because the absence of a profit-based bottom line removes the primary logic by which private employees are governed.

Attention to administrative burdens is not built into the DNA of either government culture or government processes. But such a norm is possible. For example, state agencies that deal with businesses face consistent pressure in many states and countries to adopt a lighter regulatory touch and reduce burdens by techniques such as one-stop shopping for small businesses. During the Bush and Obama years, the Department of Agriculture showed a similar attentiveness to burdens that were limiting the take-up of SNAP benefits.

The designers of Social Security were acutely aware of the existential risks that burdens, placed on both employers and beneficiaries, posed to the success of the program and worked to reduce burdens both in design and implementation. Some European countries have adopted programs to reduce administrative burdens on citizens, though these are episodic and attached to broader antiregulatory initiatives that benefit businesses.[18] Germany offers an example: the federal government has taken a model used to estimate business costs of regulation and applied it to individual interactions with state regulations such as finding nursing care or registering a vehicle.[19]

In aggregate, however, the language or concepts of administrative burden are not impressed on public managers or frontline employees in the way, for example, that the language and concepts of strategic planning or performance measurement have become ubiquitous. Public managers do not face administrative burden equivalents to routine cost-benefit analyses, performance reporting requirements, or audits. The incentives and sanctions such managers face shape the work environment of the street-level bureaucrats who deliver services.[20] Collectively, managers and frontline employees may observe rules and barriers excluding citizens, have ideas for how to fix this problem, but feel that they have little license to act on these motivations.

Even if public organizations put procedures in place that help public managers target burdens, street-level bureaucrats retain discretion that allow them to increase or reduce burdens, often in ways that reinforce inequalities. Processes to direct attention to burden therefore have to be supported by other motivators. In the example of Social Security, employees were trained to adopt a cultural assumption that claimants had a right to benefits, and the job of the bureaucrat was to ensure access to that right. Here, the organizational culture made the value of access a motivator that informed the use of frontline discretion.

Cultivating a professional norm to assess burdens in public services need not be limited to public organizations. We have focused on the role of government in reducing burdens, but we have also documented the role of nongovernmental third parties. We have seen how a desire to reduce burdens can be incentivized in for-profit situations. The example of the tax preparation industry in expanding access to the EITC is at least partly due to the profits to be made from making it easy for customers to maximize their returns. For nonprofits, the motivation can be a mixture of altruistic and financial motivations, such as nonprofits that receive government payments to help people to sign on to public health insurance but were already intent on serving that population.

The Medicare program, in contrast, points to the ways in which third parties, specifically private health insurers, have exacerbated rather than reduced administrative burdens for beneficiaries. Reducing administrative burdens for EITC beneficiaries was a mechanism to increase profits for tax preparation firms. In contrast, the administrative burdens that beneficiaries in the Medicare program face, the confusion the burdens create, and the resulting poor choices by beneficiaries actually enhance private health insurer profits.

Recognizing the importance of third parties in administrative burdens calls for a rethinking of the regulatory role of the state. With devolution, or the reliance on contractors and third parties to provide services historically provided directly by the government, the state has struggled to articulate its purpose.[21] The concept of administrative burden points to a logical way for the state to maintain a reliance on third parties to provide government services but to maintain older values such as due process, equity, procedural fairness, and customer service. The state could better monitor and regulate how citizens experience burden in their interactions with public services, even if private actors provide those services.

The reliance on nongovernmental contract organizations to provide public services makes the content of those contracts all the more important. Service providers should face explicit expectations about how they impose burdens in the same way they are accountable to fiscal and performance expectations. Of course, many contractors already care about such burdens because they care about their clients and need little prodding. However, a regulatory approach to burdens would balance the emphasis on performance measures that can serve as a source of burdens as contractors seek to perversely improve measured performance.[22] Regulating burdens created by third parties, however, requires an investment in administrative capacity.

Without strong organizational processes, culture, and motivation to pay attention to burdens, organizations and employees are apt to simply reinforce the status quo. When burdens are necessary and beneficial, the status quo is a positive outcome. When burdens could be reduced to benefit American's political and social welfare, not attending to them limits the possibility for government to improve lives.[23] Thus, techniques to reduce burden are of limited value if they are not introduced in a setting where people will use them.

Tools for Assessing and Reducing Administrative Burdens

A starting principle for the design and management of administrative burdens is that programs should be designed to be simple, their processes accessible and respectful of the people they encounter. Consistent with these principles, certain questions are necessary to diagnosing administrative burdens in an existing program (see table 10.1). Any program administrator should know the answer to these questions or quickly start asking them. Many of the questions on learning and compliance costs are objective and require tracking each step of government interactions with the people they serve. In other contexts, private organizations map the "user journey" to

Table 10.1 *Diagnostic Questions About Administrative Burdens*

Take-up: What is take-up rate for eligible beneficiaries?

Inequality: Does take-up rate vary across populations?

Learning costs
  Is it easy for potential participants to
  · find out about the program?
  · establish if they are eligible?
  · understand what benefits are provided?
  · learn about application processes?

Compliance costs
  How many questions and forms are there to complete?
  How much documentation is needed?
  Does the participant have to input the same information multiple times?
  Is the information sought already captured via administrative data?
  Is it possible to serve the person in a less intrusive way, such as phone
    rather than in-person interviews?
  Do applicants have easily accessible help?
  How frequent is reenrollment?
  How much time must people commit to the process? What are the
    bottlenecks?
  What are the financial costs?

Psychological costs
  Are interactions stressful?
  Do people receive respectful treatment?
  Do people enjoy some autonomy in the interaction?

Source: Authors' compilation.

identify problems and negative experiences. What we propose is similar.

Where should policymakers and public managers concentrate their attention? Focus on the bottlenecks where burdens are meaningfully affecting people and limiting their ability to access services. If the problem is learning costs, ensure that the right information flows to the right people. But sometimes information is not enough; people also need a helping hand. Recall the example of the FAFSA experiment discussed in the introduction—those given more information but no additional help did not do better in applying for federal student loans.[24] The compliance costs were great enough that they also needed direct help with the process. Compliance costs can also be reduced via

Table 10.2 *Techniques to Reduce Administrative Burdens in Program Design*

Favor more universal over means-tested program designs

Design fewer and simpler conditions to receive benefits, such as elimination
  of asset tests

Curtail choice to limit cognitive demands

Reduce recertification time periods

Label programs in positive terms to reduce stigma

Establish a default option to reduce learning and compliance costs—can be
  achieved by auto-enrollment or presumptive eligibility

Source: Authors' compilation.

process simplification—such as one-stop shopping—or by shifting
burdens onto the state through techniques such as auto-enrollment.
Psychological costs are the most difficult to address because they
may be associated with broader stigma of societal beliefs. However,
public managers can look for ways to minimize negative messages
that people receive in their interactions with the state.

Although questions about psychological costs are more subjective,
they can be collected via surveys. The simple questions posed in
table 10.1 could be framed in more specific way depending on the
nature of the program. A step further would be to convert the answers
into performance indicators that reflect burdens, such as participant
assessments of respectful treatment, objective measures of delays
such as length of time to process applications, or wait times at offices.

Table 10.2 summarizes some of the techniques identified in this
book to reduce burdens in the program design stage. Given that our
focus is on a limited range of encounters in the U.S. setting, and social
policies in particular, both tables 10.1 and 10.2 should be seen as a
starting point rather than a definitive list. The list for other types of
interactions, such as those with police, would be different.

Even within this limited context, it is clear that state interactions
with people can be designed by policymakers and administrators
to be more or less onerous. For example, Social Security has strict
administrative rules and documentation requirements, but almost
all administrative burdens fall on the state rather than the beneficiary. This was how the first program administrators designed it. The
state takes responsibility for collecting employment and earnings
data, meaning that applicants do not need to provide the lifetime

of detailed income documentation needed to ensure the program achieves a near-zero error rate. In short, it is a complex program, but one designed to feel simple.

One basic design choice is how the default for participating in a program is established: is the eligible beneficiary automatically included in a program or not? In the private sector, the success of this technique has been extensively documented. The best-known example is retirement accounts for new employees: when the default is enrollment, rather than requiring the employee to opt in, participation is substantially higher.[25] This is, in fact, how Social Security works. For other public programs, an analogous way to establish a default of inclusion is via auto-enrollment, under which the state draws on existing administrative data to identify if individuals meet eligibility criteria and enroll those who do.

Presumptive eligibility is a less aggressive way of establishing inclusion, allowing those who appear to be eligible to participate pending full documentation. If appropriate, the state can undertake additional verification, or make the individual responsible for doing so. A technique such as auto-enrollment dramatically reduces the psychological costs of opting in as well as learning and compliance costs. Some of these costs might rise if the individual chooses to stay in the program, but the barriers to entering the program are significantly reduced. Administrative data, therefore, can be actively used to shift the administrative burden for completing applications from the individual to the state and has already been successfully used in areas such as voter registration (see chapter 2).

Medicaid reform in Wisconsin involved two governors from opposing parties using auto-enrollment to target specific groups; Governor Doyle auto-enrolled newly eligible health insurance beneficiaries; Governor Walker used administrative data to automatically reenroll existing beneficiaries whose income fell well below the threshold for eligibility. Individuals can always opt out of a program, and some may be enrolled inappropriately (because the administrative data used to enroll them may be out of date). But for a great many, auto-enrollment will eliminate the problem of underenrollment due to doubts about eligibility or a difficult application process.

Auto-enrollment is but one example of how information technology and administrative data can also play a role in reducing burdens.

Online systems can easily share individual information to reduce learning costs and allow for online applications or pre-fill applications to reduce compliance costs. Estonia pioneered the once-only principle: the idea that citizens share information with the state once, rather than again and again. Estonia's model had been successful because it was supported by public opinion in favor of digital democracy as well as by a massive investment in secure digital portals that can share information when a citizen tries to pay taxes, open a business, or go to a doctor.[26]

By investing in data systems that can integrate data across programs, the state can both reduce the need for applicants to provide the same data multiple times and improve accuracy. For example, information based on state tax returns is more likely to be accurate than self-reported income data in verifying eligibility.

We offer positive examples of how a mixture of administrative data and technology can be used to reduce burdens, but there is also a dark side, in that automated systems might be used to intrusively target people and rob administrators of flexibility to ameliorate burdens when the circumstances require it.[27] Technology can offer both great promise and great risk; it can be used to reduce burdens but can also enhance them. Technology, or any other innovation, will only reduce burdens if that is the goal of those controlling it.

Another lesson for practice is that linking benefits across programs makes take-up more likely and burdens substantially lower for beneficiaries. A simple approach to exploit this insight is to use a single form for multiple programs where eligibility overlaps. Alternatively, governments could auto-enroll those who have demonstrated eligibility from one program into another with equivalent eligibility requirements. The corollary is also true. Delinking benefits from one another reduces take-up. An unintended consequence is illustrated by the 1996 welfare reform, which delinked SNAP and Medicaid from those enrolled in the Aid to Families with Dependent Children (AFDC) program. Those who were used to receiving health insurance and food supports as a function of their AFDC benefits now had to find out about and gain access to these programs separately. As chapter 6 recounts, the increase in learning and compliance costs led to a predictable decline in program enrollment.

Other relatively simple administrative changes can reduce burden during implementation (see table 10.3). One insight from the qualitative part of the Wisconsin Medicaid case is that interactive effects are likely between different forms of burden reduction. For example, the potential of outreach becomes much greater if combined with allowing third parties to actively enroll individuals rather than simply inform them of their eligibility, or with online application processes that allow outreach workers to enroll individuals outside traditional settings. In addition, program simplification around the brand of BadgerCare lessened burdens not only by reducing the number of forms an applicant had to complete, but also by facilitating marketing and outreach efforts around a single easily identified nonstigmatizing program. Any approach to reducing burdens should therefore consider how different techniques can work together.

A discussion of techniques to reduce burden raises the issue of capacity. The right professional norms motivate administrators to help, but they also need the ability to act on those motivations. Both professional norms and capacity depend in large part on the willingness of elected officials to allow administrative professionals the autonomy and resources to manage burdens.

The history of Social Security helps us understand how investments in capacity can generate large payoffs. It succeeded because Congress gave administrative professionals in the new organization enough independence, and ultimately resources, to build a well-trained corps of employees dedicated to ensuring beneficiaries had easy access to the program. Of course, as we describe in chapter 9, this may be undone given that Congress has increasingly targeted the Social Security Administration (SSA) with large budget cuts even as the pool of beneficiaries has grown significantly.

The IRS offers an instructive contrast to SSA's historical capacity. The IRS currently plays a large role in administering social programs, partly because programs like the EITC are implemented through the tax code, and partly because tax records make the IRS the lynchpin of administrative data in the federal government. However, Congress has not set it up to succeed in this role. National Taxpayer Advocate Nina Olson has called for a significant overhaul in both professional norms and capacity to reflect new IRS responsibilities: "By explicitly recognizing the IRS's role as a benefits administrator in its

Table 10.3 *Techniques to Reduce Administrative Burdens in Program Implementation*

Learning costs
· Make information and application processes accessible, online, and easily searchable
· Use simple language, understandable to the target audience, and multiple language options
· Provide calculators to estimate benefits
· Communicate choices in simple terms, such as categorize options in gold, silver, bronze
· Provide reminders (texts, mail, phone): the poor may move frequently, or may be inclined to ignore documents that look like bills, but many own smart phones
· Use outreach campaigns to shape public perceptions of a program and provide information

Compliance costs
· Integrate multiple forms with similar questions into one
· Allow multiple options for documentation to be accessible
· Allow standard deductions (such as medical expenses) rather than require extensive documentation
· Use administrative data to verify status and pre-fill forms
· Allow online or phone interviews/submission in addition to in-person options
· Solicit responses and documentation only to the degree necessary to perform task, or legally mandated
· Provide enrollment help: auto-completion, phone, or in-person help, either via public actors or third parties
· Make administrative centers geographically accessible
· Provide help outside the traditional nine-to-five bracket
· Allow third parties to enroll at point of contact (hospitals, churches, community groups)

Psychological costs
· Send messages of welcome and inclusion to potential participants
· Build a cultural ethic based on respectful interaction and an ethic of help
· Give individuals the opportunity to articulate their story and provide feedback
· Offer participants Ombudsman or other clear mechanisms to express dissatisfaction

Source: Authors' compilation.

mission statement, the IRS will have to rethink how it conducts major aspects of its work. To fulfill this aspect of its mission, it will have to hire employees whose skills are better suited for this educational and compliance work. Thus, for the EITC and other tax provisions specifically targeted to the low-income population, the IRS will have to hire or train employees with skills that are drawn from the social work profession."[28]

Although we offer suggestions to shift administrative burden onto the state, such a shift is not a free lunch. These techniques demand smart and capable government coupled with investments in information technology and administrative data, as well as a willingness to let professionals use those tools. The IRS has become leery of maintaining its unasked-for role in the welfare state in large part because it has not received the types of resources to make the changes that Olson envisages.[29] Instead, it has faced both dramatically declining budgets and personnel, and the risk of political blame when politicians decide to target waste and fraud in programs like the EITC. Much of the reputational risks it has encountered arise from its social welfare or regulatory functions rather than its original tax collection function.

Burdens Beyond the United States

One limitation of our approach is that we focus on burden from a U.S. perspective, particularly on the politics of U.S. social policy. This allows us to consider a set of related policies in a specific domain, to dig into the policy details and the political context. But does the concept of burdens travel beyond the polarized setting of the United States?

Just as regulatory burdens occur worldwide, it is also reasonable to expect that administrative burdens will impose learning, compliance, and psychological costs on citizens in different settings. The degree to which burdens are constructed, consequential, and distributive in any particular setting is an empirical question. Although we do not attempt a comprehensive review, enough evidence exists to underline the relevance of administrative burden in other countries, suggesting that the effect may even be more pronounced in poorer countries.

One example is Carolyn Heinrich's examination of an ambitious cash transfer program aimed at eleven million South African children. Potential recipients experienced significant compliance costs, such as extensive documentation requirements, delay at welfare offices, and learning costs exacerbated by changes in the policy rules.[30] As a result, most beneficiaries experienced disruptions in cash transfers, and four in five of those disruptions were made in error. Eligible beneficiaries lost resources, which had a negative effect of adolescent outcomes, resulting in greater rates of sexual activity, alcohol consumption, and criminal behavior.

An analysis of another cash transfer program in India found that only one-third of eligible citizens were enrolled. A field experiment showed that different types of intervention improved access. Simply providing information increased enrollment but only for those literate enough to read the information. Providing help in filling out forms or working directly with bureaucracies to claim benefits had large positive effects, increasing applications by 41 percent and 70 percent respectively, and especially benefiting more vulnerable women who were illiterate, lacked political connections, or had household autonomy.[31]

In Pakistan, Nisar documents the burdens that gender nonconforming individuals face in accessing identity documents, documents that have become increasingly necessary to get a job, claim property rights, access welfare services, or negotiate encounters at security checkpoints.[32] More broadly, Nisar argues that administrative burdens provide an ideal conceptual framework for understanding the experience of marginalized groups in their interactions with the state. Our study of the United States focuses on conceptions of deservingness that intersect with gender, class, and race. Research in other settings can usefully document how the social construction of deservingness and the ensuing psychological costs vary by context.[33]

Such examples illustrate Heinrich's point that the "bite" of administrative burden may be even larger in poorer countries, given that the state has less ability to identify and resolve burdens, and individuals with lower human capital, such as literacy and familiarity in dealing with bureaucratic procedures, are less able to overcome burdens. In the context of India, Akhil Gupta goes even further, suggesting that the red tape that people encounter is a form of structural violence that is responsible for the slow rate of progress for the poor.[34]

This is not to say that administrative burdens do not feature in richer countries. The ways in which they arise might look different. For example, Sebastian Jilke, Wouter Van Dooren, and Sabine Rys use an ingenious design to demonstrate how people encounter learning costs differently in public and private settings. Fictional retirees sent requests for information to Belgian nursing-homes, some with typically Flemish names, some with Arab-sounding names. Private providers were about 20 percentage points less likely to provide information to the Arab applicants. The findings confirm that the selective use of help to minimize learning costs is one tool organizations can use to create a discriminatory effect, and, in this setting at least, private actors were more willing to use it to limit access to public services.[35]

Although limited, such examples suggest that the administrative burden framework we propose is relevant in quite different settings.

Conclusion

The primary goal of this book is to develop and document the concept of administrative burden. It might be tempting to treat our analysis as an attack on government itself. After all, we frame administrative burden in terms of costs and largely negative outcomes for citizens. Are burdens not just one more dispiriting testament to the failures of the public sector? Such an interpretation misses the point. Just as diagnosing a disease is not an attack on the patient, identifying burdens is not an attack on government. Rather, the diagnosis allows us to distinguish between burdens that are necessary or unnecessary and to understand that shifting burdens away from citizens requires adequate administrative capacity. It offers us a framework to improve governance.

If we suppose that elected officials view good government as something that will generate a positive electoral return, the merits of the evidence-based approach we propose is plain. Even if politicians are indifferent to public-sector outcomes, they may discover that tools that hurt good governance are costly in the long run. For example, governments shifted from a spoils system that provided short-term partisan gain to a civil service system that offered long-term competence.[36] If we assume willingness to adopt an evidence-based approach, policymakers, public managers, and third parties need the conceptual language of burdens, empirical documentation of their effects, and the ability to draw a connection to political values.

Governing is ultimately a meeting of the state and the people it serves. There are multiple reasons to ensure that this interaction is no more onerous than it should be: it is good politics not to irritate people; it ensures that individuals are willing to engage with, rather than become disaffected by, government; and, it allows government policies to reach their target audience. It is also the right thing to do. This simple principle of governing appears to have been lost, with burdens being best understood—and most effectively used—by political actors seeking to make government dysfunctional. If government is to do big things, if it is to provide a measure of support and security to the people it serves, or even if it settles for the more modest goal of competence, it needs to master the governance of burdens.

NOTES

Introduction

1. Scott 2001.
2. The sharp-eyed reader may notice that we sometimes use the term *administrative burden* and sometimes *administrative burdens*. The singular is intended to capture the idea of burden as a theoretical concept; the plural reflects the fact that, in practice, burdens are multiple rather than singular.
3. Though often modified, the original quote comes from a dissenting opinion by Holmes in *Compania General de Tabacos v. Collector* 275 U.S. 87 (1927).
4. Sunstein 2013.
5. Benzarti 2017.
6. Jones and Saad 2013; Becker 2013.
7. Associated Press 1944.
8. Dynarski, Scott-Clayton, and Wiederspan 2013; Goldrick-Rab 2016.
9. Hoxby and Avery 2012.
10. Fix, Passel, and Sucher 2003.
11. Gonzalez-Barrera et al. 2013.
12. Nakamura 2013.
13. Heinrich, Hoddinott, and Samson 2017.
14. Spear 1968, 84.
15. Breitman and Kraut 1987, 8.
16. Ibid.
17. Ibid.
18. Knight 1992.
19. On Supplemental Social Insurance, Elder and Powers 2006; on SNAP, Food and Nutrition Service 2007; on Unemployment Insurance, Kroft 2008; on Medicaid, Somers et al. 2012.
20. IRS 2016a, 2016b.
21. ASPE 2007, 19.
22. Hoxby and Turner 2012.

23. Bettinger et al. 2012.
24. Wyman 1985, 67.
25. Breitman and Kraut 1987, 133. At the same time, the State Department added even more barriers to the process. Applications had to be reviewed by Immigration and Naturalization Service, the FBI, Army intelligence, Navy intelligence, and the State Department to assess the candidate's suitability, which took three to six weeks. The additional time involved was not inconsequential. Visas expired at the end of the fiscal year. If the visa was not processed and transportation was not acquired, the applicant had to start again in the new fiscal year (135–36).
26. Wyman 1984, 127.
27. Ibid., 14.
28. Wyman 1984, 190.
29. Breitman and Kraut 1987, 27.
30. The 40 percent figure does not reflect the 2018 tax changes that increased the standard deduction, reducing the number of people who need to take more detailed deductions. It is therefore an underestimate of the proportion of taxpayers who would benefit from return-free filing.
31. Day 2014.
32. Stross 2010.
33. Day 2013.
34. Day 2014.
35. Majoo 2015.
36. Cannon 1980.
37. Goolsbee 2006.
38. Day 2014; Majoo 2015.
39. Wilson 1989; Kaufman 1977.
40. This point is a logical descendent of Terry Moe's argument that public agencies may be structured to be less-than-functional to ensure responsiveness to all groups, especially those that oppose the mission and design of the agency (1989).

Chapter 1: Understanding Administrative Burden

1. Nichols and Zeckhauser 1982, 366–77.
2. For an overview, see Baicker, Congdon, and Mullainathan 2012; Shafir 2013.
3. Shafir 2013.
4. Choi et al. 2004.
5. Jolls, Sunstein, and Thaler 1998; Thaler and Sunstein 2008.
6. Thaler acknowledges that rules might be designed to deliberately lead to worse outcomes for people and has suggested calling them "sludge" (2018). We view our work as a framework for understanding how "sludge" functions in the public sector.
7. Leggett 2014, 8.
8. Bozeman 2000, 12.
9. Bozeman and Feeney 2011, 48.
10. For a summary of this body of research, see Bozeman and Feeney 2011. More recent work has examined the effects of compliance burdens on citizen satisfaction (see, for example, Kaufmann and Tummers 2017).

11. On the intersection, see Brodkin and Majmundar 2010; Fossett and Thompson 2006; on disentitlement, see Lipsky 1980; on equity, see Piven and Cloward 1971.
12. For an example of the application of the administrative burden framework to organizations in the context of understanding the challenges that food producers seeking organic certification face, see Carter, Scott, and Mahallati 2017.
13. Besley 2015; OECD 2007.
14. For examples of efforts to reduce burdens on individuals rather than businesses, see OECD 2012.
15. Eubanks 2018.
16. Burden et al. 2012.
17. Heckman and Smith 2003; Bartlett, Burstein, and Hamilton 2004.
18. Bartlett, Burstein, and Hamilton 2004.
19. On distance, Warlick 1982. Distance from an administrative center also imposes compliance costs in terms of the time and effort it takes to travel there. On barriers; Heckman and Smith 2003.
20. Zedlewski et al. 1993; Currie and Gruber 1996.
21. Budd and McCall 1997; Keiser and Miller 2010; Kopczuk and Pop-Eleches 2007.
22. On take-up, Bhargava and Manoli 2015; Daponte, Sanders, and Taylor 1999; on aid, Hoxby and Avery 2012.
23. The existing empirical evidence may still underestimate the effects of compliance costs in one key way. In some cases, the estimated effects of changes in take-up due to eligibility changes may partly reflect reductions in compliance costs (Hanratty 2006). A prime example is eliminating asset requirements for eligibility. This in turn removes the need for an asset test, and the need for the claimant to provide documentation on assets. Any resulting increase in take-up will be credited to the change in eligibility, but some portion of it likely has to do with reduced application compliance costs.
24. Brien and Swann 2001.
25. Wolfe and Scrivner 2005.
26. Brodkin and Majmundar 2010; Ewalt and Jennings 2004.
27. Hanratty 2006; Kabbani and Wilde 2003; Ratcliffe, McKernan, and Finegold 2008.
28. Leininger et al. 2011.
29. Kopczuk and Pop-Eleches 2007; Schwabisch 2012.
30. Aizer 2003.
31. Schanzenbach 2009.
32. See chapter 3; see also Dorn, Hill, and Hogan 2009.
33. Deci and Ryan 1985.
34. Lind and Tyler 1988.
35. Soss 1999a; Bruch, Marx Ferree, and Soss 2010.
36. Van Ryzin 2011.
37. Moffitt 1983.
38. Katz 1986; Horan and Austin 1974; Piven and Cloward 1971; Schneider and Ingram 1997.
39. Mettler 2011.
40. Stuber and Schlesinger 2006.
41. Bartlett, Burstein, and Hamilton 2004.
42. Piven and Cloward 1971.

43. On applications, Bartlett, Burstein, and Hamilton 2004.
44. Brodkin 1992; Soss 1999b.
45. Lipsky 1980; Soss 1999b.
46. Dias and Maynard-Moody 2007.
47. Goodsell, 1977.
48. Lipsky 1980.
49. Soss 1999a.
50. Dias and Maynard-Moody 2007; Lipsky 1980; Soss 1999b.
51. Pinquart and Sorensen 2003.
52. Thorin and Irvin 1992.
53. Yetter 2016.
54. Nieder 2013.
55. Ratcliffe, McKernan, and Finegold 2008; Schanzenbach 2009.
56. Bhargava and Manoli 2015.
57. Kincheloe, Frates, and Brown 2007; Ratcliffe, McKernan, and Finegold 2008.
58. Bruch, Marx Ferree, and Soss 2010; Mettler and Soss 2004.
59. Mettler 2002, 352.
60. Campbell 2003; Kumlin and Rothstein 2005.
61. Soss 1999a.
62. Campbell 2003.
63. Mettler 2005.
64. Bruch, Marx Ferree, and Soss 2010.
65. On social programs, Aizer 2003; Brodkin and Majmundar 2010; Heckman and Smith 2003; on education, Hoxby and Avery 2012; on voting registration, Rigby and Springer 2011; on immigration, Fix, Passel, and Sucher 2003.
66. Mullainathan and Shafir 2013; see also Gennetian and Shafir 2015.
67. Mani et al. 2013.
68. Schneider and Ingram 1997.
69. Marr and Murray 2016.
70. Barnes and Henley 2018; Brodkin and Lipsky 1983; Lipsky 1980.
71. Moynihan and Soss 2014; Tummers 2013.
72. Bozeman and Feeney 2011.
73. Lasswell 1936.
74. For an excellent categorization of the array of public values relevant for public services, see Jørgensen and Bozeman 2007.
75. Wilson 1989.
76. Brodkin 1987.
77. Hanratty 2006.
78. Wichowsky and Moynihan 2008.
79. Soss et al. 2011.
80. Miller and Schofield 2008; Phillips 1969.
81. Soss, Fording, and Schram 2011.
82. Moe 1989.
83. Lineberry 1977.

84. Hacker 2004, see also Thompson 2012.
85. Hacker 2004, 243.
86. Lascoumes and Le Gales 2007.
87. Edelman 1985.
88. Hacker 2004.
89. Klarner, Mao, and Buchanan 2007.
90. Keiser and Soss 1998.
91. Piven and Cloward 1971; Brodkin and Lipsky 1983; Brodkin 2011; Soss, Fording, and Schram 2011.
92. For example, when the origins of red tape are considered, benign neglect and historical accident are more prominent explanations than deliberate political choice (see Moynihan and Herd 2010).
93. Drawing from the organizational and behavioral perspective of Robert Kahn, Daniel Katz, and Barbara Gutek (1976), Carolyn Heinrich skillfully illuminates how burdens are created by multiple-directional encounters within government and between government, individuals and third-parties (2016).
94. Becker 2014, 10.
95. Keiser and Miller 2010.
96. Their tactics included an advertisement of Uncle Sam providing a gynecological exam to a college student, and campus parties where students were encouraged to demonstrate their independence from government by signing pledges to opt-out of Obamacare.
97. Soss, Fording, and Schram 2011.
98. Creswell 2013.
99. Marshall 1964.
100. *Goldberg, Commissioner of Social Services of the City of New York v. Kelly, et al.*, 397 U.S. 254 (1970).
101. CBPP 2016a.

Chapter 2: The Resurgence of Burdens in Voting: Race, Burdens, and Access to Political Rights

1. On taxation, Bechtel, Hangartner, and Schmid 2016; Martin 2003; Mueller and Stratmann 2003; Wichowsky 2012; on rules, Avery and Peffley 2005.
2. *Shelby County, Alabama v. Holder, Attorney General et al.*, No. 12-96 (570 U.S. ___, 2013), https://www.supremecourt.gov/opinions/12pdf/12-96_6k47.pdf (accessed June 28, 2018).
3. The White House 2017.
4. Foner 2011.
5. Lawson 1999.
6. Goluboff and Lithwick 2011.
7. Lawson 1999, 90.
8. Ibid.
9. Onion 2013.

10. Lawson 1999.
11. Keyssar 2009, 212.
12. Keyssar 2009.
13. Shannon et al. 2017.
14. Estimates are based on the Current Population Survey, based on analysis by Barry Burden, and shared with the authors.
15. Hasen 2012.
16. Berman 2011.
17. Moynihan and Roberts 2010; Rutenberg 2015, see also Berman 2015.
18. Alvarez, Hall, and Llewellyn 2007.
19. Ansolabehere and Konisky 2006.
20. Burden et al. 2014.
21. Braconnier, Dormagen, and Pons 2017.
22. Street et al. 2015.
23. Burden et al. 2014.
24. Flavelle 2015.
25. Knack 1995.
26. Cha and Kennedy 2014.
27. Holbein and Hillygus 2016.
28. Alvarez et al. 2009.
29. Weiser and Norden 2011, 23.
30. Cooper 2011.
31. Herron and Smith 2013.
32. Berman 2015.
33. Stuart 2004.
34. Berman 2015.
35. Goel et al. 2016.
36. Sullivan and Smith 2016.
37. Graham 2016.
38. Haspel and Knotts 2005.
39. Brady and McNulty 2011; McNulty, Dowling, and Ariotti 2009.
40. Burden et al. 2016.
41. Gerber, Huber, and Hill 2013.
42. Burden et al. 2014.
43. National Council of State Legislatures 2017.
44. Commission on Federal Election Reform 2005.
45. The Brennan Center 2016.
46. Mentzer 2011.
47. Frank 2014.
48. Maciag 2013.
49. Hobby et al. 2015.
50. Valentino and Neuner 2017.
51. Alvarez et al. 2009.
52. GAO 2014b.

53. Cecil 2017.
54. Keyssar 2009.
55. Flavelle 2015.
56. Barreto, Cohen-Marks, and Woods 2009.
57. Avery and Peffley 2005.
58. Braconnier, Dormagen, and Pons 2017.
59. Fresh 2018.
60. Rigby and Springer 2011.
61. Burden et al. 2017.
62. Berinsky 2005.
63. Burden et al. 2014, 2017; Rigby and Springer 2011.
64. Fullmer 2014. Elliott Fullmer (2013) suggests that the effects of early voting are conditioned on the nature and location of early voting polling places, offering evidence that early voting sites can also improve turnout for minorities and younger voters if they are widely available in their community.
65. Opoien 2016. Madison benefited from aggressive efforts by county and city officials to expand the early voting sites, along with public service announcements to encourage early voting. The City of Milwaukee, which has less resources and a lower income population, did not see the same efforts.
66. Burden et al. 2014.
67. Barreto, Sanchez, and Walker 2012, 2009.
68. Burden 2015.
69. Sobel 2014.
70. White, Nathan, and Faller 2015.
71. On IDs, Atkeson et al. 2010; Cobb, Greiner, and Quinn 2012; on discretion, Alvarez et al. 2009; Atkeson et al. 2010.
72. Alvarez, Bailey, and Katz 2008; see also GAO 2014b, which found strict voter ID laws in Kansas and Tennessee reduced black turnout to a greater degree than white turnout. Zoltan Hajnal, Nazita Lajevardi, and Lindsay Nielsen compared the turnout gap between whites and nonwhites, claiming that strict voter ID laws have a large negative effect on blacks, Hispanics, and mixed-race voters, and also depressed Democratic turnout more than Republican turnout relative for general elections (2017). However, Justin Grimmer and his colleagues criticize this analysis, arguing that the data and analysis support no definitive conclusions about the causal relationship between voter ID laws and turnout of different groups (2017).
73. Wilson and Brewer 2013.
74. Bentele and O'Brien 2013, 1094.
75. Commission on Federal Election Reform 2005; Presidential Commission on Election Administration 2014.
76. Colvin 2016. An analysis of the 2016 voting data by David Cottrell, Michael Herron, and Sean Westwood disputed this claim, concluding that "the expansive voter fraud concerns espoused by Donald Trump and those allied with him are not grounded in any observable features of the 2016 election" (2018, 1).
77. For example, Lyndon Johnson won a Senate seat partly because followers stuffed ballot boxes (Caro 1990).

78. Levitt 2014; Khan and Carson 2012; Minnite 2010.
79. Levitt 2007; see also Sharad Goel and colleagues, who after examining 130 million 2012 ballots estimate that just 0.02 percent were double votes (2016).
80. Saul 2012.
81. Edelson et al. 2017.
82. Minnite 2010.
83. Lipton and Urbina 2007.
84. Levitt 2007, 16.
85. Alquist, Mayer, and Jackman 2014. About 2.5 percent of the population say they have been involved in voter fraud, equivalent to those who claim to have been abducted by otherworldly creatures.
86. Christensen and Schultz 2014.
87. Presidential Commission on Election Administration 2014.
88. Levitt 2007; Moynihan 2004.
89. Bentele and O'Brien 2013.
90. Ibid.
91. Hayes 2012.
92. Bentele and O'Brien 2013; Fogarty et al. 2015.
93. Fogarty et al. 2015, 2.
94. Bentele and O'Brien 2013.
95. McKee 2015.
96. Wilson and Brewer 2013.
97. Ibid.
98. Wilson, Brewer, and Rosenbluth 2014.
99. Banks and Hicks 2016.
100. Mendez and Grose 2018.
101. Ansolabehere and Persily 2008.
102. *Frank v. Walker*, 768 F.3d 744 (7th Cir. 2014) (Posner, R., dissenting).
103. Drum 2014.
104. Douglas 2014.
105. Eidelson 2016.
106. Wines and Blinder 2016.
107. Universal registration was opposed by all Republicans in the Oregon state senate. Republican Governors, Chris Christie in New Jersey and Tim Pawlenty in Minnesota, vetoed plans similar to those of Oregon. Pawlenty argued that "registering to vote should be a voluntary, intentional act." Christie raised the specter of voter fraud. Such an objection is also hard to sustain. The movement for voter IDs was based on the logic that the process of providing information for driver's licenses and other state-issue ID reduced the potential for fraud in elections, and that such processes are surely more secure and reliable than information collected by third parties in registration drives. The same benefits arise from universal registration. Indeed, one benefit of universal registration would be to remove the need for the current reliance on registration drives that are prone to errors and at the heart of many accusations about fraud.
108. Brennan Center 2016.
109. Liebelson 2014.

Chapter 3: False Claims and Targeted Burdens: The Case of Abortion Restrictions

1. On credibility of Guttmacher, see Cunningham 2015. However, an important caveat to the one in three statistics is that they are based on 2008 abortion rates, and abortions have declined since then, though more exact estimates do not appear to be available.
2. Jerman, Jones, and Onda 2016.
3. Ibid.
4. Upadhyay et al. 2015.
5. *Jane Roe, et al. v. Henry Wade, District Attorney of Dallas County*, 410 U.S. 113 (1973).
6. *Whole Women's Health, et al. v. John Hellerstedt, Commissioner, Texas Department of State Health Services, et al.*, No. 15-274 (579 U.S. ___, 2016), https://www.supremecourt.gov/oral_arguments/argument_transcripts/2015/15-274_d18e.pdf (accessed June 28, 2018).
7. Jones, Finer, and Singh 2010.
8. Jones, Upadhyay, and Weitz 2013.
9. Ibid.
10. Linnane 2013.
11. Tavernise 2016.
12. Jones, Upadhyay, and Weitz 2013.
13. Dennis and Blanchard 2012.
14. Carmon 2015.
15. Kaye, Suellentrop, and Sloup 2009.
16. Kumar, Hessini and Mitchell, 2009, 628.
17. Sanger 2017.
18. Kumar, Hessini, and Mitchell 2009.
19. Major and Gramzow 1999.
20. Finer et al. 2005.
21. Mercier et al. 2015, 6–7.
22. Doe 2013.
23. Linnane 2013.
24. Joffe 2014.
25. *Whole Women's Health v. Hellerstedt.*
26. Cauterucci 2015.
27. Medoff 2015.
28. Upadhyay et al. 2014.
29. Grossman et al. 2015.
30. Stephens-Davidowitz 2016.
31. GAO 2014a.
32. Weitz et al. 2013.
33. Bright 2007.
34. Mercier et al. 2015, 5.
35. Mercier et al. 2015, 5.
36. Joffe 2014.
37. Mississippi State Department of Health 2016.

38. Fernandez 2014.

39. *Planned Parenthood Arizona, Inc. v. Humble,* 753 F.3d 905 (9th Cir. 2014).

40. *Whole Women's Health v. Hellerstedt,* 48.

41. Bazelon 2010.

42. Dennis and Blanchard 2012.

43. Dennis, Manski, and Blanchard 2012.

44. S.C. Reg. 61–12 § 501.

45. 25 Texas Admin. Code § 139.51.

46. S.C. Reg. 61–12 § 501.

47. Upadhyay et al. 2015.

48. Raymond and Grimes 2012.

49. APA Taskforce 2008.

50. Herd et al. 2016.

51. On goals, Upadhyay, Biggs, and Foster 2015; on violence, Roberts et al. 2014.

52. McDorman et al. 2016.

53. Eckholm 2014.

54. Alford and Eckholm 2014.

55. Grimes et al. 2006.

56. Alford and Eckholm 2014.

57. Eckholm 2014.

58. Texas Office of the Governor 2016.

59. Cummings 2005.

60. McCubbins and Schwartz 1984.

61. *Harris, Secretary of Health and Human Services v. Cora McRae, et al.,* 448 U.S. 297 (1980); William L. Webster, Attorney General of Missouri, et al. v. Reproductive Health Services, et al., 492 U.S. 490 (1989); *Planned Parenthood of Southeastern Pennsylvania, et al. v. Robert P. Casey, et al.,* 505 U.S. 833 (1992).

62. *Planned Parenthood v. Casey.*

63. *Frank v. Walker,* 768 F.3d 744 (7th Cir. 2014) (Posner, R., dissenting).

64. Ibid.

65. Davidson 2014.

66. *Whole Women's Health v. Hellerstedt.*

67. Ibid.

68. Ibid.

69. Liptak 2016.

Chapter 4: The Affordable Care Act: Federalism as a Source of Burdens

1. ASPE 2016.

2. OIG HHS 2016, 6.

3. Desilver 2013.

4. Ibid.

5. Medicaid and CHIP Learning Collaborative 2014.

6. Dorn 2014a.

7. Ibid.
8. Ibid.
9. Weiss and Sheedy 2015.
10. OIG HHS 2016.
11. Ibid.
12. Ibid., 28.
13. Brooks et al. 2016.
14. Ibid.
15. Haberkorn 2018.
16. Holahan et al. 2015.
17. Ibid.
18. Kenney et al. 2016.
19. Pradhan 2016.
20. Gary Cohen, *Testimony to the House Committee on Oversight and Government Reform Subcommittee on Energy Policy, Healthcare and Entitlements/Subcommittee on Economic Growth, Job Creation, and Regulatory Affairs*, 113 Cong., 1st sess., May 21, 2013.
21. Collins et al. 2016.
22. Ibid.
23. Dropp and Nyhan 2017.
24. Dorn 2014b.
25. Collins et al. 2016.
26. Dorn 2014b.
27. ConsumersUnion 2009.
28. Garfield and Young 2015.
29. Scott 2015.
30. Families USA 2012.
31. Pollitz, Tolbert, and Semanskee 2016.
32. Ibid.
33. Gary Cohen, *Testimony to the House Committee on Oversight and Government Reform Subcommittee on Energy Policy, Healthcare and Entitlements/Subcommittee on Economic Growth, Job Creation, and Regulatory Affairs*, 113 Cong., 1st sess., May 21, 2013.
34. Pollitz, Tolbert, and Semanskee 2016.
35. Blumberg and Holohan 2015.
36. Pollitz, Tolbert, and Ma 2015.
37. Ibid.
38. Brooks et al. 2016.
39. Healthcare for America Now 2013.
40. Kusnetz 2013.
41. Ibid.
42. Healthcare for America Now 2013.
43. Kusnetz 2013.
44. Tenn. Public Acts, public chapter 377, senate bill 1145, 2013. A federal court struck down the overly broad language of the act in 2015 as an infringement on free speech rights.
45. Perry 2013.

46. Large, diffuse public service networks with infrequent working relationship are more successful when directed by a central network actor, which they label network administrative organization (Provan and Kenis 2008).

47. On the ineffectiveness of such groups in Wisconsin, see Friedsam, Kaplan, and Eskrich 2014.

48. Wishner, Spencer, and Wengle 2014; see also Provan and Kenis 2008, who point to the important of previous working relationships to network success.

49. Ibid.

50. Hill, Wilkinson and Courtot 2014.

51. Giovannelli and Curran 2016.

52. Ibid.; Brooks et al. 2016.

53. The examples are cited at the Center on Budget and Policy Priorities website (see "Sabotage Watch: Tracking Efforts to Undermine the ACA," last updated June 26, 2018, https://www.cbpp.org/sabotage-watch-tracking-efforts-to-undermine-the-aca).

54. CMS 2018.

55. ASPE 2016.

56. *National Federation of Independent Business, et al. v. Kathleen Sebelius, Secretary of Health and Human Services, et al., Department of Health and Human Services, et al. v. Florida, et al., Florida, et al. v. Department of Health and Human Services, et al.,* 567 U.S. 519 (2012).

57. Weiss and Sheedy 2015.

58. Brooks et al. 2016.

59. Ibid.

60. Weiss and Sheedy 2015.

61. Brooks et al. 2016.

62. Weiss and Sheedy 2015.

63. Brooks et al. 2016.

64. Ibid.

65. Guyer, Schwartz, and Artiga 2013.

66. Families USA 2012; Brooks et al. 2016; Gonzales 2016.

67. Brooks et al. 2016.

68. Ibid.

69. State of Michigan 2016.

70. Wisconsin Council on Children and Families 2016.

71. Pear 2017.

72. Weixel 2018

73. Goodnough 2018.

74. Garfield et al. 2018.

75. Ibid.

76. Ibid.

77. Raymond 2018.

78. Ibid.

79. For a detailed breakdown of eligibility rules, see Brooks et al. 2016.

80. Artiga, Rudowitz, and Tolbert 2016.

81. Ibid.

82. Kenney et al. 2016.

Chapter 5: Negotiating the Medicare Maze

1. Gornick et al. 1996.
2. Kaiser Family Foundation 2012.
3. For a discussion of the evidence on choice overload, see Scheibehenne, Greifeneder, and Todd 2010; Chernev, Böckenholt, and Goodman 2010. Debate about a real aggregate effect on choice overload aside, it can be triggered under certain conditions. Given that the role of cognition is central to choice overload, it seems reasonable to assume that cognitive decline is one of those conditions. Empirical evidence appears to support this point in the context of health insurance (see, for example, McWilliams et al. 2011). Richard Thaler and Cass Sunstein also discuss Medicare Part D in their book *Nudge*, in part considering the consequences of choice overload (2008).
4. Stevens 1996; SSA 2015.
5. Gornick et al. 1996.
6. Finkelstein and McKnight 2008.
7. Gornick et al. 1996.
8. Jacobson et al. 2015.
9. GAO 1994; Short and Vistnes 1992.
10. Moon and Herd 2002.
11. Maestas, Schroeder, and Goldman 2009.
12. GAO 2001.
13. Maestas, Schroeder, and Goldman 2009.
14. McGuire, Newhouse, and Sinaiko 2011.
15. Jacobson et al. 2015; Moon and Herd 2002; Herd 2005.
16. Biles, Nicholas, and Cooper 2004; Herd 2005.
17. Medicare Payment Advisory Commission 2016; Zarabozo and Harrison 2009.
18. Afendulis, Sinaiko, and Frank 2015; McWilliams et al. 2011.
19. McWilliams et al. 2011.
20. Wuppermann, Bauhoff, and Grabka 2014.
21. Frank and Lamiraud 2009; McWilliams et al. 2011; Wuppermann, Bauhoff, and Grabka 2014.
22. Jacobson et al. 2014, 12.
23. Medicare Payment Advisory Commission 2012, 2016.
24. Hoadley et al. 2006.
25. Oliver, Lee and Lipton 2004.
26. Herd 2005.
27. GAO 2006.
28. Herd 2005.
29. Besedeš et al. 2012.
30. Barnes et al. 2012.
31. Heiss et al. 2013.
32. Alemayehu and Warner 2004.
33. CMS 2018.
34. Cubanski et al. 2014.
35. Cooper and Gould 2013.

36. SSA 2016b.
37. Johnson and Smeeding 2012.
38. U.S. Census Bureau 2018.
39. Jacobson et al. 2014.
40. Seeman et al. 2010.
41. National Center for Health Statistics 2014.
42. Langa et al. 2008; Ritchie, Artero, and Touchon 2001.
43. Chan and Elbel 2012.
44. Winter et al. 2006.
45. Kuye, Frank, and McWilliams 2013.
46. McWilliams et al. 2011.
47. Ibid.
48. Moon and Herd 2002.
49. Van de Water 2014.
50. McGuire, Newhouse, and Sinaiko 2011.
51. Handel and Kolstad 2015.
52. Hanoch et al. 2009; Hanoch et al. 2011.
53. Frank and Lamiraud 2009; McWilliams et al. 2011.
54. Neuman et al. 2007.
55. Jilke, Van Ryzin and Ven de Walle 2016.
56. Kling et al. 2012.
57. Abaluck and Gruber 2011.
58. Ibid.
59. Heiss et al. 2013.
60. Handel and Kolstad 2015.
61. Smith 2014.
62. Kling et al. 2012.
63. Thaler and Sunstein 2008.
64. Zhang, Baik, and Newhouse 2015.
65. Dickson 2014.
66. Medicare Payment Advisory Commission 2012
67. Medicare Rights Center 2018.

Chapter 6: Bipartisan Fixes and Partisan Blame: Cycles of Burdens in SNAP

1. Rank and Hirschl 2005, 2009.
2. Ganong and Liebman 2013; Food and Nutrition Service 2016.
3. Rosenbaum and Keith-Jennings 2016.
4. On self-sufficiency, Hoynes, Schanzenbach, and Almond 2016; on recidivism, Tuttle 2018.
5. The comments came in the context of a week-long special theme across various Fox News shows of *The Great Food Stamp Binge*, which presented an unemployed, able-bodied Californian surfer as the face of SNAP (Edwards 2013).

6. Lowry 2017.
7. Ganong and Liebman 2013; Haider, Jacknowitz, and Schoeni 2003; Food and Nutrition Service 2014; Wolkwitz and Leftin 2008; Wu 2009.
8. Hanson and Oliveira 2012.
9. Food and Nutrition Service 2016.
10. Ganong and Liebman 2013.
11. Zedlewski and Brauner 1999; Zedlewski and Gruber, 2001.
12. Bartlett, Burstein, and Hamilton 2004.
13. Daponte, Sanders, and Taylor 1999.
14. GAO 1999; see also Quint, Widom, and Moore 2001.
15. Ibid., 28.
16. Ibid.
17. Van Hook and Balistreri 2006.
18. Food and Nutrition Service 2014.
19. Food and Nutrition Service 2010.
20. Ganong and Liebman 2013.
21. Ibid.
22. Kabbani and Wilde 2003: Kornfeld 2002.
23. Ribar, Edelhoch, and Liu 2008.
24. Currie and Grogger 2001; Ribar, Edelhoch, and Liu 2008; Hanratty 2006.
25. Food and Nutrition Service 2010.
26. Hanratty 2006.
27. CBPP 2016b.
28. Schwabisch 2012.
29. Schanzenbach, 2009.
30. Mills et al. 2014.
31. Bartlett, Burstein, and Hamilton 2004.
32. Lopez-Landin 2013, 11.
33. Bartlett, Burstein, and Hamilton 2004.
34. Lopez-Landin 2013, 8.
35. Ibid.
36. Ibid., 8.
37. Ibid., 10.
38. Bartlett, Burstein, and Hamilton 2004.
39. Currie and Grogger 2001, Danielson and Klerman 2006; Kabbani and Wilde 2003; on stigma, Ratcliffe, McKernan, and Finegold 2008; Schanzenbach 2009.
40. Greenridge 2017.
41. Rozsa 2016.
42. Food and Nutrition Service 2016.
43. Food and Nutrition Service 2013.
44. Tuttle 2016. SNAP funding has long been understood to be fungible at the household level, meaning that each extra SNAP dollar gives the household the freedom to spend money from other sources in different ways, such as increasing their consumption on other goods, such as entertainment, utilities, clothes and

transportation. Neo-classical economic theory suggests that households will make only small net investments on food as a result of SNAP (see Tuttle 2016, 5–7). Therefore, the finding that SNAP significantly increases food consumption undercuts one concern about the effectiveness of SNAP in reducing hunger.

45. Rosenbaum and Keith-Jennings 2016.
46. Samuels 2018.
47. Brown et al. 2013.
48. For a letter to state commissioners over SNAP programs from November 30, 2017, see https://www.usda.gov/sites/default/files/documents/lipps-snap-letter.pdf.
49. Dewey 2018.
50. Land 2018.
51. Ibid.
52. Delaney 2018.
53. Kogan and Shapiro 2015.
54. National Council of State Legislatures 2017.
55. Covert and Israel 2016.
56. O'Connor 2017.
57. Soss 2017.
58. Anderson and Butcher 2016.
59. Diane Whitmore Schanzenbach, *Testimony Before the House Committee on Agriculture, Pros and Cons of Restricting Food Stamp Purchases*, 115 Cong., 1st sess., February 16, 2017, https://www.brookings.edu/testimonies/pros-and-cons-of-restricting-snap-purchases (accessed June 28, 2018).
60. Ibid.
61. Freeland-Graves and Nitzke 2013.
62. Daniel 2016.
63. Ganong and Liebman 2013; Haider, Jacknowitz, and Schoeni 2003; Wolkwitz and Leftin 2008; Wu 2009.
64. Eslami 2010.
65. U.S. Census Bureau 2014.
66. Ibid.
67. Langa et al. 2008; Ritchie, Artero, and Touchon 2001.
68. Stern et al. 1994.
69. Machlin and Carper 2014.
70. Neuman et al. 2015.
71. Jones 2014.
72. National Council on Aging 2018.
73. Jones 2014.
74. Pew Charitable Trusts 2014.
75. Mills et al. 2014.
76. Seeman et al. 2010.
77. National Center for Health Statistics 2014.
78. CDC 2013.
79. Ibid.
80. Food and Nutrition Service 2005.

Chapter 7: Mending Medicaid: The Politics of Shifting Burdens at the State Level

1. This chapter is drawn heavily from collaborative work with Hope Harvey and Tom DeLeire. Data for the case study were collected from twenty-four interviews of state and local elected officials, their staff, administrators, and stakeholders involved in changes in the programs. Unless otherwise cited, quotes in the chapter come from these interviews. Program documentation was also analyzed to establish a timeline of changes and the nature of those changes. These included all state operations memos from 1999 to 2012 that referred to Medicaid, BadgerCare, and BadgerCare Plus eligibility procedures, all available application forms from 1999 to 2011; state eligibility handbooks; Department of Health Services internal documents archived at the Wisconsin Historical Society; state audits and external of the program (Gavin et al. 2003; Sirica 2001; Swart, Troia, and Ellegard 2004); and waiver requests submitted to the federal Centers for Medicare and Medicaid Services by the state and federal responses to these waiver requests. For more detailed information on data sources, see Herd et al. 2013.

2. We focus on the governorship because the legislature delegated key details on program changes to the executive branch.

3. See Cohodes et al. 2014; Levine and Schanzenbach 2009; Miller and Wherry 2017.

4. O'Brien and Robertson 2018.

5. Kaiser Commission on Medicaid and the Uninsured 2010a.

6. Guyer, Schwartz, and Artiga 2013.

7. For exceptions, see Fossett and Thompson 2006; Stuber and Kronebusch 2004.

8. Kaiser Commission on Medicaid and the Uninsured 2010a; Shore-Sheppard 2008; Somers et al. 2012.

9. Kenney et al. 2016.

10. The Department of Health Services was formerly part of the Department of Health and Family Services, which was split into two agencies during the Doyle administration. For the sake of simplicity, we refer to the Department of Health Services, though in some cases we are referring to the former department.

11. Kaiser Commission on Medicaid and the Uninsured 2010b.

12. Moynihan, Herd, and Harvey 2015.

13. Sirica 2001, 5.

14. Herd et al. 2013.

15. A limit on BadgerCare spending that distinguishes it from an entitlement program is the inclusion of an enrollment threshold to be enacted if enrollment was projected to exceed budgeted levels.

16. Kronebusch 2001.

17. Thompson 2012.

18. Swart, Troia, and Ellegard 2004.

19. Leininger et al. 2011; Schanzenbach 2009.

20. Gavin et al. 2003.

21. Ibid.

22. The Kaiser Commission on Medicaid and the Uninsured identified these and other state practices that have significantly increased Medicaid enrollment rates (2010b).
23. Thompson 2012.
24. Gavin et al. 2003.
25. Thompson 2012.
26. Espeseth and Riportella 2006.
27. Wisconsin Department of Health and Family Services 2006.
28. Ibid.
29. Dorn, Hill, and Hogan 2009.
30. The vast majority of the previously eligible were family members of enrollees (see DeLeire et al. 2012).
31. DeLeire and Friedsam 2010, 5.
32. Mendel-Clemens 2004.
33. DeLeire and Friedsam 2010.
34. Hynes and Oliver 2010, 17.
35. Ibid., 26.
36. Wisconsin Healthcare Public Relations and Marketing Society 2010, 14.
37. Stuber and Kronebusch 2004.
38. Kaiser Commission on Medicaid and the Uninsured 2013.
39. Center for Healthcare Research and Transformation 2011; Hynes and Oliver 2010.
40. Hynes and Oliver 2010, 27.
41. Ibid.
42. Leininger et al. 2011; Herd et al. 2013.
43. Governor's Commission on Waste, Fraud, and Abuse 2012, 13.
44. Scott Walker, Letter to the Joint Committee on Finance, September 30, 2011, Wisconsin Department of Health Services, http://archives.whcawical.org/whca-docs/DHS%20Sept%2030%20Report.pdf (accessed August 1, 2018), 3.
45. Artiga, Ubri, and Zur 2017.
46. Wright et al. 2005.
47. Friedsam, Kaplan, and Eskrich 2014.
48. Wisconsin Council on Children and Families 2016.
49. Wisconsin Department of Health Services and Wisconsin Commissioner of Insurance 2014.
50. Friedsam, Kaplan, and Eskrich 2014.
51. Albertoni 2011.
52. Wisconsin Council on Children and Families 2016.
53. Boulton 2018.
54. Ibid.
55. Garfield et al. 2018.
56. Boulton 2018
57. Weixel 2018.
58. The Medicaid Act seeks to enable each state "to furnish medical assistance" to individuals "whose income and resources are insufficient to meet the costs of necessary medical services" and to provide "rehabilitation and other services to help such families and individuals attain or retain capability for independence or self-care." The law

specifies that waivers are only to be provided to the extent they facilitate the objectives of the Medicaid Act.

59. CMS 2018.
60. Pierson 2018.
61. Thompson 2012.
62. Moynihan, Herd, and Rigby 2016.
63. Thompson 2012.

Chapter 8: The Earned Income Tax Credit: Benefiting Business by Reducing Burdens on the Working Poor

1. Friedman (1962) saw the mix of existing welfare programs as amounting to a guaranteed income, but one with the worst possible incentives for labor market participation. By contrast, a negative income tax tied welfare support to work. In 1967, Friedman wrote: "If we lived in a hypothetical world in which there were not governmental welfare programs at all and in which all assistance to the destitute was by private charity, the case for introducing a negative income tax would be far weaker than the case for substituting it for present programs. For such a world, I might very well not favor it … [But] the Left, if it accepts the program, will find that it has bought a Trojan Horse." It is doubtful that the Left has regretted embracing the EITC, but its enduring popularity and growth relative to other welfare programs offers some support from Friedman's prediction that it would displace other programs.

2. IRS 2016a, 2016b; see also "About EITC," https://www.eitc.irs.gov/eitc-central/abouteitc.

3. For a strong overview of the evolving politics of welfare, see Weaver 2000.

4. See Newman 2003. Christopher Howard further argues that the EITC benefits from being ambiguous—it can satisfy multiple sets of values at the same time (1997).

5. Individuals pay federal and other types of taxes in addition to the federal income tax, such as federal payroll taxes, and state and local sales and income taxes.

6. Holtz and Scholz 2006.

7. Grogger 2003; Meyer 2002; Meyer and Rosenbaum 1999.

8. Meyer 2002.

9. Meyer and Rosenbaum 1999.

10. Grogger 2003.

11. Hoynes and Patel 2015.

12. IRS 2016a. Twenty states have state EITC programs with total spending around $2 billion on refundable state EITC credits. The Supplemental Nutrition Assistance Program currently has total annual spending that is parallel to the EITC. But SNAP is not, strictly speaking, an income support program.

13. Short 2014.

14. Hoynes and Patel 2015.

15. Baughman 2012; Dahl and Lochner 2012; Michelmore 2013; Strully, Rehkopf, and Xuan 2010.

16. Scholz 1994.
17. Holtzblatt and McCubbin 2004; Plueger 2009.
18. Bhargava and Manoli 2015.
19. Ibid.
20. Halpern-Meekin et al. 2015.
21. Chetty and Saez 2013.
22. Nina Olson, *Written Testimony to the House Subcommittee on Financial Services and General Government Committee on Appropriations, Internal Revenue Service Oversight,* 113 Cong., 2nd sess., February 26, 2014.
23. Plueger 2009.
24. Bhargava and Manoli 2015.
25. Campos 2014.
26. Bhargava and Manoli 2015.
27. Ventry 2000, 992.
28. Sykes et al. 2015, 259.
29. Piven 1998; Piven and Cloward 1971.
30. Mink 1998.
31. The most detailed analysis on this point comes from a series of qualitative studies. See, for example, Sykes et al. 2015, 259; see also Halpern-Meekin et al. 2015, 69: "Among our households, there is no stigma to walking through those [tax-preparers] doors.... At H&R Block, one is a taxpayer, a client."
32. Ventry 2000. All of these proposals drew some inspiration from Milton Friedman's ideas for a negative income tax.
33. Quadagno 1990. Although the minimum income guarantee was by no means the only reason for the failure of the Family Assistance Plan (race, cultural beliefs, and shifting notions of citizenship played critical roles), it was a significant reason.
34. Ventry 2000, 985; see also Betram 2007.
35. Ibid.
36. Burke and Burke 1974, 147.
37. Indeed, Vincent Burke and Vee Burke conclude that "white Southerners feared that FAP's guaranteed income would shrink the supply of cheap labor, bankrupt marginal industry, boost the cost of locally produced goods and services, increase taxes and put more blacks into political office" (1974, 147).
38. Long 1972, 9.
39. Robertson 1988.
40. Quadagno 1990.
41. Ibid., 20.
42. Howard 1997; Ventry 2000.
43. Howard 1997, 891.
44. Ventry 2000.
45. Ibid.
46. The new provisions added a 10 percent supplement to wages up to $4,000 for taxpayers with children, and phased out over the $4,000 to $8,000 income range (Holtz and Scholz 2006).
47. Pierson 2000.
48. Ventry 2000.

49. Weaver 2000; Ventry 2000; Toner 1986.
50. Mufson 1990.
51. *St. Petersburg Times* 1993; Tang 1994.
52. Salwen 1993.
53. Ibid.
54. Rosenbaum 1993.
55. Waltman 2000. Though the Democrats had made a trade-off expanding the EITC at the cost of raising the minimum wage, they eventually were able to pass an unexpected minimum wage increase in 1996, in the midst of the presidential election. This expansion is illustrative of the difficulty of holding off increases in the minimum wage, given its popular resonance and the consequent 80 percent public support for its expansion. Senator Robert Dole was blindsided by a procedural move that allowed Democrats to put the minimum wage on the agenda. Democrats attached amendments that would raise the minimum wage to almost any bill that came forward, effectively making every day a debate over the minimum wage, and forcing Republicans to vote against a popular policy. Eventually, Dole resigned to run for president and Trent Lott became majority leader. At this point, after threats of more guerrilla tactics from Democrats, a bill was finally passed to expand the minimum wage. But it also included nearly $19 billion in tax cuts for small businesses.
56. Betram 2007.
57. Institute for a Competitive Workforce 2007, 19.
58. Ibid., 9.
59. The EPI we cite is the Employment Policies Institute, not to be confused with the Economic Policy Institute, which strongly supports the EITC.
60. Employment Policies Institute, "About Us," http://www.epionline.org/aboutepi/ (accessed July 18, 2018).
61. Lipton 2014.
62. Strom 2010.
63. Lipton 2014.
64. Adams 2011.
65. Donohue 2005.
66. See, for example, Evanstim 2003; Garcia 2005; Doehrel 2006.
67. Institute for a Competitive Workforce 2007, 2.
68. Ibid, 2.
69. James Gaffigan, *Testimony to the House Committee on Ways and Means/Subcommittee on Human Resources*, 104 Cong., 1st sess., June 15, 1995.
70. Smeeding et al. 2000.
71. Leigh 2010.
72. Kopczuk and Pop-Eleches 2007.
73. Ibid.
74. Ibid.
75. Ibid.
76. Get It Back Campaign 2016.
77. Cobb 2014.
78. One might wonder about the validity of a survey presented to citizens by an organization called the Tax Institute (2015) that frames almost every query in terms of

tax fraud, and provides no meaningful background information on questions that citizens do not have information on—for example, that tax preparers are expected to provide more detailed information on returns precisely because they have a record of greater error than self-filers. Although presenting itself as the "independent research and analysis division" of H&R Block, the research is designed to align closely with H&R Block's explicit policy positions.

79. GAO 2014c; see also Olson, *Written Testimony*.

80. Nina Olson, *Written Testimony to the House Subcommittee on Financial Services and General Government Committee on Appropriations, Internal Revenue Service Oversight*, 113 Cong., 2nd sess., February 26, 2014; GAO 2016.

81. John Koskinen, *Written Statement to the House Ways and Means Committee, The State of the IRS*, 113 Cong., 2nd sess., February 5, 2014.

82. Book, Williams, and Holub 2018.

83. Olson, *Written Testimony*, 32.

84. Ibid.

85. GAO 2016.

86. Two-year bans for noncompliance are salient because of the tendency for EITC claimants to not respond to audits. A 2006–2008 EITC compliance study found that 14.6 percent of those audited failed to respond, compared to 2.9 percent for all other taxpayers (IRS 2014).

87. National Taxpayer Advocate 2007.

88. Ibid.

89. National Taxpayer Advocate 2012.

90. Debot, Horton, and Marr 2017.

91. Ventry 2000, 983.

92. Ibid.

93. Treasury Inspector General for Tax Administration 2011; Olson, *Written Testimony*, 31.

94. Ventry 2000.

95. Greenstein, Wancheck, and Marr 2014; Maag, Peters, and Edelstein 2016. For example, multigenerational families may have to provide birth certificates for more than one generation to establish a proof of relationship (GAO 2016).

96. Chait 2014.

97. On the American Enterprise Institute, Mathur 2015; on the American Action Forum, Gitis 2014.

Chapter 9: Social Security: How the Biggest Bookkeeping Organization in the World Banished Burdens

1. In a 2010 poll of self-identified Tea Party members, 62 percent indicated that we spend the right amount of money on programs like Social Security and Medicare (New York Times/CBS News Poll 2010, 26).

2. We are not discussing the Disability Insurance (DI) portion of the program in this chapter, which suffers from the more typical administrative burdens associated with a more tightly targeted program. DI especially struggles from the challenge of determining what qualifies as an eligible disability.

3. CBPP 2016c.

4. Wilson 1989, 100.

5. SSA 1965.

6. Huse 1938, 4.

7. Fukuyama 2013.

8. Quadagno 1984.

9. Ibid.

10. Ibid.

11. Wyatt and Wandel 1937.

12. On his opposition, Bellush 1968; Berkowitz and DeWitt 2009; on his speech, Associated Press 1936.

13. Puckett 2009.

14. Ibid.

15. McKinley and Frase 1970, 18, 28, 49; Puckett 2009.

16. Ibid.

17. Puckett 2009.

18. Bellush 1968.

19. Quadagno 1988.

20. Wilson 1989, 99; see also Puckett 2010.

21. Bellush 1968.

22. Ingraham 1995.

23. McKinley and Frase 1970; Puckett 2010.

24. Corson 1938.

25. Kumlin and Rothstein 2005.

26. Corson 1942, 408–09.

27. Cates 1983, 15.

28. Corson 1942, 408.

29. Altmeyer 1966, 11.

30. Alter 2007, 315.

31. Corson 1938, 6.

32. Corson 1942, 402.

33. DeWitt 2010.

34. Ibid.

35. Kessler-Harris 1995; Quadagno 1988.

36. Quadagno 1988.

37. Altmeyer 1966; DeWitt 2010.

38. U.S. Senate Committee on Finance 1939, 17–18.

39. Christgau 1960.

40. Altmeyer 1966, vii.

41. Skocpol 1992.

42. Fay and Wasserman 1938.

43. Corson 1938; SSA 1965.

44. Commission on Economic Security 1937, 209.

45. Alter 2007.

46. Corson 1938.
47. U.S. House of Representatives 1935, 112–13.
48. Broughton 1940.
49. Puckett 2010.
50. Altmeyer 1958; Corson 1938; Puckett 2009, 2010.
51. Altmeyer 1958; Corson 1938; Puckett 2009.
52. Broughton 1940.
53. Ibid., 13.
54. Corson 1938.
55. Puckett 2010.
56. Corson 1938; Puckett 2010.
57. Puckett 2009.
58. Sheppard 2004.
59. Ibid.
60. Corson 1938; Altmeyer 1958.
61. Huse 1938, 8.
62. SSA 1965.
63. Carpenter and Krause 2012.
64. Puckett 2010; Pogge 1952.
65. Cohen 1985, 21.
66. Wyatt and Wandel 1937.
67. Bellush 1968; Alter 2007.
68. Derthick 1979.
69. SSA 2016a.
70. Bortz 1967.
71. OIG SSA 2014a, 1.
72. Brown et al. 2013; Romig 2016.
73. OIG SSA 2014a.
74. Romig 2016.
75. SSA 2016a.
76. Romig 2016.
77. Davidson 2016.
78. OIG SSA 2014a.
79. Romig 2016.
80. Ibid.
81. OIG SSA 2014a.
82. Ibid.
83. Ibid.
84. Romig 2016.
85. Brown et al. 2013.
86. Ibid.
87. OIG SSA 2016.
88. OIG SSA 2014b.

89. CBPP 2017.
90. Ibid.
91. Bortz 1967.
92. Campbell 2003.
93. Schlesinger 1958, 315.
94. de Schweinitz 1944, 26.

Chapter 10: Toward an Evidence-Based Approach to Administrative Burden

1. The obvious exceptions are in the intensely politicized domains of abortion and elections, but even here, burdens are framed most often through the prism of values, such as access, or fraud, or in a way specific to the policy domain, such as voter suppression.
2. Samuels 2018.
3. Verma 2018.
4. Mettler 2011.
5. Winkler 2011.
6. Soss 1999a.
7. An important caveat that the universalism is itself a relative notion. The original version of Social Security cut across income groups, but to a much more limited degree across racial groups.
8. Hacker 2004.
9. Reitman 2014.
10. See, for example, Speaker Paul Ryan's Commission on Evidence-Based Policy (https://www.cep.gov).
11. Brodkin and Lipsky 1983.
12. Heinrich 2007; Moynihan 2008; Vining and Weimer 2015.
13. *Whole Women's Health v. Cole*, No. 14-50928 (5th Cir., 2015).
14. *Whole Women's Health v. Hellerstedt*.
15. *Planned Parenthood Arizona, Inc. v. Humble*, 753 F.3d 905 (9th Cir., 2014), 913.
16. *Whole Women's Health v. Hellerstedt*.
17. Rainey 2009.
18. OECD 2012.
19. Nationaler Normenkontrollat 2013.
20. Lipsky 1980.
21. Heinrich, Lynn, and Milward 2010.
22. Soss, Fording, and Schram 2011.
23. Barry Bozeman made essentially the same observations for red tape (2000).
24. Bettinger et al. 2012
25. Choi et al. 2004.
26. Heller 2017.
27. Eubanks 2018.
28. Olson 2015, 15.

29. Hickman 2016.
30. Heinrich 2016; see also Heinrich, Hoddinott, and Sampson 2017.
31. Gupta 2017.
32. Nisar 2018.
33. Masood and Nisar 2018.
34. Gupta 2012.
35. Jilke, Van Dooren, and Rys 2018.
36. Gailmard and Patty 2012.

REFERENCES

Abaluck, Jason, and Jonathan Gruber. 2011. "Choice Inconsistencies Among the Elderly: Evidence from Plan Choice in the Medicare Part D Program." *American Economic Review* 101(4): 1180–210.

Adams, Susan. 2011. "Obama Nominee Pulled Back on Minimum Wage Defense." *Forbes*, August 31. Accessed June 21, 2018. https://www.forbes.com/sites /susanadams/2011/08/31/obama-nominee-pulled-back-on-minimum-wage -defense/#3e85f97447f7.

Afendulis, Christopher, Anna Sinaiko, and Richard Frank. 2015. "Dominated Choices and Medicare Advantage Enrollment." *Journal of Economic Behavior and Organization* 119 (November): 72–83.

Aizer, Anna. 2003. "Low Take-Up in Medicaid: Does Outreach Matter and for Whom?" *American Economic Review Papers and Proceedings* 93(2): 238–41.

Albertoni, Rich. 2011. "Administrative Renewals." Operations Memo. Madison: Wisconsin Department of Health Services.

Alemayehu, Berhanu, and Kenneth Warner. 2004. "The Lifetime Distribution of Healthcare Costs." *Health Services Research* 39(3): 627–42.

Alford, Jeremy, and Erik Eckholm. 2014. "With New Bill, Abortion Limits Spread in South." *New York Times*, May 21. Accessed June 21, 2018. http://www.nytimes.com /2014/05/22/us/politics/new-bill-spreads-abortion-limits-in-south.html.

Alquist, John S., Kenneth R. Mayer, and Simon Jackman. 2014. "Alien Abduction and Voter Impersonation in the 2012 US General Election: Evidence from a Survey List Experiment." *Election Law Journal* 13(4): 460–75.

Alter, Jonathan. 2007. *The Defining Moment: FDR's Hundred Days and the Triumph of Hope*. New York: Simon and Schuster.

Altmeyer, Arthur J. 1958. "The Wisconsin Idea and Social Security." *Wisconsin Magazine of History* 42(1): 19–25.

———. 1966. *The Formative Years of Social Security*. Madison: University of Wisconsin Press.

Alvarez, R. Michael, Stephen Ansolabehere, Adam Berinsky, Gabriel Lenz, Charles Stewart III, and Thad Hall. 2009. *2008 Survey of the Performance of American*

Elections: Final Report. Washington, D.C.: Pew Center for the States. Accessed June 21, 2018. http://www.pewtrusts.org/en/research-and-analysis/reports /2009/03/26/2008-survey-of-the-performance-of-american-elections.

Alvarez, R. Michael, Delia Bailey, and Jonathan Katz. 2008. "The Effect of Voter Identification Laws on Turnout." *Social Science* working paper no. 1267R. Pasadena: California Institute of Technology. Accessed June 21, 2018. http:// jkatz.caltech.edu/research/files/wp1267R.pdf.

Alvarez, R. Michael, Thad E. Hall, and Morgan Llewellyn. 2007. "How Hard Can It Be: Do Citizens Think It Is Difficult to Register to Vote." *Stanford Law & Policy Review* 18(2): 383–409.

American Psychological Association Taskforce on Mental Health and Abortion (APA Taskforce). 2008. *Report of the APA Taskforce on Mental Health and Abortion.* Washington, D.C.: American Psychological Association.

Anderson, Patricia M., and Kristin F. Butcher. 2016. "The Relationships Among SNAP Benefits, Grocery Spending, Diet Quality, and the Adequacy of Low-Income Families' Resources." Washington, D.C.: Center on Budget and Policy Priorities.

Ansolabehere, Stephen, and David M. Konisky. 2006. "The Introduction of Voter Registration and Its Effect on Turnout." *Political Analysis* 14(1): 83–100.

Ansolabehere, Stephen, and Nathaniel Persily. 2008. "Vote Fraud in the Eye of the Beholder: The Role of Public Opinion in the Challenge to Voter Identification Requirements." *Harvard Law Review* 121(7): 1737–74.

Artiga, Samantha, Robin Rudowitz, and Jennifer Tolbert. 2016. "Outreach and Enrollment Strategies for Reaching the Medicaid Eligible but Uninsured Population." San Francisco: Kaiser Family Foundation. Accessed June 21, 2018. https://www.kff.org/medicaid/issue-brief/outreach-and-enrollment-strategies -for-reaching-the-medicaid-eligible-but-uninsured-population.

Artiga, Samantha, Petry Ubri, and Julia Zur. 2017. "The Effects of Premiums and Cost Sharing on Low-Income Populations: Updated Review of Research Find-ings." San Francisco: Kaiser Family Foundation. Accessed July 18, 2018. https:// www.kff.org/medicaid/issue-brief/the-effects-of-premiums-and-cost-sharing -on-low-income-populations-updated-review-of-research-findings/.

Assistant Secretary for Planning and Evaluation (ASPE). 2007. *Indicators of Welfare Dependence, Annual Report to Congress.* Washington: U.S. Department of Health and Human Services.

———. 2016. "Health Insurance Coverage and the Affordable Care Act, 2010–2016." *ASPE* Issue Brief. Washington: U.S. Department of Health and Human Services.

Associated Press. 1936. "Text of Gov. Landon's Milwaukee Address on Economic Security." *New York Times*, September 27.

———. 1944. "Tax Form Baffles Even Prof. Einstein." *New York Times*, March 11, A1.

Atkeson, Lonna Rae, Lisa A. Bryant, Thad E. Hall, Kyle L. Saunders, and R. Michael Alvarez. 2010. "A New Barrier to Participation: Heterogeneous Application of Voter Identification Policies." *Electoral Studies* 29(1): 66–73.

Avery, James, and Mark Peffley. 2005. "Voter Registration Requirements, Voter Turnout, and Welfare Eligibility Policy: Class Bias Matters." *State Politics and Policy Quarterly* 5(1): 47–67.

Baicker, Katherine, William J. Congdon, and Sendhil Mullainathan. 2012. "Health Insurance Coverage and Take-Up: Lessons from Behavioral Economics." *Milbank Quarterly* 90(1): 107–34.

Banks, Antoine, and Heather Hicks. 2016. "Fear and Implicit Racism: Whites' Support for Voter ID Laws." *Political Psychology* 37(5): 641–58.

Barnes, Andrew, Yaniv Hanoch, Stacey Wood, Pi-Ju Liu, and Thomas Rice. 2012. "One Fish, Two Fish, Red Fish, Blue Fish: Effects of Price Frames, Brand Names, and Choice Set Size on Medicare Part D Insurance Plan Decisions." *Medical Care Research and Review* 69(4): 460–73.

Barnes, Carolyn Y., and Julia R. Henley. 2018. "'They Are Underpaid and Understaffed': How Clients Interpret Encounters with Street-Level Bureaucrats." *Journal of Public Administration Research and Theory* 28(2): 165–81.

Barreto, Matt A., Mara Cohen-Marks, and Nathan D. Woods. 2009. "Are All Precincts Created Equal? The Prevalence of Low-Quality Precincts in Low-Income and Minority Communities." *Political Research Quarterly* 62(3): 445–58.

Barreto, Matt A., Gabriel R. Sanchez, and Hannah Walker. 2012. "Rates of Possession of Valid Photo Identification, and Public Knowledge of Voter ID Law in Pennsylvania." Expert Report Submitted on Behalf of Plaintiffs in *Applewhite, et al. v. Commonwealth of Pennsylvania et al.*, No. 330 MD 2012. Accessed June 21, 2018. https://www.pubintlaw.org/wp-content/uploads/2012/05/Voter-ID -expert-report-Matt-Barreto.pdf.

Bartlett, Susan, Nancy Burstein, and William Hamilton. 2004. "Food Stamp Program Access Study." Washington: U.S. Department of Agriculture, Economic Research Service. Accessed June 21, 2018. https://www.ers.usda.gov/publications /pub-details/?pubid=43407.

Baughman, Reagan A. 2012. "The Effects of State EITC Expansion on Children's Health." Issue Brief no. 48. Durham: University of New Hampshire, Carsey Institute.

Bazelon, Emily. 2010. "The New Abortion Providers." *New York Times*, July 14. Accessed June 21, 2018. http://www.nytimes.com/2010/07/18/magazine /18abortion-t.html.

Bechtel, Michael. M., Dominik Hangartner, and Lukas Schmid. 2016. "Does Compulsory Voting Increase Support for Leftist Policy?" *American Journal of Political Science* 60(3): 752–67.

Becker, Bernie. 2013. "Pew: IRS Least Popular of Federal Agencies." *The Hill*, October 21. Accessed June 21, 2018. http://thehill.com/policy/finance /329713-pew-irs-least-popular-among-federal-agencies.

Becker, Howard S. 2014. *What About Mozart? What About Murder?: Reasoning from Cases*. Chicago: University of Chicago Press.

Bellush, Bernard. 1968. *He Walked Alone: A Biography of John Gilbert Winant*. Berlin: Mouton de Gruyter.

Bentele, Keith G., and Erin E. O'Brien. 2013. "Jim Crow 2.0? Why States Consider and Adopt Restrictive Voter Access Policies." *Perspectives on Politics* 11(4): 1088–116.

Benzarti, Youssef. 2017. "How Taxing Is Tax Filing: Using Revealed Preferences to Estimate Compliance Costs." *NBER* working paper no. 23903. Cambridge, Mass.: National Bureau of Economic Research.

Berinsky, Adam J. 2005. "The Perverse Consequences of Electoral Reform in the United States." *American Politics Research* 33(4): 471–91.

Berkowitz, Edward D., and Larry DeWitt. 2009. "Social Security from the New Deal to the Great Society: Expanding the Public Domain." In *Conservatism and American Political Development,* edited by Brian Glenn and Steven Teles. New York: Oxford University Press.

Berman, Ari. 2011. "The GOP War on Voting." *Rolling Stone,* August 30. Accessed June 21, 2018. http://www.rollingstone.com/politics/news/the-gop-war-on -voting-20110830.

———. 2015. *Give Us the Ballot: The Modern Struggle for Voting Rights in America.* London: Macmillan.

Besedeš, Tibor, Cary Deck, Sudipta Sarangi, and Mikael Shor. 2012. "Age Effects and Heuristics in Decision Making." *Review of Economics and Statistics* 94(2): 580–95.

Besley, Timothy. 2015. "Law, Regulation, and the Business Climate: The Nature and Influence of the World Bank Doing Business Project." *Journal of Economic Perspectives* 29(3): 99–120.

Betram, Eva C. 2007. "The Institutional Origins of 'Workfarist' Social Policy." *Studies in American Political Development* 21(2): 203–39.

Bettinger, Eric, Bridget Long, Philip Oreopoulos, and Lisa Sanbonmatsu. 2012. "The Role of Application Assistance and Information in College Decisions: Results from the H&R Block FASFA Experiment." *Quarterly Journal of Economic* 127(3): 1205–42.

Bhargava, Saurabh, and Dayanand Manoli. 2015. "Why Are Benefits Left on the Table? Assessing the Role of Information, Complexity, and Stigma on Take-Up with an IRS Field Experiment." *American Economic Review* 105(11): 1–42.

Biles, Brian, Lauren Hersch Nicholas, and Barbara S. Cooper. 2004. "The Cost of Privatization: Extra Payments to Medicare Advantage Plans—2005 Update." Issue Brief. New York: Commonwealth Fund.

Blumberg, Linda J., and John Holahan. 2015. "After King v. Burwell: Next Steps for the Affordable Care Act." Washington, D.C.: The Urban Institute. Accessed June 21, 2018. https://www.urban.org/research/publication/after-king-v -burwell-next-steps-affordable-care-act.

Book, Leslie, David Williams, and Krista Holub. 2018. "Insights from Behavioral Economics Can Improve the Administration of the EITC." *Virginia Tax Review* 37: 177–242.

Bortz, Abe. 1967. "Historical Interview with John J. Corson." *Social Security History.* Washington: Social Security Administration. Accessed June 21, 2018. https:// www.ssa.gov/history/corsonoral.html.

Boulton, Guy. 2018. "Proposed Work Requirements Could Add Uncertainties to Wisconsin's Medicaid System." *Milwaukee Journal Sentinel,* March 28. Accessed June 21, 2018. https://www.jsonline.com/story/money/business/health-care /2018/03/28/wisconsin-among-states-seeking-federal-approval-work -requirements-some-people-covered-medicaid-but-o/460672002.

Bozeman, Barry. 2000. *Bureaucracy and Red Tape.* Upper Saddle River, N.J.: Prentice Hall.

Bozeman, Barry, and Mary K. Feeney. 2011. *Rules and Red Tape: A Prism for Public Administration Research and Theory.* Armonk, N.Y.: ME Sharp.

Braconnier, Céline, Jean-Yves Dormagen, and Vincent Pons. 2017. "Voter Registration Costs and Disenfranchisement: Experimental Evidence from France." *American Political Science Review* 111(3): 584–604.

Brady, Henry E., and John E. McNulty. 2011. "Turning Out to Vote: The Costs of Finding and Getting to the Polling Place." *American Political Science Review* 105(1): 115–34.

Breitman, Richard, and Alan M. Kraut. 1987. *American Refugee Policy and European Jewry, 1933–1945.* Bloomington: Indiana University Press.

Brennan Center. 2016. "The Case for Automatic Voter Registration." New York: Brennan Center. Accessed June 21, 2018. http://www.brennancenter.org/sites/default/files/publications/Case_for_Automatic_Voter_Registration.pdf.

Brien, Michael, and Christopher Swann. 2001. "Prenatal WIC Participation and Infant Health: Selection and Maternal Fixed Effects." *Thomas Jefferson Center* discussion paper no. 295. Charlottesville: University of Virginia.

Bright, Leonard. 2007. "Does Person-Organization Fit Mediate the Relationship Between Public Service Motivation and the Job Performance of Public Employees?" *Review of Public Personnel Administration* 27(4): 361–79.

Brodkin, Evelyn. 1987. "Policy Politics: If We Can't Govern, Can We Manage?" *Political Science Quarterly* 102(4): 571–87.

———. 1992. "The Organization of Disputes: The Bureaucratic Construction of Welfare Rights and Wrongs." *Studies in Law, Politics, and Society* 12: 53–76.

———. 2011. "Policy Work: Street-Level Organizations Under New Managerialism." *Journal of Public Administration Research and Theory* 21(Supplement 2): i199–201.

Brodkin, Evelyn, and Michael Lipsky. 1983. "Quality Control in AFDC as an Administrative Strategy." *Social Service Review* 57(1): 1–34.

Brodkin, Evelyn, and Malay Majmundar. 2010. "Administrative Exclusion: Organizations and the Hidden Costs of Welfare Claiming." *Journal of Public Administration Research and Theory* 20(4): 827–48.

Brooks, Tricia, Sean Miskell, Samantha Artiga, Elizabeth Cornachione, and Alexandra Gates. 2016. "Medicaid and CHIP Eligibility, Enrollment, Renewal, and Cost-Sharing Policies as of January 2016: Findings from a 50-State Survey." San Francisco: Kaiser Family Foundation. Accessed June 21, 2018. https://www.kff.org/medicaid/report/medicaid-and-chip-eligibility-enrollment-renewal-and-cost-sharing-policies-as-of-january-2016-findings-from-a-50-state-survey.

Broughton, Philip. 1940. "Wage Reports Must Be Right." *Social Security Bulletin* 3(8): 10–17. Accessed June 21, 2018. https://www.ssa.gov/policy/docs/ssb/v3n8/v3n8p10.pdf.

Brown, Kay, Gale Harris, Nhi Nguyen, and Michael Pahr. 2013. "Temporary Assistance for Needy Families: Potential Options to Improve Performance and Oversight." GAO-13-431. Washington: Government Accountability Office. Accessed June 21, 2018. http://www.gao.gov/assets/660/654614.pdf.

Bruch, Sarah K., Myra Marx Ferree, and Joe Soss. 2010. "From Policy to Polity Democracy, Paternalism, and the Incorporation of Disadvantaged Citizens." *American Sociological Review* 75(2): 205–26.

Budd, John, and Brian McCall. 1997. "The Effect of Unions on the Receipt of Unemployment Insurance Benefits." *Industrial & Labor Relations Review* 50(3): 478–91.

Burden, Barry C. 2015. "Expert Report: *North Carolina State Conference of the NAACP v. McCrory, et al.*" Case No. 1:13-cv-00658-TDS-JEP (MDNC). Accessed June 21, 2018. https://cdn.theatlantic.com/assets/media/files/41187c5df0d29acea8_q1m6bhevg.pdf.

Burden, Barry C., David T. Canon, Kenneth R. Mayer, and Donald P. Moynihan. 2012. "The Effect of Administrative Burden on Bureaucratic Perception of Policies: Evidence from Election Administration." *Public Administration Review* 72(5): 741–51.

———. 2014. "Election Laws, Mobilization, and Turnout: The Unanticipated Consequences of Election Reform." *American Journal of Political Science* 58(1): 95–109.

———. 2017. "The Complicated Partisan Effects of State Election Laws." *Political Research Quarterly* 70(3): 564–76.

Burden, Barry, Jason Fletcher, Pam Herd, Brad Jones, and Donald Moynihan. 2016. "How Different Forms of Health Matter to Political Participation: The Roles of Cognitive, Physical, and General Health." *Journal of Politics* 79(1): 166–78.

Burke, Vincent J., and Vee Burke. 1974. *Nixon's Good Deed: Welfare Reform.* New York: Columbia University Press.

Campbell, Andrea Louise. 2003. *How Policies Make Citizens: Senior Political Activism and the American Welfare State.* Princeton, N.J.: Princeton University Press.

Campos, Nora. 2014. *The Path to Earned Income Tax Credit Participation: Are Community Coalitions Beneficial?* Dallas: University of Texas.

Cannon, Lou. 1980. "The Leader He Was, the Leader He Wasn't." *Washington Post.* April 26.

Carmon, Irin. 2015. "Shuttered: The End of Abortion Access in Red America." *MSNBC,* October 21. Accessed June 21, 2018. http://www.msnbc.com/shuttered.

Caro, Robert A. 1990. *The Years of Lyndon Johnson: Means of Ascent.* New York: Alfred A Knopf.

Carpenter, Daniel P., and George A. Krause. 2012. "Reputation and Public Administration." *Public Administration Review* 72(1): 26–32.

Carter, David A., Tyler P. Scott, and Nadia Mahallati. 2017. "Balancing Barriers to Entry and Administrative Burdens in Voluntary Regulation." *Perspectives on Public Management and Governance.* Published online September 27. DOI: 10.1093/ppmgov/gvx005.

Cates, Jerry. 1983. *Insuring Inequality: Administrative Leadership in Social Security, 1935–54.* Ann Arbor: University of Michigan Press.

Cauterucci, Christina. 2015. "Shuttering Texas Abortion Clinics Means More Second-Term Abortions." *Slate,* October 5. Accessed June 21, 2018. http://www.slate.com/blogs/xx_factor/2015/10/05/as_texas_abortion_clinics_close_second_term_abortions_will_spike.html.

Cecil, Guy. 2017. "Voter Suppression Analysis." May 3. Chicago: Civis Analytics. Accessed June 21, 2018. http://www.demos.org/publication/voter-suppression -analysis-civis-analytics.

Center on Budget and Policy Priorities (CBPP). 2016a. "Introduction to the Federal Budget Policy Process." Policy Basics. Washington, D.C.: CBPP. Accessed June 21, 2018. http://www.cbpp.org/sites/default/files/atoms/files/3-7-03bud.pdf.

———. 2016b. "SNAP Online: A Review of State Government SNAP Websites." Washington, D.C.: CBPP. Accessed June 21, 2018. http://www.cbpp.org/research /food-assistance/snap-online-a-review-of-state-government-snap-websites.

———. 2016c. "Top Ten Facts About Social Security." Policy Basics. Washington, D.C.: CBPP. Accessed June 21, 2018. http://www.cbpp.org/research/social-security /policy-basics-top-ten-facts-about-social-security.

———. 2017. "A Quick Guide to SNAP Eligibility and Benefits." Washington, D.C.: CBPP. Accessed June 21, 2018. https://www.cbpp.org/sites/default/files/atoms /files/11-18-08fa.pdf.

Center for Healthcare Research and Transformation. 2011. "Medicaid Enrollment and Eligibility Practice Opportunities." Accessed June 21, 2018. http://www.chrt.org /publication/medicaid-enrollment-eligibility-practice-opportunities.

Centers for Disease Control and Prevention (CDC). 2013. *The State of Aging and Health in America 2013*. Hyattsville, Md.: U.S. Department of Health and Human Services. Accessed June 21, 2018. https://www.cdc.gov/aging/pdf/state-aging -health-in-america-2013.pdf.

Cha, J. Mijin, and Liz Kennedy. 2014. *Millions to the Polls: Practical Policies to Fulfill the Freedom to Vote for All Americans*. New York: Demos.

Chait, Jonathan. 2014. "Obama to Republicans: You're Right, Let's Expand the Earned Income Tax Credit." *New York Magazine*, March 4. Accessed July 20, 2018. http:// nymag.com/daily/intelligencer/2014/03/obama-to-gop-youre-right-lets -expand-eitc.html.

Chan, Sewin, and Brian Elbel. 2012. "Low Cognitive Ability and Poor Skill with Numbers May Prevent Many from Enrolling in Medicare Supplemental Coverage." *Health Affairs* 31(8): 1847–54.

Chernev, Alexander, Ulf Böckenholt, and Joseph Goodman. 2010. "Commentary on Scheibehenne, Greifeneder, and Todd Choice Overload: Is There Anything to It?" *Journal of Consumer Research* 37(3): 426–28.

Chetty, Raj, and Emmanual Saez. 2013. "Teaching the Tax Code: Earnings Responses to an Experiment with EITC Recipients." *American Economic Journal: Applied Economics* 5(1): 1–31.

Choi, James, David Laibson, Brigitte Madrian, and Andrew Metrick. 2004. "Saving for Retirement on the Path of Least Resistance." Working paper no. 04-08A0405B. Washington: National Bureau of Labor Statistics.

Christensen, Ray, and Thomas J. Schultz. 2014. "Identifying Election Fraud Using Orphan and Low Propensity Voters." *American Politics Research* 42(2): 311–37.

Christgau, Victor. 1960. "Old-Age, Survivors, and Disability Insurance After Twenty-Five Years." *Social Security Bulletin* 23(8): 20–30.

Cobb, Rachael V., D. James Greiner, and Kevin M. Quinn. 2012. "Can Voter ID Laws Be Administered in a Race-Neutral Manner? Evidence from the City of Boston in 2008." *Quarterly Journal of Political Science* 7(1): 1–33.

Cobb, William. 2014. "H&R Block Addresses EITC Improper Payments and Related Fraud." *Tax Notes Today*, November 11. Accessed June 21, 2018. http://www.taxanalysts.org/content/hr-block-addresses-eitc-improper-payments-and-related-fraud.

Cohen, Wilbur. 1985. "The Early Days of Social Security." *Social Security History*. Washington: Social Security Administration. Accessed June 21, 2018. https://www.ssa.gov/history/50wc.html.

Cohodes, Sarah R., Daniel S. Grossman, Samuel A. Kleiner, and Michael F. Lovenheim. 2014. "The Effect of Child Health Insurance Access on Schooling: Evidence from Public Insurance Expansions." *NBER* working paper no. 20178. Cambridge, Mass.: National Bureau of Economic Research.

Collins, Sara R., Munira Z. Gunja, Michelle M. Doty, and Sophie Beutel. 2016. "Who Are the Remaining Uninsured and Why Haven't They Signed Up for Coverage?" Issue Brief no. 24. New York: Commonwealth Fund.

Colvin, Jill. 2016. "Trump Wrongly Insists Voter Fraud Is 'Very, Very Common.'" Associated Press, October 18. Accessed June 21, 2018. http://bigstory.ap.org/article/93d1908f2a324c3492dd117f1712b14e/trump-wrongly-insists-voter-fraud-very-very-common.

Commission on Economic Security. 1937. *Social Security in America*. Publication no. 20. Washington: Government Printing Office. Accessed June 21, 2018. https://www.ssa.gov/history/reports/ces/cesbook.html.

Commission on Federal Election Reform. 2005. *Building Confidence in US Elections: Report of the Commission on Federal Election Reform*. Washington, D.C.: American University, Center for Democracy and Election Management. Accessed June 21, 2018. https://www.eac.gov/assets/1/6/Exhibit%20M.PDF.

ConsumersUnion. 2009. "Simplifying Health Insurance Choices." Health Policy Brief. Yonkers, N.Y.: ConsumersUnion. Accessed July 18, 2018. https://consumersunion.org/pdf/SimplifyingHealthInsuranceChoices-CU-FINAL-June2009.pdf.

Cooper, David, and Elise Gould. 2013. "Financial Security of Elderly Americans at Risk." Briefing Paper no. 362. Washington, D.C.: Employee Policy Institute. Accessed June 21, 2018. http://www.epi.org/publication/economic-security-elderly-americans-risk.

Cooper, Michael. 2011. "New State Rules Raise Hurdles at Voting Booth." *New York Times*, October 3. http://www.nytimes.com/2011/10/03/us/new-state-laws-are-limiting-access-for-voters.html.

Corson, John. 1938. "Administering Old-Age Insurance." *Social Security Bulletin* 1: 3–6.
———. 1942. "Social Insurance: Its Nature and Characteristics as Exemplified by the Old Age and Survivor's Insurance System." *Social Service Review* 16(3): 401–13.

Cottrell, David, Michael C. Herron, and Sean J. Westwood. 2018. "An Exploration of Donald Trump's Allegations of Massive Voter Fraud in the 2016 General Election." *Electoral Studies* 51(February): 123–42.

Covert, Bryce, and Josh Israel. 2016. "Drug Testing Welfare Recipients is a Popular New Policy that Costs States Millions. Here Are the Results." Thinkprogress.com, February 19. Accessed June 21, 2018. https://thinkprogress.org/drug-testing -welfare-recipients-is-a-popular-new-policy-that-cost-states-millions-here -are-the-cf829257adeo.

Creswell, J. W. 2013. *Qualitative Inquiry and Research Design: Choosing Among Five Approaches*, 3rd ed. Thousand Oaks, Calif.: Sage Publications.

Cubanski, Juliette, Christina Swoope, Anthony Damico, and Tricia Neuman. 2014. *How Much Is Enough? Out-of-Pocket Spending Among Medicare Beneficiaries.* San Francisco: Kaiser Family Foundation.

Cummings, Jeanne. 2005. "In Abortion Fight, Little-Known Group Has Guiding Hand." *Wall Street Journal*, November 30. Accessed June 21, 2018. http:// www.wsj.com/articles/SB113331435902109731.

Cunningham, Paige. 2015. "Both Sides of Abortion Debate Get Data from Same Source." *Washington Examiner*, October 20. Accessed June 21, 2018. http:// www.washingtonexaminer.com/both-sides-of-abortion-debate-get-data -from-same-source/article/2572477.

Currie, Janet. 2004. "The Take Up of Social Benefits." *NBER* working paper no. 10488. Cambridge, Mass.: National Bureau of Economic Research.

Currie, Janet, and Jeffrey Grogger. 2001. "Explaining Recent Declines in Food Stamp Program Participation." *Brookings-Wharton Papers on Urban Affairs* (2001): 203–44. Accessed June 21, 2018. https://muse.jhu.edu/article/35588/pdf.

Currie, Janet, and Jonathan Gruber. 1996. "Health Insurance Eligibility, Utilization of Medical Care, and Child Health." *Quarterly Journal of Economics* 111(2): 431–66.

Dahl, Gordon B., and Lance Lochner. 2012. "The Impact of Family Income on Child Achievement: Evidence from the Earned Income Tax Credit." *American Economic Review* 102(5): 1927–56.

Daniel, Caitlin. 2016. "A Hidden Cost to Giving Kids Their Vegetables." *New York Times*, February 16. Accessed June 21, 2018. https://www.nytimes.com/2016/02/16 /opinion/why-poor-children-cant-be-picky-eaters.html.

Danielson, Caroline, and Jacob Alex Klerman. 2006. *Why Did the Food Stamp Caseload Decline (and Rise?): Effects of Policies and the Economy.* Madison: University of Wisconsin, Institute for Research on Poverty.

Daponte, Beth Osborne, Seth Sanders, and Lowell Taylor. 1999. "Why Do Low-Income Households Not Use Food Stamps? Evidence from an Experiment." *Journal of Human Resources* 34(3): 612–28.

Davidson, Amy. 2014. "Fractions of Women in Texas." *New York Times*, October 5. Accessed June 21, 2018. https://www.newyorker.com/news/amy-davidson /texas-abortion-law-women.

Davidson, Joe. 2016. "Closed Social Security Offices, Furloughed Staff Under GOP Cuts, Agency Warns." *Washington Post*, August 9. Accessed June 21, 2018. https://www.washingtonpost.com/news/powerpost/wp/2016/08/09 /closed-social-security-offices-furloughed-staff-under-gop-cuts-agency-warns /?utm_term=.5455bd833f20.

Day, Liz. 2013. "How the Maker of TurboTax Fought Free, Simple Tax Filing." *ProPublica,* March 26. Accessed June 21, 2018. https://www.propublica.org /article/how-the-maker-of-turbotax-fought-free-simple-tax-filing.

———. 2014. "TurboTax Maker Linked to 'Grassroots' Campaign Against Free, Simple Tax Filing." *ProPublica,* April 14. Accessed June 21, 2018. https:// www.propublica.org/article/turbotax-maker-linked-to-grassroots -campaign-against-free-simple-tax-filing.

de Schweinitz, Karl. 1944. "The Basic Skill in Social Security." *Social Security Bulletin* 7(1): 24–31. Accessed June 21, 2018. https://www.ssa.gov/policy/docs/ssb/v7n1 /v7n1p24.pdf.

Debot, Brandon, Emily Horton, and Chuck Marr. 2017. "Trump Budget Continues Multi-Year Assault on IRS Funding Despite Mnuchin's Call for More Resources." Center for Budget and Policy Priorities, March 17. Accessed June 21, 2018. https:// www.cbpp.org/sites/default/files/atoms/files/3-14-17bud.pdf.

Deci, Edward, and Richard Ryan. 1985. *Self-Determination.* Hoboken, N.J.: John Wiley & Sons.

Delaney, Arthur. 2018. "Republicans Say People Would Kick Themselves Off Food Stamps Under Their New Bill." *Huffington Post,* April 18. Accessed June 21, 2018. https://www.huffingtonpost.com/entry/republicans-food-stamps_us _5ad76c97e4b029ebe0205215.

DeLeire, Thomas, and Donna Friedsam. 2010. "Enrollment, Take-Up, Exit, and Churning: Has BadgerCare Plus Improved Access to and Continuity of Coverage?" Madison: University of Wisconsin Population Health Institute.

DeLeire, Thomas, Lindsey Leininger, Laura Dague, Shannon Mok, and Donna Friedsam. 2012. "Wisconsin's Experience with Auto-Enrollment: Lessons for Other States." *Medicare and Medicaid Research Review* 2(2): E1–20.

Dennis, Amanda, and Kelly Blanchard. 2012. "A Mystery Caller Evaluation of Medicaid Staff Responses About State Coverage of Abortion Care." *Women's Health Issues* 22(2): 143–48.

Dennis, Amanda, Ruth Manski, and Kelly Blanchard. 2012. "Looking Back at the Hyde Amendment and Looking Forward to Restoring Public Funding." Repro- ductive Laws for the 21st Century Papers. Washington, D.C.: Center for Women's Policy Studies.

Derthick, Martha. 1979. *Policymaking for Social Security.* Washington, D.C.: Brookings Institution Press.

Desilver, Drew. 2013. "Most Uninsured Americans Live in States that Won't Run Their Own Obamacare Exchanges." *Pew Research Center,* September 19. Accessed June 21, 2018. http://www.pewresearch.org/fact-tank/2013/09/19 /most-uninsured-americans-live-in-states-that-wont-run-their-own -obamacare-exchanges.

Dewey, Caitlin. 2018. "GOP Proposes Stricter Work Requirements for Food Stamp Recipients, a Step Toward a Major Overhaul of the Social Safety Net." *Washington Post,* April 12. Accessed June 21, 2018. https://www.washingtonpost.com/news /wonk/wp/2018/04/12/gop-proposes-stricter-work-requirements-for-food -stamp-recipients-a-step-toward-a-major-overhaul-of-the-social-safety-net.

DeWitt, Larry. 2010. "The Decision to Exclude Agricultural and Domestic Workers from the 1935 Social Security Act." *Social Security Bulletin* 7(4): 49–68.

Dias, Janice, and Stephen Maynard-Moody. 2007. "For-Profit Welfare: Contracts, Conflicts, and the Performance Paradox." *Journal of Public Administration Research and Theory* 17(2): 189–211.

Dickson, Virgil. 2014. "Drug, Insurer Groups Battle Medicare Part D Cost-Control Measure." *Modern Healthcare*, February 26. Accessed June 21, 2018. http://www.modernhealthcare.com/article/20140226/NEWS/302269943.

Doe, Mary Jane. 2013. "The Horrors of Getting an Abortion Under Current Wisconsin State Law." *Isthmus*, February 6. Accessed June 21, 2018. http://isthmus.com/opinion/opinion/the-horrors-of-getting-an-abortion-under-current-wisconsin-law.

Doehrel, Andrew. 2006. "Should Voters Approve a Minimum Wage Increase?" *Columbus Dispatch*, October 13.

Donohue, Thomas 2005. "Statement on the Need for Comprehensive Immigration Reform: Serving Our National Economy Before the U.S. Senate Committee on the Judiciary Subcommittee on Immigration, Border Security and Citizenship U.S. Senate Committee on the Judiciary." Washington: U.S. Chamber of Commerce. Accessed June 21, 2018. https://www.uschamber.com/sites/default/files/legacy/testimony/tjdimmigrationtestimony52605final.pdf.

Dorn, Stan. 2014a. "Marketplace Enrollment Procedures: Early Barriers to Participation and Options for Surmounting Them." Washington, D.C.: The Urban Institute. Accessed June 21, 2018. http://www.urban.org/sites/default/files/alfresco/publication-pdfs/2000038-Marketplace-Enrollment-Procedures-Early-Barriers-to-Participation.pdf.

——. 2014b. "Public Education, Outreach and Application Assistance." Washington, D.C.: The Urban Institute. Accessed June 21, 2018. https://www.urban.org/research/publication/public-education-outreach-and-application-assistance.

Dorn, Stan, Ian Hill, and Sara Hogan. 2009. "The Secrets of Massachusetts' Success: Why 97 Percent of State Residents Have Health Coverage." Washington, D.C.: The Urban Institute. Accessed June 21, 2018. http://www.urban.org/research/publication/secrets-massachusetts-success-why-97-percent-state-residents-have-health-coverage.

Douglas, Joshua A. 2014. "The Right to Vote: A State Right." *Slate*, January 21. Accessed June 21, 2018. http://www.slate.com/articles/news_and_politics/jurisprudence/2014/01/voting_rights_state_courts_should_be_fighting_strict_voter_id_laws.html.

Dropp, Kyle, and Brendan Nyhan. 2017. "One-Third Don't Know Obamacare and Affordable Care Act Are the Same." *New York Times*, February 7. Accessed June 21, 2018. https://www.nytimes.com/2017/02/07/upshot/one-third-dont-know-obamacare-and-affordable-care-act-are-the-same.html.

Drum, Kevin. 2014. "Here's Why Wisconsin's Voter ID Law Got Struck Down." *Mother Jones*, April 30. Accessed June 21, 2018. http://www.motherjones.com/kevin-drum/2014/04/heres-why-wisconsins-voter-id-law-got-struck-down.

Dynarski, Susan, Judith Scott-Clayton, and Mark Wiederspan. 2013. "Simplifying Tax Incentives and Aid for College: Progress and Prospects." *Tax Policy and the Economy* 27(1): 161–202.

Eckholm, Erik. 2014. "Alabama's Requirement for Abortion Clinic Doctors Is Ruled Unconstitutional." *New York Times*, August 4. Accessed June 21, 2018. http://www.nytimes.com/2014/08/05/us/alabamas-requirement-for-abortion-clinic-doctors-is-ruled-unconstitutional.html.

Edelman, Murray. 1985. *The Symbolic Uses of Politics*, 2nd ed. Chicago: University of Illinois Press.

Edelson, Jack, Alexander Alduncin, Christopher Crewson, James A Sieja, and Joseph Uscinski. 2017. "The Effect of Motivated Reasoning on Belief in Election Fraud." *Political Research Quarterly* 70(4): 933–46.

Edwards, David. 2013. "O' Reilly: Food Stamps Are 'Encouraging Parasites' to 'Take as Much as They Want.'" *Raw Story*, August 13. Accessed July 18, 2018. https://www.rawstory.com/2013/08/oreilly-food-stamps-are-encouraging-parasites-to-take-as-much-as-they-want/.

Eidelson, Josh. 2016. "The Texas Voter ID Fight Keeps Getting Weirder." *Bloomberg*, September 29. Accessed June 21, 2018. http://www.bloomberg.com/politics/articles/2016-09-29/texas-voter-id-fight-keeps-getting-weirder.

Elder, Todd, and Elizabeth Powers. 2006. "The Incredible Shrinking Program." *Research on Aging* 28(3): 341–58.

Eslami, Esa. 2010. *State Trends in Supplemental Nutrition Assistance Program Eligibility and Participation Among Elderly Individuals*. Washington, D.C.: Mathematica Policy Research. Accessed June 21, 2018. https://www.mathematica-mpr.com/our-publications-and-findings/publications/state-trends-in-supplemental-nutrition-assistance-program-eligibility-and-participation-among.

Espeseth, Allison Hales, and Roberta Riportella. 2006. "Wisconsin's Recent BadgerCare Enrollment Decline: How Administrative Rules Can Set Off Unanticipated Change." *The Journal of Ambulatory Care Management* 29(4): 300–09.

Eubanks, Virginia. 2018. *Automating Inequality: How High-Tech Tools Profile, Police, and Punish the Poor*. New York: St. Martin's Press.

Evanstim, Tim. 2003. "Coalition Pushes for Better Wages for Indianapolis Area." *Indianapolis Star*, April 4.

Ewalt, Jo Ann, and Edward Jennings. 2004. "Administration, Governance, and Policy Tools in Welfare Policy Implementation." *Public Administration Review* 64(4): 449–62.

Families USA. 2012. "Brokers and Agents and Health Insurance Exchanges." Washington, D.C.: Families USA. Accessed June 21, 2018. http://familiesusa.org/sites/default/files/product_documents/Exchanges-Brokers-and-Agents.pdf.

Fay, Joseph L., and Max J. Wasserman. "1938. Accounting Operations of the Bureau of Old-Age Insurance." *Social Security Bulletin* 1(6): 24–28. Accessed June 21, 2018. https://www.ssa.gov/history/fay638.html.

Fernandez, Manny. 2014. "Decision Allows Abortion Law, Forcing 13 Texas Clinics to Close." *New York Times*, October 2. Accessed June 21, 2018. http://www.nytimes.com /2014/10/03/us/appeals-court-ruling-closes-13-abortion-clinics-in-texas.html.

Finer, Lawrence B., Lori F. Frohwirth, Lindsay A. Dauphinee, Susheela Singh, and Ann M. Moore. 2005. "Reasons US Women Have Abortions: Quantitative and Qualitative Perspectives." *Perspectives on Sexual and Reproductive Health* 37(3): 110–18.

Finkelstein, Amy, and Robin McKnight. 2008. "What Did Medicare Do? The Initial Impact of Medicare on Mortality and Out of Pocket Medical Spending." *Journal of Public Economics* 92(7): 1644–68.

Fix, Michael, Jeffrey Passel, and Kenneth Sucher. 2003. "Trends in Naturalization. Immigrant Families and Workers." Facts and Perspectives Brief. Washington, D.C.: The Urban Institute.

Flavelle, Christopher. 2015. "The Voting Law That's Being Ignored." *Bloomberg*, April 6. Accessed June 21, 2018. https://www.bloomberg.com/view/articles /2015-04-06/the-voting-law-that-s-being-ignored.

Fogarty, Brian J., Jessica Curtis, Patricia Frances Gouzien, David C. Kimball, and Eric C. Vorst. 2015. "News Attention to Voter Fraud in the 2008 and 2012 US Elections." *Research & Politics* 2(2): 1–8.

Foner, Eric. 2011. *Reconstruction: America's Unfinished Revolution, 1863–1877*. New York: Harper Collins.

Food and Nutrition Service. 2005. "Combined Application Projects: Guidance for States Developing Projects." Washington: U.S. Department of Agriculture. Accessed June 21, 2018. http://www.fns.usda.gov/sites/default/files /CAPsDevelopmentGuidance.pdf.

———. 2007. *Reaching Those in Need: Food Stamp Participation Rates in 2005*. Washington: U.S. Department of Agriculture.

———. 2010. *Enhancing Supplemental Nutrition Assistance Program (SNAP) Certification: SNAP Modernization Efforts*. Washington: U.S. Department of Agriculture. Accessed June 21, 2018. http://www.fns.usda.gov/sites/default/files /EnhancedCertification_Vol1Final.pdf.

———. 2013. "The Extent of Trafficking in the Supplemental Nutrition Assistance Program: 2009–2011." Washington: U.S. Department of Agriculture. Accessed June 21, 2018. https://www.fns.usda.gov/sites/default/files/Trafficking2009.pdf.

———. 2014. *Trends in Supplemental Nutrition Assistance Program Participation Rates: Fiscal Year 2010 to Fiscal Year 2012*. Washington: U.S. Department of Agriculture. Accessed June 21, 2018. http://www.fns.usda.gov/sites/default/files/ops /Trends2010-2012.pdf.

———. 2016. *SNAP Quality Control Error Rates*. Washington: U.S. Department of Agriculture. Accessed June 21, 2018. http://www.fns.usda.gov/snap/snap -quality-control-error-rates.

Fossett, James, and Frank Thompson. 2006. "Administrative Responsiveness to the Disadvantaged: The Case of Children's Health Insurance." *Journal of Public Administration Research and Theory* 16(3): 369–92.

Frank, Richard G., and Karine Lamiraud. 2009. "Choice, Price Competition and Complexity in Markets for Health Insurance." *Journal of Economic Behavior and Organization* 71(2): 550–62.

Frank, Ruthelle. 2014. "Wisconsin's New Voter ID Law Could Keep Me from Voting at 87." *The Guardian*, September 24. Accessed June 21, 2018. https://www.theguardian.com/commentisfree/2014/sep/24/wisconsin-new-voter-id-law-woman-denied-right-87.

Freeland-Graves, Jeanne H., and Susan Nitzke. 2013. "Position of the Academy of Nutrition and Dietetics: Total Diet Approach to Healthy Eating." *Journal of the Academy of Nutrition and Dietetics* 113(2): 307–17. Accessed July 18, 2018. https://jandonline.org/article/S2212-2672(12)01993-4/abstract.

Fresh, Adriane. 2018. "The Effect of the Voting Rights Act on Enfranchisement: Evidence from North Carolina." *Journal of Politics* 80(2): 713–18.

Friedman, Milton. 1962. *Capitalism and Freedom*. Chicago: University of Chicago Press.

———. 1967. "The Case for the Negative Income Tax." *National Review*, March 7.

Friedsam, Donna, Tom Kaplan, and Sarah Eskrich. 2014. "State-Level Field Network Study of the Implementation of the Affordable Care Act." Albany: State University of New York, Nelson A. Rockefeller Institute of Government. Accessed June 21, 2018. http://www.rockinst.org/aca/states/wisconsin/2014–08-Wisconsin_Round_One.pdf.

Fukuyama, Francis. 2013. "The Decay of American Political Institutions." *American Interest*, December 8. Accessed June 21, 2018. http://www.the-american-interest.com/2013/12/08/the-decay-of-american-political-institutions.

Fullmer, Elliott. 2013. "At Your Convenience: New Perspectives on Early Voting in the United States." Ph.D. diss., Georgetown University.

———. 2014. "The Site Gap Racial Inequalities in Early Voting Access." *American Politics Research* 43(2): 283–303.

Gailmard, Sean, and John W. Patty. 2012. *Learning While Governing: Information, Accountability, and Executive Branch Institutions*. Chicago: University of Chicago Press.

Ganong, Peter, and Jeffrey B. Liebman. 2013. "The Decline, Rebound, and Further Rise in SNAP Enrollment: Disentangling Business Cycle Fluctuations and Policy Changes." *NBER* working paper no. 19363. Cambridge, Mass.: National Bureau of Economic Research.

Garcia, Jason. 2005. "Effort Mounts for 'Living Wage.'" *Orlando Sentinel*, April 11.

Garfield, Rachel, Robin Rudowitz, MaryBeth Musucemi, and Anthony Damico. 2018. "Implications of Work Requirement in Medicaid: What Does the Data Say." Issue Brief, June 12. San Francisco: Kaiser Family Foundation. Accessed June 21, 2018. https://www.kff.org/medicaid/issue-brief/implications-of-work-requirements-in-medicaid-what-does-the-data-say.

Garfield, Rachel, and Katherine Young. 2015. "Adults Who Remained Uninsured at the End of 2014." Issue Brief, January 29. San Francisco: Kaiser Family Foundation. Accessed June 21, 2018. https://www.kff.org/health-reform/issue-brief/adults-who-remained-uninsured-at-the-end-of-2014.

Gavin, N., Nathan David West, Nancy F. Lenfestey, and Jamie Chriqui. 2003. *Evaluation of the BadgerCare Medicaid Demonstration*. Research Triangle Park, NC: RTI International.

Gennetian, Lisa A., and Eldar Shafir. 2015. "The Persistence of Poverty in the Context of Financial Instability: A Behavioral Perspective." *Journal of Policy Analysis and Management* 34(4): 904–36.

Gerber, Alan S., Gregory A. Huber, and Seth J. Hill. 2013. "Identifying the Effect of All-Mail Elections on Turnout: Staggered Reform in the Evergreen State." *Political Science Research and Methods* 1(1): 91–116.

Get It Back Campaign. 2016. "Refund Anticipation Loans." Accessed June 21, 2018. http://www.eitcoutreach.org/learn/tax-filing/rals.

Giovannelli, Justin, and Emily Curran. 2016. "Factors Affecting Healthcare Enrollment Through States Marketplaces: Observations on the ACA's Third Open Enrollment Period." New York: Commonwealth Fund. Accessed June 21, 2018. http://www.commonwealthfund.org//media/files/publications/issue-brief /2016/jul/1887_giovannelli_factors_affecting_enrollment_rb_v3.pdf.

Gitis, Ben. 2014. "Primer: Earned Income Tax Credit and the Minimum Wage." Washington, D.C.: American Action Forum. Accessed June 21, 2018. http:// americanactionforum.org/research/primer-earned-income-tax-credit-and -the-minimum-wage.

Goel, Sharad, Marc Meredith, Michael Morse, David Rothschild, and Houshmand Shirani-Mehr. 2016. "One Person, One Vote: Estimating the Prevalence of Double Voting in US Presidential Elections." Cambridge, Mass.: Scholars at Harvard. Accessed June 21, 2018. https://scholar.harvard.edu/morse/publications /one-person-one-vote-estimating-prevalence-double-voting-us-presidential -elections.

Goldrick-Rab, Sara. 2016. *Paying the Price: College Costs, Financial Aid, and the Betrayal of the American Dream*. Chicago: University of Chicago Press.

Goluboff, Risa, and Dahlia Lithwick. 2011. "A Fraudulent Case: The Ugly Parallels Between Jim Crow and Modern Vote-Suppression Laws." *Slate*, October 20. Accessed June 21, 2018. http://www.slate.com/articles/news_and_politics /jurisprudence/2011/10/voter_id_laws_their_proponents_should_have_to _answer_for_the_ugl.html.

Gonzalez, Shelby. 2016. "Louisiana Blazing Trail for Streamlined Medicaid Enrollment." *Off the Charts* (Center for Budget and Policy Priorities blog), July 12. Accessed June 21, 2018. http://www.cbpp.org/blog/louisiana-blazing-trail -for-streamlined-medicaid-enrollment.

Gonzalez-Barrera, Ana, Mark Hugo Lopez, Jeffrey S. Passel, and Paul Taylor. 2013. "The Path Not Taken: Two-Thirds of Legal Mexican Immigrants Are Not U.S. Citizens." Washington, D.C.: Pew Research Center.

Goodnough, Abby. 2018. "Kentucky Rushes to Remake Medicaid as Other States Prepare to Follow." *New York Times*, February 10. Accessed June 21, 2018. https://www.nytimes.com/2018/02/10/health/kentucky-medicaid-work -requirement.html

Goodsell, Charles. 1977. "Bureaucratic Manipulations of Physical Symbols: An Empirical Study." *American Journal of Political Science* 2(1): 79–91.

Goolsbee, Austan. 2006. "The 'Simple Return': Reducing America's Tax Burden Through Return-Free Filing." *Hamilton Project* discussion paper no. 2006-04. Washington, D.C.: Brookings Institution.

Gornick, Marian E., Paul W. Eggers, Thomas W. Reilly, Renee M. Mentnech, Leslye K. Fitterman, and Lawrence E. Kecken. 1996. "Effects of Race and Income on Mortality and Use of Services Among Medicare Beneficiaries." *New England Journal of Medicine* 335(September): 791–99.

Governor's Commission on Waste, Fraud, and Abuse. 2012. *Reforming Government, Eliminating Waste, Saving Taxpayer Dollars.* Accessed July 18, 2018. https:// www.innovations.harvard.edu/sites/default/files/opex/documents/Waste %20Fraud%20Abuse%20Commission%20Final%20Report%2C%20Wisconsin %2C%202012.pdf.

Graham, David. 2016. "Ohio's Questionable Vote Purge." *The Atlantic*, June 3. Accessed June 21, 2018. https://www.theatlantic.com/politics/archive/2016 /06/ohio-voter-purge/485357.

Greenridge, Kaitlyn. 2017. "The 1040 Nightmare." *New York Times*, April 9, SR10.

Greenstein, Robert, John Wancheck, and Chuck Marr. 2014. *Reducing Overpayments in the Earned Income Tax Credit.* Washington, D.C.: Center for Budget and Policy Priorities.

Grimes, David A., Janie Benson, Susheela Singh, Mariana Romero, Bela Ganatra, Friday E. Okonofua, and Iqbal H. Shah. 2006. "Unsafe Abortion: The Preventable Pandemic." *The Lancet* 368(9550): 1908–19.

Grimmer, Justin, Eitan Hersh, Marc Meredith, Jonathan Mummolo, and Clayton Nall. 2017. "Comment on 'Voter Identification Laws and the Suppression of Minority Votes.'" Stanford, Calif.: Stanford University. Accessed June 21, 2018. http://web.stanford.edu/jgrimmer/comment_final.pdf.

Grogger, Jeffrey. 2003. "The Effects of Time Limits, The EITC, and Other Policy Changes on Welfare Use, Work, and Income Among Female-Headed Families." *Review of Economics and Statistics* 85(2): 394–408.

Grossman, Daniel, Kari White, Liza Fuentes, Kristine Hopkins, Amanda Stevenson, Sara Yeatman, and Joseph E. Potter. 2015. "Knowledge, Opinion and Experience Related to Abortion Self-Induction in Texas." Texas Policy Evaluation Project, Research Brief. Paper presented at the North American Forum on Family Planning, Chicago (November 14).

Gupta, Akhil. 2012. *Red Tape: Bureaucracy, Structural Violence, and Poverty in India.* Durham, N.C.: Duke University Press.

Gupta, Sarika. 2017. "Perils of Paperwork: The Impact of Information and Application Assistance on Welfare Program Take-Up in India." Unpublished paper, Harvard University. Accessed June 21, 2018. https://www.dropbox.com/s /shhlxta7hopixmw/Gupta_JMP_11.15.pdf.

Guttmacher Institute. 2017. "An Overview of Abortion Laws." New York: Guttmacher Institute, July 1. Accessed October 12, 2017. https://www.guttmacher.org/state-policy/explore/overview-abortion-laws.

Guyer, Jocelyn, Tanya Schwartz, and Samantha Artiga. 2013. "Fast Track to Coverage: Facilitating Enrollment of Eligible People into the Medicaid Expansion." Issue Brief, November 19. San Francisco: Kaiser Family Foundation. Accessed June 21, 2018. https://www.kff.org/medicaid/issue-brief/fast-track-to-coverage-facilitating-enrollment-of-eligible-people-into-the-medicaid-expansion.

Haberkorn, Jennifer. 2018. "Trump's Secret Plan to Scrap Obamacare." *Politico*, January 10. Accessed August 1, 2018. https://www.politico.com/story/2018/01/10/trump-obamacare-secret-plan-278145.

Hacker, Jacob. 2004. "Privatizing Risk Without Privatizing the Welfare State: The Hidden Politics of Social Policy Retrenchment in the United States." *American Political Science Review* 98(2): 243–60.

Haider, Steven J., Alison Jacknowitz, and Robert F. Schoeni. 2003. "Food Stamps and the Elderly: Why Is Participation So Low?" *Journal of Human Resources* 38(Supplement): 1080–111.

Hajnal, Zoltan, Nazita Lajevardi, and Lindsay Nielson. 2017. "Voter Identification Laws and the Suppression of Minority Votes." *Journal of Politics* 79(2): 363–79.

Halpern-Meekin, Sarah, Kathryn Edin, Laura Tach, and Jennifer Sykes. 2015. *It's Not Like I'm Poor: How Working-Class Families Make Ends Meet in a Post-Welfare World.* Oakland: University of California Press.

Handel, Benjamin R., and Jonathan T. Kolstad. 2015. "Health Insurance for 'Humans': Information Frictions, Plan Choice, and Consumer Welfare." *American Economic Review* 105(8): 2449–500.

Hanoch, Yaniv, Thomas Rice, Janet Cummings, and Stacey Wood. 2009. "How Much Choice Is Too Much? The Case of the Medicare Prescription Drug Benefit." *Health Services Research* 44(4): 1157–68.

Hanoch, Yaniv, Stacey Wood, Andrew Barnes, Pi-Ju Liu, and Thomas Rice. 2011. "Choosing the Right Medicare Prescription Drug Plan: The Effect of Age, Strategy Selection, and Choice Set Size." *Health Psychology* 30(6): 719–27.

Hanratty, Maria. 2006. "Has the Food Stamp Program Become More Accessible? Impacts of Recent Changes in Reporting Requirements and Asset Eligibility Limits." *Journal of Policy Analysis and Management* 25(3): 603–21.

Hanson, Kenneth, and Victor Oliveira. 2012. "How Economic Conditions Affect Participation in USDA Nutrition Assistance Programs." Economic Information Bulletin no. 100. Washington: U.S. Department of Agriculture, Economic Research Service.

Hasen, Richard L. 2012. *The Voting Wars: From Florida 2000 to the Next Election Meltdown.* New Haven, Conn.: Yale University Press.

Haspel, Moshe, and H. Gibbs Knotts. 2005. "Location, Location, Location: Precinct Placement and the Costs of Voting." *Journal of Politics* 67(2): 560–73.

Hayes, Stephen. 2012. "High Noon in Wisconsin." *Weekly Standard,* May 28. Accessed June 21, 2018. http://www.weeklystandard.com/articles/high-noon-wisconsin _645176.html.

Healthcare for America Now. 2013. "Anti-Obamacare States Try to Throw Navigators Off Course: An Analysis of Sabotage Tactics that Could Deny Affordable Healthcare to Millions." September. Accessed June 21, 2018. http://healthcareforamericanow.org.

Heckman, James, and Jeffrey Smith. 2003. "The Determinants of Participation in a Social Program: Evidence from a Prototypical Job Training Program." *NBER* working paper no. w9818. Cambridge, Mass.: National Bureau of Economic Research.

Heinrich, Carolyn J. 2007. "Evidence-Based Policy and Performance Management: Challenges and Prospects in Two Parallel Movements." *American Review of Public Administration* 37(3): 255–77.

———. 2016. "The Bite of Administrative Burden: A Theoretical and Empirical Investigation." *Journal of Public Administration Research and Theory* 26(3): 403–20.

Heinrich, Carolyn J., John Hoddinott, and Michael Samson. 2017. "Reducing Adolescent Risky Behaviors in a High-Risk Context: The Effects of Unconditional Cash Transfers in South Africa." *Economic Development and Cultural Change* 64(4): 619–52.

Heinrich, Carolyn, Laurence Lynn, and H. Brinton Milward. 2010. "A State of Agents? Sharpening the Debate and Evidence over the Extent and Impact of the Transformation of Governance." *Journal of Public Administration Research and Theory* 20(Supplement 1): 3–19.

Heiss, Florian, Adam Leive, Daniel McFadden, and Joachim Winter. 2013. "Plan Selection in Medicare Part D: Evidence from Administrative Data." *Journal of Health Economics* 32(6): 1325–44.

Heller, Nathan. 2017. "Estonia, the Digital Republic." *New Yorker,* December 18/25.

Herd, Pamela. 2005. "Universalism Without the Targeting: Privatizing the Old Age Welfare State." *Gerontologist* 45(3): 292–98.

Herd, Pamela, Thomas DeLeire, Hope Harvey, and Donald P. Moynihan. 2013. "Shifting Administrative Burden to the State: The Case of Medicaid Take-Up." *Public Administration Review* 73(Supplement 1): S69–81.

Herd, Pamela, Jenny Higgins, Kamil Sicinski, and Irina Merkurievna. 2016. "The Implications of Unintended Pregnancies for Mental Health in Later Life." *American Journal of Public Health* 106(3): 421–29.

Herron, Michael C., and Daniel A. Smith. 2013. "The Effects of House Bill 1355 on Voter Registration in Florida." *State Politics & Policy Quarterly* 13(3): 279–305.

Hickman, Kristin. 2016. "Pursuing a Single Mission: Or Something Closer to it for the IRS." *Columbia Journal of Tax Law* 7(1): 169–93.

Hill, Ian, Margaret Wilkinson, and Brigette Courtot. 2014. "The Launch of the Affordable Care Act in Selected States: Outreach, Education and Enrollment Assistance." Washington, D.C.: The Urban Institute. Accessed June 21, 2018.

https://www.urban.org/sites/default/files/publication/22341/413039-The -Launch-of-the-Affordable-Care-Act-in-Eight-States-Outreach-Education -and-Enrollment-Assistance.PDF.

Hoadley, Jack, Elizabeth Hargrave, Juliette Cubanski, and Tricia Neuman. 2006. "An In-Depth Examination of Formularies and Other Features of Medicare Drug Plans." New York: Kaiser Family Foundation. Accessed June 21, 2018. http://globalag.igc.org/health/us/2006/kffvariations.pdf.

Hobby, Governor Bill, Cong Huang, David Llanos, Chris Mainka, Kwok-Wai Wan, Ching-Hsing Wang, and Isaiah Warner. 2015. "The Texas Voter ID Law and the 2014 Election: A Study of Texas's 23rd Congressional District." Houston: University of Houston, Hobby School of Public Affairs.

Holahan, John, Linda J. Blumberg, Erik Wengle, Ian Hill, Rebecca Peters, and Patricia Solleveld. 2015. "Factors That Contributed to Low Marketplace Enrollment Rates in Five States in 2015." Washington, D.C.: The Urban Institute. Accessed June 21, 2018. https://www.urban.org/sites/default/files/publication/72441 /2000488-Factors-That-Contributed-To-Low-Marketplace-Enrollment-In -Five-States-In-2015.pdf.

Holbein, John B., and D. Sunshine Hillygus. 2016. "Making Young Voters: The Impact of Preregistration on Youth Turnout." *American Journal of Political Science* 60(2): 364–82.

Holtz, V. Joseph, and John Karl Scholz. 2006. "Examining the Effect of the Earned Income Tax Credit on the Labor Market Participation of Families on Welfare." *NBER* working paper no. 11968. Cambridge, Mass.: National Bureau of Economic Research.

Holtzblatt, Janet, and Janet McCubbin. 2004. "Complicated Lives: Tax Administrative Issues Affecting Low-Income Filers." In *The Crisis in Tax Administration*, edited by Henry Aaron and Joel Slemrod. Washington, D.C.: Brookings Institution Press.

Horan, Patrick, and Patricia L. Austin. 1974. "The Social Bases of Welfare Stigma." *Social Problems* 21(5): 648–57.

Howard, Christopher. 1997. *The Hidden Welfare State: Tax Expenditures and Social Policy in the United States*. Princeton, N.J.: Princeton University Press.

Hoxby, Caroline M., and Christopher Avery. 2012. "The Missing One-Offs: The Hidden Supply of High-Achieving, Low Income Students." *NBER* working paper no. 18586. Cambridge, Mass.: National Bureau of Economic Research.

Hoxby, Caroline, and Sarah Turner. 2012. "Expanding College Opportunities for Low-Income, High-Achieving Students." *NBER* working paper no. 18728. Cambridge, Mass.: National Bureau of Economic Research.

Hoynes, Hilary, and Ankur J. Patel. 2015. "Effective Tax Policy for Reducing Inequality? The Earned Income Tax Credit and the Distribution of Income." *NBER* working paper no. 21340. Cambridge, Mass.: National Bureau of Economic Research.

Hoynes, Hilary, Diane Whitmore Schanzenbach, and Douglas Almond. 2016. "Long-Run Impacts of Childhood Access to the Safety Net." *American Economic Review* 106(4): 903–34.

Huse, Robert. 1938. "Public Relations in the Administration of Social Legislation." *Social Security Bulletin* 1: 3–5. https://www.ssa.gov/policy/docs/ssb/v1n10/v1n10p3.pdf.

Hynes, Emma, and Thomas Oliver. 2010. *Wisconsin's BadgerCare Plus Health Coverage Program*. Madison: University of Wisconsin Population Health Institute.

Ingraham, Patricia. 1995. *The Foundation of Merit*. Baltimore, Md.: Johns Hopkins University Press.

Institute for a Competitive Workforce. 2007. "Community Building Through the Earned Income Tax Credit." Washington: U.S. Chamber of Commerce. Accessed June 21, 2018. https://www.uschamberfoundation.org/sites/default/files/publication/edu/ICW_EITCToolkitrdc.pdf.

Internal Revenue Service (IRS). 2014. "Compliance Estimates for the Earned Income Tax Credit Claimed on 2006–2008 Returns." Publication 5162. Washington: U.S. Department of the Treasury. Accessed June 21, 2018. http://www.irs.gov/pub/irs-soi/EITCComplianceStudyTY2006-2008.pdf.

———. 2016a. "Earned Income Tax Credit Statistics." Accessed June 21, 2018. https://www.irs.gov/credits-deductions/individuals/earned-income-tax-credit/earned-income-tax-credit-statistics.

———. 2016b. "EITC Participation Rate by State." Accessed June 21, 2018. https://www.eitc.irs.gov/eitc-central/participation-rate/eitc-participation-rate-by-states.

———. 2018. "Understanding Your CP09 Notice." Accessed July 1, 2018. https://www.irs.gov/individuals/understanding-your-cp09-notice.

Jacobson, Gretchen, Marsha Gold, Anthony Damico, Tricia Neuman, and Giselle Casillas. 2015. *Medicare Advantage 2016 Data Spotlight: Overview of Plan Changes*. Issue Brief, December 3. San Francisco: Kaiser Family Foundation. Accessed June 21, 2018. https://www.kff.org/medicare/issue-brief/medicare-advantage-2016-data-spotlight-overview-of-plan-changes.

Jacobson, Gretchen, Christina Swoope, Michael Perry, and Mary C. Slosar. 2014. *How Are Seniors Choosing and Changing Health Insurance Plans?* San Francisco: Kaiser Family Foundation.

Jerman, Jenna, Rachel K. Jones, and Tsuyoshi Onda. 2016. "Characteristics of US Abortion Patients in 2014 and Changes Since 2008." New York: Guttmacher Institute. Accessed June 21, 2018. https://www.guttmacher.org/sites/default/files/report_pdf/characteristics-us-abortion-patients-2014.pdf.

Jilke, Sebastian, Wouter Van Dooren, and Sabine Rys. 2018. "Discrimination and Administrative Burden in Public Service Markets: Does a Public–Private Difference Exist?" *Journal of Public Administration Research and Theory* 28(3): 423–39.

Jilke, Sebastian, Gregg Van Ryzin, and Steven Van de Walle. 2016. "Responses to Decline in Marketized Services: An Experimental Evaluation of Choice Overload." *Journal of Public Administration Research and Theory* 26(1): 421–32.

Joffe, Carole. 2014. "The Hidden Costs of Abortion." *Rewire*, October 14. Accessed June 21, 2018. https://rewire.news/article/2014/10/15/hidden-costs-abortion-restrictions.

Johnson, David, and Tim Smeeding. 2012. "A Consumer's Guide to Interpreting Various US Poverty Measures." *Fast Focus* no. 14–2012. Accessed June 21, 2018. https://www.irp.wisc.edu/publications/fastfocus/pdfs/FF14-2012.pdf.

Jolls, Christine, Cass R. Sunstein, and Richard H. Thaler. 1998. "A Behavioral Approach to Law and Economics." *Stanford Law Review* 50(5): 1471–550.

Jones, Jeffrey, and Lydia Saad. 2013. "Americans Sour on IRS, Rate CDC and FBI Most Positively." Gallup, May 23. Accessed June 21, 2018. https://news.gallup.com/poll/162764/americans-views-irs-sharply-negative-2009.aspx.

Jones, Rachel K., Lawrence B. Finer, and Susheela Singh. 2010. "Characteristics of U.S. Abortion Patients, 2008." New York: Guttmacher Institute. Accessed June 21, 2018. http://nyfamilylife.org/wp-content/uploads/2013/11/US-Abortion-Patients.pdf.

Jones, Rachel K., Ushma D. Upadhyay, and Tracy A. Weitz. 2013. "At What Cost? Payment for Abortion Care by US Women." *Women's Health Issues* 23(3): 173–78.

Jones, Ty. 2014. "SNAP's Excess Medical Expense Deduction. Targeting Food Assistance to Low-Income Seniors and Individuals with Disabilities." Washington, D.C.: Center on Budget and Policy Priorities. Accessed June 21, 2018. https://www.cbpp.org/sites/default/files/atoms/files/8-20-14fa.pdf.

Jørgensen, Torben Beck, and Barry Bozeman. 2007. "Public Values: An Inventory." *Administration and Society* 39(3): 354–81.

Kabbani, Nader S., and Parke E. Wilde. 2003. "Short Recertification Periods in the U.S. Food Stamp Program." *Journal of Human Resources* 38(Special Issue): 1112–38.

Kahn, Robert L., Daniel Katz, and Barbara Gutek. 1976. "Bureaucratic Encounters—An Evaluation of Government Services." *The Journal of Applied Behavioral Science* 12(2): 178–98.

Kaiser Commission on Medicaid and the Uninsured. 2010a. "Medicaid: A Primer." San Francisco: Kaiser Family Foundation. Accessed June 21, 2018. https://www.kff.org/medicaid/upload/7334-04.pdf.

———. 2010b. "Optimizing Medicaid Enrollment: Spotlight on Technology, Wisconsin's ACCESS Internet Portal." San Francisco: Kaiser Family Foundation. Accessed June 21, 2018. https://www.kff.org/medicaid/upload/8119.pdf.

———. 2013."Key Lessons from Medicaid and CHIP for Outreach and Enrollment Under the Affordable Care Act." San Francisco: Kaiser Family Foundation. Accessed October 3, 2018. https://www.kff.org/report-section/key-lessons-outreach-and-enrollment-aca-issue-brief.

Kaiser Family Foundation. 2012. "Key Findings from the Kaiser Family Foundation 2012 National Survey of Seniors." San Francisco: Kaiser Family Foundation. Accessed June 21, 2018. https://kaiserfamilyfoundation.files.wordpress.com/2013/01/8374.pdf.

Katz, Michael. 1986. *In the Shadow of the Poorhouse: A Social History of Welfare in America.* New York: Basic Books.

Kaufman, Herbert. 1977. *Red Tape: Its Origins, Uses, and Abuses.* Washington, D.C.: Brookings Institution Press.

Kaufmann, Wesley, and Lars Tummers. 2017. "The Negative Effect of Red Tape on Procedural Satisfaction." *Public Management Review* 19(9): 1311–27.

Kaye, Kelleen, Katherine Suellentrop, and Corinna Sloup. 2009. *The Fog Zone: How Misperceptions, Magical Thinking, and Ambivalence Put Young Adults at Risk for Unplanned Pregnancy*. Washington, D.C.: National Campaign to Prevent Teen and Unplanned Pregnancy.

Keiser, Lael R., and Susan M. Miller. 2010. "Impact of Organized Interests on Eligibility Determination: The Case of Veterans' Disability Compensation." *Journal of Public Administration Research and Theory* 20(2): 505–31.

Keiser, Lael R., and Joe Soss. 1998. "With Good Cause: Bureaucratic Discretion and the Politics of Child Support Enforcement." *American Journal of Political Science* 42(4): 1133–56.

Kenney, Genevieve M., Jennifer Haley, Clare Pan, Victoria Lynch, and Matthew Buettgens. 2016. "Children's Coverage Climb Continues: Uninsurance and Medicaid/CHIP Eligibility and Participation Under the ACA." Washington, D.C.: The Urban Institute. Accessed June 21, 2018. http://www.urban.org/sites/default/files/alfresco/publication-pdfs/2000787-Childrens-Coverage-Climb-Continues-Uninsurance-and-Medicaid-CHIP-Eligibility-and-Participation-Under-the-ACA.pdf.

Kessler-Harris, Alice. 1995. "Designing Old Women and Fools." In *US History as Women's history: New Feminist Essays*, edited by Linda K. Kerber, Alice Kessler-Harris, and Kathryn Kish Sklar. Chapel Hill: University of North Carolina Press.

Keyssar, Alexander. 2009. *The Right to Vote: The Contested History of Democracy in the United States*. New York: Basic Books.

Khan, Natasha, and Corbin Carson. 2012. "Election Day Impersonation, an Impetus for Voter ID Laws, a Rarity, Data Show." *Washington Post*, August 11.

Kincheloe, Jennifer, Janice Frates, and E. Richard Brown. 2007. "Determinants of Children's Participation in California's Medicaid and SCHIP Programs." *Health Services Research* 42(2): 847–66.

Klarner, Carl, Xiaotong Mao, and Stan Buchanan. 2007. "Business Interest Group Power and Temporary Assistance to Needy Families." *Social Science Quarterly* 88(1): 104–19.

Kling, Jeffrey R., Sendhil Mullainathan, Eldar Shafir, Lee Vermeulen, and Marian Wrobel. 2012. "Comparison Friction: Experimental Evidence from Medicare Drug Plans." *Quarterly Journal of Economics* 127(1): 199–235.

Knack, Stephen. 1995. "Does "Motor-Voter" Work? Evidence from State-Level Data." *Journal of Politics* 57(3): 796–811.

Knight, Jack. 1992. *Institutions and Social Conflict*. Cambridge: Cambridge University Press.

Kogan, Richard, and Isaac Shapiro. 2015. "Congressional Budget Plans Get Two-Thirds of Cuts From Programs for People with Low or Moderate Incomes." Washington, D.C.: Center on Budget and Policy Priorities.

Kopczuk, Wojciech, and Cristian Pop-Eleches. 2007. "Electronic Filing, Tax Preparers and Participation in the Earned Income Tax Credit." *Journal of Public Economics* 91(7–8): 1351–67.

Kornfeld, Robert. 2002. "Explaining Recent Trends in Food Stamp Program Caseloads." *E-FAN Report* no. 02–008. Washington: U.S. Department of Agriculture, Economic Research Service.

Kroft, Kory. 2008. "Take-Up, Social Multipliers and Optimal Social Insurance." *Journal of Public Economics* 92(3–4): 722–37.

Kronebusch, Karl. 2001. "Medicaid for Children: Federal Mandates, Welfare Reform, and Policy Backsliding." *Health Affairs* 20(1): 97–111.

Kumar, Anuradha, Leila Hessini, and Ellen Mitchell. 2009. "Conceptualising Abortion Stigma." *Culture, Health & Sexuality* 11(6): 625–39.

Kumlin, Staffan, and Bo Rothstein. 2005. "Making and Breaking Social Capital the Impact of Welfare-State Institutions." *Comparative Political Studies* 38(4): 339–65.

Kusnetz, Nicholas. 2013. "Obamacare's Hidden Battle: Insurance Agents Push State Regulation of Guides to New Marketplaces." Washington, D.C.: Center for Public Integrity. Accessed June 21, 2018. https://www.publicintegrity.org/2013/08/09/13144/obamacares-hidden-battle-insurance-agents-push-state-regulation-guides-new.

Kuye, Ifedayo, Richard Frank, and Michael McWilliams. 2013. "Cognition and Take-Up of Subsidized Drug Benefits by Medicare Beneficiaries." *JAMA Internal Medicine* 173(12): 1100–107.

Land, Stephanie. 2018. "The Only Work the Farm Bill Will Create Is Paperwork." *Talk Poverty*, April 20. Accessed June 21, 2018. https://talkpoverty.org/2018/04/20/work-farm-bill-will-create-paperwork.

Langa, Kenneth M., Eric B. Larson, Jason H. Karlawish, David M. Cutler, Mohammed U. Kabeto, Scott Y. Kim, and Allison B. Rosen. 2008. "Trends in the Prevalence and Mortality of Cognitive Impairment in the United States: Is There Evidence of a Compression of Cognitive Morbidity?" *Alzheimer's & Dementia* 4(1): 134–44.

Lascoumes, Pierre, and Patrick Le Gales. 2007. "Understanding Public Policy Through Its Instruments—From the Nature of Instruments to the Sociology of Public Policy Instrumentation." *Governance* 20(1): 1–21.

Lasswell, Harold, D. 1936. *Politics: Who Gets What, When, How.* New York: Peter Smith.

Lawson, Steven F. 1999. *Black Ballots: Voting Rights in the South, 1944–1969.* Lanham, Md.: Lexington Books.

Leggett, Will. 2014. "The Politics of Behaviour Change: Nudge, Neoliberalism and the State." *Policy and Politics* 42(1): 3–19.

Leigh, Andrew. 2010. "Who Benefits from the Earned Income Tax Credit? Incidence Among Recipients, Coworkers and Firms." *B.E. Journal of Economic Analysis & Policy* 10(1). Published online May 21. DOI: 10.2202/1935-1682.1994.

Leininger, Lindsey, Donna Friedsam, Kristen Voskuil, and Thomas DeLeire. 2011. *The Target Efficiency of Online Medicaid/CHIP Enrollment: An Evaluation of Wisconsin's ACCESS Internet Portal.* Princeton, N.J.: Robert Wood Johnson Foundation State Health Access Reform Evaluation.

Levine, Phillip B., and Diane W. Schanzenbach. 2009. "The Impact of Children's Public Health Insurance Expansions on Educational Outcomes." *Forum for Health Economics and Policy* 12(1). DOI:10.2202/1558-9544.1137.

Levitt, Justin. 2007. "The Truth About Voter Fraud." New York: Brennan Center for Justice. Accessed June 21, 2018. http://www.brennancenter.org/sites/default /files/legacy/The%20Truth%20About%20Voter%20Fraud.pdf.

———. 2014. "Electoral Integrity: The Confidence Game." *New York University Law Review* 89(October): 70–86. Accessed June 21, 2018. http://www.nyulawreview .org/issues/volume-89-online-symposium/electoral-integrity-confidence-game.

Library of Congress. 2018. "A Monthly Check to You for the Rest of Your Life" (poster). Accessed July 1, 2018. http://www.loc.gov/pictures/item/92500634/.

Liebelson, Dana. 2014. "The Supreme Court Gutted the Voting Rights Act. What Happened Next in These 8 States Will Not Shock You." *Mother Jones*, April 8. Accessed June 21, 2018. http://www.motherjones.com/politics/2014/04 /republican-voting-rights-supreme-court-id.

Lind, E. Allan, and Tom R. Tyler. 1988. *The Social Psychology of Procedural Justice*. New York City: Plenum Publishing.

Lineberry, Robert. 1977. *American Public Policy: What Government Does and What Difference It Makes*. New York: Harper & Row.

Linnane, Rory. 2013. "Wisconsin Law Increases Abortion Delays, Risks." *Cap Times*, January 30. Accessed June 21, 2018. http://host.madison.com/ct/news/local /health_med_fit/wisconsin-law-increases-abortion-delays-risks/article _ab120798-6a4a-11e2-9dd7-0019bb2963f4.html.

Lipsky, Michael. 1980. *Street-Level Bureaucracy: Dilemmas of the Individual in Public Services*. New York: Russell Sage Foundation.

———. 1984. "Bureaucratic Disentitlement in Social Welfare Programs." *Social Service Review* 58(1): 3–27.

Liptak, Adam. 2016. "Supreme Court Strikes Down Texas Abortion Restrictions." *New York Times*, June 27.

Lipton, Eric. 2014. "Fight over Minimum Wage Illustrates Web of Industry Ties." *New York Times*, February 9.

Lipton, Eric, and Ian Urbina. 2007. "In 5-Year Effort, Scant Evidence of Voter Fraud." *New York Times*, April 12. Accessed June 21, 2018. http://www.nytimes.com/2007 /04/12/washington/12fraud.html.

Long, Russell. 1972. *Welfare Cheating: Address of Hon. Russell B. Long, Chairman, Committee on Finance, and Supporting Material*. 99th Cong., 2nd sess., Committee Print 75–077. Washington: Government Printing Office.

Lopez-Landin, Hiram. 2013. "SNAP Access Barriers Faced by Low Income 50–59 Year Olds." *AARP Foundation*, April. Accessed September 26, 2018. https://www.aarp.org /content/dam/aarp/aarp-foundation/2013-pdfs/SNAP_White_Paper_Mar _2013.pdf.

Lowry, Bryan. 2017. "Agriculture Secretary, in KC, Praises Trump's Deal-Making, Hints at Food Stamp Change." *Kansas City Star*, April 27. Accessed June 21, 2018. http://www.kansascity.com/news/politics-government/article147262554.html.

Maag, Elaine, Elizabeth Peters, and Sara Edelstein. 2016. "Increasing Family Complexity and Volatility: The Difficulty in Determining Child Tax Benefits." Washington, D.C. The Tax Policy Center. Accessed June 21, 2018. https://www.urban.org/sites

/default/files/publication/78271/2000641-increasing-family-complexity-and
-volatility-the-difficulty-in-determining-child-tax-benefits.pdf.

Machlin, Steven R., and Kelly Carper. 2014. "Out-of-Pocket Healthcare Expenses
by Age and Insurance Coverage, 2011." Statistical Brief no. 441. Rockville, Md.:
Agency for Healthcare Research and Quality. Accessed June 21, 2018. https://
meps.ahrq.gov/data_files/publications/st441/stat441.pdf.

Maciag, Mike. 2013. "Analysis: Who's Moving to Your State?" *Governing*, September 25.
Accessed June 21, 2018. http://www.governing.com/blogs/by-the-numbers
/residents-moving-to-new-state-demographics-mobility-data-2012.html.

Maestas, Nicole, Mathis Schroeder, and Dana Goldman. 2009. "Price Variation in
Markets with Homogenous Goods: The Case of Medigap." *NBER* working paper
no. 14679. Cambridge, Mass.: National Bureau of Economic Research.

Majoo, Farhad. 2015. "Would You Let the I.R.S. Prepare Your Taxes?" *New York Times*,
April 15.

Major, Brenda, and Richard H. Gramzow. 1999. "Abortion as Stigma: Cognitive
and Emotional Implications of Concealment." *Journal of Personality and Social
Psychology* 77(4): 735–45.

Mani, Anandi, Sendhil Mullainathan, Eldar Shafir, and Jiaying Zhao. 2013. "Poverty
Impedes Cognitive Function." *Science* 341(6149): 976–80.

Marr, Chuck, and Cecile Murray. 2016. "IRS Funding Components Compromise
Taxpayer Service and Weaken Enforcement." Washington, D.C.: Center for
Budget and Policy Priorities. Accessed June 21, 2018. https://www.cbpp.org
/sites/default/files/atoms/files/6-25-14tax.pdf.

Marshall, Thomas H. 1964. *Class, Citizenship and Social Development.* New York:
Doubleday.

Martin, Paul S. 2003. "Voting's Rewards: Voter Turnout, Attentive Publics, and
Congressional Allocation of Federal Money." *American Journal of Political Science*
47(1): 110–12.

Masood, Ayesha, and Muhammad Nisar. 2018. "'It Is Like Being Crushed Between
Two Stones': Administrative Burden of Maternity Benefits in Pakistan." Paper
presented at the 22nd Annual International Research Society for Public
Management Conference, Edinburgh (April 11–13). Accessed June 21, 2018.
https://irspm2018.exordo.com/files/papers/81/final_draft/Administrative
_Burden_Masood_and_Nisar.pdf.

Mathur, Aparna. 2015. "Why Raising the Minimum Wage Is Riskier than Expanding
the EITC." Washington, D.C.: American Enterprise Institute. Accessed June 21,
2018. http://www.aei.org/publication/why-raising-minimum-wages-is-riskier
-than-expanding-the-eitc.

McCubbins, Mathew D., and Thomas Schwartz. 1984. "Congressional Oversight
Overlooked: Police Patrols Versus Fire Alarms." *American Journal of Political
Science* 28(1): 165–79.

McDorman, Marian F., Eugene Declercq, Howard Cabral, and Christine Morton.
2016. "Recent Increases in the US Mortality Rate." *Obstetrics & Gynecology*
123(1): 1–10.

McGuire, Thomas G., Joseph P. Newhouse, and Anna D. Sinaiko. 2011. "An Economic History of Medicare Part C." *Milbank Quarterly* 89(2): 289–332.

McKee, Seth C. 2015. "Politics Is Local: State Legislator Voting on Restrictive Voter Identification Legislation." *Research & Politics* 2(1): 1–7.

McKinley, Charles, and Robert Frase. 1970. *Launching Social Security: A Capture-and-Record Account, 1935–1937*. Madison: University of Wisconsin Press.

McNulty, John E., Conor M. Dowling, and Margaret H. Ariotti. 2009. "Driving Saints to Sin: How Increasing the Difficulty of Voting Dissuades Even the Most Motivated Voters." *Political Analysis* 17(4): 435–55.

McWilliams, J. Michael, Christopher Afendulis, Thomas McGuire, and Bruce Landon. 2011. "Complex Medicare Advantage Choices May Overwhelm Seniors—Especially Those with Impaired Decision Making." *Health Affairs* 30(9): 1786–94.

Medicaid and CHIP Learning Collaborative. 2014. "Federally Facilitated Marketplace Eligibility & Enrollment Learning Collaborative: Marketplace Renewal & Interaction with Medicaid/CHIP." MAC Learning Collaborative Presentation, Washington (September 10). Accessed June 21, 2018. https://www.medicaid .gov/state-resource-center/mac-learning-collaboratives/downloads/rnwls -intrsctns.pdf.

Medicare Payment Advisory Commission. 2012. *Report to the Congress: Medicare Payment Policy*. Washington: MedPac. Accessed June 21, 2018. http://www.medpac.gov /docs/default-source/reports/march-2012-report-to-the-congress-medicare -payment-policy.pdf.

———. 2016. *Report to Congress: Medicare and the Healthcare Delivery System*. Washington: MedPac. Accessed June 21, 2018. http://www.medpac.gov/docs/default-source /reports/june-2016-report-to-the-congress-medicare-and-the-health-care -delivery-system.pdf.

Medicare Rights Center. 2018. "Advance Notice of Methodological Changes for Calendar Year (CY) 2019 for Medicare Advantage (MA) Capitation Rates, Part C and Part D Payment Policies and 2019 Call Letter." Washington, March 5. Accessed June 21, 2018. https://www.medicarerights.org/pdf/030518-2019 -call-letter-comments.pdf.

Medoff, Marshall. 2015. "The Impact of State Abortion Policy on the Price of an Abortion." *Behavior and Social Issues* 24(1): 56–67.

Mendel-Clemens, Amy. 2004. "Food Stamp and Medicaid Self-Assessment Internet Based Tool." Operations Memo. Madison: Wisconsin Department of Health Services.

Mendez, Matthew S., and Christian R. Grose. 2018 "Doubling Down: Inequality in Responsiveness and the Policy Preferences of Elected Officials." *Legislative Studies Quarterly*. Published online June 12. DOI: 10.1111/lsq.12204.

Mentzer, Robert. 2011. "Voter ID Becomes Law of Unintended Consequences." *Wausau Daily Herald* [Wisconsin], December 4.

Mercier, Rebecca J., Mara Buchbinder, Amy Bryant, and Laura Britton. 2015. "The Experiences and Adaptations of Abortion Providers Practicing Under a New TRAP Law: A Qualitative Study." *Contraception* 91(6): 507–12.

Mettler, Suzanne B. 2002. "Bringing the State Back in to Civic Engagement: Policy Feedback Effects of the GI Bill for World War II Veterans." *American Political Science Review* 96(2): 351–65.

———. 2005. *Soldiers to Citizens: The G.I. Bill and the Making of the Greatest Generation.* New York: Oxford University Press.

———. 2011. *The Submerged State: How Invisible Government Policies Undermine American Democracy.* Chicago: University of Chicago Press.

Mettler, Suzanne, and Joe Soss. 2004. "The Consequences of Public Policy for Democratic Citizenship: Bridging Policy Studies and Mass Politics." *Perspectives on Politics* 2(1): 55–73.

Meyer, Bruce D. 2002. "Labor Supply at the Extensive and Intensive Margins: The EITC, Welfare, and Hours Worked." *American Economic Review* 92(2): 373–79.

Meyer, Bruce D., and Dan T. Rosenbaum. 1999. "Welfare, the Earned Income Tax Credit, and the Labor Supply of Single Mothers." *NBER* working paper no. 7363. Cambridge, Mass.: National Bureau of Economic Research.

Michelmore, Katherine. 2013. "The Effect of Income on Educational Attainment: Evidence from State Earned Income Tax Credit Expansions." Working Paper. Ann Arbor: University of Michigan.

Miller, Gary, and Norman Schofield. 2008. "The Transformation of the Republican and Democratic Party Coalitions in the US." *Perspectives on Politics* 6(3): 433–50.

Miller, Sarah M., and Laura R. Wherry. 2017. "The Long-Term Health Effects of Early Life Medicaid Coverage." *SSRN* working paper no. 2466691. DOI:10.2139/ssrn.2466691.

Mills, Gregory, Tracy Vericker, Heather Koball, Kye Lippold, Laura Wheaton, and Sam Elkin. 2014. "Understanding the Rates, Causes, and Costs of Churning in SNAP." Paper presented at the annual meeting of the Association of Public Policy and Management, Miami (November 13).

Mink, Gwendolyn. 1998. *Welfare's End.* Ithaca, N.Y.: Cornell University Press.

Minnite, Lorraine Carol. 2010. *The Myth of Voter Fraud.* Ithaca, N.Y.: Cornell University Press.

Mississippi State Department of Health. 2016. "Minimum Standards of Operation for an Abortion Facility." Jackson: Mississippi State Department of Health. Accessed June 21, 2018. http://msdh.ms.gov/msdhsite/_static/resources/108.pdf.

Moe, Terry. 1989. "The Politics of Bureaucratic Structure." In *Can the Government Govern?* edited by John E. Chubb and Paul E. Petersen. Washington, D.C: The Brookings Institution.

Moffitt, Robert A. 1983. "An Economic Model of Welfare Stigma." *American Economic Review* 73(5): 1023–35.

Moon, Marilyn, and Pamela Herd. 2002. *A Place at the Table: Women's Needs and Medicare Reform.* New York: Century Foundation.

Moynihan, Donald P. 2004. "Building Secure Elections: E-Voting, Security, and Systems Theory." *Public Administration Review* 64(5): 515–28.

———. 2008. *The Dynamics of Performance Management: Constructing Information and Reform.* Washington, D.C.: Georgetown University Press.

Moynihan, Donald P., and Pamela Herd. 2010. "Red Tape and Democracy: How Rules Affect Citizenship Rights." *American Review of Public Administration* 40(6): 654–70.

Moynihan, Donald P., Pamela Herd, and Hope Harvey. 2015. "Administrative Burden: Learning, Psychological, and Compliance Costs in Citizen-State Interactions." *Journal of Public Administration Research and Theory* 25(1): 43–69.

Moynihan, Donald P., Pamela Herd, and Elizabeth Rigby. 2016. "Policymaking by Other Means: Do States Use Administrative Barriers to Limit Access to Medicaid?" *Administration & Society* 48(4): 497–524.

Moynihan, Donald P., and Alasdair S. Roberts. 2010. "The Triumph of Loyalty over Competence: The Bush Administration and the Exhaustion of the Politicized Presidency." *Public Administration Review* 70(4): 572–81.

Moynihan, Donald P., and Joe Soss. 2014. "Policy Feedback and the Politics of Administration." *Public Administration Review* 74(3): 320–32.

Mueller, Dennis C., and Thomas Stratmann. 2003. "The Economic Effects of Democratic Participation." *Journal of Public Economics* 87(9–10): 2129–55.

Mufson, Steven. 1990. "Most Americans Would Feel the Pinch." *Washington Post*, October 1.

Mullainathan, Sendhil, and Eldar Shafir. 2013. *Scarcity: Why Having So Little Means So Much*. New York: Times Books.

Nakamura, David. 2013. "Senators to Release Immigration Plan, Including a Path to Citizenship." *Washington Post*, April 16. Accessed June 21, 2018. https://www.washingtonpost.com/politics/senators-to-release-immigration-plan-including-a-path-to-citizenship/2013/04/15/67914cee-a5e2-11e2-8302-3c7e0ea97057_story.html.

National Center for Health Statistics. 2014. *Health, United States, 2013: With Special Feature on Prescription Drugs*. Report no. 2014-1232. Hyattsville, Md.: U.S. Department of Health and Human Services.

National Council of State Legislatures. 2017. "Drug Testing for Welfare Recipients and Public Assistance." Accessed June 21, 2018. http://www.ncsl.org/research/human-services/drug-testing-and-public-assistance.aspx.

———. 2018. "Voter Identification Requirement | Voter ID Laws." Accessed June 21, 2018. http://www.ncsl.org/research/elections-and-campaigns/voter-id.aspx.

National Council on Aging. 2018. "Maximizing the SNAP Medical Expense Deduction for Older Adults." Arlington, Va.: National Council on Aging. Accessed July 18, 2018. https://www.ncoa.org/wp-content/uploads/SNAPshots-Medical-Deduction.pdf.

National Taxpayer Advocate. 2007. "The IRS EIC Audit Process—A Challenge for Taxpayers." Washington: Taxpayer Advocate Service. Accessed July 18, 2018. https://taxpayeradvocate.irs.gov/Media/Default/Documents/ResearchStudies/eitc_audits_challenge_tps_ra_dec2007.pdf.

———. 2012. "Virtual Face-to-Face Audits: A Prescription for Curing the IRS's Ailing Correspondence Examination Process." Washington: Taxpayer Advocate Service. Accessed July 18, 2018. https://taxpayeradvocate.irs.gov/news/virtual-face-to-face-audits-a-prescription-for-curing-the-irs's-ailing-correspondence-examination-process.

Nationaler Normenkontrollat. 2013. *Transparency of Costs Improved Focus on Future Burden Reduction*. Annual Report. Bonn: Die Bundesregierung. Accessed June 21, 2018. https://www.normenkontrollrat.bund.de/Webs/NKR/Content/EN/Publikationen/2013_07_04_jahresbericht_2013_en.pdf.

Neuman, Patricia, Juliette Cubanski, Jennifer Huang, and Anthony Damico. 2015. "The Rising Cost of Living Longer: Analysis of Medicare Spending by Age for Beneficiaries in Traditional Medicare." San Francisco: Kaiser Family Foundation. Accessed June 21, 2018. http://files.kff.org/attachment/report-the-rising-cost-of-living-longer-analysis-of-medicare-spending-by-age-for-beneficiaries-in-traditional-medicare.

Neuman, Patricia, Michelle Kitchman Strollo, Stuart Guterman, William H. Rogers, Angela Li, Angie Mae Rodday, and Dana Gelb Safran. 2007. "Medicare Prescription Drug Benefit Progress Report: Findings from a 2006 National Survey of Seniors." *Health Affairs* 26(5): w630–43.

Newman, Abraham L. 2003. "When Opportunity Knocks: Economic Liberalisation and Stealth Welfare in the United States." *Journal of Social Policy* 32(2): 179–97.

New York Times/CBS News Poll. 2010. "National Survey of Tea Party Supporters." Accessed June 21, 2018. https://www.nytimes.com/interactive/projects/documents/new-york-timescbs-news-poll-national-survey-of-tea-party-supporters.

Nichols, Albert L., and Richard J. Zeckhauser. 1982. "Targeting Transfers Through Restrictions on Recipients." *American Economic Review* 72(2): 372–77.

Nieder, Dana. 2013. "Adding (Bureaucratic) Insult to 'Permanent' Injury." *Uncommon Sense* (blog), March 13. Accessed July 18, 2018. https://niederfamily.blogspot.com/search?q=Let+me+prove+to+you+how+different+my+daughter+is+and+how+many+special+needs+she+has+and+how+it+is+permanent%2C+it's+permanent%2C+and+why+must+I+keep+telling+you+that+she+can't+walk+for+long+and+her+balance+isn't+great+and+everything+is+more+work+for+her.

Nisar, Muhammad. 2018. "Children of a Lesser God: Administrative Burden and Social Equity in Citizen-State Interactions." *Journal of Public Administration Research and Theory* 28(1): 104–19.

O'Brien, Rourke, and Cassandra L. Robertson. 2018. "Early Life Medicaid Coverage and Intergenerational Economic Mobility." *Journal of Health and Social Behavior* 59(2): 300–15.

O'Connor, Anahad. 2017. "In the Shopping Cart of a Food Stamp Household: Lots of Soda." *New York Times*, January 13, A1.

Office of Inspector General (OIG HHS). 2016. *Healthcare.gov: CMS Management of the Federal Marketplace, a Case Study*. OEI-06-14-00350. Washington: U.S. Department of Health and Human Services. Accessed June 21, 2018. https://oig.hhs.gov/oei/reports/oei-06-14-00350.pdf.

Office of the Inspector General (OIG SSA). 2014a. "The Social Security Administration's Completion of Program Integrity Workloads." August 18. Washington: U.S. Social Security Administration. Accessed July 18, 2018. https://oig.ssa.gov/sites/default/files/audit/full/pdf/A-07-14-24071.pdf.

——. 2014b. "The Social Security Administration's Reduction in Field Office Operating Hours." August 7. Washington: U.S. Social Security Administration. Accessed June 21, 2018. http://oig.ssa.gov/sites/default/files/audit/full/pdf /A-01-14-14039.pdf.

——. 2016. "Customer Waiting Times in the Social Security Administration's Field Offices." December 5. Washington: U.S. Social Security Administration. Accessed June 21, 2018. https://oig.ssa.gov/sites/default/files/audit/full/pdf /A-04-17-50216.pdf.

Oliver, Thomas R., Philip R. Lee, and Helene L. Lipton. 2004. "A Political History of Medicare and Prescription Drug Coverage." *Milbank Quarterly* 82(2): 283–354.

Olson, Nina. 2015. "IRS Future State: The National Taxpayer Advocate's Vision for a Taxpayer-Centric 21st Century Tax Administration." Washington: Taxpayer Advocate Service. Accessed June 21, 2018. https://taxpayeradvocate.irs.gov /Media/Default/Documents/2016-ARC/ARC16_Volume1_SpecialFocus.pdf.

Onion, Rebecca. 2013. "Take the Impossible 'Literacy' Test Louisiana Gave Black Voters in the 1960s." *Slate*, June 28. Accessed June 21, 2018. http://www.slate.com /blogs/the_vault/2013/06/28/voting_rights_and_the_supreme_court_the _impossible_literacy_test_louisiana.html.

Opoien, Jessie. 2016. "Why Did Wisconsin See Its Lowest Presidential Election Turnout in 20 Years." November 11, *Capital Times*. Accessed June 21, 2018. http://host.madison.com/ct/news/local/govt-and-politics/election-matters /why-did-wisconsin-see-its-lowest-presidential-election-voter-turnout/article _6dd2887f-e1fc-5ed8-a454-284d37204669.html.

Organization for Economic Cooperation and Development (OECD). 2007. *Cutting Red Tape: Comparing Administrative Burdens Across Countries.* Paris: OECD. Accessed June 21, 2018. http://www.paca-online.org/cop/docs/OECD_Cutting _Red_Tape_Comparing_Administrative_Burdens_across_Countries.pdf.

——. 2012. "Cutting Administrative Burdens on Citizens: Implementation Challenges and Opportunities." Budapest: OECD. Accessed June 21, 2018. http://www.oecd.org/gov/regulatory-policy/50444905.pdf.

Pear, Robert. 2017. "Trump Administration Will Support Work Requirements for Medicaid." *New York Times*, November 7, A19.

Perry, Travis. 2013. "Obamacare Navigator Under Fire for Arrest Warrant." *Kansas Watchdog*, October 16. Accessed June 21, 2018. http://watchdog.org/110877 /obamacare-navigator-under-fire-for-arrest-warrant.

Pew Charitable Trusts. 2014. "Online Voting Available to Nearly Half of Eligible Voters." *Election Initiatives*, September 30. Accessed June 21, 2018. http:// www.pewtrusts.org/en/research-and-analysis/analysis/2014/09/30 /online-registration-now-available-to-nearly-half-of-eligible-voters.

Phillips, Kevin. 1969. *The Emerging Republican Majority.* New Rochelle, N.Y.: Arlington House.

Pierson, Brendan. 2018. "Medicaid Work Rules Face Tough Legal Challenges, Experts Say." Reuters, January 25. Accessed June 21, 2018. https://www.reuters.com /article/us-usa-healthcare-medicaid-analysis/medicaid-work-rules-face-tough -legal-challenges-experts-say-idUSKBN1FE33P.

Pierson, Paul. 2000. "Increasing Returns, Path Dependence, and the Study of Politics." *American Political Science Review* 94(2): 251–67.

Pinquart, Martin, and Silvia Sörensen. 2003. "Differences Between Caregivers and Noncaregivers in Psychological Health and Physical Health: A Meta-Analysis." *Psychology and Aging* 18(2): 250–67.

Piven, Frances Fox. 1998. "Welfare and Work." *Social Justice* 25(1): 67–82.

Piven, Frances Fox, and Richard A. Cloward. 1971. *Regulating the Poor: The Functions of Public Welfare*. New York: Vintage.

Plueger, Dean. 2009. "Earned Income Tax Credit Participation Rate for Tax Year 2005." Paper presented at the 2009 IRS Research Conference, Washington (July 8–9). Accessed June 21, 2018. https://www.irs.gov/statistics/soi-tax-stats-2009-irs-research-conference.

Pogge, Oscar C. 1952. "After Fifteen Years: A Report on Old-Age and Survivors Insurance." *Social Security Bulletin* 15(1): 3–14.

Pollitz, Karen, Jennifer Tolbert, and Rosa Ma. 2015. "2015 Survey of Health Insurance Marketplace Assister Programs and Brokers." San Francisco: Kaiser Family Foundation. Accessed June 21, 2018. https://www.kff.org/health-reform/report/2015-survey-of-health-insurance-marketplace-assister-programs-and-brokers/.

Pollitz, Karen, Jennifer Tolbert, and Ashley Semanskee. 2016. "2016 Survey of Health Insurance Marketplace Assister Programs and Brokers." San Francisco: Kaiser Family Foundation. Accessed July 18, 2018. https://www.kff.org/health-reform/report/2016-survey-of-health-insurance-marketplace-assister-programs-and-brokers/.

Pradhan, Rachana. 2016. "Kentucky Begins Dismantling Obamacare Exchange." *Politico*, January 12. Accessed June 21, 2018. http://www.politico.com/story/2016/01/kentucky-dismantle-obamacare-exchange-217629.

Presidential Commission on Election Administration. 2014. *The American Voting Experience: Report and Recommendations of the Presidential Commission on Election Administration*. Washington: Government Printing Office.

Provan, Keith G., and Patrick Kenis. 2008. "Modes of Network Governance: Structure, Management, and Effectiveness." *Journal of Public Administration Research and Theory* 18(2): 229–52.

Puckett, Caroline. 2009. "The Story of the Social Security Number." *Social Security Bulletin* 69(2): 55–74. Accessed June 21, 2018. https://www.ssa.gov/policy/docs/ssb/v69n2/v69n2p55.html.

———. 2010. "Administering Social Security: Challenges Yesterday and Today." *Social Security Bulletin* 70(3): 27–78.

Quadagno, Jill. 1984. "Welfare Capitalism and the Social Security Act of 1935." *American Sociological Review* 49(5): 632–47.

———. 1988. *The Transformation of Old Age Security: Class and Politics in the American Welfare State*. Chicago: University of Chicago Press.

———. 1990. "Race, Class, and Gender in the US Welfare State: Nixon's Failed Family Assistance Plan." *American Sociological Review* 55(1): 11–28.

Quint, Janet, and Rebecca Widom with Lindsay Moore. 2001. "Post-TANF Food Stamp and Medicaid Benefits: Factors That Aid or Impede Their Receipt."

New York: Manpower Demonstration Research Corporation. Accessed June 21, 2018. https://www.mdrc.org/sites/default/files/full_476.pdf.

Rainey, Hal G. 2009. *Understanding and Managing Public Organizations*, 4th ed. New York: John Wiley & Sons.

Rank, Mark R., and Thomas A. Hirschl. 2005. "Likelihood of Using Food Stamps During the Adulthood Years." *Journal of Nutrition Education and Behavior* 37(3): 137–46.

———. 2009. "Estimating the Risk of Food Stamp Use and Impoverishment During Childhood." *Archives of Pediatrics & Adolescent Medicine* 163(11): 994–99.

Ratcliffe, Caroline, Signe-Mary McKernan, and Kenneth Finegold. 2008. "Effects of Food Stamp and TANF Policies on Food Stamp Receipt." *Social Service Review* 82(2): 291–334.

Raymond, Adam K. 2018. "Michigan's Proposed Medicaid Work Requirement Comes with a Racist Twist." *New York Magazine*, May 3. Accessed June 21, 2018. http://nymag.com/daily/intelligencer/2018/05/michigans-medicaid-work-requirement-comes-with-racist-twist.html.

Raymond, Elizabeth G., and David A. Grimes. 2012. "The Comparative Safety of Legal Induced Abortion and Childbirth in the United States." *Obstetrics & Gynecology* 119(2): 215–19.

Reitman, Janet. 2014. "The Stealth War on Abortion." *Rolling Stone Magazine*, January 15. Accessed June 21, 2018. http://www.rollingstone.com/politics/news/the-stealth-war-on-abortion-20140115.

Ribar, David C., Marilyn Edelhoch, and Qiduan Liu. 2008. "Watching the Clocks the Role of Food Stamp Recertification and TANF Time Limits in Caseload Dynamics." *Journal of Human Resources* 43(1): 208–38.

Rigby, Elizabeth, and Melanie J. Springer. 2011. "Does Electoral Reform Increase (or Decrease) Political Equality?" *Political Research Quarterly* 64(2): 420–34.

Ritchie Karen, Sylvanie Artero, and Jacques Touchon. 2001. "Classification Criteria for Mild Cognitive Impairment: A Population-Based Validation Study." *Neurology* 56(1): 27–42.

Roberts, Sarah C.M., M. Antonia Biggs, Karuna S. Chibber, Heather Gould, Corinne H. Rocca, and Diana Greene Foster. 2014. "Risk of Violence from the Man Involved in the Pregnancy After Receiving or Being Denied an Abortion." *BMC Medicine* 12(1): 144–51.

Robertson, David Brian. 1988. "Planned Incapacity to Succeed? Policy-Making Structure and Policy Failure." *Review of Policy Research* 8(2): 241–63.

Romig, Kathleen. 2016. "Budget Cuts Squeeze Social Security Administration Even as Workloads Reach Record Highs." Policy Futures, June 3. Washington, D.C.: Center on Budget and Policy Priorities. Accessed June 21, 2018. https://www.cbpp.org/research/retirement-security/budget-cuts-squeeze-social-security-administration-even-as-workloads.

Rosenbaum, David. 1993. "The Budget Bill." *New York Times*, August 3.

Rosenbaum, Dottie, and Brynne Keith-Jennings. 2016. "SNAP Costs and Caseloads Declining: Trends Expected to Continue." Washington, D.C.: Center for Budget and Policy Priorities. Accessed June 21, 2018. https://www.cbpp.org/sites/default/files/atoms/files/11-20-13fa.pdf.

Rozsa, Matthew. 2016. "Fox News Apologizes for Getting a Report on Food Stamp Fraud So Very, Very Wrong." *Salon*, December 30. Accessed June 21, 2018. http://www.salon.com/2016/12/30/fox-news-apologizes-for-getting-a-report-on-food-stamp-fraud-so-very-very-wrong.

Rutenberg, Jim. 2015. "A Dream Undone: Inside the 50-year Campaign to Roll Back the Voting Rights Act." *New York Times*, July 29. Accessed June 21, 2018. http://www.nytimes.com/2015/07/29/magazine/voting-rights-act-dream-undone.html.

Salwen, Kevin. 1993. "Business Groups Prepare to Square off against Clinton on Minimum Wage Issue." *Wall Street Journal*, February 8.

Samuels, Robert. 2018. "Wisconsin Is the GOP Model for 'Welfare Reform.' But as Work Requirements Grow, So Does One Family's Desperation." *Washington Post*, April 22. Accessed June 21, 2018. https://www.washingtonpost.com/politics/you-ever-think-the-government-just-dont-want-to-help-as-requirements-for-welfare-grow-so-does-one-familys-desperation/2018/04/22/351cb27a-2315-11e8-badd-7c9f29a55815_story.html.

Sanger, Carol. 2017. *About Abortion: Terminating Pregnancy in Twenty-First Century America*. Boston, Mass.: Harvard University Press

Saul, Stephanie. 2012. "Conservative Groups Focus on Registration in Swing States." *New York Times*, September 16, A1.

Schanzenbach, Diane Whitmore. 2009. "Experimental Estimates of the Barriers to Food Stamp Enrollment." Madison, Wisc.: Institute for Research on Poverty.

Scheibehenne, Benjamin, Rainer Greifeneder, and Peter M. Todd. 2010. "Can There Ever Be Too Many Options? A Meta-Analytic Review of Choice Overload." *Journal of Consumer Research* 37(3): 409–25.

Schlesinger, Arthur, Jr. 1958. *The Coming of the New Deal: 1933–1935, The Age of Roosevelt*, vol. 2. New York: Houghton Mifflin Harcourt.

Schneider, Anne L., and Helen M. Ingram. 1997. *Policy Design for Democracy*. Lawrence: University Press of Kansas.

Scholz, John Karl. 1994. "The Earned Income Tax Credit: Participation, Compliance, and Antipoverty Effectiveness." *National Tax Journal* 47(1): 63–87.

Schwabish, Jonathan. 2012. "The Impact of Online Food Stamp Applications on Participation." Paper presented at the annual meeting of the Association of Public Policy and Management, Baltimore, Md. (November 8–10).

Scott, Dylan. 2015. "Why Do Millions of People Mistakenly Think They Don't Qualify for Obamacare?" *Talking Points Memo*, February 20. Accessed June 21, 2018. http://talkingpointsmemo.com/dc/obamacare-eligible-think-they-dont-qualify.

Scott, Janny. 2001. "A Nation Challenged: The Paperwork; Awash in Grief After Attack, Adrift in a Sea of Paperwork." *New York Times*, November 20.

Seeman, Teresa E., Sharon S. Merkin, Eileen M. Crimmins, and Arun S. Karlamangla. 2010. "Disability Trends Among Older Americans: National Health and Nutrition Examination Surveys, 1988–1994 and 1999–2004." *American Journal of Public Health* 100(1): 100–107.

Shafir, Eldar, ed. 2013. *The Behavioral Foundations of Public Policy*. Princeton, N.J.: Princeton University Press.

Shannon, Sarah K.S., Christopher Uggen, Jason Schnittker, Melissa Thompson, Sara Wakefield, and Michael Massoglia. 2017. "The Growth, Scope, and Spatial Distribution of People with Felony Records in the United States, 1948–2010." *Demography* 54(5): 1795–818.

Sheppard, Si. 2004. *The Buying of the Presidency: Franklin Roosevelt, the New Deal and the Election of 1936*. Santa Barbara, Calif.: Praeger Press.

Shore-Sheppard, Lara D. 2008. "Stemming the Tide? The Effect of Expanding Medicaid Eligibility on Health Insurance Coverage." *BE Journal of Economic Analysis & Policy* 8(2): Article 6.

Short, Kathleen. 2014. "The Supplemental Poverty Measure: 2013." *Current Population Reports*, series p60, no. 251. Washington: Government Printing Office. Accessed June 21, 2018. https://www.census.gov/content/dam/Census/library/publications /2014/demo/p60-251.pdf.

Short, Pamela E., and Jessica P. Vistnes. 1992. "Multiple Sources of Medicare Supplementary Insurance." *Inquiry* 29(1): 33–43.

Sirica, Coimbra. 2001. "The Origins and Implementation of BadgerCare." New York: Milbank Memorial Fund. Accessed June 21, 2018. https://www.milbank.org /wp-content/uploads/2001/01/The-Origins-and-Implementation-of -BadgerCare.pdf.

Skocpol, Theda. 1992. *Protecting Mothers and Soldiers: The Political Origins of Social Policy in the United States*. Cambridge: Belknap Press.

Smeeding, Timothy, Katherin Ross Phillips, Michael O'Connor, and Michael Simon. 2010. "The EITC: Expectation, Knowledge, Use, and Economic and Social Mobility." *National Tax Journal* 53(4): 1187–209.

Smith, Aaron. 2014. "Older Adults and Technology Use." April 3. Washington, D.C.: Pew Research Center. Accessed June 21, 2018. http://www.pewinternet.org /2014/04/03/older-adults-and-technology-use.

Sobel, Richard. 2014. "The High Cost of 'Free' Photo Voter Identification Cards." Cambridge, Mass.: Charles Hamilton Houston Institute for Race and Justice, Harvard University Law School.

Social Security Board. 1935. "A Monthly Check to You for the Rest of Your Life" (poster). Available through the Library of Congress, accessed July 1, 2018. http://www.loc.gov/pictures/item/92500634/.

Somers, Ben, Rick Kronick, Kenneth Finegold, Rosa Po, Karyn Schwartz, and Sherry Glied. 2012. "Understanding Participation Rates in Medicaid: Implications for the Affordable Care Act." *Public Health* 93(1): 67–74.

Soss, Joe. 1999a. "Lessons of Welfare: Policy Design, Political Learning, and Political Action." *American Political Science Review* 93(2): 363–80.

———. 1999b. "Welfare Application Encounters Subordination, Satisfaction, and the Puzzle of Client Evaluations." *Administration & Society* 31(1): 50–94.

———. 2017. "Food Stamp Fables." *Jacobin*, January 16. Accessed June 21, 2018. https://www.jacobinmag.com/2017/01/food-stamps-snap-welfare-soda -new-york-times.

Soss, Joe, Richard C. Fording, and Sanford Schram. 2011. *Disciplining the Poor: Neoliberal Paternalism and the Persistent Power of Race.* Chicago: University of Chicago Press.

Spear, Sheldon. 1968. "The United States and the Persecution of the Jews in Germany, 1933–1939." *Jewish Social Studies* 30(4): 215–42.

St. Petersburg Times. 1993. "Social Security Changes Under Study." January 31.

State of Michigan. 2016. *Michigan Adult Coverage Demonstration: Section 1115 Annual Report.* Lansing: Department of Health and Human Services. Accessed June 21, 2018. https://www.medicaid.gov/Medicaid-CHIP-Program-Information /By-Topics/Waivers/1115/downloads/mi/Healthy-Michigan/mi-healthy -michigan-annual-report-DY6.pdf.

Stephens-Davidowitz, Seth. 2016. "The Return of the D.I.Y. Abortion." *New York Times*, March 5. Accessed June 21, 2018. http://www.nytimes.com/2016/03/06 /opinion/sunday/the-return-of-the-diy-abortion.html.

Stern, Yaakov, Barry Gurland, Thomas K. Tatemichi, Ming Xin Tang, David Wilder, and Richard Mayeux. 1994. "Influence of Education and Occupation on the Incidence of Alzheimer's Disease." *Journal of the American Medical Association* 271(13): 1004–10.

Stevens, Rosemary. 1996. "Healthcare in the 1960s." *Healthcare Financing Review* 1(2): 11–22.

Street, Alex, Thomas Murray, John Blitzer, and Rajan Patel. 2015. "Estimating Voter Registration Deadline Effects with Web Search Data." *Political Analysis* 23(2): 225–41.

Strom, Stephanie. 2010. "Nonprofit Advocate Carves Out a For-Profit Niche." *New York Times*, June 18.

Stross, Randall. 2010. "Why Can't the I.R.S. Fill in the Blanks?" *New York Times*, January 23.

Strully, Kate W., David H. Rehkopf, and Ziming Xuan. 2010. "Effects of Prenatal Poverty on Infant Health State Earned Income Tax Credits and Birth Weight." *American Sociological Review* 75(4): 534–62.

Stuart, Guy. 2004. "Databases, Felons, and Voting: Bias and Partisanship of the Florida Felons List I the 2000 Elections." *Political Science Quarterly* 119(3): 453–75.

Stuber, Jennifer, and Karl Kronebusch. 2004. "Stigma and Other Determinants of Participation in TANF and Medicaid." *Journal of Policy Analysis and Management* 23(3): 509–30.

Stuber, Jennifer, and Mark Schlesinger. 2006. "Sources of Stigma for Means-Tested Government Programs." *Social Science & Medicine* 63(4): 933–45.

Sullivan, Andy, and Grant Smith. 2016. "Use It or Lose It: Occasional Ohio Voters May Be Shut Out in November." Reuters, June 2. Accessed June 21, 2018. http:// www.reuters.com/article/us-usa-votingrights-ohio-insight-idUSKCN0YO19D.

Sunstein, Cass. 2013. *Simpler: The Future of Government.* New York: Simon & Schuster.

Swart, Chris, Nina Troia, and Dorothy Ellegaard. 2004. *BadgerCare Evaluation.* Madison: Wisconsin Department of Health and Family Services, Office of Strategic Finance Evaluation Section.

Sykes, Jennifer, Katrin Kriz, Kathryn Edin, and Sarah Halpern-Meekin. 2015. "Dignity and Dreams: What the Earned Income Tax Credit (EITC) Means to Low-Income Families." *American Sociological Review* 80(2): 243–67.

Tang, Terry. 1994. "Raising the Minimum and Maximizing Jobs." *Seattle Times*, January 9.

Tavernise, Sabrina. 2016. "New FDA Guidelines Ease Access to Abortion Pill." *New York Times*, March 31, A1.

Tax Institute at H&R Block. 2015. *Consumer Tax Fraud: Sources and Solutions.* Accessed June 21, 2018. http://newsroom.hrblock.com/wp-content/uploads/2015/03/TTI-2015-Fraud-Survey.pdf.

Texas Office of the Governor. 2016. "Governor Abbott's Statement on Supreme Court's HB 2 Ruling." Press release, June 27. Accessed June 21, 2018. http://gov.texas.gov/news/press-release/22427.

Thaler, Richard. 2018. "Nudge, Not Sludge." *Science* 361(6401): 431.

Thaler, Richard, and Cass Sunstein. 2008. *Nudge: Improving Decisions About Health, Wealth and Happiness.* New Haven, Conn.: Yale University Press.

Thompson, Frank. 2012. *Medicaid Politics: Federalism, Policy Durability and Health Reform.* Washington, D.C.: Georgetown University Press.

Thorin, Elizabeth J. and Larry K. Irvin. 1992. "Family Stress Associated with Transition to Adulthood of Young People with Severe Disabilities." *Journal of the Association for Persons with Severe Handicaps* 17(1): 31–39.

Toner, Robin. 1986. "Major Help Found in Tax Bill for Low-Income Households." *New York Times*, August 21.

Treasury Inspector General for Tax Administration. 2011. "Reduction Targets and Strategies Have Not Been Established to Reduce the Billions of Dollars in Improper Earned Income Tax Credit Payments Each." Report no. 2011-40-023. Washington: U.S. Department of the Treasury. Accessed June 21, 2018. https://www.treasury.gov/tigta/auditreports/2011reports/201140023fr.pdf.

Tummers, Lars. 2013. *Policy Alienation and the Power of Professionals: Confronting New Policies.* Cheltenham, U.K.: Edward Elgar Publishing.

Tuttle, Charlotte. 2016. "The Stimulus Act of 2009 and Its Effect on Food-At-Home Spending by SNAP Participants." Economic Research Report no. 213. Washington: U.S. Department of Agriculture, Food and Nutrition Services. https://www.ers.usda.gov/webdocs/publications/74686/60328_err213.pdf.

Tuttle, Cody. 2018. "Snapping Back: Food Stamp Bans and Criminal Recidivism." *SSRN.* Published online March 29. DOI: 10.2139/ssrn.2845435.

U.S. Census Bureau. 2014. *Income and Poverty in the United States: 2013.* Washington: Government Printing Office.

———. 2018. *The Supplemental Poverty Measure: 2017.* Accessed September 21, 2018. https://www.census.gov/content/dam/census/library/publications/2018/demo/p60-265.pdf.

U.S. Centers for Medicare and Medicaid Services (CMS). 2015. "Choosing a Medigap Policy: A Guide to Health Insurance for People with Medicare."

Washington: Government Printing Office. Accessed June 21, 2018. http://
www.medicaresupplementplans.com/pdf/Choosing_A_Medigap_Policy
_A_Guide_to_Health_Insurance_for_People_with_Medicare.pdf.

———. 2018. "State Medicaid Director Letter SMD 18-002, RE: Opportunities to
Promote Work and Community Engagement Among Medicaid Beneficiaries."
Washington: U.S. Department of Health and Human Services, January 11.
Accessed July 18, 2018. https://www.medicaid.gov/federal-policy-guidance
/downloads/smd18002.pdf.

U.S. General Accounting Office (GAO). 1994. "Health Insurance for the Elderly:
Owning Duplicate Policies Is Costly and Unnecessary." HEHS-94-185.
Washington: Government Printing Office.

———. 1999. *Food Stamp Program: Various Factors Have Led to Declining Participation*.
Washington: Government Printing Office. Accessed June 21, 2018. http://
www.gao.gov/assets/230/227751.pdf.

———. 2001. "Medigap Insurance: Plans Are Widely Available But Have Limited
Benefits and May Have High Costs." GAO-01-941. Washington: Government
Printing Office.

U.S. Government Accountability Office (GAO). 2006. "Medicare Part D: Prescription
Drug Plan Sponsor Call Center Responses Were Prompt, But Not Consistently
Accurate." GAO-06-710. Washington: Government Printing Office.

———. 2013. "Social Security Administration: Long-Term Strategy Needed to Address
Key Management Challenges." GAO-13-459. Washington: Government Printing
Office. Accessed June 21, 2018. http://www.gao.gov/assets/660/654863.pdf.

———. 2014a. "Health Insurance Exchanges: Coverage of Non-Excepted Abortion
Services by Qualified Health Plans." GAO-14-742R. Washington: Government
Printing Office.

———. 2014b. "Issues Related to State Voter Identification Laws." GAO-14–634.
Washington: Government Printing Office.

———. 2014c. "Paid Tax Return Preparers: In a Limited Study, Preparers Made
Significant Errors." GAO-14-467T. Washington: Government Printing Office.

———. 2016. *Refundable Tax Credits: Comprehensive Compliance Strategy and Expanded
Use of Data Could Strengthen IRS's Efforts to Address Noncompliance*. GAO-16–475.
Washington: Government Printing Office.

U.S. House of Representatives. 1935. *Hearings Before Committee on Ways and Means
74th Congress, First Session on H.R. 4120, a Bill to Alleviate the Hazards of Old Age,
Unemployment, Illness, and Dependency, to Establish a Social Insurance Board in the
Department of Labor, to Raise Revenue, and for Other Purposes*. January 21–31 and February 1–12. Accessed June 21, 2018. https://www.ssa.gov/history/hquotes2.html.

U.S. Senate Committee on Finance. 1939. *Hearings on the Social Security Amendments:
H.R. 6635, An Act to Amend the Social Security Act, and for Other Purposes*. June 12,
13, 14, 15, 20, and 29, 1939. Washington: Government Printing Office. Accessed
June 21, 2018. https://babel.hathitrust.org/cgi/pt?id=mdp.39015012363464
;view=1up;seq=17

U.S. Social Security Administration (SSA). 1965. "Social Security Act: 30 Years of Building." OASIS 11: 24–29. Washington: Government Printing Office. Accessed June 21, 2018. https://www.ssa.gov/history/oasis/august1965.pdf.

———. 2015. *Annual Statistical Supplement, 2014.* Washington: Government Printing Office. Accessed June 26, 2018. https://www.ssa.gov/policy/docs/statcomps/supplement/2014/supplement14.pdf.

———. 2016a. *Annual Statistical Supplement, 2015.* SSA Publication no. 13-11700. Washington: Government Printing Office. Accessed June 21, 2018. https://www.ssa.gov/policy/docs/statcomps/supplement/2015/supplement15.pdf.

———. 2016b. "Income of the Aged Chartbook, 2014." SSA Publication no. 13-11727. Washington: Government Printing Office. Accessed June 21, 2018. https://www.ssa.gov/policy/docs/chartbooks/income_aged/2014/iac14.pdf.

Upadhyay, Ushma D., M. Antonia Biggs, and Diana Greene Foster. 2015. "The Effect of Abortion on Having and Achieving Aspirational One-Year Plans." *BMC Women's Health* 15(November): 102. DOI: 10.1186/s12905-015-0259-1.

Upadhyay, Ushma D., Sheila Desai, Vera Zlidar, Tracy A. Weitz, Daniel Grossman, Patricia Anderson, and Diana Taylor. 2015. "Incidence of Emergency Department Visits and Complications After Abortion." *Obstetrics & Gynecology* 125(1): 175–83.

Upadhyay, Ushma D., Tracy A. Weitz, Rachel K. Jones, Rana E. Barar, and Diana Greene Foster. 2014. "Denial of Abortion Because of Provider Gestational Age Limits in the United States." *American Journal of Public Health* 104(9): 1687–94.

Valentino, Nicholas A., and Fabian G. Neuner. 2017. "Why the Sky Didn't Fall: Mobilizing Anger in Reaction to Voter ID Laws." *Political Psychology* 38(2): 331–50.

Van de Water, Paul. 2014. "Medicare in Ryan's 2015 Budget." Washington, D.C.: Center for Budget and Policy Priorities.

Van Hook, Jennifer, and Kelly Stamper Balistreri. 2006. "Ineligible Parents, Eligible Children: Food Stamps Receipt, Allotments, and Food Insecurity Among Children of Immigrants." *Social Science Research* 35(1): 228–51.

Van Ryzin, Gregg. 2011. "Outcomes, Process, and Trust of Civil Servants." *Journal of Public Administration Research and Theory* 21(4): 745–60.

Ventry, Dennis J., Jr. 2000. "The Collision of Tax and Welfare Politics: The Political History of the Earned Income Tax Credit, 1969–99." *National Tax Journal* 53(4): 983–1026.

Verma, Seema. 2018. "Making Medicaid a Pathway out of Poverty." *Washington Post,* February 4.

Vining, Aidan R., and David L. Weimer. 2015. "Policy Analysis." In *International Encyclopedia of the Social and Behavioral Sciences,* 2nd ed., edited by James D. Wright. Oxford: Elsevier.

Waltman, Jerold. 2000. *The Politics of the Minimum Wage.* Urbana: University of Illinois Press.

Warlick, Jennifer L. 1982. "Participation of the Aged in SSI." *Journal of Human Resources* 17(2): 236–60.

Weaver, R. Kent. 2000. *Ending Welfare as We Know It.* Washington, D.C.: Brookings Institution Press.

Weiser, Wendy R., and Lawrence Norden. 2011. *Voting Changes in 2012*. New York: Brennan Center for Justice.

Weiss, Alice M., and Kaitlin Sheedy. 2015. "State Enrollment Experience: Implementing Health Coverage Eligibility and Enrollment Systems under the ACA." Washington, D.C.: National Academy for State Health Policy. Accessed June 21, 2018. http://www.nashp.org/state-enrollment-experience-implementing-health-coverage-eligibility-and-enrollment-systems-under-the-aca.

Weitz, Tracy A., Diana Taylor, Sheila Desai, Ushma D. Upadhyay, Jeff Waldman, Molly F. Battistelli, and Eleanor A. Drey. 2013. "Safety of Aspiration Abortion Performed by Nurse Practitioners, Certified Nurse Midwives, and Physician Assistants Under a California Legal Waiver." *American Journal of Public Health* 103(3): 454–61.

Weixel, Nathaniel. 2018. "New Hampshire Wins Approval for Medicaid Work Requirements." *The Hill*, May 7. Accessed June 21, 2018. http://thehill.com/policy/healthcare/medicaid/386566-new-hampshire-wins-approval-to-imose-medicaid-work-requirements.

White, Ariel R., Noah L. Nathan, and Julie K. Faller. 2015. "What Do I Need to Vote? Bureaucratic Discretion and Discrimination by Local Election Officials." *American Political Science Review* 109(1): 129–42.

The White House. 2017. "Presidential Executive Order on the Establishment of Presidential Advisory Commission on Election Integrity." May 11. Accessed June 27, 2018. https://www.whitehouse.gov/presidential-actions/presidential-executive-order-establishment-presidential-advisory-commission-election-integrity.

Wichowsky, Amber. 2012. "Competition, Party Dollars, and Income Bias in Voter Turnout, 1980–2008." *Journal of Politics* 74(2): 446–59.

Wichowsky, Amber, and Donald P. Moynihan. 2008. "Measuring How Administration Shapes Citizenship: A Policy Feedback Perspective on Performance Management." *Public Administration Review* 68(5): 908–20.

Wilson, David C., and Paul R. Brewer. 2013. "The Foundations of Public Opinion on Voter ID Laws Political Predispositions, Racial Resentment, and Information Effects." *Public Opinion Quarterly* 77(4): 962–84.

Wilson, David C., Paul R. Brewer, and Phoebe Theodora Rosenbluth. 2014. "Racial Imagery and Support for Voter ID Laws." *Race and Social Problems* 6(4): 365–71.

Wilson, James. 1989. *Bureaucracy, What Government Agencies Do and Why They Do It*. New York: HarperCollins.

Wines, Michael, and Alan Blinder. 2016. "Federal Appeals Court Strikes Down Voter ID Requirement." *New York Times*, July 29.

Winkler, Adam. 2011. *Gunfight: The Battle Over the Right to Bear Arms in America*. New York: W. W. Norton.

Winter, Joachim, Rowilma Balza, Frank Caro, Florian Heiss, Byung-hill Jun, Rose Matzkin, and Daniel McFadden. 2006. "Medicare Prescription Drug Coverage: Consumer Information and Preferences." *Proceedings of the National Academy of Sciences of the United States of America* 103(20): 7929–34.

Wisconsin Council for Children and Families. 2016. "Healthcare for Kids: How Wisconsin Lost and Could Regain Its National Prominence." July 12.

Madison: Wisconsin Council for Children and Families. Accessed June 21, 2018. http://www.wccf.org/assets/WI-Child-Medicaid-Participation-Report.pdf.

Wisconsin Department of Health and Family Services. 2006. "Framework for the Annual Report of the State Children's Health Insurance Plans Under Title XXI of the Social Security Act 2004/2005." Madison: Wisconsin Department of Health and Family Services.

Wisconsin Department of Health Services and Wisconsin Commissioner of Insurance. 2014. "The Wisconsin Health Insurance Market and Wisconsin Entitlement Reforms, Wisconsin's Unique Approach to Operationalizing the Affordable Care Act." P-00634A (3/14). Madison: Wisconsin Department of Health Services. Accessed June 21, 2018. https://www.dhs.wisconsin.gov/publications/p0/p00634a.pdf.

Wisconsin Healthcare Public Relations and Marketing Society. 2010. "Reaching the Finish Line; A Primer for Healthcare Advocates Using Wisconsin's Experience." Madison (October 12–14, 2010).

Wishner, Jane B., Anna C. Spencer, and Erik Wengle. 2014. "Analyzing Different Enrollment Outcomes in Select States That Used the Federally Facilitated Marketplace in 2014." Washington, D.C.: The Urban Institute. Accessed June 21, 2018. http://www.urban.org/sites/default/files/alfresco/publication-pdfs/2000014-Analyzing-Different-Enrollment-Outcomes-in-Select-States-that-Used-the-Federally-Facilitated-Marketplace-in-2014.pdf.

Wolfe, Barbara, and Scott Scrivner. 2005. "The Devil May Be in the Details." *Journal of Policy Analysis and Management* 24(3): 499–522.

Wolkwitz, Kari, and Joshua Leftin. 2008. *Characteristics of Food Stamp Households: Fiscal Year 2007.* Report no. FSP-08-CHAR. Washington: U.S. Department of Agriculture, Food and Nutrition Service.

Wright, Bill J., Matthew J. Carlson, Tina Edlund, Jennifer DeVoe, Charles Gallia, and Jeanene Smith. 2005. "The Impact of Increased Cost Sharing on Medicaid Enrollees." *Health Affairs* 24(4): 1106–16.

Wu, April Yanyuan. 2009. "Why Do So Few Elderly Use Food Stamps?" Chicago: University of Chicago, Harris School of Public Policy.

Wuppermann, Amelie C., Sebastian Bauhoff, and Markus Grabka. 2014 "The Price Sensitivity of Health Plan Choice: Evidence from Retirees in the German Social Health Insurance." *Netspar* discussion paper no. 02/2014–013. Tilburg: Network for Studies on Pensions, Aging and Retirement.

Wyatt, Birchard, and William H. Wandel. 1937. *The Social Security Act in Operation: A Practical Guide to the Federal and Federal-State Social Security Programs.* Washington, D.C.: Graphic Arts Press.

Wyman, David S. 1984. *The Abandonment of the Jews: America and the Holocaust, 1941–1945.* New York: Pantheon Books.

———. 1985. *Paper Walls: America and the Refugee Crisis 1938–1941.* New York: Pantheon Books.

Yetter, Deborah. 2016. "Red Tape Snarls Kentuy Program for the Disable." *Courier Journal,* November 19. Accessed June 21, 2018. https://www.courier-journal.com/story/news/politics/2016/11/19/red-tape-snarls-ky-program-disabled/93285224.

Zarabozo, Carlos, and Scott Harrison. 2009. "Payment Policy and the Growth of Medicare Advantage." *Health Affairs* 28(1): w55–w67.

Zedlewski, Sheila R., and Sarah Brauner. 1999. "Are the Steep Declines in Food Stamp Participation Linked to Falling Welfare Caseloads?" Washington, D.C.: The Urban Institute.

Zedlewski, Sheila R., with Amelia Gruber. 2001. "Former Welfare Families and the Food Stamp Program: The Exodus Continues." Washington, D.C.: The Urban Institute.

Zedlewski, Sheila, John Holahan, Linda Blumberg, and Colin Winterbottom. 1993. "The Distributional Effects of Alternative Healthcare Financing Options." In *Building Blocks for Change: How Healthcare Affects Our Future*, edited by Jack A. Meyer and Sharon S. Carroll. Washington, D.C.: Economic and Social Research Institute.

Zhang, Yuting, Seo Hyon Baik, and Joseph P. Newhouse. 2015. "Use of Intelligent Assignment to Medicare Part D Plans for People with Schizophrenia Could Produce Substantial Savings." *Health Affairs* 34(3): 455–60.

INDEX

Boldface numbers refer to figures and tables.

Medicaid in Wisconsin: all-kids goal and
BadgerCare Plus under Governor
Doyle, 172–83; changes in administrative burdens during Doyle administration, **174–75,** 175–83, 260; changes
in administrative burdens during
Thompson administration, **169–70;**
changes in administrative burdens
during Walker administration, 183–89,
185, 260; community outreach and
enrollment, 182–83; evolution of
political preferences and administrative burdens, 165–67, 189–90; express
enrollment, expansion of, 178; insurance verification forms, shifting the
burden of, 175–77; "making work pay"
under Governor Thompson, 167–72;
marketing and all-kids branding,
181–82; one-time auto enrollment,
177–78; online access for applicants,
180–81; program and form simplification, 178–80
Medicare: aggregate impact of burdens
on beneficiaries, 131–37; burdens in,
122; choice in, emergence of, 124–25,
127; choices between Medigap plans,
126; expanding benefits and the role
of private insurers, 127–31; financial
risks of poor choices, 131, 133–34;
increasing burdens and learning
costs in, 121–23, 140–41; increasing
choice and burdens, relationship of,
129–31; learning costs amid cognitive
declines, 134–35; the limits of choice,
135–37; Medicare Advantage (Part C),
127–29, 136; the Medicare maze, **132;**
overview of, 123–24; policy options
to reduce learning costs, 138–40;
prescription drug benefit (Part D),
129–31, 137; reform of, probability
of, 140; SNAP outreach among older
adults, potential for, 160
Medicare Modernization Act of 2003, 129
Medicare Modernization Act of 2004, 127

Medigap insurance, 124–25, **126,** 127, 138
Mettler, Suzanne, 244
Michigan: Medicaid in, 115, 117
Mills, Vincent, 221
Minnesota: the Affordable Care Act in,
103
Mississippi: abortion providers in,
burdens placed on, 83–85; voter
registration in, 69; voting in, 57
Missouri: SNAP program in, 156
Moe, Terry, 270n40
Montana: the Affordable Care Act in, 101
Moore, Stephen, 212

NARAL Pro-Choice America, 90
National Association of Manufacturers,
202
National Federation of Independent
Businesses, 202
*National Federation of Independent
Businesses v. Sebelius,* 112, 186
National Restaurant Association, 202
National Rifle Association, 245–46
National Voter Registration Act (NVRA)
of 1993, 48, 51
Navigator Program, 107–11
Nebraska: SSA field office staff
reductions in, 234
neutrality, 36
New Hampshire: Medicaid in, 189;
voting in, 57
New Jersey: the Affordable Care Act in, 101
New York: the Affordable Care Act in, 100;
SNAP program in, 156; voting in, 54
Nickles, Don, 210
Nieder, Dana, 27–28
Nielsen, Lindsay, 275n72
Nisar, Muhammad, 265
Nixon, Richard, 191, 198–99
nongovernmental actors: abortion
providers, burdens on, 82–87, **84;**
the Earned Income Tax Credit and,
196; Medicare and, 121–23, 127–31,
140–41; Medigap insurance plans

through, 124–27; navigators to
address administrative burdens of
the Affordable Care Act, 97, 106–11;
outreach for Medicaid in Wisconsin,
participation in, 171, 182–83; role of,
37–39; voter registration and, 51–52
North Carolina: voter ID law, judicial
action regarding, 67–68; voter
registration in, 58, 69; voting in, 59
NVRA. *See* National Voter Registration
Act of 1993

Obama, Barack, 20, 57, 96, 212
Obamacare. *See* Affordable Care Act
(ACA) of 2010
O'Brien, Erin, 61
Ohio: voter registration in, 53; voting
in, 59
Old-Age and Survivors Insurance (OASI).
See Social Security
Old-Age Assistance (OAA) program,
222, 224
older adults: learning costs amid cogni-
tive declines, 134–35, 158–60; the
Supplemental Nutrition Assistance
Program (SNAP) and, 157–62
Olson, Nina, 262, 264
Omnibus Reconciliation Act of 1990, 125
opacity, 36
Oregon: voter registration in, 68; voting
in, 55
O'Reilly, Bill, 144
Organization for Economic Cooperation
and Development (OECD), 20

Paperwork Reduction Act of 1980, 20
partisanship: the Affordable Care Act
and, 96, 98, 109–11; burdening voters,
voter ID and, 63–65; the politics of
administrative burdens and, 243–47;
voting and, 48–49
Patient Protection and Affordable Care
Act (ACA) of 2010. *See* Affordable Care
Act (ACA) of 2010
Pawlenty, Tim, 276n107

Pennsylvania: voter ID law, judicial
action regarding, 67
Personal Responsibility and Work
Opportunity Act (PRWORA) of 1996,
143, 145
Peterson, Bobby, 189
Planned Parenthood, 90
Planned Parenthood v. Casey, 90–92
policymaking: rationality in, 249–51;
transparency in, 247–49; via
administrative burdens, 35–36, 87
political participation: administrative
burdens and, 29–30; facilitated by
Social Security, 238. *See also* voting
politics of abortion, 72–73, 93–94;
administrative burdens as, 87–90;
the role of the courts in, 90–93
politics of administrative burdens:
administrative capacity, 31–33;
ideology/partisanship and, 243–47;
policymaking and, 242–47; political
beliefs and, 33–37; political choice,
burdens as the product of, 8–12;
rationality in policymaking and,
249–51; third parties, role of, 37–39;
transparency in policymaking and,
247–49
politics of burdening voters, 60; fraud,
assessing the threat of, 60–64; the
judiciary and the role of evidence
in weighing burdens, 65–68;
partisanship and race, voter ID laws
and, 63–65
Posner, Richard, 66–67, 91–92, 253
poverty: the Earned Income Tax Credit
and, 194; health care costs and, 133–34;
impact of Social Security on, 237
Price, Tom, 101, 103
PRWORA. *See* Personal Responsibility
and Work Opportunity Act (PRWORA)
of 1966
psychological costs, 2, 25–29; abortions,
for providers of, 83; abortions, for
women seeking, 77–81; administrative
burdens in SNAP and, **147,** 151–53;